Converting the Saxons

Utilizing a "crusading ethos," from 772 to 804 AD, Charlemagne, King of the Franks, waged war against the continental Saxons to integrate them within the growing Frankish Empire and facilitate their conversion to Christianity. While substantial research has been produced concerning various components of Carolingian history, this work offers a unique examination of Charlemagne's Saxon Wars as a case study for understanding methods of conversion used in the Christianization of Europe, as well as their significance for subsequent conversion strategies employed around the globe.

Converting the Saxons builds on prior scholarly research, is grounded in primary sources, and is contextualized with a robust historical introduction. Throughout the text, particular emphasis is given to Christian encounters with paganism and the way paganism was interpreted, confronted, and transformed. Within those encounters, we observe myriad forces of coercion and incentivization used in societal religious conversion, demonstrating the need for a serious reconsideration of the standard narratives surrounding Christian missions.

This book provides a scholarly and accessible resource for students and researchers interested in transhistorical methods of conversion, the history of Christianity, Early Medieval paganism, Colonial religious encounters, and the nature of religious conversion.

Joshua M. Cragle has an MSc in Social and Cultural Anthropology from the University of Amsterdam, where he conducted research on historical and contemporary Germanic/Norse paganism. He formerly worked as a Social Science Field Researcher for the University of Michigan as well as taught history in China. His previous publications primarily concern philosophy, Early Medieval religion, and paganism and can be found in *The Pomegranate* and *Journal of Thought*. He currently works at the University of Colorado-Boulder.

Converting the Saxons

A Study of Violence and Religion in Early
Medieval Germany

Joshua M. Cragle

Routledge
Taylor & Francis Group

LONDON AND NEW YORK

First published 2024
by Routledge
4 Park Square, Milton Park, Abingdon, Oxon OX14 4RN

and by Routledge
605 Third Avenue, New York, NY 10158

Routledge is an imprint of the Taylor & Francis Group, an informa business

British Library Cataloguing-in-Publication Data
A catalogue record for this book is available from the British Library

ISBN: 978-1-032-45896-0 (hbk)
ISBN: 978-1-032-45897-7 (pbk)
ISBN: 978-1-003-37915-7 (ebk)

DOI: 10.4324/9781003379157

Typeset in Times New Roman
by codeMantra

To my wife Mary.
For tolerating me spending the last 15 years living in the eighth century.
And to my brother Mikey, of whom I am immensely proud.

Contents

Maps

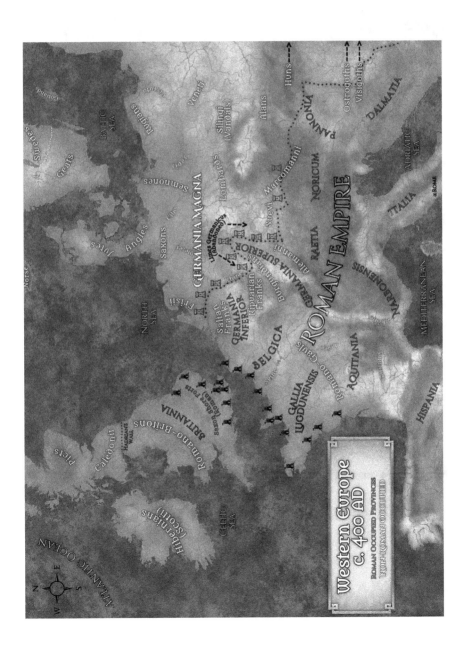

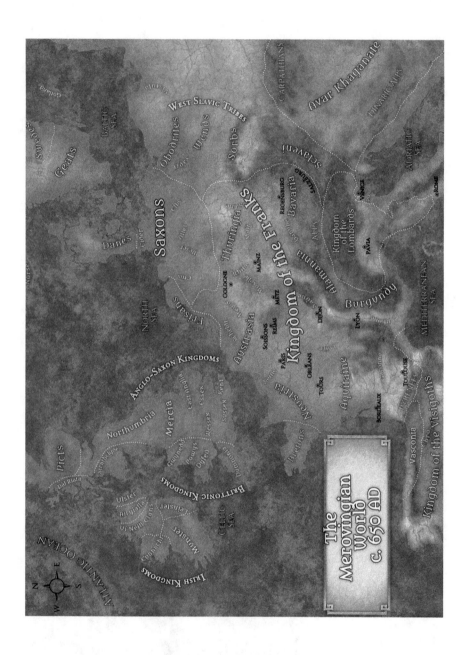

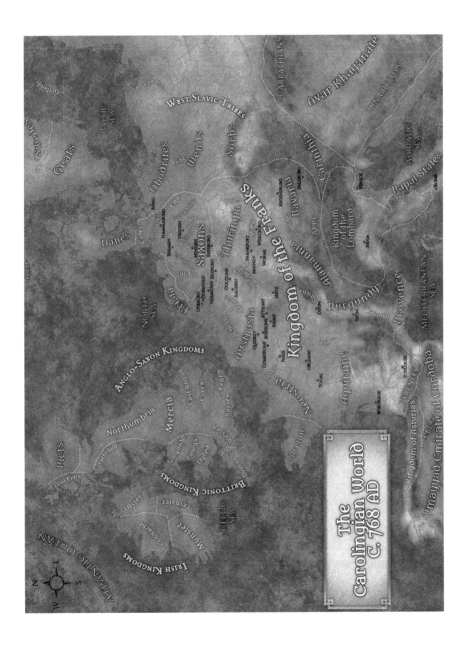

The Carolingian World
C. 768 AD

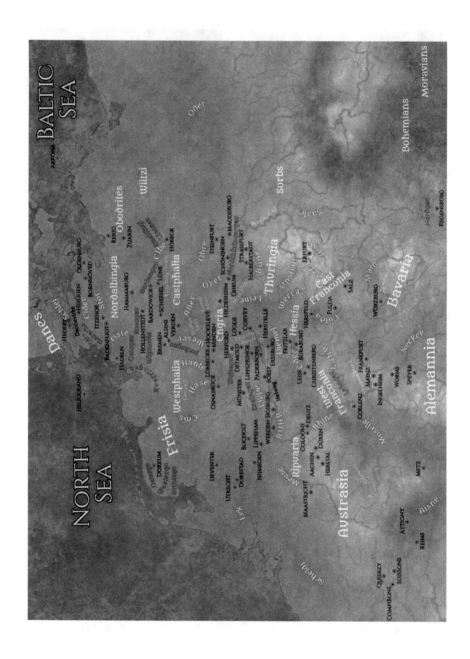

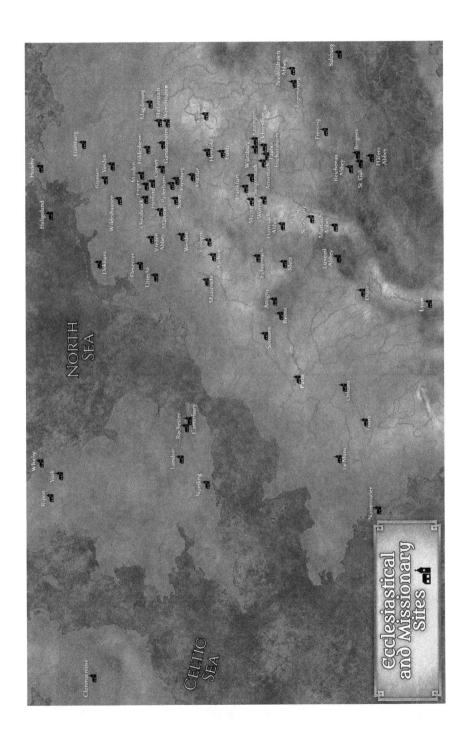

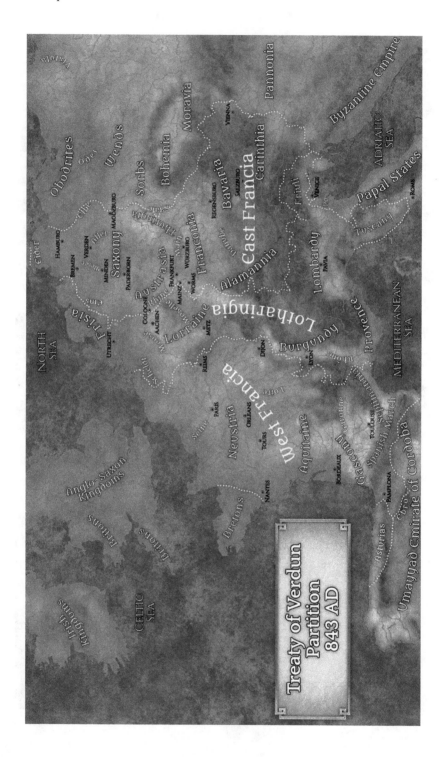

Acknowledgments

Many thanks to Dr. Kyle Wilkison of Colin College for his encouragement during the initial "idea phase" for this book and to my dear friends Brian King and Jon Mount, scholars in their own right, who offered support throughout the writing process and gave useful advice on improving the maps.

I would also like to express my gratitude to Michael Greenwood and Louis Nicholson-Pallett. The advice, commitment, and labor of the Routledge editorial team have been incredibly helpful in navigating the publishing process, as well as in improving the text. I would also sincerely like to include my thanks here to Kathrin Immanuel and the copyeditor.

My wife, Mary, deserves special appreciation. She allowed me the space necessary for finishing this project, as well as utilized her linguistic expertise to proofread the text, offering many useful edits. My son, Orin, who just turned seven months old, has also provided a much-needed lesson in time management, as well as the motivation necessary to endure.

Abbreviations

AB:	*Annals of St. Bertin*
AF:	*Annals of Fulda*
LHF:	*Liber Historiae Francorum*
OE:	Old English
OHG:	Old High German
ON:	Old Norse
OS:	Old Saxon
RFA:	*Royal Frankish Annals*

Introduction

Despite all inherent contradictions, since the advent of European Colonialism, Christianity has often been labeled the "White man's religion." If Christendom was a global phenomenon, Europe was its beating heart.[1] The association of Christianity with Europe resulted primarily from three processes: (1) the Christianization of Europe; (2) the expansion of Islam that shifted the intellectual center of Christianity away from North Africa, Greece, and Asia Minor toward the West; and (3) Colonial missionary endeavors associated with imperialism that occurred worldwide between the fifteenth and the early twentieth centuries.[2]

While most modern Westerners are familiar with the more horrific elements of Colonialism, such as the decimation of Native American populations by smallpox or the systematic enslavement of Africans, the role of religious conversion as a fundamental component of European imperialism has been less understood. This lack of clarity regarding Colonial conversion narratives comes *not* from a failure of discussion but from representations of conversion in overly simplified, progressive, positivist, and triumphal forms.[3] Fundamental to these presentations is the paternalist notion that, while there is much to lament in the darker corners of Colonial history, the West can ultimately take pride in having improved indigenous societies via civilization and Christianity.[4] The "savage" became the "citizen," while, simultaneously, "the heathen" received the gift of salvation, narrowly escaping the devil's grasp and eternal damnation in the fires of hell.[5] How had European societies come to these conclusions?

Common justifications presented in contemporary Western education and popular culture often blame racism alongside an ethos of religious intolerance that developed in Europe via the Crusades, Inquisition, witch trials, and sectional wars of religion. Thereafter, during Colonialism, this racist crusading ethos facilitated the destruction or transformation of non-Christian indigenous societies around the globe. Very few historians would challenge these basic premises. However, they fail in one capacity: by ignoring the prior thousand years and the critical elements of Antiquity and the Early Middle Ages that made a crusading ethos possible. To understand Colonial Christianization, we must understand the methods by which Europeans *themselves* became Christians.

Akin to having encountered general Colonial narratives, when Western students graduate from high school or attain a college degree, most will have learned

DOI: 10.4324/9781003379157-1

something about the growth of Christianity or specific conversion events. For example, the conversion of Constantine, names of prominent missionaries, excerpts from St. Augustine, heretical sects, and Roman encounters with pagan "barbarians" often make it into the curriculum. However, beyond discussing singular conversion *events* or studying snippets of theology, very little is taught concerning the *processes* by which Christianity became a central component of European life. Instead, the general narrative is often reduced down to something like this: Jesus was crucified, his followers spread his teachings throughout the Roman world, Christians faced cruel persecutions, Constantine converted, missionaries continued to spread the word, and paganism (which outside of Greco-Roman mythology is virtually never discussed) was eradicated (which was a good thing), at which point Europe was a "pure" Christian civilization (albeit riddled with heretics). Thereafter, during the "Age of Exploration," European missionaries spread the gospel across the globe, growing Christendom by the millions with the evident truth of their message.

Historically rooted in models of "sacred history" and promoted by "true believers," this general narrative of European Christianization to which many Westerners are (or were) exposed is neat, progressive, and triumphalist.[6] However, the reality behind the more palatable presentation is, in actuality, rather messy. Perhaps the non-romantic nature of European Christianization, coupled with a general ignorance of what preceded it, is why these processes tend to be ignored.[7] However, the consequences of that neglect are significant, which is where a study of Charlemagne's conquest and conversion of the Saxons proves helpful.

At first glance, Charlemagne's conquest of the Saxons may seem like nothing more than a footnote in a never-ending story of empire-building. It can generally be summarized as such: between the late eighth and early ninth centuries, the Frankish King "Charles the Great" waged war against the Saxons intermittently for over 30 years, resulting in Saxony being integrated within the Frankish Empire as a newly Christianized region. However, upon closer inspection, Charlemagne's Saxon Wars allow us to observe various conversion strategies and methods working together simultaneously. The lessons therein help us understand the multidimensional nature of societal religious transformation and give insight into what "conversion" *actually* meant.

The Challenges of Understanding Religious Conversion

Contemporary understandings of conversion have been highly beholden to Reformation theological conclusions and the widespread influence of American evangelicalism, wherein conversion is a transformative *individual* experience or event.[8] The convert is "born again," either through a conscious choice rooted in spiritual understanding or by the instigation of a seismic moment; Saul's sudden encounter on the road to Damascus is the archetypal example.[9] Psychological studies have further upheld conversion as an emotional and a profound (sometimes mystical) experience, notably since William James published *The Varieties of Religious Experience* in 1902.[10] However, as many scholars have noted, understanding conversion in terms of the individual is, at best, only a small part of the picture, one that ignores the vast majority of historical, sociological, and anthropological conversion scenarios, which tend to be dominated by gradual, dynamic, and complex conversion processes involving groups of people under various forms of strain.[11]

As Lewis Rambo has detailed, whether we consider the conversion of individuals or societies, each must be seen as bound by obligations tied to micro and macro contexts (micro being: family, friends, community, etc. and macro being: broad political, religious, economic, and environmental systems).[12] When these contexts are considered, the experiential explanation of conversion becomes much less pronounced compared to the more prominently observed forces of incentivization and coercion. A number of these "push and pull" factors can be observed in the Frankish Christianization of Saxony, including conversion by:

1 **Violence:** war, massacres, and capital punishment (alongside the fear these instilled). Violence was intensified by notions of cosmic war and the consequent demonization of pagans.
2 **Gifts:** of gold, land, titles, and resources to elite members of society.
3 **Legal enforcement:** via mandates and punishments criminalizing pagan, heretical, or "inappropriate" customs.
4 **Slavery:** and the forced "reeducation" of child oblates or hostages.
5 **Economic exploitation:** through mandatory tithing and labor requirements to support the Church.
6 **Eradicating paganism**: via the destruction and appropriation of pagan cult sites.
7 **Geographic restructuring:** creating new (often fortified) religious communities promoting urbanization and a new geography of power in which the Church played a central role. This was coupled with massive deportations and Frankish colonization.
8 **Promoting a cult of the saints:** intended to commandeer devotion given to pagan deities and economically enhance the power of bishops and noble families.
9 **Marriage and political alliance:** resulting in the fusion of elite Franco-Saxon families into a new interconnected Christianized ruling class.
10 **Theological persuasion:** undertaken by missionaries evangelizing in dangerous territory who faced the daunting challenge of communicating their message comprehensibly. This process was aided by good works, including missionaries providing for marginalized members of society (such as slaves, criminals, or the poor).

Except for those persuaded by theology, each method radically differs from the spiritual notion of "conversion by interior change," often used to explain conversion in the history of religious missions.[13] Instead, rather than being a matter of belief, conversion traditionally implied to whom or what an individual owed their allegiance.[14] That allegiance could be given freely, incentivized, or compelled. Critically, allegiance came with strings attached, most notably, a renunciation of prior religious loyalties and obligations to perform rituals and behaviors, signifying the convert's new place of belonging within the Church. Understanding fundamental Christian principles and doctrines was seldom necessary for inclusion, indicating that many converts could only be considered nominally Christian. This is especially true concerning rural populations, most of whom were illiterate and dependent upon intermediaries for receiving the Christian message. As a result, conversion was typically a "top-down" affair undertaken by those in power (the ruler, nobles, and clergy), who wielded economic and military might while simultaneously controlling the production and dissemination of religious knowledge.

This work explores the processes mentioned above as they relate to Charlemagne's Saxon Wars in detail. However, while the context is Early Medieval "Germanic" Europe, the conversion techniques discussed became the blueprint by which subsequent peoples were brought within Christendom.

Outline

The text is divided (somewhat) chronologically into three parts. **Part One: Origins** contains five chapters establishing the historical context leading up to Charlemagne's conquest of Saxony. Chapters 1–3 introduce the reader to Franco-Saxon origins and their historical interactions from antiquity to the death of Charlemagne's father, Pippin III. By the end of Chapter 3, readers will have an understanding of key conflict points between Franks and Saxons, including rising religious tensions and the increasing pressure on Saxons to convert to Christianity. Chapter 4 focuses on the question: what were Saxons being converted from? This brief overview of Saxon paganism bleeds into Chapter 5, which chronicles pagan encounters during the establishment of the Church in Germany. Chapter 5 concludes with the encroachment of missionaries into Saxony and a broader look at methods of conversion leading up to Charlemagne's rule.

Part Two: Charlemagne's Saxon Wars contains four chapters, each addressing a particular phase of the conflict. Chapter 6 discusses the outbreak of the war, the escalation of religious tensions, early missionary endeavors in Saxony, and Saxon revolts from 772 to 777, while Chapter 7 chronicles the continued Saxon revolts in Westphalia led by the Saxon warlord Widukind. The progress of Christianization in Saxony between 777 and 785 is also discussed by addressing Saxon capitularies, missionary activities, the development of ecclesiastical institutions, and the final submission and conversion of Widukind. Chapters 8 and 9 trace the movement of the conflict into the north of Saxony and deal with the challenges of Saxon political integration and increasing tensions between Franco-Saxons and their Danish and Slavic neighbors up to Charlemagne's death in 814.

Part Three: Consequences also contains four chapters, the first of which (Chapter 10) concerns Franco-Saxon relations during the reign of Charlemagne's son Louis the Pious. The chapter focuses on the continued political integration of Saxony within the Frankish Empire and on Louis' successful courtship of Saxon loyalty amid a period of significant turmoil. Chapter 11 shifts focus back to the continued Christianization of Saxony, particularly the religious endeavors fostered by Louis the Pious, his grandsons, and the Saxon nobility, including the establishment of new ecclesiastical centers, missionary deployments, the acquisition of relics, and the production of the Old Saxon *Heliand*. Chapter 12 returns to the political crisis facing the Frankish Empire in the aftermath of Louis the Pious' death. The resulting Frankish civil war makes up the first half of the chapter, followed by a discussion of the final Saxon rebellion stemming from the Frankish conquest led by the so-called *Stellinga*. The chapter concludes by addressing the macro consequences affecting Saxony post-Frankish conquest, including increased militarization in response to Vikings, Slavs, and Magyars, economic developments related to urbanization, the establishment of new Saxon ecclesiastical institutions, and missionary enterprises aimed toward converting the Slavs and Danes. The Conclusion returns us to our initial concern by summarizing the methods of conversion employed in the religious transformation of Saxony while relating them to the broader historical context of global Christian missions.

A Note on Methods and Translations

I have approached this study chiefly as a historian, that is, by relying upon relevant primary sources. However, simultaneously, I have tried to bring an anthropological approach by utilizing archaeological, linguistic, and comparative socio-cultural insights when appropriate. As for the sources, throughout the text, basic introductions to authors and texts crucial to the topic are provided, alongside necessary endnotes. Nevertheless, specific sources and translations have been indispensable and require upfront acknowledgment. Chief among these is the *Royal Frankish Annals* (*Annales regni Francorum*), which include original (and revised) entries by Frankish court scholars chronicling significant events in the Frankish world between 741 and 829. An edited Latin edition can be found online via the *Monumenta Germaniae Historica* (MGH). However, I have primarily relied upon reputable English and German source translations. Regarding the *Royal Frankish Annals*, that would include Bernhard Scholz and Barbara Rogers-Gardner's book *Carolingian Chronicles*, an English translation also containing Nithard's four books on the turbulent period following the death of Charlemagne (814–843). Also, indispensable (though tragically out of print) has been P.D. King's *Charlemagne: Translated Sources*, which includes key entries from several of the so-called minor annals, miscellaneous sources, translations of Carolingian capitularies, letters, *Lives* of contemporary popes, and the Astronomer's *Life of the Emperor Louis*.

Timothy Reuter's translation of the *Annals of Fulda*, Janet Nelson's *The Annals of St. Bertin*, and Sydney Painter's translation of Einhard's *Vita Karoli Magni* (*The Life of Charlemagne*) have also been valuable. Supplementing each of these is Paul Dutton's *Carolingian Civilization*, an excellent collection of primary sources and excerpts.

In addition to source translations focusing primarily on Carolingian political and military events, several others have been critical for understanding earlier Frankish (Merovingian) history, including Lewis Thorpe's translation of Gregory of Tours' *The History of the Franks*, J.M. Wallace-Hadrill's *The Fourth Book of the Chronicle of Fredegar*, and Bernard Bachrach's *Liber Historiae Francorum* (*The Book of the History of the Franks*). These Frankish reports have been aided by a wider pool of translated sources, including many from antiquity, various collections of letters, biographical histories, Old Saxon texts, Ottonian Chronicles, Church histories, and hagiographical reports (including C.H. Talbot's incredibly useful collection, *The Anglo-Saxon Missionaries in Germany*). Without the labor of the countless scholars who tirelessly translated these texts for wider public access, this study would have taken infinitely longer to complete. It is with immense gratitude that I have utilized their work in the pages ahead.

Notes

1 Heather, *Christendom*, xiii & Neill, *A History of Christian Missions*, 207
2 Ibid. 218–219 & Hawk & Twiss, "An American Hermeneutic of Colonization," 52
3 La Barre, *The Ghost Dance*, 33; Gose, "Converting the Ancestors," 141 & Larkin & Meyer, "Pentecostalism, Islam and Culture," 292–293
4 Rambo, *Understanding Religious Conversion*, 75; Hawk & Twiss, "An American Hermeneutic of Colonization," 47–50; Lalitha, "Postcolonial Feminism," 79 & Smith et al., *Evangelical Postcolonial Conversations*, 45
5 Lindenfeld, *World Christianity and Indigenous Experience*, 2 & 112
6 Cusack, *Conversion among the Germanic Peoples*, 2–18 & 173–175; Heather, *Christendom*, xvii–xxii & 123–124 & Armstrong, *Fields of Blood*, 156
7 Jacoby, *Strange Gods*, 31
8 Buckser, "Social Conversion and Group Definition in Jewish Copenhagen," 80–81; Rambo, Anthropology and the Study of Conversion," 213 & Heather, *Christendom*, 60
9 Rambo, *Understanding Religious Conversion*, 15; Jacoby, *Strange Gods*, xviii; Glazier, "Limin wid Jah," 149 & Butler et al., *Religion in American Life*, 334
10 Ibid. 9 & James, *The Varieties of Religious Experience*, 217
11 Ibid. 1–5 & 8 & 44 & 60 & "Anthropology and the Study of Conversion," 213; Jacoby, *Strange Gods*, xiv & xix; Austin-Broos, "The Anthropology of Conversion," 2; Coleman, "Continuous Conversion?", 16–18; Anderson, "Constraint and Freedom in Icelandic Conversion," 130; Glazier, "Limin wid Jah," 154 & Greer, "Conversion and Identity," 177
12 Ibid. 21–22
13 Cusack, *Conversion among the Germanic Peoples*, 7
14 Armstrong, *Fields of Blood*, 245, and note here the etymological origins of "religion," which stems from the Latin *religare*, meaning "to bind fast," that is, to "obligate." See La Barre, *The Ghost Dance*, 9

Part I
Origins

1   The Kingdom of the Franks

Part I: An Introduction to Early Frankish History

People who came to be known as "Franks" began their ascent to power during what German scholars once called the *Völkerwanderung*, "the wandering of peoples," generally dated between 400 and 600 CE.[1] Their ancestral precursors were among the many Germanic tribes situated east of the Roman's Rhenish frontier, the *Limes Germanicus*.[2] In 406 CE, that frontier system of fortifications collapsed and was overrun by Germanic migrants and invaders, including (among others) Vandals, Suevi, and Alans.[3] It was a collapse that followed centuries of conflict, trade, and shifting alliances with various Germanic peoples and coincided with several factors that ultimately led to the disintegration of the Western Roman Empire. The (symbolic) end came in 476 CE when Emperor Romulus Augustus was deposed by the warlord Odoacer and his diverse army of "barbarians."[4] However, this convenient classification point merely represents the climax of a gradual process of decline. The incompetence of late Roman Emperors, disloyalty within the government, intermittent civil war, population decline, an over-reliance upon slavery, inflation, loss of tax revenue (e.g., from African grain), increasing use of mercenaries (*foederati*) in the army (leading to its degradation), and the overextension of the Empire were all significant contributors to Rome's decent.[5]

In addition, radical social changes came with the adoption of Christianity following the reigns of Constantine and Theodosius in the late fourth century CE.[6] That change disrupted the practices of ancient cults, facilitated the persecution of pagans, and brought about the destruction and appropriation of their idols and temples.[7] For some, the Empire's decline could be attributed to these religious disruptions alone, as it seemed the gods were furious at having been abandoned.[8] Indeed, this was a popular enough sentiment that early Christian writers felt compelled to argue against it, most notably in St. Augustine's *City of God* and Orosius' *Seven Books of History against the Pagans*.[9]

Altogether these myriad factors contributed to a fragmented and weakened empire, which some Germanic peoples capitalized on. By the sixth century, several new kingdoms had sprung up across Western Europe and North Africa, replacing imperial rule.[10] These new kingdoms did not go unchallenged, and both Gothic and Vandal power collapsed following the reclamation campaigns of Emperor

DOI: 10.4324/9781003379157-3

Justinian.[11] Yet, ultimately, Justinian's goal of restoration couldn't be sustained, and renewed Roman authority didn't linger long.[12] Within that context, the Franks began their ascent, ultimately becoming the primary inheritors of the Roman legacy, the dominant political power in the West, and a key contributor to the expansion of Christianity in Europe.[13]

Frankish Origins

What was meant by the ethnonym "Frank"? In his *Etymologies*, the influential seventh-century scholar Isidore of Seville claimed that some believed the Franks acquired their name from "a certain chieftain of theirs," while others thought it derived from "the brutality of their behavior, for their behavior is wild, with a natural ferocity of spirit."[14] Modern scholars lean toward the latter of these explanations and believe "Frank" originally denoted something akin to "fierce," "free," or "brave."[15] Therefore, "Franks" could be interpreted as "free," "bold," or "brave ones."[16] However, the term did not always refer to specific tribal groups, and sometimes, "Frank" may have been a "trans-ethnic political identity," indicating adherence to Frankish (Salic) law, or used more broadly by Romans as a term for their Rhenish enemies.[17]

In their earliest form, Franks are mentioned in Antiquity with references to groups of tribes (e.g., Salli, Ripuari, Chatti, Bructeri, Batavi, and Chamavi) situated on the Lower and Middle Rhine or inhabiting the river valleys of the Elbe and Main.[18] Yet, by the time the Western Roman Empire began to crumble, Franks could be generally relegated to three groups: Salians, situated primarily in the Low Countries where the Ijssel flows into the Zuider Zee; Ripuarians (*Rheinfranken*) of the Middle Rhine; and Hessians (*populus Hassiorum*), located to the south on the River Main.[19] Of these groups, it was the Salians who emerged as dominant sometime in the fourth or fifth century CE and from whom sprang the ambitious Merovingian dynasty.[20]

As the Franks expanded west, they intermingled, assimilated, and fused with local Gallo-Roman populations.[21] Tribal affiliations were fluid, and ethnicity in Early Medieval Europe was much fuzzier than claimed by later scholars searching for "pure" continuities between tribes and nations.[22] Franks spoke variants of West Germanic, including Old Low Franconian, Rhenish Franconian, and other variants of Low and Old High German.[23] However, eventually, their tongues fused with the "Vulgar Latin" of the Gallo-Romans, forming the foundations of Old French.[24]

Expansion also brought increasing exposure to Roman influence, particularly in Frankish constructions of their origins, which (in part) sought to emulate the grandeur of Rome's foundation myths.[25] For example, one prominent tale placed Frankish origins among the ancient Trojans.[26] This was a popular story among seventh- and eighth-century Franks who, according to the *Chronicle of Fredegar*, claimed the Franks were descendants of King Priam of Troy.[27] However, an alternative myth was proposed earlier by the sixth-century Gallo-Roman bishop Gregory of Tours.[28] In his *Ten Books of History*, Gregory claimed the Franks originally migrated from Pannonia before settling along the Rhine.[29] The Pannonia and Trojan stories were later merged and replicated in the eighth-century *Liber Historiae Francorum*. However, none of these accounts should be interpreted as historically reliable.[30] That is not to say they do not speak to some cultural memory regarding earlier migrations from the east (notably those of the Goths and Huns), which had genuine ramifications for Frankish developments.

We get a historical sense of place for early Frankish groups primarily through their interactions with the Romans. For example, there are indicators in the first century CE, during the Batavian revolts along the Rhine delta, of "proto-Franks" participating in the Roman army as auxiliary units and making up significant portions of the imperial bodyguard.[31] A few centuries later, some of these groups settled in various Western enclaves as *laeti* (non-Roman settlers granted land in exchange for military service).

By 358, Salian Franks were also acting as *foederati* in exchange for settlement in Toxandria (now South Holland and North Belgium).[32] Many Franks thereafter became prominent generals in the Roman army.[33] However, Franco-Roman relations were not always cordial. In 240, during the reign of Emperor Aurelian, Franks were defeated in battle by the Romans outside Mainz.[34] They fought again in 355 when Ripuarian Franks took control of Cologne (*Colonia*), the capital of the Roman province *Germania Inferior*.[35] Even the Salian settlement in Toxandria a few years later followed bitter conflicts with Emperor Julian.[36] Simultaneously, we are given reports of Frankish pirates vanquished by Romans in the Mediterranean and Frankish captives used for gruesome entertainment in Roman arenas.[37]

Despite intermittent conflict, Roman influence on the Franks continued manifesting in their material culture and social customs. Roman iconography decorated Frankish coinage (e.g., Romulus and Remus), and Roman ideas helped mold Frankish Salic law, a fusion of Roman and Germanic legal customs composed in Latin between 507 and 511 CE.[38] When the Rhineland defenses collapsed in 406, Franks fought *against* the invaders in defense of Roman territory.[39] However, we are told in the *Liber Historiae Francourm* that following this event, some Franks revolted and began executing Roman tax collectors, which required a Roman army to march against them.[40] Nevertheless, again, in defense of the Empire, Franks (as well as Saxons) stood with Aetius and the Romans at the Battle of the Catalaunian Plains in 451, which stopped Attila and the onslaught of the Huns.[41] Soon after, when the Merovingian dynasty consolidated power in the 450s, the Franks and Rome drew closer with the conversion of the Frankish king Clovis to Christianity.[42]

Early Frankish Paganism

Before Clovis, Franks were adherents to a form of Germanic paganism (likely supplemented with Roman and Celtic influences).[43] We know very little about the deities they worshiped, but in part, they belonged to the "Cult of Odin," the eccentric god of war, wisdom, and poetry who appears in various guises across the Germanic/Norse world.[44] Of their goddesses, we know virtually nothing, although some of the votive *Matronae* stones found throughout the Rhineland may have belonged to proto-Frankish clans.[45] The influence of imported mystery cults on early Frankish paganism should also be considered, given that sanctuaries dedicated to Isis and Mithras have been discovered in Mainz.[46] However, how influential these were outside of imperial centers is difficult to surmise. This question is also relevant for the adoption of Roman or Celtic deities, although archaeological and historical evidence makes their wider influence more likely.[47]

Much of what constituted pre-Christian Frankish customs also remains elusive. Nevertheless, we are not left wandering entirely adrift. Akin to customs found elsewhere in pre-Christian Europe, Franks venerated their ancestors, erected idols of their gods, ritually ate horses, made use of magic amulets, practiced witchcraft, and utilized animal and human sacrifice.[48] Some sacrifices were made before crossing rivers, presumably in the hope of securing safe passage.[49]

In his *Gallic Wars*, Julius Caesar recorded religious customs of the Suevi, a tribe whose descendants included the Chatti (proto-Franks).[50] From Caesar, we learn that the Suevi cast lots and used divination before battle, perhaps a custom that lingered among later Franks.[51] According to Gregory of Tours, Frankish pagans also made sacrifices to idols they molded in the likeness of woodland and river animals.[52] In fifth-century Western Francia, condemnation was also voiced by Caesarius of Arles, who called for the destruction of "profane trees" considered sacred to locals.[53] However, whether these refer to trees associated with "Romano-Celtic paganism" or "Franco-Germanic paganism" is unclear. Regardless, the "cult of trees" continued to be condemned during Frankish Synods and councils over the following three centuries, suggesting it proved especially difficult to extirpate.[54]

In the *Chronicle of Fredegar*, Merovingians claimed divine descent from Merowech, a demi-god of sorts whose mother was impregnated by a sea creature.[55] However, following the conversion of the Franks to Christianity, these early pagan associations were abandoned or minimized. They were replaced by epic migration myths designed to place Franks on par with the Romans, such as the one mentioned concerning the Trojans.

The Conversion of Clovis

The first significant move away from paganism came with Clovis (Clodovech/ Chlodwig), a Salian warlord ultimately responsible for establishing the Franks as a more unified power.[56] The chronicler of the *Liber Historiae Francorum* hailed him as the greatest of kings.[57] However, recent scholars have been less doting. Indeed, British historian Charles Oman called Clovis "morally far the worst of all the Teutonic founders of kingdoms."[58] Oman's criticism is not unjustified. After all, Clovis' ascendancy *was* accomplished via schemes and treachery, including assassinating his family members and rivals among the Salians and Ripuarians.[59] However, he was also an effective commander, and a significant victory came in 486 when Clovis defeated the governor-general Syagrius at Soissons (whom he had executed), which removed the remnants of Roman rule in Gaul.[60] The Franks then took control largely of what is now France, while Clovis extended Frankish suzerainty east by defeating the Thuringians in battle and making them tributaries.

It was sometime between 496 and 507, at the behest of his Burgundian wife Clotilde, and following a victory in battle against the Alamanni, that Clovis converted to Christianity.[61] Specifically, Clovis converted to Roman Catholicism, placing the Franks at odds with other Germanic peoples who mostly converted to Homoean Arianism—a Christian sect rejecting the Catholic (Nicene) interpretation of the divine unity of God the Father and Christ the Son.[62] Clovis' conversion had not come easy. He spent most of his early life as a staunch pagan and, according to Gregory of Tours, may have even allowed his troops to plunder churches.[63] In addition, Clotilde frequently pleaded for the conversion of her husband, and the couple fought on two occasions concerning Clotilde's decision to baptize their children.[64] Clovis was also unsuccessfully courted by Arian missionaries (although he may have dabbled in Arianism for a bit, perhaps influenced by his Arian sister Lanthechild).[65]

According to Gregory, it was only during war with the Alamanni that Clovis was forced out of necessity to accept what he had been reluctant to.[66] The warlord vowed to the Christian God that if he helped Clovis achieve victory in battle, Clovis would receive baptism in return.[67] After winning the battle, Clovis upheld his end of the bargain and was baptized on Christmas Day by Bishop Remigius at Rheims (alongside 3,000 of his retainers).[68] During this process, the bishop allegedly instructed Clovis, the "new Constantine," to "worship what you have burnt" and "burn what you have been wont to worship."[69]

While the war may have played a role in Clovis' conversion, much of later history credited Clotilde with facilitating his change of heart. Indeed, in Normandy, she was made a saint, one to be invoked by wives suffering the company of "iniquitous husbands."[70] However, political considerations were also powerful motivators, and by converting to Roman Catholicism, Clovis secured the support of the Gallo-Roman aristocracy within his kingdom, garnered East Roman support against his Visigothic (Arian) enemies, and ensured stronger ties among the Franks, Rome, and papacy.[71] Clovis also benefited from the organizational structure of Romano-Christian culture, which he soon began to emulate via policy. Indeed, it was Clovis who instituted Salic law, promoted royal patronage of saints' cults, and began employing bishops as counts, granting them extensive secular and spiritual powers.[72] Bishops, in turn, were expected to be useful to the king. This began a system of patronage given to the Church by which monastic centers gained vast endowments and clerics acquired special privileges. These endowments to early Merovingian bishops, in turn, perpetuated a hierarchical system in which connection to the nobility came to be seen as nearness to God, ergo *status* rather than *learning* equated to sanctity.[73] In the future, it would be a rare occurrence indeed for an individual of lower social status to be made bishop, an observation increasingly true for becoming a member of European monastic communities (both male and female).[74]

These religious changes profoundly affected how elite Franks conceptualized themselves, notably as being chosen by God as the rightful inheritors of the Roman legacy.[75] That fusion of "Roman imperialist ethos" and divine destiny would instill in the Franks what Jeff Sypeck has called a particularly "muscular, Old Testament brand of Christianity."[76]

The Merovingians

Following Clovis' conversion, the Franks achieved significant military victories, notably over the Burgundians in 500 and Alaric's Visigoths at Vouillé in 507.[77] Yet, Clovis' guardianship eventually ended, and after reigning for 30 years, he died in 511 and was buried in Paris at the Abbey of Saint Genevieve, which he had founded only a few years prior.[78]

The Merovingians succeeding Clovis continued his work of expansion, Christianization, and consolidation.[79] By 530/31, Theuderic and Chlotar (Clovis' sons) conquered the Thuringians along the River Unstrut.[80] That victory was followed in 534 by the overthrow of the Burgundians, which placed Franks in control of territory in Provence.[81] Theuderic also repelled a Scandinavian invasion of the Lower Rhineland, led supposedly by the Danish king Hygelac, a ruler typically associated with the legend of Beowulf.[82] However, according to the *Liber Historiae Francorum*, the real credit goes to Theuderic's son Theudebert, who pursued the Danes, defeated them, and killed their king.[83] Only a few years later, in 536, Theudebert also conquered Alamannia, a region that would remain predominantly pagan (and somewhat autonomous) until the mid-eighth-century reign of Charles Martel (see Chapter 5).[84]

By way of conquest, "Francia" thereafter came to represent the land between the Seine and the Rhine, consisting of Austrasia, "the eastern land" between the Rhine and the Meuse, and Neustria, the newer Frankish lands between the Meuse and the Loire.[85] The so-called long-haired kings had expanded their authority over many enemies. Yet, by the seventh century, their hold on power was being challenged from within by an aspiring family known as the Carolingians, an Austrasian clan deriving its name from the prominent use of "Karl" (Lat. "Karolus" or "Charles") among its members.[86]

The Carolingian Ascent

Carolingian origins lay within the Frankish nobility where, as early as the 630s, they managed to secure influence by maintaining hold of the position "Mayor of the Palace" (*major domus*).[87] The precise meaning of that title remains somewhat confused, and although its origins harken back to Roman senatorial estate administrators, scholars continue to debate the extent of its functions.[88] Nevertheless, by the late Merovingian Age, the "Mayor of the Palace" appears to have been responsible for royal administrative duties, military actions, and oversight of the king's household.[89] As the power of the Merovingian kings deteriorated, those of the "Mayors" grew until they became de facto rulers of the realm.[90]

The final blow to Merovingian authority was initiated by Pippin III ("Pippin the Short"), a son of the influential Mayor of the Palace, Charles Martel.[91] In 751, Pippin led a successful coup against King Childeric III, ending Merovingian rule.[92] Pope Zacharias supposedly supported the overthrow to secure Frankish support against the Lombards, a wish the Franks would later fulfill. Following Zacharias' acknowledgment, Pippin gathered an assembly of nobles, secured their support, and was anointed King of the Franks by St. Boniface at Soissons, ushering in a new Frankish dynasty.[93] However, scholars question whether Pippin acquired papal support *before* the Carolingian takeover. That notion may have been written in hindsight as justification for the coup.[94] Nevertheless, Pippin's rule was further symbolically sanctioned in 754 when Pope Stephen II staged a second anointing in Paris at the Basilica of St. Denis, where he proclaimed Pippin "Patrician of the Romans."[95] It was a title he would take seriously, as would his eldest son Charles.

Charlemagne

The man known as Charlemagne, or Charles the Great, was born on April 2, 742 (or 748?) to Pippin III and his wife Bertrada, a daughter of the influential Count of Laon.[96] History has mostly remembered Charles fondly, often romantically, and only in recent scholarship (with some exceptions), critically.[97] As Matthias Becher has written, Charles "is inextricably bound to the idea of historical greatness."[98] Or, in the words of Richard Fletcher, "Charlemagne was incontestably the greatest ruler of early Medieval Europe."[99] For many, he is the "Father of Europe" or Western civilization.[100] Charles Oman called him "the common pride of Christendom."[101] Per the French nobility of the fifteenth century, he was undeniably worthy of sainthood.[102] The tenth-century Saxon chronicler Widukind of Corvey hailed Charles as the mightiest and wisest of kings.[103] In the twelfth-century epic, *The Song of Roland*, Charles even took on the guise of "a bearded sage who fought alongside angels for God," which served as poetic inspiration for crusaders.[104] For many, he was undoubtedly *the* archetypal Christian ruler.[105]

In more recent periods, Charles has been explicitly connected with notions of international unity, learning, and peace.[106] At the same time, he has been a convenient tool of nationalism, having been claimed as a folk hero by France, Germany, and Belgium.[107] For imperialists, his conquests served as inspiration as well as propaganda.[108] He found admiration from both Napoleon and Hitler. However, Charles has not entirely escaped denigration. For example, sixteenth-century French historian Etienne Pasquier was little pleased with the grandiose myths of a man he deemed a tyrant.[109] Likewise, Voltaire believed Charles was a remnant of a darker age—a vestige of barbarian violence, ignorance, and religious fanaticism.[110]

As may be surmised by the multifaceted use of his legacy, the reality of who Charles the Great *actually* was is significantly more complex than has often been portrayed. He was, as E.C. Metzenthin noted in 1923, one of those "double-natured men" rooted in a seemingly paradoxical period of history.[111]

Much of what we know concerning Charles' personality stems from a biography, the *Vita Karoli Magni*, written by the scholar Einhard sometime between 817 and 836.[112] In Einhard's work, modeled on Suetonius' second-century *Lives of the Twelve Caesars*, we are presented with a man who cherished Christian literature above all others but still revered heroic "heathen" poems of bygone days.[113] We see a man who, when he wasn't hunting, swimming, courting, or feasting, could be found codifying laws, initiating educational reforms, commissioning architectural works, gazing at the stars, or spending time with his beloved daughters (who had a bit of a mischievous reputation).[114] Although he never quite mastered the art of writing, Charles was an exceptionally well-learned man of his time. He was undoubtedly familiar with the classic works of the period, such as Boethius' *Consolation of Philosophy* or Isidore's *Etymologies*.[115]

The forging of Charles' character began at a young age. As early as 6 years old, he would have started training for war by learning traditional skills of the nobility, including weaponry, horse riding, and hunting.[116] As youth gave way to manhood, his studies expanded with knowledge of statecraft and courtly life; he witnessed the military campaigns of his father in Aquitaine and those against the Saxons. He even accompanied his father on his later campaigns in Aquitaine, brutal and devastating endeavors that must have lingered in Charles' memory during his own conquests.[117]

If Charles managed to maintain a working relationship with his father, his closeness with his brother Carloman could easily be questioned.[118] It is generally believed that the two were not very fond of each other and that Charles grew distant from his brother when Carloman refused to aid him in putting down a revolt in Aquitaine.[119] As a result, Charles was little displeased when Carloman conveniently died in December 771 (possibly from a hemorrhage) at the early age of 20, just shortly after their joint succession to the throne in 768.[120]

Whether or not Charles played a role in the death of his brother has long been a source of scholarly intrigue. However, while the possibility cannot be dismissed, no concrete evidence supports it. Whatever the case might be, Charles almost surely knew the death of his brother was imminent (from reports, rumors, or direct involvement) because immediately after the event, he annexed his brother's realm (ignoring the inheritance rights of Carloman's sons), which caused his brother's wife and children to flee south to the Kingdom of Lombards and seek refuge with its ruler Desiderius. Charles responded to their flight by ending his diplomatic ties with the Lombards, which he demonstrated by sending his Lombard wife Desiderata back to her father (Desiderius).[121]

Returning his bride was not particularly problematic for Charles because they had married back in 770 in defiance of the Pope. Yet, with her dismissal, Franco-Papal relations on the matter were salvaged.[122] It also didn't take long for Charles to find a more politically suitable bride, the future Queen Hildegard, who was only 13 years of age (not particularly unusual for the time).[123] Hildegard brought with her significant connections to Bavaria and Alamannia, which were valuable for Charles in the aftermath of Carloman's death.[124] As the sole ruler of the realm, securing the loyalty of various regional noble and ecclesiastical factions was critical, allowing Charles to prepare for his broader ambitions. Much of what constituted those ambitions will be explored in the chapters ahead.

Part II: Frankish Society

Frankish Geography

By the Carolingian ascendancy, Francia had become a fusion of Germanic, Gallo-Roman, and Christian cultures. It was a diverse realm composed of myriad tribes and peoples. Geographically, the kingdom consisted of Neustria (between the Seine and the Loire), west Francia (between the Seine and the Meuse), middle Francia (between the Meuse and the Rhine), and eastern Francia (Hesse, Thuringia, and Alamannia).[125] To the northwest lay hostile Frisians and Saxons, to the south a relatively independent Bavaria, while in the west, the Romanized region of Aquitaine continued to resist Frankish rule.[126] Further to the southwest, the Spanish border was an area of shifting leadership with varying levels of loyalty, while the mountainous Basque country remained eternally hostile. Similarly, staunch resistance could be found among the Bretons of the northwest coast.[127]

A key component of Frankish geography and economy was the kingdom's access to significant trade ports.[128] Quentovic, situated near Montreuil-sur-Mer across from the southern coast of Britain, was the earliest of these.[129] However, it was supplemented by the Frisian port of Dorestad (*Durstede*), which the Franks commandeered in the early eighth century and turned into a tolling station.[130] Dorestad also gave the Franks access to trade networks connecting the North Sea and Baltic and became an important center for minting coinage.[131] Frankish commerce was also enhanced by the Frisian market of Domburg, located on the island of Walcheren in Zeeland.[132] While further south, along the Rhine, the Franks controlled Mainz (the former capital of *Germania superior*), which became a busy hub for trade and minting coinage.[133] Mainz was also intimately connected with the slave trade, the stock of which often came from Slavic lands (the word "slave" is derived from *Slav* or *Sclavus*).[134]

Slaves were sometimes transported to Mainz (or Venice) and sold to Jewish or Arab merchants who hauled their acquisitions back to Spain.[135] Slavery, though common, was a complex system in the Carolingian world. While captives were routinely sold for transport abroad, they were more often used as bondsmen for labor on Frankish estates.[136] Regulations stipulated who could be enslaved, who could not, and where and to whom they could be sold.[137] For example, selling Christians to pagans or Jews was forbidden, although these regulations were often ignored. During the eighth and ninth centuries, the slave trade expanded. For the present work, one is forced to wonder what role the Saxon Wars played in that expansion.[138] The conflict occurred from the end of the eighth century until the early ninth, and Frankish raiding and hostage-taking during the war are well attested.[139] In addition, like most Slavs, Saxons were predominantly pagan and, therefore, free game for slavers wanting to avoid the taboo of capturing Christians. There was also already a precedent for Saxon slaves in Francia during the Merovingian era, as is attested by Gregory of Tours.[140]

The "guilt-free" enslavement of "heathens" was no mere historical aberration. On the contrary, the sentiment became more prominent over the following centuries, climaxing in countless societies during the Colonial quest for free land and labor (see Conclusion).[141] The justifications were typically two-fold: a refusal of "savages" to convert absolved invaders of their enslavement *of* and violence *toward* indigenous peoples (which could be done with reference to biblical precedents), and further, one's conscience could be assuaged by understanding that enslavement of pagans inevitably leads to their exposure to Christianity and possible conversion.[142] Put bluntly, slavery could save souls.

Political and Social Structure

Power within Francia was centralized on the monarch. On several occasions, Charlemagne required all males older than 12 to swear an oath of fealty over sacred relics.[143] Once sworn, an oath was not broken lightly. Treason was punishable by death, blinding, banishment, or slavery.[144] In addition, the fact that oaths were sworn over relics sacralized the occasion. Allegiance to the king, a divine representative of God, was not simply a political statement but a religious obligation.

Frankish society was strictly hierarchical; "class" structures were rigidly enforced. One was born noble, free, or enslaved, and the opinions of lower classes counted for very little.[145] Frankish Salic law, and the punishments therein, also varied significantly based on social status, and those accused of crimes often faced the daunting task of proving their innocence via "ordeals."[146] If the accused failed to find supporters to vouch for their innocence, sticking a hand into boiling water (with the hope of avoiding injury), casting lots, or an arranged duel was expected to harness "the judgment of God" (*iudicium dei*).[147] This reliance upon structured legal action was fundamental to the Frankish desire to avoid the never-ending problem of feuding.[148]

For enacting laws and dispensing justice, the king relied upon several royal officials, especially counts. Counts acted as territorial representatives of the king, although their power varied considerably depending on the size and location of their county. For example, those situated in the borderlands were more militarized due to the threat of raiding.[149] However, regardless of locale, a count's duties were extensive and might require levying armies, holding assemblies, passing judgment in legal proceedings, administering law, enforcing capitularies, or collecting fines and taxes.[150] They were assisted in administering law and "high justice" by legal assessors known as *scabini*, while lower-level village-related crimes were dealt with by vicars (representatives) and hundredmen (administrators who held jurisdiction over smaller territories).[151] The power and corruption of counts were meant to be kept in check by *missi dominici*, ecclesiastical and royal officials who traveled throughout the realm to ensure adherence to the king's will.[152] These officials were assigned *missatica* (inspection zones), typically comprising six to ten counties.[153]

If the king was otherwise engaged, trials at court were overseen by the "count of the palace." The king was further aided in establishing justice throughout his domain by a chancellor responsible for drafting royal charters.[154] Many of the other serious affairs fell to the royal chamberlain and seneschal.[155] The seneschal was considered the senior court official; their duties included overseeing the king's household, for example, the acquisition and maintenance of provisions.[156] Meanwhile, the royal chamberlain absorbed the functions of the former Mayor of the Palace, including management of the treasury, oversight of royal gifts, and collecting fines and taxes.[157] Together, these officials ensured the safety of the king and the enactment of his will.

Methods of War

Warfare was endemic in Frankish society. Hardly a year passed by without the mustering of troops.[158] By what means were campaigns fought, and who took part in them?

During the Merovingian era, Franks spread terror among their enemies with throwing axes called *fransiska*.[159] These came in handy for immobilizing enemy shields in which they were prone to get stuck. Despite their widespread use, by the Carolingian Age, throwing axes had fallen out of favor and were replaced by *scramasax* short swords.[160] The Franks also increasingly made use of light-weight long swords (*spathae*), which (because of their efficiency, length, and ease of use) gradually replaced the *seax* (see Chapter 2).[161] However, swords were incredibly expensive and took hundreds of man hours in complex labor to complete.[162] As a result, their use was typically reserved for the nobility.[163] Nevertheless, Francia had some of the best blacksmiths in Europe, and Frankish blades were sought after by their enemies well into the Viking Age.[164] Consequently, the sale of Frankish weapons was highly regulated to maintain a technological advantage.[165]

Standard Frankish infantrymen relied primarily on spears, such as the common "winged lance" type (*Flügellanzen*), while others employed short iron daggers (*seax*), long D-shaped yew bows, slings, and axes.[166] For protection, upper-class warriors adorned leather shirts (sometimes covered with a cuirass), various conical helmets (one being the *spangenhelm*), armored gauntlets, and oval, round, and concave wooden shields reinforced with metal and leather.[167] Those who could afford it might protect their legs and arms with iron greaves, gauntlets, or armguards.[168] While many of these items were the privilege of the wealthy, wooden shields were not expensive or difficult to construct and would have been widely available.[169]

Infantry composed the core of the Frankish army. Conscripts from subjugated areas bolstered their ranks, many coming from Bavaria and Alamannia. Beyond their use in fighting, infantrymen often occupied enemy strongholds and built fortified camps (*castra*) on the frontier.[170] Carolingian warfare focused primarily on capturing and garrisoning strongholds; in general, open battles were to be avoided.[171] When engaging in siege warfare, the enemy was starved out, or if time was short, walls or gates (the most vulnerable points) were battered with siege engines and projectiles and then stormed with ladders.[172]

By the middle of the eighth century, mounted warfare was also a critical component of Frankish military might. Those able to afford the lucrative cost of outfitting a horse (equivalent to the worth of 20 cattle) could be used as cavalrymen.[173] Carolingians utilized elite heavily armored Breton cavalry, which often rode in tightly packed formations and fought with javelins, lances, and swords.[174] Vast landholders and members of the nobility also made up rapid strike cavalry and elite units known as *scarae*, which, as Pierre Riche has noted, "played a decisive role in the conquest of Saxony."[175] As early as the seventh century, Frankish cavalrymen also utilized stirrups, an innovation gleaned from the Avars, which used the horse's momentum and allowed for easier movement of a lance or sword.[176]

War was also a vital aspect of Frankish governance. Frankish kings needed to keep counts (of which there were roughly 300) and nobles happy with a steady supply of loot (including livestock, precious goods, and slaves), which necessitated a near-constant state of war and rapine.[177] Frankish nobles began training for combat as soon as they entered puberty, after which they participated in the ravenous "game of war."[178] However, pillaging was not relegated to upper classes; such was the right of men on the march when entering enemy territory.[179] As Bachrach has noted, in the Early Middle Ages, there were few hardline "rules of engagement" concerning the treatment of enemy civilians.[180] Scorched-earth tactics were particularly encouraged when fighting pagans or heretics, whose decimation could be equated to "holy work."[181] Charlemagne's ninth-century biographer, Notger the Stammerer, proudly proclaimed the Frankish sword was ever "ready for attacking pagans."[182] Massacres, burning villages, destroying crops, slaughtering livestock, rape, and executions were routine. Such measures were used mercilessly in Aquitaine, Brittany, and Saxony.[183]

By the reign of Charlemagne, the Carolingian army is estimated to have contained 30,000–100,000 infantry and roughly 3,000 cavalrymen, of which only a small part was used at any given time.[184] These units were mustered from various regional levies, conscripts, bishoprics, household troops of the nobility and royal family, and mercenaries.[185] The king kept desertion and truancy in check by decreeing the death penalty and confiscation of property for anyone who left the army without permission. Hefty fines were also given to noblemen who failed to show up when called upon; social ostracism and the prospects of disgrace were also powerful constraints.[186]

To keep the army engaged and fit for handling the landscapes of war, tactical drilling was constant. Learning battle formations and signals (e.g., from banners, trumpets, or drums), how to employ surprise attacks or feign retreats, and engaging in effective siege warfare were all critical for ensuring victory.[187] Reconnaissance and intelligence gathering were also required to understand enemy terrain, movements, fortification weak points, and troop numbers. Such information could be acquired through various means, including by scouting, interviewing merchants and locals, or interrogating enemy prisoners.[188]

As for Charlemagne, by most accounts, he was a brilliant and resourceful military tactician.[189] He was educated in the martial lessons of Antiquity, including influential works such as Vegetius' *Epitoma mei militaris*.[190] He would divide his armies to force his enemy to fight on multiple fronts and is credited with directing rapid advances into hostile territory, including unorthodox night and winter marches.[191] His armies' baggage train was also heavily regulated, with consideration given to organizing the logistical components of a campaign. For example, oats had to be harvested during the spring to feed horses brought with the army.[192] Soldiers also needed to be fed, which required sufficient resources for maintaining battle readiness.[193] Consequently, domesticated animals and wagons stocked with supplies for cooking, daily repairs, fording rivers, and more accompanied the army on campaign. As did the servants and laborers responsible for them.[194] Given this dependency upon basic survival goods, supply lines were maintained by land and water.[195] Crossing a river posed serious challenges; therefore, repairing bridges was crucial for ensuring successful supply chains and troop movements.[196]

Because of these practical obstacles, Charlemagne loathed anything brought on campaign deemed excessive or ostentatious, and he criticized any display of luxury by his commanders. Only members of the Church were allowed to flaunt their wealth to demonstrate the prestige of the Church and inspire the army.[197] Bishops or priests might also carry sacred relics, granting the army spiritual favor.[198] In addition, they heard confessions or led soldiers in prayer and sang psalms before battle to swell their courage and remind them God was on their side.[199] Songs or chants might also keep armies in line while marching; therefore, they served organizational and spiritual functions.[200]

While on campaign, the king and his retinue often stayed at royal estates (*Konigslandschafen* or *Pfalzen*).[201] In the early Carolingian era, Frankfurt, Ingelheim, Paderborn, Herstal, and Aachen were the most notable.[202] Together, these constituted a distinct "geography of power" (*Herrschaftsgeographie*) by which the ruler's authority could be projected.[203]

During the reign of Charlemagne, the most significant royal estate was undoubtedly Aachen.[204] The attraction to Aachen was the healing power of its hot springs. Originally a Celtic pagan site (called *Aquae Granni*, "the waters of Granus"), by the first century CE, it had developed into baths for Roman troops stationed nearby, whereafter (by the fifth century) the area had transformed into a locale sacred to Christians.[205] With the Carolingian ascent, Aachen gained the admiration of Charlemagne's father, Pippin, who had a residence erected there in the mid-eighth century.[206] Charlemagne replicated his father's attraction to the site, and, in the early 790s, he placed Odo of Metz and his biographer Einhard in charge of developing the local complex, notably with the addition of a new palace and cathedral/chapel.[207] Today nothing remains of the palace, but visitors to Aachen can still stand in awe of the cathedral. The structure is an architectural marvel, which Odo appears to have partially modeled on Justinian's sixth-century church of St. Vitale in Ravenna.[208] By 794, construction of the newer Aachen facilities had progressed well enough that Charlemagne felt comfortable residing there nearly every following winter.[209] While construction continued for over a decade, Aachen increasingly became an imperial center, which contemporaries were proud to call the "new Jerusalem" or "second Rome."[210]

Daily Life

Frankish life was subject to the cycles of nature.[211] During the summer, people and animals busied themselves with farm work and producing goods to prepare for winter hibernation when food might become scarce.[212] Summer was also a time of military campaigning when horses could feed off the land, and men didn't have to worry about freezing during the night. Although, even in summer, soldiers had the rains to contend with, and flooding rivers were always a concern. Sudden climate change could spell disaster, leading to the eradication of domesticated animals, disease, and the decimation of crops.[213] Lightning strikes burned villages to the ground, and famine halted armies on the march. Life expectancy was short. Early childhood mortality rates were high (3/10 died before age 1); males might live into their mid-40s, women roughly 35 (possibly due to child-birth or iron deficiency).[214]

Frankish families populated the landscape with villages, stone manors, castles, and strongholds. The realm was connected loosely by a few roads and paths criss-crossing the wilderness, including some left by the Romans.[215] Travel and communication were slow and difficult.[216] Economic resources were limited. Nevertheless, merchants plied their wares, and women adorned market stalls with crafts. Each navigated a commerce system reliant upon both bartering and coinage.[217]

Fashion statements mattered even at the lowest levels of society. Men grew long mustaches over shaved chins, while women concealed their hair behind veils or hoods, donned ornamental brooches, and, in Riche's words, cultivated beauty in "service to God."[218] Everyone had their role in ensuring the continuance of social harmony and the fulfillment of God's plan (this was *ordo mundi*, the "order of the world"), and it was well understood that idle hands made for the Devil's play-thing.[219] The supernatural permeated all life. There was no separation between spir-itual and mundane—no compartmentalization of one's religion.

Conclusion

Over roughly 250 years, the Merovingian and Carolingian dynasties transformed a loosely connected conglomeration of tribes into an imperial kingdom that domi-nated Western Europe. This was no small feat in the dynamic and competitive envi-ronment of the post-Roman West. Frankish success was due not only to military prowess but also to the partial adoption of Roman models of law, governance, and religion. Each was used to bolster an infrastructure that maintained social order and enhanced the royal family's power. Nevertheless, myriad challenges remained, including the continued Christianization of the realm and the defeat of peripheral enemies whose religious affiliations were altogether different. Increasingly promi-nent among those foes were the Saxons.

Notes

1 Davies, *Europe*, 217–218; Mackay, *Atlas of Medieval Europe*, 8; Thompson, *Feudal Germany*, XI; James, "The Northern World in the Dark Ages," 64; Cantor, *The Civili-zation of the Middle Ages*, 89 & Holland, *Germany*, 12–13
2 Henderson, *A History of Germany in the Middle Ages*, 28
3 Musset, *The Germanic Invasions*, 23; Green, *Language and History in the Early Ger-manic World*, 195 & Brown, "The Transformation of the Roman Mediterranean," 2–3
4 Baldoli, *A History of Italy*, 2–5 & Halsall, *Barbarian Migrations and the Roman West*, 457
5 Fletcher, *The Conversion of Europe*, 17; Naylor, *North Africa*, 47; Wickham, *The Inheritance of Rome*, 23; Geary, *Before France and Germany*, 21–22; Backman, *The Worlds of Medieval Europe*, 14–16; Bachrach, *Warfare in Medieval Europe*, 99–100 & Cantor, *The Civilization of the Middle Ages*, 41–45
6 Durant, *Caesar and Christ*, 667–668

7 Fletcher, *The Conversion of Europe*, 38

8 Chadwick, "The Early Christian Community," 41–42 and the most famous early modern critic (though typically rejected) of Christianity's negative impacts on the Roman Empire comes from the eighteenth-century historian Edward Gibbons. See Gibbons, *The History of the Decline and Fall of the Roman Empire*, 436–437; Jacoby, *Strange Gods*, xvi; Armstrong, *Fields of Blood*, 163 & Heather, *Christendom*, 131

9 Orosius, *Seven Books of History against the Pagans*, 8–13

10 Vitensis, *Victor of Vita*, 3–6

11 Brown, "The Transformation of the Roman Mediterranean," 7

12 Halsall, *Barbarian Migrations and the Roman West*, 512

13 Mackay, *Atlas of Medieval Europe*, 9 & Geary, *Before France and Germany*, 89

14 Barney et al., *The Etymologies of Isidore of Seville*, 198. From *The Etymologies of Isidore of Seville*, © Stephen A. Barney, W. J. Lewis, J. A. Beach and Oliver Berghof, 2006. Reproduced with the permission of Cambridge University Press through PLS Clear.

15 Funck-Brentano, *A History of Gaul*, 178–179; James, *The Franks*, 6–7 & Cusack, *Conversion among the Germanic Peoples*, 68

16 Reinhardt, *Germany: 2000 Years V.I*, 28; Nelson, *King and Emperor*, 15; Nielsen, *The Germanic Languages*, 48; Halsall, *Barbarian Migrations and the Roman West*, 62 & Geary, *Before France and Germany*, 78

17 Faulkner, *Law and Authority in the Early Middle Ages*, 9–10 & Drew, *The Laws of the Salian Franks*, 30–31 & 180

18 Musset, *The Germanic Invasions*, 69; Falk, *Franks and Saracens*, 34 & Wood, *The Merovingian Kingdoms*, 38

19 Faulkner, *Law and Authority in the Early Middle Ages*, 16; Oman, *The Dark Ages*, 49; Buse, *The Regions of Germany*, 98 & Holland, *Germany*, 24

20 Musset, *The Germanic Invasions*, 70; Miller, *Ethnogenesis and Frankish Origins*, 284–285 & Geary, *Before France and Germany*, 80

21 Durant, *The Age of Faith*, 93 & Wemple, *Women in Frankish Society*, 9

22 Halsall, *Barbarian Migrations and the Roman West*, 12–15 & 36–40; Geary, *Before France and Germany*, 53 & Nelson, *Charles the Bald*, 2

23 James, *The Franks*, 6–7 & Fortson, *Indo-European Language and Culture*, 323

24 Algeo, *The Origins and Development of the English Language*, 67; Pounds, *An Historical Geography of Europe*, 186 & Schrijver, *Language Contact and the Origins of the Germanic Languages*, 111

25 Falk, *Franks and Saracens*, 41

26 Ozment, *A Mighty Fortress*, 36 & McKitterick, *History and Memory in the Carolingian World*, 8–15

27 Derks, *Ethnic Constructs in Antiquity*, 327–328; Geary, *Before France and Germany*, 77 & James, "The Northern World in the Dark Ages," 95

28 Thorpe, *Gregory of Tours' History of the Franks*, 7

29 Ibid. 125

30 Bachrach, *Liber Historiae Francorum*, 23–24

31 France, *Warfare in the Dark Ages*, 136–139

32 Halsall, *Barbarian Migrations and the Roman West*, 152–153; Geary, *Before France and Germany*, 64 & Musset, *The Germanic Invasions*, 72–73

33 Wolfram, *The Roman Empire and its Germanic Peoples*, 65–66; Wickham, *The Inheritance of Rome*, 47 & Halsall, *Barbarian Migrations and the Roman West*, 187

34 Durant, *The Age of Faith*, 88

35 Marcellinus, *Ammianus Marcellinus*, 210–211 & Pounds, *An Historical Geography of Europe*, 154

36 Marcellinus, *The Roman History of Ammianus Marcellinus*, 127 & 235

37 Geary, *Before France and Germany*, 78–79 & Hummer, "Franks and Alamanni," 10

38 Drew, *The Laws of the Salian Franks*, 8
39 Halsall, *Barbarian Migrations and the Roman West*, 211 & 399 & Geary, *Before France and Germany*, 79
40 Bachrach, *Liber Historiae Francorum*, 25–26
41 Jones, *The Cambridge Illustrated History of France*, 46–47; Faulkner, *Law and Authority in the Early Middle Ages*, 14 & Jordanes, *The Origin and Deeds of the Goths*, 59–60
42 Ozment, *A Mighty Fortress*, 37 & Geary, *Before France and Germany*, 86
43 Höpken, "Religion, Cult, and Burial Customs," 258–260
44 Miller, *Ethnogenesis and Frankish Origins*, 277–278; Simek, *Dictionary of Northern Mythology*, 240 & Wallace-Hadrill, *The Frankish Church*, 22
45 Höpken, "Religion, Cult, and Burial Customs," 259–260
46 Ibid. 256–260
47 Wallace-Hadrill, *The Frankish Church*, 18–19
48 Bachrach, *Liber Historiae Francorum*, 29; Fletcher, *The Conversion of Europe*, 102; Dryakhlov, "The Amulets of German Merovingian Aristocracy," 207–215; Wood, "Pagan Religions and Superstitions East of the Rhine," 259 & 261; Arrhenius, "Kinship and Social Relations," 56 & Welch, "Pre-Christian Practices in the Anglo-Saxon World," 870
49 Grimm, *Teutonic Mythology V.I*, 45
50 Pounds, *An Historical Geography of Europe*, 99 & Halsall, *Barbarian Migrations and the Roman West*, 118
51 Hammond, *The Gallic Wars*, 33
52 Thorpe, *Gregory of Tours' History of the Franks*, 125
53 Filotas, *Pagan Survivals*, 213–214
54 Ibid. 214–216
55 Wood, *The Merovingian Kingdoms*, 37; Backman, *The Worlds of Medieval Europe*, 69 & Cantor, *The Civilization of the Middle Ages*, 112
56 Goetz, *Life in the Middle Ages*, 27 & France, *Warfare in the Dark Ages*, 142–143
57 Bachrach, *Liber Historiae Francorum*, 31
58 Oman, *The Dark Ages*, 55
59 Halsall, *Barbarian Migrations and the Roman West*, 307 & Geary, *Before France and Germany*, 87–88
60 Wolfram, *The Roman Empire and its Germanic Peoples*, 199 & 203 & Bachrach, *Liber Historiae Francorum*, 33
61 Farmer, *The Oxford Dictionary of Saints*, 95
62 Wood, *The Merovingian Kingdoms*, 41–42 & & Russell, *The Germanization of Early Medieval Christianity*, 138
63 Thorpe, *Gregory of Tours' History of the Franks*, 139
64 Ibid. 141–142 & Bachrach, *Liber Historiae Francorum*, 38–46
65 Fletcher, *The Conversion of Europe*, 104–105; Wood, "Christianization and the Dissemination of Christian Teaching," 713 & Heather, *Christendom*, 191–192
66 Thorpe, *Gregory of Tours' History of the Franks*, 143–144
67 Bennett, *Medieval Europe*, 37
68 Reinhardt, *Germany: 2000 Years V.1*, 30 & Geary, *Before France and Germany*, 85
69 Thorpe, *Gregory of Tours' History of the Franks*, 144 & Bachrach, *Liber Historiae Francorum*, 46
70 Farmer, *The Oxford Dictionary of Saints*, 95
71 Russell, *The Germanization of Early Medieval Christianity*, 17; Wallace-Hadrill, *The Frankish Church*, 25 & Heather, *Christendom*, 193
72 Riche, *Daily Life in the World of Charlemagne*, 32 & Van Dam, "Merovingian Gaul and the Frankish Conquests," 213
73 Geary, *Before France and Germany*, 123–124

74 Thompson, *Feudal Germany*, 10–11; Goetz, *Life in the Middle Ages*, 61 & 84–85; Wemple, *Women in Frankish Society*, 172; Raaijmakers, *The Making of the Monastic Community of Fulda*, 11 & Milis, *The Pagan Middle Ages*, 16

75 Geary, *Before France and Germany*, 123–124 & Costambeys, *The Carolingian World*, 299

76 Sypeck, *Becoming Charlemagne*, 8

77 Wood, *The Merovingian Kingdoms*, 44 & Reinhardt, *Germany: 2000 Years V.I*, 30

78 Thorpe, *Gregory of Tours' History of the Franks*, 17

79 James, "The Northern World in the Dark Ages," 70–71

80 Flierman, *Saxon identities*, 59 & Oman, *The Dark Ages*, 93

81 Halsall, *Barbarian Migrations and the Roman West*, 303 & Geary, *Before France and Germany*, 117

82 Hedeager, "Scandinavia," 501–502; Oman, *The Dark Ages*, 93 & Cusack, "Between Land and Sea," 4

83 Bachrach, *Liber Historiae Francorum*, 56–57

84 Musset, *The Germanic Invasions*, 79

85 Geary, *Before France and Germany*, 119–120

86 Kibler et al., *Medieval France*, 83

87 Sypeck, *Becoming Charlemagne*, 7–8 & Costambeys, *The Carolingian World*, 34

88 Kahler, *The Germans*, 41

89 Durant, *The Age of Faith*, 460 & Oman, *The Dark Ages*, 101

90 Geary, *Before France and Germany*, 200 & Gibbs, *Medieval German Literature*, 24–25

91 Oman, *The Dark Ages*, 264

92 Reuter, *Germany in the Early Middle Ages*, 22

93 Jones, *The Cambridge Illustrated History of France*, 61

94 Costambeys, *The Carolingian World*, 34

95 Wallace-Hadrill, *The Fourth Book of the Chronicle of Fredegar*, 104

96 Nelson, *King and Emperor*, 29

97 Stofferahn, "Resonance and Discord," 7–8

98 Becher, *Charlemagne*, 1

99 Fletcher, *The Conversion of Europe*, 194

100 Geary, *Before France and Germany*, 221

101 Oman, *The Dark Ages*, 301

102 Morrissey, *Charlemagne and France*, 97

103 Bachrach, *Deeds of the Saxons*, 26

104 Sypeck, *Becoming Charlemagne*, 199–200; Campbell, *The Masks of God*, 525 & Butt, *Daily Life in the Age of Charlemagne*, 194

105 Whitton, "The Society of Northern Europe in the High Middle Ages," 118 & Neill, *A History of Christian Missions*, 67

106 Sypeck, *Becoming Charlemagne*, 203 & Milis, *The Pagan Middle Ages*, 4

107 Morrissey, *Charlemagne and France*, xvii–xviii & 83–84; Bartlett, *The Medieval World Complete*, 20 & Nelson, *Charles the Bald*, 1

108 Costambeys, *The Carolingian World*, 5

109 Morrissey, *Charlemagne and France*, 131

110 Ibid. 204–205

111 Metzenthin, "The 'Heliand': A New Approach," 503

112 Einhard, *The Life of Charlemagne*, 9–12 & Noble, *Charlemagne and Louis the Pious*, 7 & 9

113 Oman, *The Dark Ages*, 299 & 306 & Gibbs, *Medieval German Literature*, 25

114 Einhard, *The Life of Charlemagne*, 46–51 & McKinney, *The Saxon Poet's Life of Charles the Great*, 90–95 & 100

115 Kapovic, *The Indo European Languages*, 30, & Brehaut, *An Encyclopedist of the Dark Ages*, 42

116 Becher, *Charlemagne*, 44; Nelson, *King and Emperor*, 28 & Butt, *Daily Life in the Age of Charlemagne*, 149
117 Nelson, *King and Emperor*, 86–87 & Williams, *Atrocity or Apology?* 23
118 Wickham, *The Inheritance of Rome*, 377
119 Bachrach, *Charlemagne's Early Campaigns (768–777)*, 110 & 115–117 & Oman, *The Dark Ages*, 266–267
120 Ibid. 181–182
121 Riche, *The Carolingians*, 86–87 & Butt, *Daily Life in the Age of Charlemagne*, 29–30
122 Dutton, *Carolingian Civilization*, 25–26
123 Goetz, *Life in the Middle Ages*, 30 & 54–55; Wemple, *Women in Frankish Society*, 32 & Butt, *Daily Life in the Age of Charlemagne*, 31 & 58
124 Bachrach, *Charlemagne's Early Campaigns (768–777)*, 189
125 Riche, *The Carolingians*, 130–132
126 Geary, *Before France and Germany*, 201–203 & 208–210 & Noble, *Charlemagne and Louis the Pious*, 156
127 Pounds, *An Historical Geography of Europe*, 173
128 Wickham, *The Inheritance of Rome*, 230
129 Mackay, *Atlas of Medieval Europe*, 61–62 & Pounds, *An Historical Geography of Europe*, 218
130 Jellema, "Frisian Trade in the Dark Ages," 31; James, "The Northern World in the Dark Ages," 92 & Verhulst, *The Carolingian Economy*, 91–92
131 Cunliffe, *Europe between the Oceans*, 433; Hodges, "Frisians and Franks," 29–31; Lebecq, "The Northern Seas," 648 & 655 & Mackay, *Atlas of Medieval Europe*, 57 & 61
132 Wood, *The Merovingian Kingdoms*, 293–294 & Costambeys, *The Carolingian World*, 340–343
133 Nees, *Early Medieval Art*, 71 & 74
134 Durant, *The Age of Faith*, 554 & Barford, *The Early Slavs*, 167
135 Thompson, *Feudal Germany*, 395; Sypeck, *Becoming Charlemagne*, 87–88; Verhulst, "Economic organisation," 508 & Riche, *Daily Life in the World of Charlemagne*, 116–119
136 Riche, *The Carolingians*, 314
137 Percival, *The Reign of Charlemagne*, 49–50
138 Henning, "Slavery or Freedom?" 270–273 & Verhulst, *The Carolingian Economy*, 105
139 France, *Warfare in the Dark Ages*, 273–274
140 Thorpe, *Gregory of Tours' History of the Franks*, 427–428
141 Lindenfeld, *World Christianity and Indigenous Experience*, 100
142 Ibid. 55; Kling, *A History of Christian Conversion*, 326–327 & Steffen, "Religion and Violence in Christian Traditions," 115
143 Dutton, *Carolingian Civilization*, 69
144 Riche, *Daily Life in the World of Charlemagne*, 253 & 263
145 Ibid. 99; Costambeys, *The Carolingian World*, 276–277 & Backman, *The Worlds of Medieval Europe*, 151
146 Drew, *The Laws of the Salian Franks*, 45–48 & 116
147 Riche, *Daily Life in the World of Charlemagne*, 260; Green, *Language and History in the Early Germanic World*, 74; Smith, "Religion and Lay Society," 671; Drew, *The Laws of the Salian Franks*, 34–35 & 138–139 & Wallace-Hadrill, *The Fourth Book of the Chronicle of Fredegar*, 42
148 Dutton, *Carolingian Civilization*, 76; Backman, *The Worlds of Medieval Europe*, 57 & Green, *Language and History in the Early Germanic World*, 64
149 Reuter, *Germany in the Early Middle Ages*, 27–29 & Oman, *The Dark Ages*, 101
150 Riche, *The Carolingians*, 5
151 Ibid. 126–128; Ozment, *A Mighty Fortress*, 43 & Oman, *The Dark Ages*, 102

152 Reuter, *Germany in the Early Middle Ages*, 28–29; Backman, *The Worlds of Medieval Europe*, 146; Cantor, *The Civilization of the Middle Ages*, 192 & Davis, *Charlemagne's Practice of Empire*, 51–52

153 Riche, *The Carolingians*, 126–128 & Goldberg, *Struggle for Empire*, 222–223

154 Ibid. 80–82

155 Ibid. & Backman, *The Worlds of Medieval Europe*, 144

156 Green, *Language and History in Early Germanic Society*, 196–197

157 Riche, *The Carolingians*, 80–82

158 Butt, *Daily Life in the Age of Charlemagne*, 37 & McKitterick, *The Frankish Kingdoms under the Carolingians*, 78

159 Macdowall, *Germanic Warrior*, 52–53 & Bachrach, *Warfare in Medieval Europe*, 218 & 228

160 Steuer, "Thuringians and Bavarians," 121 & Butt, *Daily Life in the Age of Charlemagne*, 43

161 Bachrach, *Warfare in Medieval Europe*, 214

162 Butt, *Daily Life in the Age of Charlemagne*, 44 & 49

163 France, *Warfare in the Dark Ages*, 262–263

164 Coupland, "Carolingian Arms and Armor," 44; Verhulst, *The Carolingian Economy*, 110 & France, *Warfare in the Dark Ages*, 264–265

165 Dutton, *Carolingian Civilization*, 79

166 France, *Warfare in the Dark Ages*, 262–263 & 267–270 & Bachrach, *Warfare in Medieval Europe*, 185 & 221–223 & 228–229 & *Merovingian Military Organization*, 127

167 Ibid. 252–258 & 260–261; Coupland, "Carolingian Arms and Armor," 33–37 & 42 & Hooper, *The Cambridge Illustrated Atlas of Warfare*, 12

168 Ibid. 253 & 261–262

169 Ibid. 255–256

170 Riche, *The Carolingians*, 308

171 Langen, "Die Bedeutung von Befestigungen in den Sachsenkriegen Karls des Großen," 188–190 & Hooper, *The Cambridge Illustrated Atlas of Warfare*, 15

172 Bachrach, *Warfare in Medieval Europe*, 242 & 248

173 Last, "Die Bewaffnung der Karolingerzeit," 88–90 & Butt, *Daily Life in the Age of Charlemagne*, 47; Riche, *Daily Life in the World of Charlemagne*, 74 & Newman, *Daily Life in the Middle Ages*, 216

174 Nicolle, *The Age of Charlemagne*, 14 & France, *Warfare in the Dark Ages*, 30 and for illustrations of Frankish cavalrymen, see the depictions by Wayne Reynolds in Nicolle, *Carolingian Cavalryman, AD 768–987*, 32–41

175 Riche, *The Carolingians*, 90–91 & Hooper, *The Cambridge Illustrated Atlas of Warfare*, 13

176 Wolfram, *The Roman Empire and its Germanic Peoples*, 305; Last, "Die Bewaffnung der Karolingerzeit," 85–86 & Hooper, *The Cambridge Illustrated Atlas of Warfare*, 12–13

177 Riche, *Daily Life in the World of Charlemagne*, 80 & Hooper, *The Cambridge Illustrated Atlas of Warfare*, 15

178 Goldberg, *Struggle for Empire*, 39–42

179 Bachrach, *Warfare in Medieval Europe*, 365

180 Ibid. 374

181 Riche, *Daily Life in the World of Charlemagne*, 80 & Aslan, "Cosmic War in Religious Traditions," 264

182 Noble, *Charlemagne and Louis the Pious*, 88

183 Riche, *Daily Life in the World of Charlemagne*, 78–79

184 Nicolle, *The Age of Charlemagne*, 7; Riche, *The Carolingians*, 89–91 & Butt, *Daily Life in the Age of Charlemagne*, 40–41

185 Bachrach, *Warfare in Medieval Europe*, 107–109

186 Ibid. 328 & Butt, *Daily Life in the Age of Charlemagne*, 46
187 Goldberg, *Struggle for Empire*, 42; Bachrach, *Charlemagne's Early Campaigns (768–777)*, 445 & France, *Warfare in the Dark Ages*, 256
188 Bachrach, *Warfare in Medieval Europe*, 351–354
189 Dutton, *Carolingian Civilization*, 79
190 Last, "Die Bewaffnung der Karolingerzeit," 77–78 & Bachrach, *Warfare in Medieval Europe*, 380–381
191 Nicolle, *The Age of Charlemagne* 13 & Hooper, *The Cambridge Illustrated Atlas of Warfare*, 16
192 Bachrach, *Warfare in Medieval Europe*, 158–159 & Butt, *Daily Life in the Age of Charlemagne*, 34
193 Ibid. 157
194 Hooper, *The Cambridge Illustrated Atlas of Warfare*, 17; Butt, *Daily Life in the Age of Charlemagne*, 49–50 & Bachrach, *Charlemagne's Early Campaigns (768–777)*, 240
195 Ibid.
196 Ibid. 114 & Verhulst, *The Carolingian Economy*, 94
197 Nicolle, *The Conquest of Saxony*, 32–37
198 Bachrach, *Warfare in Medieval Europe*, 323
199 Ibid. 324–325
200 Ibid. 320
201 Wamers, "Carolingian Pfalzen and Law," 150–151 & Loyn et al., *The Reign of Charlemagne*, 64–73
202 Ibid. 153–154 & Altet, *The Early Middle Ages*, 128
203 Ibid. 151
204 Nelson, "Religion and Politics in the Reign of Charlemagne," 22
205 Jeep, *Medieval Germany*, 1; Ring, *Northern Europe*, 1; Kibler et al., *Medieval France*, 17 and Charles' father Pippin reportedly had the springs of Aachen "exorcized" by slaying a demonic figure there, see Noble, *Charlemagne and Louis the Pious*, 109–110 & Raiswell & Winter, *The Medieval Devil*, 123–124
206 Ibid.
207 Ring, *Northern Europe*, 3
208 Ibid. & Altet, *The Early Middle Ages*, 10 & 128 & 131–137
209 Butt, *Daily Life in the Age of Charlemagne*, 27
210 Kibler et al., *Medieval France*, 17
211 Backman, *The Worlds of Medieval Europe*, 152–153
212 Goetz, *Life in the Middle Ages*, 16 & Butt, *Daily Life in the Age of Charlemagne*, 67–69 & 80–81
213 Dutton, *Carolingian Civilization*, 85
214 Goetz, *Life in the Middle Ages*, 17; Wemple, *Women in Frankish Society*, 101–102 & Butt, *Daily Life in the Age of Charlemagne*, 60–61
215 These tended to be infested by wolves and bandits. See Backman, *The Worlds of Medieval Europe*, 155 & Bachrach, *Warfare in Medieval Europe*, 44–45
216 Cantor, *The Civilization of the Middle Ages*, 187 & Butt, *Daily Life in the Age of Charlemagne*, 54
217 Verhulst, *The Carolingian Economy*, 97
218 Riche, *The Carolingians*, 338
219 Backman, *The Worlds of Medieval Europe*, 95 & Cosman, *Medieval Wordbook*, 175

2 The Early Saxons

Origins

Like their Frankish neighbors, Saxon origins are riddled with unanswered questions, myths, and often murky or contradictory historical reports. The earliest of these stems from Ptolemy's mid-second-century *Geographia*. In his work, the Greek scholar references *Saxones* in northern Germany between the Elbe and the south of Jutland (the "Cimbrian peninsula"), near Suevi, Chauci, and Frisians.[1] However, some scholars argue that Ptolemy's *Saxones* do not refer to Saxons at all but are instead a corruption of *Aviones* or *Axones*, an altogether different people Tacitus referred to in his first-century *Germania*.[2]

Whatever the case concerning Ptolemy, we are given other clues by early Roman writers who situated Saxons and their precursors in the North German Plain between the Elbe and the Weser and along the North Sea coastland.[3] To the Romans, Saxons were one of the *gentes ultra Rheneum*, "people beyond the Rhine," dwelling within the province of *Germania magna*.[4]

Later sources postulated more elaborate origins. In his tenth-century *Deeds of the Saxons*, the Saxon monk Widukind of Corvey suggested, not unreasonably, that his people descended from the Danes.[5] However, he also noted that some believed Saxons were descended from Greek or Macedonian survivors associated with the army of Alexander the Great, which was dispersed following the conqueror's death.[6] Widukind adds with more conviction that the Saxons came to their homeland by ship, eventually settling at Hadeln.[7]

Widukind's mention of Hadeln as the original site of Saxon settlement was taken directly from the ninth-century *Translatio s. Alexandri*, written partially by the monk Rudolf of Fulda.[8] Rudolf also speculated that the Saxons had arrived by sea, having come from Britain (a tale also replicated by the eleventh-century chronicler Adam of Bremen).[9] Unfortunately, as we will see with other examples, Rudolf and Widukind's accounts of Saxon origins are unreliable.[10] The primary concerns are three-fold: both authors copied heavily from earlier works, political considerations guided their writing, and neither shied away from purely imaginative inventions.[11]

For modern scholars, Roman reports and archaeological data have proven more reliable for understanding Saxon origins. The Romans first encountered Saxons (or "proto-Saxons") in 12 CE during the campaigns of the Roman general Drusus

DOI: 10.4324/9781003379157-4

when he crossed the lower Rhine and subjugated the Frisians.[12] Trade also occurred between Romans and North Sea communities since at least the second-century CE.[13]

In addition, like Franks and nearby Frisians, Saxons made up contingents in the Roman army.[14] In 356, in an oration composed by Julian the Apostate to his cousin Constantius II, Saxons (alongside Franks) lent their support to Magnentius, a Roman usurper in Gaul.[15] Similarly, Ambrose of Milan claims that, in 388, Saxons assisted Theodosius in his victory over Magnus Maximus (another usurper).[16] According to the East Roman historian Jordannes, Saxons also accompanied the Goths in migrating to Gaul in 418.[17]

Simultaneously, Saxons suffered the humiliation of being used as entertainment in Roman arenas. In a late fourth-century report by the Roman statesman Symmachus, we are told of 29 Saxons killed in this manner as part of a celebration he was hosting for his 10-year-old son. (The spectacle didn't go according to plan, and rather than fight, the Saxons opted to kill themselves by breaking one another's necks.)[18]

These myriad Roman encounters are coupled with further reports related to North Sea piracy and Saxon-Merovingian encounters (see Chapter 3), which suggest the Saxons originally migrated from Schleswig-Holstein during the second or third century CE, after which they gained control over what is now Lower Saxony via warfare subjugation, alliance, and absorption.[19] Thereafter they emerged as a conglomeration of smaller tribes from southern Jutland and northwest Germany, although their degree of political cooperation during this process is entirely unknown.[20] In addition, while the tribes who came to be called Saxons are subject to debate, their precursors likely included the Suevi, Chauci, and Anglii.[21]

The Saxon Name

Scholars also debate the origins of the ethnonym "Saxon." The most persistent theory associates it with *seax*, a common short sword the Saxons were known to use.[22] However, this hypothesis has been challenged on the basis that surrounding peoples also used the *seax* (some earlier than the Saxons) and the fact that the *seax* was not in use before the fifth century CE, at which point references had already been made to Saxons for over 100 years.[23] However, there is a possibility the name could derive from the Germanic *sahs,* meaning "knife," making "Saxons" equate to something like "the people with the knife (or knives)."[24] Widukind of Corvey made such an argument and related a (likely untrue) episode where the Saxons betrayed and murdered a host of Thuringian leaders with their knives. They gained renown for this grim deed and earned the name "Saxons" because of the multitude they killed with their knives.[25] However, most scholars agree that Widukind was molding his story based on a similar account given by the Welsh monk Nennius in his ninth-century *History of the Britons*.[26]

Another theory, though even less likely, suggests the Saxon name may be derived from *Saxnōt*, an exclusively Saxon deity believed to be something of a tribal god.[27] Yet, very little is known concerning this deity (see Chapter 4).

Terms such as *Saxones* or *Saxo* were also used somewhat haphazardly between the third and the fifth centuries to refer to general marauders participating in North Sea piracy and did not necessarily refer to a particular tribal group.[28] Concerning this last phenomenon, Isidore of Seville believed:

> The Saxon people, situated on the shores of the Ocean in impassable marshes are accomplished in strength and agility. Whence they were named (i.e. from *saxosus*, "stony") because they are a hard and very powerful kind of people, standing out above the other piratical tribes.[29]

Matthias Springer has suggested that, while it remains possible that "Saxon" derives its origins from *saxum*, meaning "rock" or "stone," Isidore's interpretation is generally doubted.[30]

Language

We are on surer ground regarding the language Saxons spoke, that is, Old Saxon (*Altsächsisch*), a variant of Ingvaeonic (North Sea Germanic), which belongs to the broader West Germanic language family.[31] Old Saxon was relatively similar to Old Frisian and Old English, noticeably different from Old Low Franconian and likely unintelligible to South "Germans" (e.g., Bavarians).[32] Between 500 and 800 CE, the High German Consonant Shift altered the speech of south (High) Germans, creating a more significant linguistic divide between them and north (low) Germans, the latter of which included the Saxons.[33]

Compared to other early Germanic languages, Old Saxon was also linguistically conservative, possibly due to less exposure to foreign influence.[34] However, even Old Saxon had regional dialects; for example, speakers on the western periphery of Saxony adopted features of Old Low Franconian due to their proximity to the Franks.[35]

Geography

Regarding the geographic composition of Saxon society, we are given very little information until the eighth century, when we encounter references to specific Saxon groups in Frankish chronicles.[36] From then on, our overall impression of Saxon society is one of fragmentation, defined by kin groups, "clans," and highly local allegiances.[37] However, possibly in response to their dealings with the Franks (or as understood/designated by them), the "Old Saxons" could be divided roughly into four notable (likely geographic rather than political) groups:

1 Westphalians, "people of the western plains" situated on the Ems and Lippe near the Teutoburg Forest.
2 Eastphalians, "people of the eastern plains" situated on the Oker and Elbe who shared a border with western Slavs.
3 Engrians, or "people of Engern," who inhabited the Weser valley and whose center was possibly Minden.

4   Nordalbingians, Saxons settled "north of the Elbe" as far as Schleswig-Holstein.[38] Nordalbingians were further divided into at least three groups: Thiatmarsgi (inhabitants of the Ditmarsch), Holsati ("people of the forest"), and Stormari ("stormy folk"), whose principal town was Hamburg (OS: *Hammaburg*), the "castle in the meadows."[39] Hamburg was situated on the Elbe with easy access to the North Sea and eventually became a vital trading center. However, other Saxon strongholds also existed in nearby Schleswig-Holstein, including Bokelburg, Kuden, and Stellerburg.[40]

In addition to settlements on the Elbe, Saxons settled along the Rhine, Weser, Aller, and Lippe rivers. The southern and western boundary of Saxon territory was loosely defined by the Teutoburg Forest and Harz Mountains, while further north lay the heather-covered Lüneburg Heath and the North Sea coastal marshlands.[41]

Early Medieval Europe was predominantly rural, but Saxony was especially so compared to Francia.[42] Geographic delineations were not set in stone. Borders were permeable, and people often settled across tribal boundaries.[43] In the south, particularly in Thuringia, territory was frequently contested between Franks and Saxons. One notable point of conflict was the *Hellweg*, a road stretching from the lower Rhine into the Teutoburg Forest.[44] Contention over the *Hellweg* was due primarily to its strategic significance in conducting war, controlling vital resources, and facilitating trade access.[45]

Political Structure

The primary political and geographical unit of Saxon society was the *Gau* (plural: *Gaue*), small territories containing several villages. Until its conquest by the Franks, Saxony may have included roughly 120 *Gaue*.[46] At the head of each *Gau* was likely an appointed nobleman, or *Fürst* (first), who was selected during assemblies for a role that included military and religious obligations.[47] According to the *Lebuini vitae* (written accounts of the missionary Lebuinus), every year, representatives of the *Gaue* would attend an assembly at a place called Marklo.[48] Each *Fürst* would attend, alongside 36 members from each *Gau*, 12 from each "free" class: *edhilingui* (nobles), *frilingi* (freemen), and *lazzi* (bondsmen)—a total of 3,700 people.[49] The assembly addressed issues of war, trade, and law. We might expect to find there an *eusago* ("law-speaker") who kept local customs alive via oral tradition.[50]

The reports on the Marklo assembly have long been a source of scholarly fascination, as well as a cause for concern.[51] Romantically inclined historians have interpreted them as evidence that the Saxons developed a kind of "proto-republic" or democracy by which representatives were elected from the bottom-up.[52] This line of argument often uses Tacitus' first-century *Germania* as supporting evidence due to its mention of similar assemblies among the ancient *Germani*.[53] The assumption is then made that the Saxons, due to their supposedly conservative nature, must have maintained these identical assemblies for roughly 800 years until the Carolingian conquest.

There is little question that the Saxons had assemblies (Old Saxon contains the word *thingstedi*, which denotes an "assembly place" or "legal assembly").[54] Assemblies were a necessary component of Early Medieval life and are widely attested in several Germanic societies.[55] Rather, the primary questions for concern are as follows: What was the composition of Saxon assemblies? Can the *Lebuini vitae* be trusted? Did Marklo even exist?

We will return to the *Lebuini vitae* in the following chapters, but a few observations are necessary here. First, if the assemblies described are accurate, the "representatives" almost certainly were chosen from the top-down rather than the bottom-up.[56] That means village freemen would not have elected representatives for their *gaue*; instead, local magnates or noblemen would have designated retainers or other notables to accompany them to assemblies and represent their "districts."[57]

Regarding trusting the Lebuinus narratives, there are good reasons for maintaining skepticism. For one, the earliest account of his life, the *Vita Lebuini antiqua*, was written over a half-century after his death (in the 840s at the earliest) and may partially represent post-conquest rather than pre-conquest Saxony.[58] The other primary account of Lebuinus' life, composed by Hucbald of St. Amand, wasn't written until the early tenth century (although it relied heavily upon the earlier *Vita Lebuini antiqua*).[59] In addition, the author of the earliest account drew from older material, notably, Bede's *Ecclesiastical History of the English People* (written c. 731), as well as the *Vita Liudgeri* (*Life of Liudger*), written by bishop Altfrid of Münster in the early ninth century.[60]

Furthermore, references to the location of Marklo given in the *Lebuini vitae* (e.g., "near the Weser") are suspiciously vague.[61] Attempts to narrow down the site's location have also not been successful. In 1931, the town of Lohe (located along the Weser between Verden and Minden) changed its name to "Marklohe" based on conjecture that it was the original Saxon Marklo. However, this assertion remains unproven.[62] An alternative location making similar claims is that of Markelo (attested as Marclo since the twelfth century), located close to Deventer (where Lebuinus had his church) in the Dutch province of Overijssel.[63] Archaeological evidence supports Markelo as a place of habitation between the seventh and the ninth centuries, but beyond this, any evidence of being a Saxon assembly site remains to be seen. Some scholars argue the name may merely be derived from that of Markhelm, a friend of Lebuinus who was part of missionary endeavors in the area.[64] (Nevertheless, today, you can visit the *Dingspeelberg*, a hill near Markelo, and get married in a quaint reconstructed grove that claims to be the Saxon assembly site.)

One final issue concerning Marklo is that the name never appears in other sources.[65] The silence is surprising given that such a place would have been a significant socio-political institution. Therefore, we would expect Frankish chronicles, notably those concerning the Saxon conquest, to mention it. Surely, Marklo would have been targeted by Charlemagne to undermine Saxon resistance.

Outside of Marklo, another controversial aspect of reports concerning the Saxons' political structure is the notion that they lacked the institution of kingship.

Although this claim appears in the *Lebuini vitae*, it is taken directly from Bede's *Ecclesiastical History*, where he claims the "Old Saxons" had no king but rather "satraps" ruling over them. Only during war was a leader chosen (by lot), and even then, when the war ended, the leader returned to being of equal status with the other "satraps."[66]

Most scholars agree that Bede's use of the term "satraps" (provincial or city governors) was likely based on his reading of the Biblical description of the five satraps set over the Philistines.[67] However, what Bede meant by using the term to describe the Saxons has been debated. As a result, scholars have generally sought alternative (mostly) Germanic and Latin terms that may equate to what Bede intended. These include the Anglo-Saxon "ealdorman" or "bretwalda," the Frankish "count," German "herzog," Latin *comes* or *dux*, and more generally, the "chieftains" or "petty kings" akin to what we find among the Early Medieval Irish.[68] Each of these terms implies localized governance and the ability to lead armed retinues. If the *gau* system existed in Saxony before the Carolingian conquest (which is not guaranteed), Bede might have been referring to local lords who governed these regional units and were simultaneously responsible for military campaigns.

Bede was correct concerning a lack of kingship in Saxony. None of the contemporary reports refer to continental Saxon kings, which surely would have been noted in Frankish chronicles (especially if they had submitted to Frankish authority). In addition, as will become apparent in the chapters ahead, the lack of a centralized authority proved to be the most problematic element for the Frankish integration of Saxony within the Carolingian Empire. However, if Saxons lacked kings, they had no shortage of nobles to whom the rest of the population was subject. Many scholars believe the Saxon nobility comprised a broad class that stood atop a strict social hierarchy.[69] Some assumptions we make about Saxon nobles may be based on their position post-Carolingian conquest. However, it seems unlikely that the conquest *created* the Saxon nobility.

The origins of the Saxon nobility are obscure, but a few theories have been proposed. They may have originated from northern invaders, prosperous farmers, or elites from earlier tribes such as the Chauci.[70] In Nordalbingia, the disparity between classes appears to have been less pronounced, which has led some scholars to postulate a northern invasion by which other Saxon peoples were subjected to an incoming dominant group.[71] Anticipating later feudalism, nobles acted as large landholders whose estates were worked by slaves, bondsmen, and free farmers.[72] As early as the seventh century CE, some of these elites were housed in hilltop strongholds, such as the Gaulskopf in the south of the Teutoburg Forest.[73]

The wealth of Saxon nobles is demonstrated in Saxon law (see Chapter 8), where the bride-price (or dowry) they paid was 300–1,200 *solidi*, equating to approximately 150–600 heads of cattle.[74] Saxon law also clarified the relative worth of an individual's life based on "class." The "man-money" (*wergeld*) to be paid to a noble was six times that of a freeman and eight times that of a bondsman.[75] According to Rudolf of Fulda, the death penalty was also instituted for anyone who married above their station, while marrying beneath one's class was considered invalid.[76]

Saxon law could be harsh. Cattle theft met with the death penalty, and according to a 746/7 letter (of praise?) written by St. Boniface to Aethelbald of Mercia, in Old Saxony, an adulteress was sometimes compelled to hang herself, after which her body was burned on a pyre that her lover was subsequently hanged over. Alternatively, an adulteress might be flogged by groups of women from village to village, beaten with rods, stripped, and cut with knives.[77] In other Germanic societies, similar infractions usually resulted in fines, and the excess of Saxon law stands out by comparison.[78]

Saxons also kept alive blood-feuds. Akin to surrounding peoples, kinship in Saxon society was woven with complex obligations, and an assault on one's kin demanded reciprocity to avoid humiliation and maintain an honorable reputation.[79] However, blood-feuds could be avoided by paying a *wergeld* or with "oath-helpers" to attest on one's behalf.

Forms of Subsistence

Unlike Franks, Saxons relied almost exclusively on a barter system for commerce. The nobility likely dominated that system.[80] Coin-based currency was little used. Domesticated animals were the heart of this economy, in which cattle (OS: *fehu*) reigned supreme.[81] While sheep, goats, chickens, pigs, and horses were utilized in the North German Plain, cattle were relied upon most.[82] Akin to systems found among the Irish, Welsh, or Nguni people of South Africa (to name just a few), cattle were essential to survival and often used as currency.[83] Lest such a system seem "backward," we ought to remember that the Latin word for currency, *pecunia*, is derived from *peacus*, meaning "cattle."[84] In like manner, the term "capital" (property) is derived from the Latin *captale*, which originally denoted livestock.[85] The Anglo-Saxon term for cattle, *feoh*, is also from which we derive the English word "fee."[86] Each of these harkens back to societies where worth and status could be correlated to the number of cattle owned.

In Saxony, cattle grazed alongside sheep in the hills and salt-marshes of the northwest coast, where a lack of good farmland required a reliance upon animal husbandry.[87] However, pastoral farming was also used further south along the Rhine.[88]

Horse rearing, a privilege of the wealthy, was particularly common in Engria.[89] Archaeological evidence indicates the high value of horses, some of which were interred in the graves of prominent men or buried alone (possibly as sacrifices).[90]

In coastal regions, some salt-tolerant crops could be cultivated, including barley, linseed, and broad beans, while those who practiced sedentary agriculture in more fruitful areas relied upon a "slash and burn" method for creating arable land.[91] Abundant natural resources used for food and other necessities were also scattered throughout the North German forests.[92] This was supplemented by a reliable fishing industry and trade access to Baltic and North Sea markets, including Dorestad in Frisia and Hedeby (Haithabu) in Denmark.[93] Despite their rural nature, Saxons had been connected to wide trade networks for centuries.[94] Roman artifacts from the second century CE and later materials from Iran have been found in North Sea communities.[95] Roman jewelry has also been found among the remains of Early Medieval North Germanic cremation graves, and Saxons serving in the Roman army are believed to have brought back Roman-crafted goods when returning home.[96] Saxons also participated in a broader network of slave-raiding, the victims of which were sometimes sold to Franks.[97]

In Saxony, land ownership was often communal although not exclusively.[98] Once settled, families filled the landscape with *Grübenhauser* (sunken pit-houses), large farm-houses with attached stables, and open long-houses, many of which utilized clay walls and thatched roofing.[99] Many dwellings were surrounded by necessary supplemental structures, such as stables, granaries, or smaller storage huts.[100] Archaeological excavations have also left clues concerning Saxon attire. Ornamental brooches, which women wore to hold up woolen dresses or as status symbols, are common Saxon artifacts.[101] According to Widukind of Corvey, Franks found Saxon fashion baffling. However, this was rooted in the "barbaric" custom of Saxon men letting their hair grow long, which was traditionally only allowed among noblemen in Francia.[102] Despite Widukind's observations, it is unlikely that Franks and Saxons differed much in their physical characteristics or dress style.[103]

Methods of War

Various accounts claim Saxons chose their warlords by lot during conflicts. The warlord was followed by a retinue of warriors (OS: *druhtfolc*).[104] In Old Saxon, a warrior (*hildescalc*) might also be called a *suerdthegan* (sword-thegn), *gisith* (warrior-companion), *wapanberand* (weapon-bearer), or *helmberand* (helmet-bearer).[105] However, most Saxon infantry wore little to no armor and, for combat, relied primarily upon spears, axes, javelins, and short swords.[106] Bachrach has estimated that, during the Carolingian era, Saxony likely contained somewhere between 36,000 and 70,000 eligible fighting men.[107] However, the size Saxon armies tended to be in the field is difficult to surmise, especially given their degree of political fragmentation.

Saxons rarely used horses in war. However, archaeological evidence has provided some exceptions, and we can presume their regular use in scouting. Like the Franks, Saxons adopted stirrups (OS: *stigerep*, "climb-rope"), harnesses, wooden saddles, and snaffle bits.[108] In addition, Saxon cavalry utilized "winged-lance" spears and the longer double-edged *spathae* swords.[109]

Unlike Franks, Saxons may have been unfamiliar with using and constructing complex siege equipment.[110] However, they were prolific builders of strongholds, usually hilltop fortresses utilizing natural features to their advantage.[111] On flatter terrain, fortified centers were often circular, sometimes containing earthen ramparts, wooden gates, and towers.[112] Examples of Saxon ring-forts can be seen on the North Sea at Pipinsburg near Geestemunde and at Stottinghausen.[113] Some scholars have suggested that most Saxon fortifications were merely used as refuge sites, but that seems unlikely.[114] Instead, using fortifications to guard strategic roads, project authority, host assemblies, and monitor river crossings is just as feasible.[115]

Regarding tactics, Saxon warlords often relied upon guerilla warfare that uti-lized ambushes and knowledge of the terrain against their enemies.[116] When pos-sible, open battle was to be avoided. However, when open battle did occur, Saxons formed masses of men to charge their enemies or used defensive shield-walls.[117] A contingent of archers could then support the infantry.[118]

Saxons also counted on the protection of their gods. Ashwood spears were enhanced with powerful runic carvings, while children were granted battle prowess through war-oriented dithematic (two-word) names such as *Hildebern* (battle-bear) or *Hathumot* (battle-courage).[119] As was sometimes customary in the Early Middle Ages, such individuals might be expected to step forward before battle to boast, shout insults, or curse their foes.[120]

War was also a method of forming kinship beyond the typical avenues of blood or marriage. This is evident in the language surrounding war-bands. Comrades in arms were called "battle-friends," while warlords were "ring-friends" (*bogwin*) or "ring-givers" (*boggebo*).[121] The Old Saxon term *treuwa* also denoted an "unflinch-ing loyalty" to one's lord.[122] In response to such devotion, a warlord would offer *mundburg*, meaning "protection" or "guardianship."[123]

Widukind of Corvey provides one account of what Saxon warfare *may* have looked like. During a battle between Saxons and Thuringians, the Saxons are said to have worn cloaks and carried long spears, small shields, and knives on their backs. They also formed a "phalanx" (presumably a shield-wall) and, before engaging the enemy with swords, rushed them and hurled their spears (which the enemy reciprocated).[124]

According to their enemies, Saxons were known for their love of war.[125] That warrior ethos is perhaps best demonstrated in a speech given by the chieftain Hathagath before a Saxon assault on a Frankish settlement:

> If the fates do not permit me to live longer, at least they grant what is sweet-est to me, namely to die with my friends. The examples of the strength of our fathers are to be found in the bodies of our friends that lie around us. They preferred to die rather than be conquered. It is better to set free your indefati-gable spirits than to give way before your enemies.[126]

The speech is likely a romantic literary invention, but such were the words of Widukind of Corvey when imagining the deeds of his ancestors.[127] However, if the speech attributed to Hathagath was merely a component of Medieval myth-making, the notion of Franco-Saxon animosity therein was not.

Conclusion

Much overlap existed between Franks and Saxons regarding material culture, social customs, and geographic habitation. However, by the Carolingian Age, significant differences were readily apparent. In contrast to Frankish governance subject to the king, Saxon society existed in a decentralized system dominated by the nobility.

Saxon spheres of influence also continued to exist primarily beyond the Rhenish frontier of the former Western Roman Empire, while the Franks had expanded into substantial swaths of Roman territory. Frankish expansion facilitated familiarity with and adoption of Roman socio-political structures, which Saxons remained less exposed to. As a result, Frankish society could advantageously utilize the geographic infrastructure, intellectual heritage, and diverse populace over which it had established hegemony. How Franks and Saxons arrived at these respective situations is critical for contextualizing Charlemagne's Saxon Wars and understanding the goals that existed therein.

Notes

1 Stevenson, *The Geography*, 63–65
2 Springer, *Die Sachsen*, 31; Tacitus, *The Agricola and The Germania*, 58 & Ehlers, *Die Integration Sachsens in das fränkische Reich*, 27
3 Cathey, "The Historical Setting of the *Heliand*," 3–4
4 Campbell, *The Anglo-Saxons*, 13; Todd, *The Early Germans*, 202 & Reuter, *Germany in the Early Middle Ages*, 53
5 Widukind, *Deeds of the Saxons*, 5–6
6 Leyser, "The German Aristocracy," 29
7 Widukind, *Deeds of the Saxons*, 5–6 & Lammers, "Die Stammesbildung bei den Sachsen," 27–28
8 Lammers, "Die Stammesbildung bei den Sachsen," 30
9 Wattenbach, *Die Übertragung des hl. Alexander von Rudolf und Meginhart*, 5–6; Banaszkiewicz, "Widukind on the Saxon Origins," 30 & 54 & Tschan, *History of the Archbishops of Hamburg-Bremen*, 8–9
10 Lammers, "Die Stammesbildung bei den Sachsen," 28 & McKitterick, *History and Memory in the Carolingian World*, 42
11 Ehlers, *Die Integration Sachsens in das fränkische Reich*, 43–44
12 Arblaster, *A History of the Low Countries*, 16–17; Jellema, "Frisian Trade in the Dark Ages," 15, & Robinson, *Old English and Its Closest Relatives*, 176–181
13 Meier, "The North Sea Coastal Area," 39 & Axboe, "Danish Kings and Dendrochronology," 225
14 Morris, "Cross-North Sea Contacts in the Roman Period," 418–42 & Cusack, "Between Sea and Land," 2
15 Springer, *Die Sachsen*, 34
16 Snyder, *The Britons*, 85
17 Wolfram, *History of the Goths*, 8 & 177
18 Glover, *Life and Letters in the Fourth Century*, 161; Springer, *Die Sachsen*, 38 & Flierman, *Saxon Identities*, 50–51
19 Reuter, *Germany in the Early Middle Ages*, 65; Musset, *The Germanic Invasions*, 97; Springer, "Location in Space and Time," 11–12; Robinson, *Old English and Its Closest Relatives*, 101–102; Lammers, "Die Stammesbildung bei den Sachsen," 54; Becher, "Non enim habent regem idem Antiqui Saxones," 3–4 & Arnold, *Medieval Germany*, 40–41
20 Halsall, *Barbarian Migrations and the Roman West*, 119–120
21 Robinson, *Old English and Its Closest Relatives*, 101–102; Todd, *The Early Germans*, 202; Musset, *The Germanic Invasions*, 86–87 & Nielsen, *The Germanic Languages*, 57
22 Ibid. 100; Buse, *The Regions of Germany*, 196 & Thompson, *Feudal Germany*, 180–181

23 Springer, *Die Sachsen*, 124–125 & "Location in Space and Time," 32; Macdowall, *Germanic Warrior*, 55

24 Ibid. 126 & 131 & Tiefenbach, *Altsächsisches Handwörterbuch*, 320

25 Widukind, *Deeds of the Saxons*, 5–6, 9–10, & 17

26 Lammers, "Die Stammesbildung bei den Sachsen," 28 & Springer, *Die Sachsen*, 80–81

27 Nciolle, *The Conquest of Saxony*, 6–9

28 Springer, "Location in Space and Time," 16 & *Die Sachsen*, 14; Todd, *The Early Germans*, 202; Flierman, *Saxon Identities*, 7–8, 35–36 & James' "The Northern World in the Dark Ages," 68

29 Barney et al., *The Etymologies of Isidore of Seville*, 197. From *The Etymologies of Isidore of Seville*, © Stephen A. Barney, W. J. Lewis, J. A. Beach and Oliver Berghof, 2006. Reproduced with the permission of Cambridge University Press through PLS Clear.

30 Springer, *Die Sachsen*, 128

31 Kapovic, *The Indo-European Languages*, 389; Gibbs, *Medieval German Literature*, 3 & 21; Schrijver, *Language Contact and the Origins of the Germanic Languages*, 61 & Rauch, *The Old Saxon Language*, 108

32 Fortson, *Indo-European Language and Culture*, 315; Algeo, *The Origins and Development of the English Language*, 69; Nielsen, *The Germanic Languages*, 3; Gallee, *Old-Saxon Texts*, VIII & Gneuss, "The Old English language," 21

33 Ibid. 393–394; König, *The Germanic Languages*, 10–11 & 73; Gibbs, *Medieval German Literature*, 2; Helfenstein, *Comparative Grammar of the Teutonic Languages*, 16; Schrijver, *Language Contact and the Origins of the Germanic Languages*, 97 & Kapovic, *The Indo European Languages*, 393–394

34 Green, *Language and History in the Early Germanic World*, 86 & Helfenstein, *Comparative Grammar of the Teutonic Languages*, 9–10

35 Versloot, "The Geography and Dialects of Old Saxon," 127; Nielsen, *The Germanic Languages*, 72 & 93 & Rauch, *The Old Saxon Language*, 105

36 Ehlers, "Könige, Klöster und der Raum," 189–191

37 Thompson, *Feudal Germany*, 168–169 & Arnold, *Medieval Germany*, 42

38 Robinson, *Old English and Its Closest Relatives*, 102–105; Howorth, "The Ethnology of the Germans (I)," 368; Oman, *The Dark Ages*, 276; Cathey, "The Historical Setting of the *Heliand*," 10–11; Dean, "Felling the Irminsul," 15; Gallee, *Old-Saxon Texts*, VII-VIII; Becher, "Non enim habent regem idem Antiqui Saxones," 18–28; Ehlers, *Die Integration Sachsens in das fränkische Reich*, 39 & Springer, *Die Sachsen*, 255

39 Howorth, "The Early Intercourse of the Danes and the Franks," 151; Tschan, *History of the Archbishops of Hamburg-Bremen*, 135–136 & Thompson, *Feudal Germany*, 168

40 Meier, "Man and Environment in the Marsh Area of Schleswig-Holstein," 63

41 Dickinson, "Rural Settlements in the German Lands," 245; Buse, *The Regions of Germany*, 112; Thompson, *Feudal Germany*, XII & 167–168; Schwikart, *Journey through Lower Saxony*, 68–69 & 88

42 Barraclough, *The Origins of Modern Germany*, 6

43 Faulkner, *Law and Authority in the Early Middle Ages*, 34–35

44 Dickinson, "The Development and Distribution of the Medieval German Town," 14 & Fried, "The Frankish Kingdoms," 145

45 Landon, "Economic Incentives for the Frankish Conquest of Saxony," 52 & Ehlers, "Könige, Klöster und der Raum," 201–202

46 Reuter, *Germany in the Early Middle Ages*, 66–67

47 Robinson, *Old English and Its Closest Relatives*, 104

48 Ehlers, "Between Marklo and Merseburg," 135

49 Cathey, *Heliand*, 9

50   Ibid.; Tiefenbach, *Altsächsisches Handwörterbuch*, 78 & Drew, *The Laws of the Salian Franks*, 20
51   Bachrach, *Charlemagne's Early Campaigns (768–777)*, 201
52   For "republican" assemblies see Lammers, "Die Stammesbildung bei den Sachsen," 44
53   Springer, "Was Lebuins Lebensbeschreibung über die Verfassung Sachsens wirklich sagt," 244–247 & 250 & Tacitus, *The Agricola and The Germania*, 50
54   Ibid. 250–258; Murphy, *The Heliand*, 122 & 172 & Tiefenbach, *Altsächsisches Handwörterbuch*, 412
55   Arblaster, *A History of the Low Countries*, 53–54; Durant, *The Age of Faith*, 486 & 504 & Brink, "Law and Legal Customs," 90–91 & 102
56   Springer, "Was Lebuins Lebensbeschreibung über die Verfassung Sachsens wirklich sagt," 250–258
57   Wood, *The Missionary Life*, 116
58   Springer, "Was Lebuins Lebensbeschreibung über die Verfassung Sachsens wirklich sagt," 241–243 & Wood, *The Missionary Life*, 116–117
59   Talbot, *The Anglo-Saxon Missionaries in Germany*, 228
60   Bachrach, *Charlemagne's Early Campaigns (768–777)*, 202–203 & Wood, *The Missionary Life*, 115
61   Talbot, *The Anglo-Saxon Missionaries in Germany*, 230 & Springer, "Was Lebuins Lebensbeschreibung über die Verfassung Sachsens wirklich sagt," 243
62   Springer, *Die Sachsen*, 135 & Bachrach, *Charlemagne's Early Campaigns (768–777)*, 203
63   Ibid. 143
64   Ibid.
65   Ibid. 142
66   Bede, *Ecclesiastical History of the English People*, 281
67   Springer, "Was Lebuins Lebensbeschreibung über die Verfassung Sachsens wirklich sagt," 243–250 & Becher, "Non enim habent regem idem Antiqui Saxones," 9–13
68   Bachrach, *Charlemagne's Early Campaigns (768–777)*, 199–200; Holland, *Germany*, 21; Becher, "Non enim habent regem idem Antiqui Saxones," 15 & James, "The Northern World in the Dark Ages," 85
69   Thompson, *Feudal Germany*, 169–170 & Lammers, "Die Stammesbildung bei den Sachsen," 46
70   The "northern invasion" theory originates with Rudolf of Fulda, was copied by Widukind of Corvey, and was later replicated by numerous historians of the twentieth century; see Goldberg, *Struggle for Empire*, 177–179; Lammers, "Die Stammesbildung bei den Sachsen," 26 & 46–47 & 49–50; Lintzel, *Untersuchungen zur Geschichte der alten Sachsen*, 66–70; Bauer, *Buße und Strafe im Frühmittelalter*, 29; Von Heung-Sik Park, "Die Stände der Lex Saxonum," 200 & Dettmer, *Der Sachsenführer Widukind*, 21–23
71   Robinson, *Old English and Its Closest Relatives*, 104 & Goldberg, "Popular Revolt," 468–475
72   Von Heung-Sik Park, "Die Stände der Lex Saxonum," 202–206
73   Steuer, "The Beginnings of Urban Economies among the Saxons," 167 & Grünewald, "Westfalen zwischen Franken und Sachsen," 21–22
74   Robinson, *Old English and Its Closest Relatives*, 104–105
75   Von Heung-Sik Park, "Die Stände der Lex Saxonum," 202 & 207; Reuter, *Germany in the Early Middle Ages*, 66–67 & Bauer, *Buße und Strafe im Frühmittelalter*, 29
76   Ibid. 208–209; Wattenbach, *Die Übertragung des hl. Alexander von Rudolf und Meginhart*, 5–6 & Springer, *Die Sachsen*, 249
77   Emerton, *The Letters of Saint Boniface*, 127–128, & Talbot, *The Anglo-Saxon Missionaries in Germany*, 123
78   Henderson, *A History of Germany in the Middle Ages*, 72

79 Geary, *Before France and Germany*, 52 & 54
80 Goldberg, *Struggle for Empire*, 204
81 Cathey, *Heliand*, 310 & Hamerow, *Early Medieval Settlements*, 129–130
82 Dörfler, "Rural Economy of the Continental Saxons," 138 & Pounds, *An Historical Geography of Europe*, 207
83 Dillon, *The Celtic Realms*, 98 & 107–109 & Meredith, *The Fortunes of Africa*, 236
84 Algeo, *The Origins and Development of the English Language*, 55–56
85 Geary, *Before France and Germany*, 46–47; Nielsen, "Urban Economy in Southern Scandinavia," 205
86 Cosman, *Medieval Wordbook*, 90 & Fortson, *Indo-European Language and Culture*, 19
87 Bremmer, *Introduction to Old Frisian*, 2
88 Reuter, *Germany in the Early Middle Ages*, 95–96 & Meier, "Man and Environment in the Marsh Area of Schleswig-Holstein," 64
89 Dean, "Felling the Irminsul," 20
90 Zimmerman & Jöns, "Cultural Contacts between the Baltic, the North Sea Region and Scandinavia," 251–252
91 Geary, *Before France and Germany*, 45
92 Dörfler, "Rural Economy of the Continental Saxons," 141
93 Steuer, "The Beginnings of Urban Economies among the Saxons," 171
94 Landon, "Economic Incentives for the Frankish Conquest of Saxony," 51–52
95 Pounds, *An Historical Geography of Europe*, 166–167
96 Halsall, *Barbarian Migrations and the Roman West*, 130 & 158; Geary, *Before France and Germany*, 21 & 58–60 & Nees, *Early Medieval Art*, 77–78
97 Steuer, "The Beginnings of Urban Economies among the Saxons," 171
98 Ausenda, "Jural Relations among the Old Saxons," 113–114
99 Grünewald, "Westfalen zwischen Franken und Sachsen," 23; Schreg, "Farmsteads in early medieval Germany," 254–261; Hamerow, *Early Medieval Settlements*, 14–15 & 31–32; Fehring, *The Archaeology of Medieval Germany*, 163–165 & Both, "Eine sächsische Hofwüstung," 101
100 Both, "Eine sächsische Hofwüstung," 109
101 Newman, *Daily Life in the Middle Ages*, 126; Koch, "Friesisch-sächsische Beziehungen zur Merowingerzeit," 67, 79–82 & Laux, "Kleine karolingische und ottonische Scheibenfibeln," 15–16
102 Wickham, *The Inheritance of Rome*, 113 & Dutton, *Charlemagne's Mustache*, 12 & 23–28
103 Hennessey et al., *Fashion*, 40–47 & Flierman, *Saxon Identities*, 45–46
104 Widukind, *Deeds of the Saxons*, 25
105 Cathey, *Heliand*, 326–327 & 347; Murphy, *The Heliand*, 5; Rauch, *The Old Saxon Language*, 311 & Tiefenbach, *Altsächsisches Handwörterbuch*, 157
106 Newman, *Daily Life in the Middle Ages*, 224
107 Bachrach, *Charlemagne's Early Campaigns (768–777)*, 209–210
108 Nicolle, *The Age of Charlemagne*, 19 & France, *Warfare in the Dark Ages*, 58
109 Bachrach, *Charlemagne's Early Campaigns (768–777)*, 206–207
110 Scholz, *Carolingian Chronicles*, 9
111 Heine, "Archäologische Burgenforschung in Südniedersachsen," 263–268
112 Nicolle, *The Conquest of Saxony*, 39–41
113 Ibid. & Butt, *Daily Life in the Age, of Charlemagne*, 38
114 Langen, "Die Bedeutung von Befestigungen in den Sachsenkriegen Karls des Großen," 188–199 & Grünewald, "Westfalen zwischen Franken und Sachsen," 23
115 Ibid.
116 Dean, "Felling the Irminsul," 18
117 Bachrach, *Charlemagne's Early Campaigns (768–777)*, 206
118 Nicolle, *The Conquest of Saxony*, 39–41; Newman, *Daily Life in the Middle Ages*, 230 & Dean, "Felling the Irminsul," 17

119 Green, *Language and History in the Early Germanic World*, 81; Barney, *Word-Hoard*, 21; Shaw, *Pagan Goddesses in the Early Germanic World*, 32 & Paxton, *Anchoress and Abbess in Ninth-Century Saxony*, 42
120 Riche, *Daily Life in the World of Charlemagne*, 80
121 Green, *Language and History in the Early Germanic World*, 68
122 Murphy, *The Heliand*, 8
123 Green, *Language and History in the Early Germanic World*, 43
124 Widukind, *Deeds of the Saxons*, 18–19
125 Lammers, "Die Stammesbildung bei den Sachsen," 38
126 Widukind, *Deeds of the Saxons*, 21. From the *Deeds of the Saxons*, © Catholic University of America Press. 2014. Reproduced with the permission of the Catholic University of America Press through PLS Clear.
127 Springer, *Die Sachsen*, 84–87

3   Early Franco-Saxon Conflict

From Antiquity up through the early Carolingian era, Franks and Saxons encountered each other in myriad ways. Sometimes they were allies; more often, they were not. Understanding these interactions as a prelude to Charlemagne's Saxon Wars is necessary for understanding the evolving Frankish political perspective. By the time Charlemagne ascended to the throne, Frankish kings tended to view Saxons as subservient people whose faithlessness to Frankish suzerainty justified campaigns against them. Punishing treason was increasingly coupled with hostile religious tensions, particularly following the career of Charlemagne's grandfather, Charles Martel.

North Sea Piracy

The disparate Roman reports concerning Franks and Saxons from Antiquity mentioned in Chapters 1 and 2 become more uniform in connection to the problem of North Sea piracy, which, by the late third century CE, Saxons (alongside Frisians, Franks, and others) are recorded participating in. These raids initially targeted the coast of Gaul but later included southeast England.[1] In response, the Romans began developing the *Litus Saxonicum*, "the Saxon Shore," which included a series of fortifications along the coasts of Gaul and Britain.[2] By the mid-280s, the Roman commander Carausius was appointed to address the piratical attacks on the coast of Gaul.[3] Carausius used his fleet stationed in Boulogne for defense while further developing the "Saxon Shore."[4] However, according to Bede, shortly after his appointment, Carausius was accused of allowing pirates to raid freely in order to collect tribute from their plunder. When Emperor Maximian heard what Carausius was doing, he ordered the commander to be executed.[5] In response, Carausius seized control of Britain and proclaimed himself "Emperor of the North." He ruled for seven years before being killed by one of his companions, after which Britain returned to Roman rule.

It would seem reasonable to conclude that the usurpation of Britain by Carausius weakened Rome's authority along the North Sea. Carausius' rule had certainly not ended North Sea piracy; instead, fourth- and fifth-century raiding proved far more devastating than the third ever was.[6] One famous report from Bishop Sidonius Apollinaris of Clermont, in the aftermath of a Saxon raid in Aquitaine, laments

DOI: 10.4324/9781003379157-5

these events. Sidonius claims that when the brutal and "ungovernable" Saxons attacked at sea, before sailing home, they would drown or crucify one in ten of their victims (chosen by lot) as a sacrifice.[7] As Flierman has discussed, this same sentiment shows up in the fourth-century poetry of Claudian and in a letter written by Bishop Ambrose of Milan, where the Saxons are depicted as enemies of Rome and a scourge of the northern seas.[8]

In response to maritime marauders, during the fourth century, the Romans appointed a *Comes Litoris Saxonici*, a "Count of the Saxon Shore," to assist in defending the North Sea coasts.[9] According to the *Notitia Dignitatum*, a fifth-century list outlining Roman military administration, the Count of the Saxon Shore oversaw nine forts in the Roman provinces of *Gallia Belgica*, *Gallia Lugunensis*, and *Britannia*.[10] By 367, these defenses collapsed due to a conspiracy orchestrated by the Picts, Scots, Attacotti, Franks, and Saxons.[11] Ammianus Marcellinus records the horror in Gaul, where Franks and Saxons were "ravaging…plundering… burning, and murdering all the prisoners they could take."[12]

Ammianus relates further episodes of Saxon raids in Gaul over the late 360s and early 370s, in which Saxon attacks are followed by Romans slaughtering those responsible.[13] However, despite Roman reprisals, Saxon pillaging continued and increasingly became focused on England. Soon, even the Count of the Saxon Shore was killed, prompting Emperor Valentinian to send Count Theodosius, "the terror of Saxony," to restore order in Britain.[14] Theodosius successfully reconquered Britain, during which he defeated the Saxons at sea and rebuilt coastal defenses.[15] However, these successes were short-lived. By 370, Saxons resumed raiding in Gaul, and within a few decades, they began to concentrate again more selectively on Britain.[16] Despite the Romano-British natives sending requests for aid to Emperor Honorius, by 410, Britain was essentially abandoned.[17] Rome's loss was the Saxons' gain, and the collapse of the Roman fleet paved the way for increased assaults.[18]

The epidemic of North Sea piracy facilitated the collapse of Rome's northern defenses, which coincided with the collapse of Rome's Rhineland frontier. The opening of the North Sea thereafter initiated a restructuring of Britain by Anglo-Saxon migrants and invaders, but it also resulted in the transformation of the environments they left behind.[19]

The Anglo-Saxon Exodus

The presence of Germanic settlers in Britain can be shown as early as the second century AD, during which they acted as *foederati* for the Romans.[20] Franks, Alamans, and Saxons were among them.[21] As a result, local Celtic inhabitants were already familiar with Germanic mercenaries by the Roman withdrawal in 406. This would explain why later accounts suggest Britons turned to Saxon mercenaries for aid.[22] According to Bede, a British king named Vortigern called upon Saxons for help repelling Picts raiding from Scotland. The Saxons "arrived in three longships" and were given lands in the east in exchange for protection.[23] These Saxons successfully dealt with the Picts, after which they sent news to their homeland, informing their kin that the land was fertile and the Britons cowardly.[24] Soon more Saxons arrived, and war erupted between them and the Britons.

Bede famously claimed the incoming migrants were "Saxons, Angles, and Jutes."[25] However, in reading Bede's account (and those in Gildas' *On the Ruin of Britain*, the *Anglo-Saxon Chronicle*, and Widukind's *Deeds of the Saxons*), what is being reflected are the political, mythological, and geographic circumstances of the chronicler's day rather than representations of the historical realities of the fifth century.[26] The size of the migration, the scope of its violence, and the portrait of homogenous tribal settlements are exaggerated. Further, the ethnic composition of the Anglo-Saxons can no longer be relegated only to Angles, Saxons, and Jutes. In addition to material culture reminiscent of northern Germany and southern Denmark, archaeological remains attest to the presence of Frankish, Frisian, Alamannic, and Thuringian settlers.[27] The majority of migrants came as farmers, not warriors.[28]

Several factors motivated the Anglo-Saxon migrations. The expansion of the Merovingian Franks may be one of them. However, Britain's fertile land and wealth were also enticing to people struggling on the frigid coasts of the North Sea. In addition, population expansion in the area between the Elbe and the Ems and environmental changes were likely contributors.[29] Environmental studies indicate that rising sea levels threatened coastal communities with flooding and decimated their means of subsistence, which coastal Frisians and Saxons responded to by building artificial mounds of clay and dung, called *terpen* (OS: *wurten*).[30] Yet, despite these constructions, archaeological evidence confirms the abandonment of coastal settlements during the migration period, including the area stretching from Frisia to the Elbe-Weser region and north into Schleswig-Holstein.[31] The abandoned land in Jutland was settled by Danes and western Slavs, while Frisians extended their territory as far as the Weser and, by the seventh century, controlled the port of Dorestad as well as Utrecht.[32] Meanwhile, the "Old Saxons" expanded into Westphalia, Hesse, and the Ruhr and Lippe Valleys.[33]

For the present study, the significance of the Anglo-Saxon migration is that it left a power vacuum along the North Sea and Baltic coasts, initiating competition among nearby peoples remaining on the continent.[34] As the "Old Saxons" expanded south and west, they came into conflict with the Franks, who sought to establish hegemony over much of Western Europe. In addition, the loss of labor, craftsmen, warriors, and ships and the disruption of coastal communities must have been significant challenges to continental Saxons. Notably, during the Carolingian Age, Saxons are never mentioned employing naval assets, suggesting their maritime prowess had dissipated (and was likely replaced by Frisians and Scandinavians).[35]

Merovingian-Saxon Encounters

After the Merovingian rise to power following the conquests of Clovis, Franks and Saxons continued to encounter each other in various contexts. One of the earliest of these occurred during the reign of the Frankish king Childeric I (458–481). In the mid-fifth century, Childeric became an ally of Rome, whereafter, in 463, he assisted the Roman ruler Aegidius of Soissons in a battle against the Visigoths at Orleans.[36] Under Aegidius' successor (Count Paul), Childeric was directed to deal with Saxon pirates near Angers, only a few miles from the confluence of the Maine and the Loire.[37] Angers had recently been captured by the warlord Odoacer and a contingent of Saxons following him.[38] According to the *Liber Historiae Franco-rum*, Odoacer, a "duke" of the Saxons, arrived by sea with a band of raiders, after which his forces burned the city and murdered its citizens.[39] This was likely the same Odoacer who later deposed Emperor Romulus Augustus, and though unclear, he may have been a Saxon himself (or possibly Thuringian).[40]

To liberate Angers, the Franco-Roman army marched out to meet Odoacer, whom they soon defeated.[41] According to Gregory of Tours, a "great war" ensued between Saxons and Romans in which the Saxons were forced to retreat, and many were killed. Simultaneously, the Franks ravaged and captured some of their nearby island settlements.[42]

Military exchanges between Franks and Saxons continued to escalate follow-ing the death of Clovis, after which the kingdom was divided and co-ruled by his four sons: Theuderic, Clodomir, Childebert I, and Chlotar I. However, while these exchanges were becoming increasingly hostile, notable exceptions exist. One of these involves a controversial episode in which the Saxons allegedly assisted the Franks in 531 (during the reign of Theuderic) with destroying the Kingdom of Thuringia, which had expanded in the aftermath of Atilla's defeat.[43] In that con-flict, thousands of Saxons led by their Duke Hathagath assisted the Franks in battle near the village of Burgscheidungen, where they defeated the Thuringians and their king Irminfrid.[44] After the victory, Franks and Saxons divided the newly conquered lands between them, with the Saxons taking control of Thuringian territory north of the Unstrut and the Franks taking the rest.[45] This, at least, is what Rudolf of Fulda claimed in the ninth century, Widukind of Corvey copied in the tenth, and Adam of Bremen replicated in the eleventh.[46]

However, as noted, Rudolf of Fulda and Widukind's accounts of early Saxon history should be approached cautiously. As Matthias Springer has discussed, Rudolf was a known document forger and may have invented the Saxon conquest of Thuringia north of the Unstrut to increase the claims of the bishopric of Halber-stadt.[47] Alternatively, Widukind likely wrote his section on early Saxon history to entertain the Abbess Matilda of Quedlinburg (the 12-year-old daughter of Otto I, to whom Widukind's work was dedicated).[48] In addition, earlier accounts that discuss the destruction of Thuringia (Gregory of Tours, the *Chronicle of Fredegar*, and the *Liber Historiae Francorum*) fail to mention Saxon participation.[49]

Regardless of Saxon participation in Thuringia, during this same period, the Saxons do appear to have formally become Frankish subjects, which is demon-strated by the fact that a tribute requirement was imposed upon them.[50] The Sax-ons remained subjects of the Franks throughout Theuderic's reign and into the reign of his son Theudebert (533–548). When Theudebert wrote to the Eastern Roman Emperor Justinian, he introduced himself as the ruler of many peoples, including the Saxons.[51] However, resentment toward Frankish rule reached a boiling point a few years later, and in 555, the Saxons revolted (*alongside the*

Thuringians).[52] That revolt opportunistically followed the death of King Theude-bald, Theudebert's son.[53]

With Theudebald's death, only the brothers Chlotar and Childebert remained to rule Francia, and Chlotar set out immediately to meet the rebels in 555/556.[54] According to Gregory, after receiving word of the revolt, Chlotar gathered an army against the Saxons, killed many of them, and "ravaged" Thuringia for lending the Saxons support.[55] This same course of events is found in the *Liber Historiae Francorum*, which claims the battle against the Saxons occurred on the Weser.[56] After his victory, Chlotar required the Saxons to resume their annual tribute payment, which amounted to 500 heads of cattle.[57]

The reinstatement of a tribute requirement exacerbated Saxon animosity, and before long, Chlotar was called upon to address another Saxon revolt. In Gregory's account, Chlotar was furious that the Saxons had abandoned their tribute obligations, so he led an army toward their territory. However, en route, he was met by Saxon messengers who proclaimed their willingness to pay tribute if the king would ensure peace. Chlotar thought the Saxon demands were reasonable, but the Austrasian nobles in his entourage distrusted the Saxons and advocated attacking them. Chlotar protested the noble's conclusions, but they wouldn't be assuaged. Instead, in what can only be described as mutiny, the nobles forced Chlotar to march into battle against the Saxons, which ended in a horrific Frankish defeat.[58]

Gregory's account has several striking features, and one is forced to wonder if the story was not just invented to remove responsibility for a Frankish defeat from the king. Alternatively, the story may be a testament to the considerable power of the Austrasian nobles.[59] It is worth noting that Chlotar was not the forgiving type. Not long after the Saxon revolt, rumors spread that the king had been killed by Saxons during his campaign, causing his son Charam to lead a rebellion of his own. When his father's army eventually captured Charam, Chlotar had his son, along-side his wife and daughters, strangled to death and burned.[60] Perhaps Chlotar didn't blame the Saxons for their actions, as there is evidence that the rebellion was insti-gated by his brother Childebert, who may have also been responsible for Charam's revolt. Nevertheless, before his death, Chlotar *was* able to reimpose the tribute requirement on the Saxons, returning them to their status as Frankish subjects.[61]

Frankish subjugation of the Saxons, as well as their expansion into Saxon ter-ritory, may have been one motivation for the participation of Saxons in the 568 Lombard invasion of Northern Italy, led by the Lombard king Alboin.[62] Gregory of Tours is again our primary source on the matter. However, a similar account was replicated by Paul the Deacon in his eighth-century *History of the Langobards*.[63] In Gregory's work, Saxons passed through Gaul en route to Italy, taking loot and slaves while wreaking havoc.[64] In response to Saxon raiding, the local commander (Mummolus) mustered forces against them, "killing many thousands."[65] Defeat motivated the Saxons to return home, but in the process, they continued to raid and steal from locals around Avignon. Their actions infuriated Mummolus, who required the Saxons to turn over the stolen goods and make restitution. Once com-pleted (in part by treachery), the Saxons were given leave to cross the Rhone and return to their lands under the domain of the Frankish king Sigibert.[66]

The Saxons traveled with women and children in this episode, suggesting it was a full-scale migration. Nevertheless, when it failed, and the Saxons returned home, they were in for a rude awakening. While they were away in Italy, King Sigibert had settled Alamannians (among others) on their abandoned territory, enraging the Saxons. The Alamanni tried to negotiate a peaceful settlement but to no avail. Instead, the Saxons planned to wipe out the squatters and claim their women, leading to two battles in which they suffered devastating defeats (20,000 dead, according to Gregory).[67]

Some scholars believe Gregory may have messed up his chronology, given that he incorrectly places Chlotar I's reign as contemporaneous with the Lombard invasion.[68] Springer has suggested the Saxons may have gone to Italy in 553, possibly *alongside* the Alamanni.[69] Whatever the case might be concerning the correct timeline, there doesn't seem to be much doubt that Saxons did, in fact, sojourn to Italy at some point during the mid-sixth century.

Later in the sixth century, further Frankish dealings with the Saxons occurred during the reign of Chlotar's son Chilperic.[70] According to the *LHF*, around 568, Chilperic went to war against the Saxons.[71] However, there is also speculation here that we may be dealing with a translation error and that "Saxons" may have originally been "Suessones," that is, inhabitants of the city of Soissons, which was under the control of Chilperic's brother (and enemy) Sigibert I.[72] Less speculative is that, by 578, Chilperic was sending *actual* Saxons to fight the Bretons and their troublesome leader Waroch. However, things went badly for the Saxons, and the Bretons defeated them. Following their loss, some survivors founded a Saxon colony in what is now Normandy, which archaeological evidence has confirmed.[73] It is presumably these same Saxons whom Gregory later calls the "Saxons of Bayeux."

During the late 560s to early 570s, Venantius Fortunatus wrote a poem concerning a group of Saxons in the Loire valley of Brittany whom Bishop Felix of Nantes baptized.[74] The poem was written mainly to praise Felix for his work, yet it also gives insight into contemporary perceptions of the Saxons and suggests that Saxons settling in Frankish territory were facing increasing pressure to convert:

> Turning to the better course those wandering in pagan error, he [Felix] fortified God's fold so that the beast would not carry them off. Those whom Eve had first infected with her sin he now restores, suckled by the rich milk of the church's breast, cultivating savage hearts with gentle words; thanks to Felix a crop grows up from the thorns. A hard race, the Saxons, living like wild animals, but you heal them holy one.[75]

We don't know enough of the context regarding the Saxons Venantius mentions to establish motives; however, not long after Venantius wrote his poem and following the violent death of Chilperic (after 584), we see Bayeux Saxons working on behalf of the Franks, primarily at the behest of Chilperic's wife, the notorious Queen Fredegund.[76]

Fredegund used Saxon mercenaries to handle some of her private feuds, one of which involved a Duke named Beppolen. In 590, Beppolen joined King Guntram of Burgundy in co-leading a campaign against the Bretons. When Fredegund heard of his involvement, she devised a scheme to eliminate her nemesis for good. The queen called upon the Bayeux Saxons and had them shave off their hair in the Breton manner, after which they acquired Breton clothing to complete their disguise.[77] The Saxons were then sent to join the *actual* Bretons and assist in stopping Beppolen's army.[78] Happily for Fredegund, the plan worked. Beppolen was killed during the battle, along with many of the Frankish soldiers who accompanied him; many of the Saxons perished as well.[79] This event was also recorded in the *Chronicle of Fredegar*. However, it fails to mention Saxon involvement (or Fredegunds, for that matter).[80]

During the Frankish civil war of 612, fought between Theudebert II and his half-brother Theuderic II of Burgundy, Saxons were also participating in Frankish political affairs.[81] During the conflict, Saxons, as well as Thuringians, gave their support to Theudebert.[82] However, they bet on the losing side.[83] Still, the conflict was devastating for both armies, as can be seen in a disturbing report from the *Chronicle of Fredegar,* which claims the fighting in one battle was so dense that the corpses of the dead didn't even have room to fall to the ground.[84]

Shortly after, during the reign of Chlotar II (613–629), Saxons were again at war with the Franks, leading a revolt against Chlotar's son Dagobert, the sub-king of Austrasia.[85] In response, Dagobert led his army across the Rhine to meet the "very rebellious" Saxons, led by a nobleman named Bertoald.[86] During the campaign, Dagobert was injured by a blow to the head.[87] When his father received word of his son's injury, he marched his army through the Ardennes to join Dagobert's forces on the banks of the Weser.[88] The subsequent events recorded in the *Liber Historiae Francorum* are in the style of an epic tradition. Chlotar crosses the Rhine, rushes to Dagobert's aid, and (wearing mail and a coat of dog skins) proceeds to duel the Saxon leader Bertoald in the middle of the Weser. Eventually, Bertoald is killed, and Dagobert hoists his head on a spear. Yet, his anger was unquenched, so he ravaged Saxon lands and executed every man taller than his sword (a spatha, typically 90–100 cm long).[89]

The account is likely exaggerated, possibly made up entirely, yet it became a part of Frankish oral tradition.[90] Chlotar's victory was even memorialized in a song, which Frankish women sang while dancing together in circles.[91] Indeed, as Janet Nelson has discussed, these were still being sung as late as the mid-ninth century in the northern French city of Meaux.[92]

When Chlotar died in 629, power passed fully to his son Dagobert, who had since recovered from his injury. According to the *Chronicle of Fredegar*, in either 631 or 632, Dagobert led an army of Franks and Burgundians east to end raiding in Thuringia by Sorbs and Wends—West Slavic peoples living partially in what is now East Germany. En route, Dagobert was met by a Saxon emissary who petitioned the king to release them from their annual tribute of 500 cattle, which they had been paying for nearly 70 years.[93] (Their petition suggests tribute had been re-imposed following their defeat by Chlotar II.)[94] In return for Dagobert removing the tribute requirement, Saxons would defend the eastern frontier against the Wends.[95] After gathering advice from his Neustrian magnates, Dagobert consented to the Saxons' terms.[96] The deal was sealed with oaths, which the Saxons (per their custom) swore over arms.[97]

Perhaps Dagobert's leniency was influenced by his marriage to a Saxon woman named Nantchildis; however, very little is known about her.[98] Regardless, the implication in the *Chronicle of Fredegar* is that Dagobert's agreement didn't pan out well for the Franks. However, it was a significant development for the Saxons, who, in addition to no longer having to pay tribute, were endowed with a sanctioned military function that bolstered their confidence. This new boldness can be seen in the 690s when Saxons took advantage of the so-called lazy kings and recaptured territory south of the Lippe and Ruhr, which the Franks had formerly conquered.[99] The Saxons also took the Frankish military outpost of Soest in Westphalia and expanded further into Thuringia.[100] The area surrounding Soest continued to be significant for developments in Saxony. It was one of the earliest Christianized Saxon regions (possibly due to St. Boniface, see Chapter 5) and was also responsible for producing the influential Ekbertine family, a noble clan that became loyal assets of the Carolingians.[101] Soest was also strategically significant due to its proximity to the *Hellweg*.[102]

In the aftermath of their expansion, Saxons were in a consistent state of hostility with the Franks for the remainder of Merovingian rule. They were not alone. According to the *Annals of Metz,* during the reign of Chilperic II (715–721), Frisians, Bavarians, Alemans, Bretons, and Gascons were also contesting Frankish rule. The Frisians, Alemans, and Bavarians had been especially troublesome, and Merovingians were far more concerned with those peoples than they had been with the Saxons. However, Saxon expansion at the end of the Merovingian period was beginning to change things. Not only had Saxons managed to retain their autonomy following the recent revolt, but they had also seized Frankish territory and kept it.

Early Carolingian-Saxon Conflict

As discussed in Chapter 1, the Carolingians originated within the Frankish nobility, gaining prominence by controlling the position of "Mayor of the Palace."[103] Their rise to power was born from struggles within Francia and in response to increased external threats, notably the Saracen advance from Spain and the eastern revolts of Frisians, Bavarians, and Saxons.[104]

The first Carolingian to meet these threats was Charles Martel, "the Hammer," an illegitimate son of Pepin of Herstal and the noblewoman Alpaida.[105] Following the death of Pepin in 714, Charles Martel was in prison due to dynastic strife and competition among the nobles of Neustria. However, by 715, he had escaped and secured declaration as "Mayor of the Palace" by the nobles of Austrasia. That declaration followed Martel's defeat of his adversaries Ragamfred and Chilperic II in April 716 at the Battle of Ambleve.[106] In the meantime, that same year, western Saxons utilized discord within Francia as an opportunity to invade the lower Rhine. According to the *Annales Petaviani*, Saxons destroyed the land of the Hattuarians, a neighboring client people of the Franks.[107] It was a serious challenge, yet only after the end of the Frankish civil war in 718 was Charles Martel able to address it.[108]

The following year Charles led a campaign against the Saxons, pushed them out of Frankish territory, and marched as far as the Weser.[109] It was the first of many campaigns "the hammer" would lead against the Saxons, and he returned in 720, followed by another campaign in 724.[110] Despite his success, it seems unlikely that Charles completely regained control over Frankish territory the Saxons had recently conquered. Indeed, the missionary Boniface (see Chapter 5) observed in the early 720s that the people of Thuringia (who were subject to the Franks) had submitted to Saxon "domination."[111] Perhaps this is why Charles was planning another campaign against the Saxons in 729, but it never came to fruition.[112]

A few years later, in October 732, Charles gained historical renown by repelling an invasion of Spanish Muslims outside Tours.[113] However, it wasn't long before Charles returned to Saxony due to a Frisian revolt. In 734, according to the *Chronicle of Fredegar*, he led a fleet against Frisians in the Westergo and Ostergo (which were also inhabited by western Saxons). Charles set up camp on the river Boorn, where he killed Bubo, the "heathen chieftain" leading the Frisian rebellion. Charles then proceeded to crush, burn, and plunder sanctuaries dedicated to the Frisian's pagan gods.[114]

The destruction of Frisian (or Saxon) shrines was a notable development that stands out from prior Franco-Saxon squabbles, and Charles' actions may have represented a growing militant Frankish Christianity, one his grandson Charlemagne inherited. Lest Martel's religious convictions be doubted, it is worth noting that it wasn't just in Saxony or Frisia that Charles supported the eradication of paganism. Throughout the 720s and 730s, he was also a patron of the Visigothic missionary Pirmin, who was busy with conversion efforts in Alamannia (see Chapter 5).

In 738, Charles returned to western Saxony, unleashing further devastation.[115] According to the *Chronicle of Fredegar*, the "detestable" and "savage" pagan Saxons had risen again in revolt (possibly due to issues of taxation). In response, Charles crossed the Rhine at its confluence with the Lippe, decimated the region, and took hostages.[116] The Saxon front remained quiet for a few years until the death of Charles Martel in 741, after which discord erupted within Francia and ignited a scramble for power. Carloman and Pippin the Short, sons of Charles Martel, struggled to maintain order over the following years as they dealt with scheming nobles and revolts in Aquitaine. At the same time, the brothers campaigned against Bavarians, Alamannians, and Saxons.[117]

Carloman and Pippin's first challenge from the Saxons came in 743/744 when, under their warlord Theodoric, they joined a Bavarian revolt led by Duke Odilo.[118] The brothers quickly engaged and defeated the Bavarians at the River Lech.[119] However, that same year, according to the *Royal Frankish Annals*, Carloman also advanced into Saxony where, by way of a treaty, he captured the Hohenseesburg (a hill-fort in Westphalia known as Sigiburg/Syburg) and forced Theodoric to submit.[120] Yet, Theodoric was still alive, and the Saxons undeterred. They soon went on the offensive, raiding and pillaging the Frankish heartland of Austrasia, which brought Carloman and Pippin into Saxony, where the Saxons were defeated, and Theodoric was captured.[121] The *Chronicle of Fredegar* adds that, in addition to being enslaved, many Saxons were baptized and given the holy sacraments.[122]

The *Fredegar* account is notable as one of the earliest in which Saxon conversions are recorded immediately following military defeat, and it may speak to a growing rise in religious-based hostilities. For clerics working in the region, the conflict was causing problems. Indeed, Boniface wrote to Pope Zacharias in October 745, grumbling about his failure to receive adequate patronage due to the disruptions of "Saxons and Frisians."[123]

With the Saxons temporarily pacified, the Franks could address more serious threats. Pippin put an end to an Alamannic revolt led by Duke Gotfrid.[124] Then in 745, the brothers turned their attention toward the Gascons of Aquitaine but were soon back fighting the Alemans. The struggle against the Alemans was persistent and fierce, which explains why, after their revolt was crushed, Carloman ordered a series of mass executions that included members of the Alamannic nobility.[125] One year later, reportedly "burning" for a life of contemplation, Carloman decided to dedicate the remainder of his days in service to God.[126] After journeying to Rome to be tonsured, he took up residence at the Abbey of Monte Cassino, where he became a monk.[127] Carolingian power centralized on Pippin the Short, who was ultimately responsible for overthrowing the Merovingians a few years later.[128]

In the meantime, rebellions continued. In 747 and 748, Pippin faced challenges from his half-brother Grifo, who had recently escaped prison in the Ardennes.[129] (Grifo's crime had supposedly been instigating a revolt among the Bavarians).[130] Following his escape, he fled to the Saxons, where he received refuge and support.[131] However, by harboring Grifo, the Saxons were essentially committing treason.[132] Pippin responded by leading an army to meet Grifo and the Saxons at the River Oker. Yet, rather than join battle, the brothers came to terms, and Grifo fled to Bavaria.[133]

The *Chronicle of Fredegar* gives us additional key details, notably, that Pippin was assisted in putting down the Saxons who harbored Grifo with the aid of Wends and Frisians, and together this coalition burnt Saxon villages, slaughtered rebels, and took slaves. In the aftermath of the carnage, the Saxons were made to swear oaths that they would resume payment of the tribute they were required to give during Chlotar's reign (but had since been free of). In addition, the Saxons allegedly "asked" for access to the Christian sacraments once they realized their rebellion was doomed.[134] Some scholars doubt the note concerning sacraments, which may be an attempt by the chronicler to avoid directly stating that the Saxons were compelled to convert.[135] Whatever the case might be, again, we see conversion following military defeat and an all-but-direct correlation between political submission and religious conversion. Yet, rather than cowing the Saxons, the restored tribute system and religious hostilities ushered in two years of rebellion, which Pippin responded to by devastating the Saxon countryside and taking more hostages.[136]

By November 751, Pippin the Short had become King of Francia after ousting the Merovingian king Childeric III, who was tonsured and exiled to a monastery.[137] Again, Saxons took advantage of the transition of power, using it as an opportunity to become more aggressive. According to a letter sent by Boniface in 752 to the new pope Stephen II, the "heathen" Saxons ravaged and burned as many as 30 churches.[138] It seems probable many Saxons associated the growth of the

Church in their territory as an extension of Frankish rule. Saxon raids were also likely the stimulus for Pippin's subsequent invasion of Saxony in 753. According to the *Royal Frankish Annals*, Pippin led an army into Saxony as far as Rehme (near Minden), where he ravaged the land, took prisoners, and collected loot.[139] He was accompanied by Bishop Hildegar of Cologne, who was killed during the campaign at the Westphalian stronghold of Iburg.[140] Nevertheless, Pippin managed to subdue the Saxons, take hostages, and require them to allow missionaries to operate freely in the region.[141] The *Chronicle of Fredegar* paints a similar picture, adding that Pippin was "furious" with the Saxons and that after crossing the Rhine, he burned the land, took men and women as prisoners, gathered loot, and killed numerous Saxons. In response, the Saxons sued for peace, once more requested the sacraments, agreed to pay a larger tribute, and promised never to rebel again.[142] The missionary requirement mentioned in the *RFA* and the sacrament requests in the *Chronicle of Fredegar* tell us (1) that Saxons had not been too keen on allowing them to operate in their region thus far and (2) that Pippin was continuing to prioritize the Christianization of the Saxons as a vital part of their submission.[143]

After pacifying the Saxons, Pippin journeyed home across the Rhine.[144] For the next five years, all was quiet concerning the Saxons, and Pippin focused on subjugating the Lombards and securing loyalty in Bavaria.[145] Yet, before his reign ended, Pippin faced another Saxon challenge in 758.[146] In response, he stormed Saxon strongholds at Sythen, unleashing further devastation.[147] The Saxons again swore their loyalty and agreed to give tribute to the king, now in the form of 300 horses.[148] Pierre Riche has hypothesized that this shift in tribute from cattle to horses may signify a growing Frankish reliance upon the use of cavalry.[149] However, other notable scholars have doubted this explanation.[150] The shift in tribute may also suggest the presence of a horse blight or simply be a logical next step in increasing the punishment burden on the Saxons. Horses were far more valuable than cattle, and a tribute of 300 horses must have seemed like a fortune to the Saxons who could provide them.

The remainder of Pippin's life was spent decimating Aquitaine, which had proved challenging to conquer since the early Merovingian period.[151] Each year, between 760 and 768, Pippin led campaigns into the region, which finally became somewhat stable just before his death on September 24, 768, in St. Denis.[152] Shortly after, On October 9, Pippin's sons Charles and Carloman were pronounced joint-kings—Charles declared at Noyon and Carloman at Soissons.[153] Within a few years, the brief reprieve from what had become an ongoing Franco-Saxon feud would end.

Conclusion

Franco-Saxon reports in Antiquity pertain to the challenges these peoples faced in navigating their relationships with Rome, which can only be defined as fickle. Franks and Saxons fought *for* and *against* the empire, fought each other as allies of the Empire, or opportunistically plagued the Empire with piracy. As the Western Empire lost control of its territories and the Merovingians expanded their domain, the Franks increasingly became drawn into affairs outside of *Germania* and into the collapsing societies of Roman Gaul, Aquitaine, and Italy. To a lesser extent, Saxons were also drawn into the wider Roman world; they established enclaves in Gaul and participated in a failed migration to Italy. However, Saxon movements remained predominantly relegated to areas along the Rhine and North Sea.

Throughout the Merovingian period, Franks and Saxons primarily existed in a state of animosity; however, degrees of cooperation can be observed. Both peoples participated in North Sea piracy and the settlement of England, while Saxons willingly worked for Franks as mercenaries during their civil wars or conflicts with Bretons and Slavs. However, the mercenary phenomenon seems to have mostly been under coercive circumstances. Bayeux Saxons probably could not say "no" to Fredegund, and Saxons who volunteered to fight the Wends during the reign of Dagobert did so to remove their tribute obligations. Tribute requirements coupled with persistent Saxon rebellions indicate that Merovingian rulers tended to view Saxons as politically subordinate, while Saxons opportunistically sought their expansion and autonomy. For the most part, Merovingian rulers kept Saxon expansion in check until the late seventh century, at which point Saxons were beginning to have more success.

With the ascent of the Carolingians, Franco-Saxon feuding continued albeit with a new emphasis by Frankish rulers on Saxons to convert to Christianity. Except for the Saxons mentioned being baptized in Gaul in the poetry of Venantius, there is virtually no indication that Merovingian rulers had any real interest in promoting the Christianization of Saxons following the conversion of Clovis. That policy change only appears to have occurred following the influence of Charles Martel, who ordered the destruction of pagan shrines and required baptism from defeated Saxon rebels. His son Pippin continued the same trend, baptizing Saxon rebels and requiring Saxon magnates to allow the free operation of missionaries in their territory. Christianization and political submission were explicitly connected. As we will see in the chapters ahead, Pippin's son Charles took that lesson to heart. He would deal with the Saxons much like his ancestors had, only with a more fervent dedication to transforming, integrating, and converting them. But what exactly were Saxons being converted from?

Notes

1 Davidson, *Gods and Myths of Northern Europe*, 129
2 The original function of these fortifications has been debated; they may have been commercial in nature, possibly Roman trade and supply centers for the British fleet. This logistical theory of origin is substantiated by archaeological evidence from Roman forts in southeast Britain, which date from the first century AD. However, it is generally agreed that, by the fourth century, these structures had become primarily defensive in nature due to North Sea raids. See Flierman, *Saxon Identities*, 28–36; Kaufmann, *The Medieval Fortress*, 73 & 78; Bachrach, *Warfare in Medieval Europe*, 37–38; Pearson, "Barbarian Piracy and the Saxon Shore," 84–85; Morris, "Cross-North Sea Contacts in the Roman Period," 425–426 & Pounds, *An Historical Geography of Europe*, 167–168
3 Musset, *The Germanic Invasions*, 68
4 Arblaster, *A History of the Low Countries*, 24

5 Bede, *Ecclesiastical History of the English People*, 51
6 Heather, *Empires and Barbarians*, 285–286
7 Campbell, *The Anglo-Saxons*, 13; Davidson, *Gods and Myths of Northern Europe*, 129 & Wolfram, *History of the Goths*, 237
8 Flierman, *Saxon Identities*, 23–24 & 28–29 & Springer, *Die Sachsen*, 37–38
9 Campbell, *The Anglo-Saxons*, 14 & Freeborn, *From Old English to Standard English*, 9
10 This source also records Saxons (alongside Franks and Alamanni) as making up a unit in the Roman army. The Saxon unit was stationed in Phoenicia. See Springer, *Die Sachsen*, 43–45; Flierman, *Saxon Identities*, 30–31 & Wickham, *The Inheritance of Rome*, 33
11 Marcellinus, *The Roman History of Ammianus Marcellinus*, 413
12 Ibid. 454
13 Ibid. 493–494 & 567
14 Springer, *Die Sachsen*, 36
15 Salway, "Roman Britain," 45–49
16 Fleming, *Britain after Rome*, 22–29
17 Salway, "Roman Britain," 45–49
18 Keegan, *A History of Warfare*, 287
19 According to Springer, the Germanic inhabitants of Britain were typically called "Saxones" by Latin writers until the ninth century, at which point some writers began referring to them as Anglisaxones or Angli Saxones, a term possibly invented by Paul the Deacon. See Springer, *Die Sachsen*, 47
20 Dillon, *The Celtic Realms*, 46–48 & Sykes, *Saxons, Vikings, and Celts*, 256–288
21 Algeo, *The Origins and Development of the English Language*, 88 & Springer, *Die Sachsen*, 35
22 Halsall, *Barbarian Migrations and the Roman West*, 197
23 Bede, *Ecclesiastical History of the English People*, 62–63
24 Ibid.
25 Ibid. & Fortson, *Indo-European Language and Culture*, 23–24
26 Ibid. 24; Widukind, *Deeds of the Saxons*, 11–12; Swanton, *The Anglo-Saxon Chronicle*, 12–13; Halsall, *Barbarian Migrations and the Roman West*, 521 & Sykes, *Saxons, Vikings, and Celts*, 277–288
27 Flierman, *Saxon Identities*, 32–35; Backman, *The Worlds of Medieval Europe*, 107; Stenton, *Anglo-Saxon England*, 14–15 & Brooks, "The Social and Political Background," 3
28 Fleming, *Britain after Rome*, 1–61
29 Owen, *The Germanic People*, 102–103
30 Pounds, *An Historical Geography of Europe*, 10–11; Meier, "Man and the Environment in the Marsh area of Schleswig-Holstein," 58; Schreg, "Farmsteads in Early Medieval Germany," 253 & James, "The Northern World in the Dark Ages," 64–65
31 Heather, *Empires and Barbarians*, 286; Nielsen, *The Germanic Languages*, 57–58; Derks, *Ethnic Constructs in Antiquity*, 321–327; Hamerow, *Early Medieval Settlements*, 109–110 & Halsall, *Barbarian Migrations and the Roman West*, 383–384
32 Robinson, *Old English and its Closest Relatives*, 176–181 & Derry, *A History of Scandinavia*, 11
33 Todd, *The Early Germans*, 203
34 Musset, *The Germanic Invasions*, 99–100
35 Bachrach, *Charlemagne's Early Campaigns (768–777)*, 205–206
36 Wells, *Barbarians to Angels*, 52 & Halsall, *Barbarian Migrations and the Roman West*, 269
37 Musset, *The Germanic Invasions*, 75 & Funck-Brentano, *A History of Gaul*, 222
38 Wood, *The Merovingian Kingdoms*, 38–39
39 Bachrach, *Liber Historiae Francorum*, 32

40 Springer, *Die Sachsen*, 53–56

41 Flierman, *Saxon Identities*, 66 & Robinson, *Old English and Its Closest Relatives*, 225

42 Thorpe, *Gregory of Tours' History of the Franks*, 132

43 Halsall, *Barbarian Migrations and the Roman West*, 395–399

44 Henderson, *A History of Germany in the Middle Ages*, 47 & Halsall, *Barbarian Migrations and the Roman West*, 392–393

45 Reuter, *Germany in the Early Middle Ages*, 65 & Springer, "Location in Space and Time," 11

46 Springer, *Die Sachsen*, 62–63; Widukind, *Deeds of the Saxons*, 5–6, 17 & Tschan, *History of the Archbishops of Hamburg-Bremen*, 8–9

47 Ibid. 69 & 73–75

48 Ibid. 75–76

49 Ibid. 61; Bachrach, *Liber Historiae Francorum*, 60 & Thorpe, *Gregory of Tours' The History of the Franks*, 167–169

50 Collins, *Charlemagne*, 44

51 Heather, *Empires and Barbarians*, 364 & Nielsen, *The Germanic Languages*, 60

52 Wood, *The Merovingian Kingdoms*, 163–164

53 James, *The Franks*, 105

54 Collins, *Charlemagne*, 44 & Springer, *Die Sachsen*, 98

55 Thorpe, *Gregory of Tours' History of the Franks*, 203

56 Bachrach, *Liber Historiae Francorum*, 69–70

57 Wood, *The Merovingian Kingdoms*, 163–164

58 Thorpe, *Gregory of Tours' History of the Franks*, 209–210

59 Bachrach, *Merovingian Military Organization*, 32

60 Bachrach, *Liber Historiae Francorum*, 72

61 Fortunatus, *Personal and Political Poems*, 32

62 Heather, *Empires and Barbarians*, 286 & Moorhead, "Ostrogothic Italy and the Lombard Invasions," 152

63 Diaconus, *History of the Langobards*, 52, 61 & 97–100 & Springer, *Die Sachsen*, 107

64 Thorpe, *Gregory of Tours' The History of the Franks*, 237–238

65 Ibid.

66 Ibid.

67 Ibid. 272–273

68 Springer, *Die Sachsen*, 105–106

69 Ibid.

70 Venantius Fortunatus claimed that Chilperic, by the judgment of God, was a "terror" to Saxons, Frisians, Danes, and Jutes, see Fortunatus, *Personal and Political Poems*, 77

71 Bachrach, *Liber Historiae Francorum*, 78–79

72 Springer, *Die Sachsen*, 111–112

73 Todd, *The Early Germans*, 204 & Lebecq, "The Northern Seas," 643

74 Roberts, *The Humblest Sparrow*, 139 & 160

75 Ibid. 158. Republished with the permission of the University of Michigan Press, from *The Humblest Sparrow*, Michael Roberts, © 2009; permission conveyed through Copyright Clearance Center, Inc.

76 Fredegund, a fierce, clever, and controversial woman, is infamous due to her feud with the Austrasian Queen Brunhild, as well as for her alleged involvement with assassinations, witchcraft, adultery, and a myriad of political schemes.

77 James, *The Franks*, 101

78 Todd, *The Early Germans*, 204

79 Flierman, *Saxon Identities*, 76–77

80 Wallace-Hadrill, *The Fourth Book of the Chronicle of Fredegar*, 10

81 Collins, *Charlemagne*, 44

82 Wood, *The Merovingian Kingdoms*, 162–164

83 Bachrach, *Merovingian Military Organization*, 82

84 Wallace-Hadrill, *The Fourth Book of the Chronicle of Fredegar*, 31–32

85 Wood, *The Merovingian Kingdoms*, 162–164

86 Bachrach, *Liber Historiae Francorum*, 97–99

87 Ibid.

88 Ibid.

89 Bachrach, *Liber Historiae Francorum*, 97–99 & The author of the later Quedlinburg annals records this story as well; however, he confuses Chlotar I with Chlotar II; see Springer, *Die Sachsen*, 99 and for the length of a spatha, see France, *Warfare in the Dark Ages*, 263

90 Bachrach, *Liber Historiae Francorum*, 20

91 Ibid. & Flierman, *Saxon Identities*, 82–83

92 Nelson, *King and Emperor*, 54

93 Wallace-Hadrill, *The Fourth Book of the Chronicle of Fredegar*, 62–63

94 Ibid. & James, *The Franks*, 105

95 Wood, *The Merovingian Kingdoms*, 162–164 & James, "The Northern World in the Dark Ages," 94

96 Collins, *Charlemagne*, 44

97 Wallice-Hadrill, *The Fourth Book of the Chronicle of Fredegar*, 62–63

98 Bachrach, *Liber Historiae Francorum*, 100–102

99 Becher, *Non enim habent regem idem Antiqui Saxones*, 28–31

100 Reuter, *Germany in the Early Middle Ages*, 65

101 Leidinger, "Zur Christianisierung des Ostmünsterlandes," 19–26

102 Ibid.

103 Hunt, *The Making of the West*, 331

104 Keegan, *A History of Warfare*, 284

105 His nickname came from comparisons to Judas Maccabeus, "the hammerer" who led a revolt against the Seleucids in the *Book of the Maccabees*. See Wallace-Hadrill, *The Fourth Book of the Chronicle of Fredegar*, 86–87 & Sypeck, *Becoming Charlemagne*, 72

106 Ibid. 88 & Bachrach, *Liber Historiae Francorum*, 112

107 Flierman, *Saxon Identities*, 84 & McKitterick, *The Frankish Kingdoms under the Carolingians*, 2

108 Oman, *The Dark Ages*, 211

109 Wallace-Hadrill, *The Fourth Book of the Chronicle of Fredegar*, 90

110 Wood, *The Merovingian Kingdoms*, 273

111 Willibald, *The Life of St. Boniface*, 64–65 & Talbot, *The Anglo-Saxon Missionaries in Germany*, 46

112 Collins, *Charlemagne*, 45–47

113 Wallace-Hadrill, *The Fourth Book of the Chronicle of Fredegar*, 91

114 Ibid. 92

115 Heather, *Empires and Barbarians*, 367

116 Wallace-Hadrill, *The Fourth Book of the Chronicle of Fredegar*, 93

117 Henderson, *A History of Germany in the Middle Ages*, 60 & Nelson, *King and Emperor*, 63

118 Wallace-Hadrill, *The Fourth Book of the Chronicle of Fredegar*, 99

119 Wood, *The Merovingian Kingdoms*, 288–289

120 Scholz, *Carolingian Chronicles*, 38–39

121 Ibid.

122 Wallace-Hadrill, *The Fourth Book of the Chronicle of Fredegar*, 99

123 Emerton, *The Letters of Saint Boniface*, 108–109

124 Wood, *The Merovingian Kingdoms*, 288–289

125 Ibid. & Fouracre, "Frankish Gaul to 814," 96

126 Wallace-Hadrill, *The Fourth Book of the Chronicle of Fredegar*, 100 & Riche, *The Carolingians*, 59

127 Ibid. 101 & Scholz, *Carolingian Chronicles*, 38–39

128 Jones, *Cambridge Illustrated History of France*, 61

129 Rembold, *Conquest and Christianization*, 10

130 Wood, *The Merovingian Kingdoms*, 288–289

131 Oman, *The Dark Ages*, 257 & Dean, "Felling the Irminsul," 16

132 Collins, *Charlemagne*, 45–47

133 Scholz, *Carolingian Chronicles*, 38–39

134 Wallace-Hadrill, *The Fourth Book of the Chronicle of Fredegar,* 101

135 Dessens, *Res Voluntaria, Non Necessaria*, 28–29

136 Robinson, *Old English and Its Closest Relatives*, 101–102

137 Wallace-Hadrill, *The Fourth Book of the Chronicle of Fredegar*, 102

138 Ibid. 152; Emerton, *The Letters of Saint Boniface*, 181 & Raaijmakers, *The Making of the Monastic Community of Fulda*, 24

139 Scholz, *Carolingian Chronicles*, 39–42

140 Nelson, *King and Emperor*, 114

141 Kosto, "Hostages in the Carolingian World," 145

142 Wallace-Hadrill, *The Fourth Book of the Chronicle of Fredegar*, 103

143 Ibid.

144 Scholz, *Carolingian Chronicles*, 39–40

145 Wallace-Hadrill, *The Fourth Book of the Chronicle of Fredegar*, 105–108

146 Fouracre, "Frankish Gaul to 814," 98–99

147 Ibid.

148 Rudolf of Fulda copied this point in his own work, see Wattenbach, *Die Übertragung des hl. Alexander von Rudolf und Meginhart*, 9–10

149 Riche, *The Carolingians*, 59

150 France, *Warfare in the Dark Ages*, 50–51 & 323–324

151 Scholz, *Carolingian Chronicles*, 44–46 & Wallace-Hadrill, *The Fourth Book of the Chronicle of Fredegar*, 109–110

152 Ibid. 83

153 Ibid. 46 & Wallace-Hadrill, *The Fourth Book of the Chronicle of Fredegar*, 121

4 Old Saxon Paganism

It has become almost mandatory that any scholarly analysis of pre-Christian "Germanic" religion begin by admitting that we know little about what it consisted of. In many ways, this is unfortunately true. There are no written records left to us by Germanic pagans. Our historical records were written by outsiders, almost always from a hostile "elite" perspective, sometimes centuries after the conversion period.[1] Further, many of the "pagan customs" that writers depict appear to be formulaic replications of earlier content, a particularly troubling pattern seen in Medieval pastoral literature.[2] In addition, although pagan artifacts have emerged from excavations in the Germanic-speaking world, these tell us very little of substance concerning beliefs, attributes of deities, or even religious affiliation.[3]

It is also problematic when we start from the assumption that there was such a thing as "Germanic Paganism" containing a standard set of deities, practices, and worldviews. Instead, the reality of pre-Christian Germanic religion was one of localized variances, all of which were dynamic and developed on their own terms (this is true for any religion).[4] In addition, as Peter Heather has noted, "Paganism" was first and foremost a "Christian intellectual construct" against which it defined itself "but which did not really exist."[5] Pagans would not have thought of themselves as "pagans."

As a result, while a comparative method is beneficial (via artifacts, linguistics, religious topography, texts, etc.), we must be wary of a copy-and-paste method used to transplant, for example, the content of thirteenth-century Icelandic sagas or *Eddas* onto the religious landscape of eighth-century Northern Germany.[6] When trying to comprehend the religious beliefs of Saxons from the eighth to the ninth centuries, we need to look for more localized clues. This holds true not only geographically but also regarding time. For example, Tacitus' oft-cited first-century *Germania* gives a romanticized overview of religious practices concerning specific groups of *Germani* that may help investigate earlier customs; however, it is unlikely to represent views or practices of Germanic peoples over 700 years later.[7] In like manner, first- to fifth-century votive stones dedicated to *Matronae* in the Rhineland can be used to establish precedent. Yet, they also display the extent to which religious syncretism (particularly the implementation of Celtic and Roman customs) was already underway among people we might label "Germanic pagans."[8] All that does not imply that continuations of belief over long periods are impossible or

DOI: 10.4324/9781003379157-6

that shared deities, stories, customs, cultural themes, and values cannot be shared across large geographic areas, which is clearly the case in much of the Germanic world.

Cosmology

According to the relatively few surviving Old Saxon texts (see Chapter 12), the Saxon world was called "Middle-Earth" or "Mid-World" (OS: *middilgard*) and, akin to themes we find in various Germanic myths, seems to have been subject to the overarching power of Fate.[9] Fate (OS: *wurd*) was ultimately responsible for the destinies of humanity, the universe, and the gods.[10] This concept is expressed in the Old Saxon term *orlag*, which denotes a "fixing from the first."[11] Saxons likely lived anxiously awaiting *reganogiskapu*, the "decree of fate."[12]

Fortune was not only bestowed upon people but, in a broader sense, *helig*, or "the supernatural gift of good fortune," could also be extended to places and objects (the word is etymologically related to the New High German *heilig*, meaning "holy").[13] A similar etymological correlation can be seen in the Anglo-Saxon *Halegmonath*, or "month of sacred rites."[14] The *heilig* concept was tied to notions of individual or communal luck and may have been interpreted somewhat like the belief in *mana* found in Polynesian religions.[15]

Beyond the decrees of Fate, fortune could also be gained by securing the favor of the gods, either through various forms of appeasement (such as sacrifice) or by committing great deeds.[16] Some of these deities can be glimpsed in the *Old Saxon Baptismal Vow*, an eighth- to ninth-century formula converts used to renounce their gods.[17] Scholars have cautioned that the formula may have been intended for pagan Thuringians; however, its usage for Saxons seems more likely.[18] Further, these are not mutually exclusive views, and settlement overlap was common between Saxons and Thuringians.

Part of the formula translated from the original "pidgin" Old Saxon:

QUESTION: Do you forsake the Devil?
RESPONDENT: I forsake the Devil
QUESTION: And all idolatry?
RESPONDENT: And I forsake idolatry
QUESTION: And all the Devil's work?
RESPONDENT: And I forsake all the Devil's works and promises, Thunear and Woden and Seaxnot and all those devils who are their followers.[19]

The renunciation of demons (equated to pagan gods) has been apparent in Christian baptism ceremonies since the beginning of the third century CE.[20] In the Saxon context, chief among these supposed devils was likely Woden. However, Bruce Lincoln has argued that the requirement to reject Thunear first may indicate that *he* was considered more important.[21] We simply do not know. In the case of Woden, the attributes attributed to him across the Germanic/Norse world are extensive. Yet, generally, he is associated with war, wisdom, healing, ecstasy, magic, and poetry.[22] Etymologically, his name denotes something like "madness," "rage," or "frenzy."[23] In Icelandic sources, he was called the "All-Father," and it is from Woden that several Anglo-Saxon nobles claimed divine descent.[24] We also find mention of Wodan (Uuodan) in the controversial second Merseburg charm, where he is invoked to heal a horse.[25] This document, along with the First Merseburg charm, was written in Old High German in the tenth century (likely) from the monastic complex of Fulda (or Merseburg in SE Saxony).[26] While Fulda was located in the Frankish-controlled *Hessenland*, the abbey was one of the early institutions involved in missionary endeavors among the Saxons. Therefore, while by no means certain, the gods/goddesses/beings recorded in the Merseburg charms may refer to those revered by pagans that Fulda missionaries encountered, which included the Saxons. Given that potentiality, we should also note that the term "balder" is mentioned in the second charm, which may refer to a deity known by the same name in Norse mythology or be an adjective meaning "bright," "lord," or "brave" (much depends on which etymological correlates we pursue).[27] D. H. Green has argued in favor of the latter explanation, suggesting that "balder" was likely used in the Merseburg charm as an "honorific title" for Woden.[28]

To return to the deities mentioned in the baptismal vow, in contrast to Wodan, who often has historical associations with the nobility, the god Thunaer (Donar/ Thor) was more often connected with "commoners."[29] German historian Kurt Reinhardt has described him as "the friendly good-natured god of peasant religion," who most clearly embodied the Icelandic notion of a "god-friend" (*fulltrui*).[30] Etymologically, "Donar" originally denoted "thunder," which the deity represented alongside other natural forces such as storms or lightning.[31] Donar was also the protector of humankind and the gods, which he defended with his giant hammer, Mjöllnir.[32]

Saxnōt (*Sahsnot/Saxneat*) is uniquely Saxon and may have been a tribal deity from whom the people claimed descent. At the very least, Anglo-Saxon nobles, such as the kings of Essex, claimed him as an ancestor in the same way they claimed Wodan.[33] The name "Saxnot" may derive from Sahsginot (sword-companion) and may be associated with war, though some scholars doubt this.[34] He may also be a form of the Germanic war-god Tiwaz, known in Old English as "Tiw" and in Old Norse as "Tyr."[35] However, his name has also been translated as "companion of the Saxons," indicating his characteristics may have been quite different.[36]

Our sources on Saxon goddesses are tragically limited. The Norse goddess Frigg (wife of Odin) is found among the Anglo-Saxons as *Frieg/Frig*, in Old Frisian as *Fria*, and Old High German as *Frikka/Friia*.[37] She may be the same deity as the fertility goddess Frija ("lady"; *Fri* or *Frôia* in OS), who is sister to the god Freyr ("lord"; OS: *Fro*) in Norse mythology.[38] Notably, the goddess Frija (Friia) is also referenced by the ninth-century Second Merseburg charm as an "enchantress," alongside female beings named Sinthgunt, Sunna (possibly the personified sun), and Fulla (or Uolla, perhaps a variation of the Norse goddess with the same name); they are all described as sisters.[39]

In a later tenth-century penitential written by Burchard of Worms, he condemns locals' belief in a witch (*striga*) called "Holda," found in various Germanic forms

as Holle, Hulle, Frau Holl, Huldr, and so forth. It is possible that Holda was originally a fertility goddess, and one theory suggests she may be a form of Frigg, that
is, "Friga holda," "the generous Friga."[40]

The goddess Hel may also be attested in the Old Saxon *Heliand* (see Chapter 12); however, this is highly debatable.[41] In Norse mythology, she is the daughter
of the mischievous trickster god Loki and is associated with death.[42] Those who
died naturally on land ("straw deaths") were sent to her frozen abode in Niflheim,
a place of anguish and hunger.[43]

It is also tempting to seek clues for Saxon goddesses in Anglo-Saxon England.
However, attested beings in Old English do not guarantee that they also existed
among "Old Saxons"; it should be remembered that the composition of Anglo-
Saxon settlers was rather diverse. As a result, without evidential correlates, we
cannot *assume* that what pertained to Anglo-Saxons necessarily pertained to Saxons on the continent. Nevertheless, they remain valuable avenues of inquiry and
worthy of consideration.

Based on the testimony of the Northumbrian monk Bede, in his early-eighth-
century *Reckoning of Time*, Anglo-Saxons celebrated *Eosturmonath* with feasts in
honor of the goddess Eostre.[44] Likewise, in the same source, a goddess named
Hretha is mentioned, to whom sacrifices were made during *Hrethmonath*.[45] Given
her possible relation to the Christian Easter, Eostre has been subject to bitter and
controversial debates that go beyond the scope of this chapter.[46] For our purposes, it
is enough to say that no early continental Germanic sources mention her. However,
she did linger in later German folklore, where Jacob Grimm famously labeled her
a "divinity of the radiant dawn."[47] We also see her in Saxon legends, such as "The
Steinkirche and the Hermit."[48]

Another possible goddess found in England is "Erce," mentioned in an Anglo-
Saxon field blessing charm as an "earth mother."[49] However, like her divine sisters,
she is shrouded in mystery. In *The Reckoning of Time*, Bede also claimed that
the night before Christmas, Anglo-Saxons celebrated *Modraniht*, "the night of the
mothers," which may refer to maternal ancestors, female spiritual beings, or goddess figures.[50]

Other powerful female beings of the Germanic world were the Valkyries, who
appear in England in an eleventh-century sermon as *waelcryge* (although this could
stem from the influence of Viking settlers).[51] Similar beings may have been known
to the "Old Saxons" as *idisi*, possibly "'battle-maidens," which are attested in the
First Merseburg Charm.[52] While the word *idisi* means "women," in the context of
the charm, they are depicted as capable of stopping armies, lending assistance to
captives, and fastening bonds or fetters to keep individuals in place.[53] Critically, all
this is done while the *idisi* are sitting down. Therefore, while *idisi* can be compared
to Valkyries, their seated position may indicate that they are more akin to the Norns
of Scandinavian mythology, that is, the female entities known as the "weavers
of Fate."[54]

Many creatures passed down in Germanic folklore likely originated in pagan
popular religion.[55] For example, Dwarfs appear in Anglo-Saxon as *dweorg*, while
Old Saxon contains the word *etan* for giants (ON: *iotun*).[56] Undoubtedly, similar

Saxon cases could be made for the presence of elves, goblins, nymphs, or other such creatures found in Anglo-Saxon medicinal charms or among the Old Norse *landvaettir* ("spirits of the land").[57] Likewise, arguments could be made for the magical power of plants and herbs, many of which seem to have been used in connection with incantations, invocations, and charms for healing or warding off evil.[58] Most famously, this can be seen with Anglo-Saxon charms found in the ninth-century collection *Bald's Leechbook* and in the late-tenth-/early-eleventh-century *Lacnunga* ("remedies").[59] However, Medieval German texts, such as the *Physica* composed by Hildegard of Bingen (the "Sibyl of the Rhine"), various German blessing formulas of the Central Middle Ages, and later Saxon folk customs, also attest to this.[60]

Of a more sinister nature, there are Old Saxon references to *wihti* ("wights"), which typically take on the guise of mischievous or demonic creatures.[61] However, perhaps the most threatening force (excluding Fate itself) was *nidhudig* (ON: *Nidhogg*), the fierce "world serpent" coiled beneath the World Tree.[62] As many scholars have argued, these entities of "lower forms of religion" (as opposed to the "high" religion of gods, doctrines, priests, temples, etc.) tended to linger longer in popular superstitions and proved harder to eradicate.[63]

Religious Practice

According to Rudolf of Fulda, Saxons worshiped their deities like Tacitus noted of the early *Germani*.[64] That is, Saxons:

> [c]onsidered it incompatible with the majesty and greatness of their gods to enclose them in temples or to represent them in human form…they consecrated groves and woods, called them by the names of their gods, and looked at their sanctuaries with silent reverence.[65]
>
> Adam of Bremen, also relying on Tacitus, replicated the same observation almost verbatim.[66]

Rudolf and Adam may have copied Tacitus.[67] However, not all their "observations" need to be deemed incorrect. While inconclusive, archaeology seems to concur with a lack of temple building among the Saxons.[68] None have been found. Although, admittedly, wooden temple structures would not have left much of a trace. However, linguistic indicators also suggest that Saxons conducted their religious customs outdoors. For example, the Old Saxon term *alah* denoted a "sacred grove," "sanctuary," or "place of worship."[69] Another controversial document, the eighth-century *Indiculus Superstitionum et Paganiarum* ("Small index of superstitions and paganism"), may also support this.[70] All we have from this source is a list of titles about pagan practices found among Saxons or Austrasian Franks; the actual content has been lost.[71] The *Indiculus* was found in the seventeenth century in the Vatican library alongside the *Old Saxon Baptismal Vow* and has since been subject to intense scrutiny and inconclusive analysis due mainly to linguistic concerns (Germanic dialectical questions and the presence of non-Germanic terms) as well as the *Index* having seemingly been influenced by earlier pastoral literature.[72] However, if we turn to one of the titles (#6), we are given the description: "the rites of the woods they call *nimidas*" (*De sacris siluarum, quae nimidas uocant*), which, in the case of *nimidas*, translates in Old Saxon to "sacred grove."[73] The same document (in title #4) refers to small huts used as sanctuaries, which presumably housed statues or images of deities (made of wood or dough).[74]

As late as the eleventh century, Saxons were still being connected with groves. Archbishop Unwan of Hamburg-Bremen claimed that northern Saxons in the marshlands, among other "pagan rites," continued to "give foolish reverence" to trees and sacred groves.[75] To combat these superstitions, the archbishop had the trees cut down and the groves destroyed, after which churches were built over their remains.[76] Despite destruction or appropriation, several groves and hills associated with deities survive in place names throughout the Germanic world, although (admittedly) differentiating pagan place names from secular or Christian ones can be frustratingly difficult.[77]

While Saxons may not have constructed temples, they built statues of their deities and erected altars and sacred pillars. According to Jacob Grimm, a statue of a Saxon war god once stood on a wall in the Westphalian town of Corvey.[78] In addition, Widukind reports that, following a battle against the Franks, the Saxons *allegedly* "constructed an altar of victory following the error of their fathers."[79]

Perhaps the most famous pagan phenomenon associated with the Saxons is that of the Irminsul. This was a sacred tree, a column, or a pillar. Attempts have been made to link the Irminsul to the god Irmin (i.e., "Irmin's Pillar") or the Germanic warlord Arminius (*Hermann Säule*/Herman's Pillar); however, it is more accurately translated simply as "great pillar."[80] According to Adam of Bremen's description (based on an earlier account by Rudolf of Fulda, see Chapter 6), Saxons worshiped:

> A stock of wood, of no small size, set up in the open. In native language, it was called Irminsul, which in Latin means universal column, as if it sustained everything.[81]

Reports such as these have sparked widespread debate regarding the nature of the Irminsul, which often include comparative accounts to sacred trees or "World Pillars" found among other peoples (e.g., Yggdrasil in Scandinavia).[82] Utilizing these examples, scholars have concluded that the Irminsul was a symbol of central importance in Saxon cosmology.[83] However, it is unclear whether or not the Irminsul was a singular cult site or referred to a type of sacred pillar of which there were many.[84] It has also been proposed that these Irminsuls may have originally been Roman-made "Jupiter columns" (Pillars of Hercules), which have been found along the Rhine. However, the bulk of Saxon territory is typically considered to have been outside the area where these columns were built. In addition, the Roman pillars were constructed from stone, while the Saxon Irminsul was made of wood.

The Irminsul associated with the Saxon wars (see Chapter 6) appears to have been situated either in or near the Saxon Eresburg fortress and was said to contain a significant treasure hoard of silver and gold.[85] In the nineteenth century, Jacob

Grimm speculated that the pillar was located somewhere in the Teutoburg Forest.[86] However, in the 1930s, Heinrich Himmler, the *Reichsführer* (commander) of the Nazi SS, hypothesized that the Irminsul once stood at the Externsteine site (a sandstone rock formation) not far from Horn-Bad Meinberg.[87] That assertion was based on the conclusions of Wilhelm Teudt, a German archaeologist and ariosophist who secured funding to excavate the site in 1934 through his *Externsteine-Stiftung* (Externsteine Foundation).[88] Yet, due to their radical ideological foundations and lack of empirical evidence, modern scholars have widely rejected Teudt and Himmler's conclusions.[89]

Today there is a replica monument of the Irminsul dating from the 1990s standing in the Harbarnsen-Irmenseul village in Lower Saxony, near Hildesheim.[90] However, despite later folklore concerning the Irminsul coming from the region around Hildesheim, like the other sites mentioned, there is very little to substantiate the area as the pillars' original location.

We will return to the Irminsul in due course, but further insight into pre-Christian Saxon religious practice can also be gleaned from Saxon material culture. Pagan symbols are found adorning pottery, furniture, brooches, and undoubtedly once decorated wooden constructions that have long since perished.[91] For example, North Germanic artifacts found in East Anglia and the bogs of Jutland (notably Thorsberg Moor) often display swastikas, which had wide-ranging cross-cultural use before their appropriation by the Nazis.[92] Even more popular are complex ornamental depictions of intertwined animal-nature motifs.[93] Some of these can be seen from fifth-sixth-century bracteates (medals worn as jewelry), for example, those found at Nebenstedt, which display animals (often serpents), possible deities, cross-gender figures (bearded men with breasts), and other hybrid-human designs.[94] While these bracteates are partially modeled on Roman imperial iconography, many are unique local innovations.[95]

Saxon artifacts occasionally contain runic inscriptions.[96] Runes, derived from the Italic alphabet, appear carved in wood, metal, and stone across the Germanic world.[97] Often they were used as magical tools, to denote ownership, or to imbue an object with power or luck.[98] In Old Saxon, the term *runa* meant "council" or "discussion," while *giruni* implied something "secret" or "mysterious."[99] Their use may have been employed by "rune-masters" or had associations with "secret wisdom," "magic songs," or "incantations."[100]

Runes were just one method by which Saxons manipulated their world through magic (OS: *mahtig*).[101] Based on the *Indiculus Superstitionum*, Saxons also utilized chants, incantations, dances, and charms.[102] Each could conjure the divine, garner protection from the gods, heal, ward off disease, or show respect.[103]

The *Indiculus* references a ritual practice called *nodfyr*, which involved "fire made from rubbing wood (*De igne fricato de ligno id est nodfyr*)."[104] This may refer to a kind of ritual in which fires were made on top of graves, be associated with "cleansing" or healing, or indicate a form of pyromancy (divination by fire).[105] The *Indiculus* also alludes to the use of amulets and an intriguing practice in which (during lunar eclipses) Saxons shouted, "Triumph Moon!"[106] However, this is one example where many correlates are found in prior and subsequent pastoral literature (e.g., Caesarius of Arles, a penitential attributed to Bede, and Burchard of Worms' *Corrector sive Medicus* section in his *Decretum*).[107] Such customs were either very widespread or copied repetitively from one text to another.[108]

Similar observations were reported in the ninth century by the Frankish monk Hrabanus Maurus, who expressed annoyance with locals believing (imitating pagan custom) that shouting at the moon during a lunar eclipse would prevent it from being devoured by monsters.[109] Rudolf of Fulda also connected Saxons to moon rituals, claiming they paid attention to the moon's cycles to determine if the time was right for specific undertakings.[110] In addition, the final title in the *Indiculus* states, "[T]hey believe…women command the moon [or swallow up the moon] that they may be able to take away the hearts of men."[111] This last custom sounds sinister; however, it could refer to a kind of love magic by which women used the moon to "captivate" the hearts of men.[112]

Saxons also made use of divination. If magic was a means of expressing agency through (performative) divine manipulation, divination was a way to understand divine action and ascertain the future.[113] Rudolf of Fulda (and later Adam of Bremen) claimed Saxons divined outcomes through ritual combat, casting lots, and heeding the flights of birds and the neighing of horses.[114] Similarly, the *Indiculus* claims Saxons read omens from "the excrement or sneezing" of birds, horses, and cattle.[115]

If magic or divination failed, Saxons could resort to ritual sacrifice. In southern Jutland, an area inhabited by proto-Danes and Saxons, human remains and artifacts suggest peat bogs were early sites of human sacrifice and material offerings (some of the remains have been exceptionally well preserved due to high concentrations of tannic acid, which disrupts the body's oxidation process).[116] Certainly, Tacitus claimed human sacrifice was an ancient practice among the *Germani* and that such had been the fate of Roman captives following the slaughter of Varus' legions in the Teutoburg Forest in 9 AD.[117] A sixth-century report written by the Gallo-Roman aristocrat Magnus Ennodius also claimed Saxons burned victims to appease the anger of their gods.[118] It has even been suggested that sacrifices took place at the Irminsul.[119]

If we return to the *Translatio sancti Alexandri*, on certain days, Saxons offered human sacrifices to their chief god Mercury, whom the Romans likely associated with Wodan.[120] Bede recorded a similar account of the Anglo-Saxons in Britain, claiming that November was known to them as *Blodmanath* (or "Blood Month") because, during that time, sacrifices were made to the gods (likely in animal rather than human form).[121] A similar term, *blotmanoth*, appears in the Essen Necrology and claims this, too, is what the Old Saxons called November.[122] The *Indiculus* contains a title (#8) referring to "the sacred rites of Mercury and Jupiter," which may also indicate sacrifices to Woden and Donar.[123]

Much to the dismay of local missionaries, the prominence of animal sacrifice among continental Saxons was common well into the conversion period.[124] Horses, in particular, played a unique role in Germanic sacrifices (including among the Saxons); however, swine, cattle, and other animals (possibly associated with specific deities) were also used.[125] There are indications in Old English that sacrifices were accompanied by a kind of dance (or *lac*).[126] The term *bledsian*, also Old

English, suggests altars were sprinkled with blood before making sacrifices, after which they could receive offerings.[127]

According to Bishop Thietmar of Merseburg, locals in southern Saxony continued to make offerings to their household deities as late as the eleventh century.[128] Perhaps elements of these sacrificial rituals survived in more recent folk customs found in Lower Saxony, Schleswig-Holstein, and Mecklenburg, where locals hung carved wooden horse heads on farm roofs to dispel evil spirits.[129]

Per Jacob Grimm, a great sacrificial feast was celebrated annually by the Old Saxons during October, which commemorated their 534 victory over the Thuringians.[130] However, this later assertion should be approached with caution, especially given the uncertainty surrounding Saxon participation in the overthrow of the Thuringians.

Funerary Customs

Saxons disposed of their dead via both cremation and inhumation. While scholars continuously debate how funerary customs correlate to religious allegiance, cremation has generally been associated with paganism and inhumation with Christianity.[131] Christians may have buried the dead believing the body needed to rise from the grave on the "Day of Judgment" and the second coming of Christ.[132] However, there are obvious exceptions, and archaeological evidence suggests that dividing funerary customs neatly along religious lines can be misleading.[133] Still, there are some patterns we can observe regarding the Saxons.

Older Saxon cemeteries have been found close to archaic Bronze and Stone Age cairns, indicating Saxons believed in an ancestral connection to the people who built them or thought they were places of spiritual significance.[134] These megalithic structures, alongside archaic burial mounds (*Gräberfeld*), can be found in relative abundance across the Saxon landscape, with a notable concentration in the heathlands near Wildeshausen.[135]

During the Merovingian period, Saxon burial customs were fairly standardized, with little of the variation commonly associated with status.[136] However, by the Carolingian Age, graves containing valuable items connected with the nobility became more frequent (the opposite of what occurred among the Franks).[137] Some burial accompaniments associated with these elites include weaponry, animals (usually dogs and horses), and young females who were possibly slaves, servants, or spouses.[138] However, the comb is the most common grave good found in Saxony, regardless of status, gender, or religion. Women were also often buried with necklaces, fibulae (brooches for fastening garments), and spinning whorls.[139]

During the Carolingian Age, we see a diversity of burial practices among the Saxons, including the continuation of urnfield burials, cremation graves, and inhumation (both with and without burial mounds).[140] Crosses can be found in Saxon graves by the end of the eighth century, and cremation appears to have been mostly in decline by the ninth.[141] That change correlates to the Frankish imposition of Christianity in Saxony. However, even as late as the mid-ninth century, despite being forbidden by Charlemagne as a pagan custom, cremation graves were still in use (evidence of which comes from Frisia, as well as Lower Saxony at Dorverden and Liebenau).[142]

As for Saxon pagan funerary customs, little is known. However, the use of sacrifices, offerings, and singing seems likely. As Roberta Frank has noted, eulogistic songs and poems (or lays) seem to have been common across the Germanic world, and Saxons (according to Paul the Deacon) were known for their songs.[143] The *Indiculus* also refers to something called *dadsisas*, which could imply a funerary "dirge" sung in honor of the dead.[144] The Saxons may have also held an autumnal festival to celebrate the dead, in addition to the seasonal or agricultural celebrations that must have occurred.[145]

Conclusion

As indicated at the outset of this chapter, much is missing from our understanding of what constituted pre-Christian Saxon religion. Even the reports we do have are subject to skepticism and wide degrees of interpretation. However, there are enough clues to indicate what Frankish Christians found troubling. Saxons were polytheistic, while Franks honored one God albeit expressed in the three forms comprising the Trinity. That God was a creator who existed *outside* His creations, while pagan Saxons saw divinity (in various forms) scattered throughout nature in groves, rivers, and woodlands.[146] The Christian God was also entirely male, and Franks seeking feminine forms of spirituality had to do so via the saints. (The exceptions here are the varied representations of Christ in feminized or androgynous forms, attested throughout Europe in literary and artistic depictions from Antiquity up through the Renaissance).[147] By contrast, Saxon pagans could revere various goddesses or female entities. The gender component was no arbitrary matter. As we will see in later chapters, feminine forms of spiritual expression outside the Church were often explicitly condemned as demonic or witchcraft.[148]

The rituals Saxons engaged in were also suspect, especially those concerning sacrifice. The only sacrifice of value for Christians was made by Christ Himself; biblically, others were no longer necessary because the blood covenant with Yahweh had been fulfilled. Yet, for Saxons, sacrifices were required to appease their gods and so continued in animal and (probably) human form. For Frankish Christians, pagan sacrifices were nothing less than a boon to Satan and an affront to God. Likewise, ritual customs associated with paganism, such as indecent dancing, singing, cross-dressing, donning animal skins, divination, chants, charms, invocations, nature worship, cremation, and so forth, were evil or, at the very least, incompatible with the Christian life. As such, they needed to be identified, rooted out, and replaced.

Notes

1 Honselmann, "Die Annahme des Christentums durch die Sachsen," 201–203; Andren, "Old Norse and Germanic Religion," 846; Kling, *A History of Christian Conversion*, 106 & Bremmer, "Old English Heroic Poetry," 78

2 Simek, "Continental Germanic Religion," 301; Rampton, *European Magic and Witchcraft*, 119; Filotas, *Pagan Survivals*, 10–11 & 57–58 & 63 & see the entirety of McNeill & Gamer, *Medieval Handbooks of Penance*

3 The so-called Paderborner Odin is a case in point. See Banghard, "Noch einmal zum 'Paderborner Odin'," 70–77

4 Shaw, *Pagan Goddesses in the Early Germanic World*, 11; Jolly, *Popular Religion in Late Saxon England*, 12 & 18–19; Effros, *Merovingian Mortuary Archaeology and the Making of the Early Middle Ages*, 86–87; Wood, "The Northern Frontier," 231 & Niles, "Pre-Christian Anglo-Saxon religion," 305

5 Heather, *Christendom*, 141

6 Pulsiano, *Medieval Scandinavia*, 149–152 & 521–525 and it is unknown to what extent Christianity and prior Roman literature influenced Icelandic sources, much of which comes from the early-thirteenth-century writing of Snorri Sturluson. See Lincoln, *Gods and Demons, Priests and Scholars*, 23

7 Tacitus, *The Agricola and The Germania*, 47–61; Tacitus' descriptions of the Germani were romanticized in order to provide a reflective critique of Roman society. See O'Brian, "Values and Ethics in Heroic Literature," 107

8 Shaw, *Pagan Goddesses in the Early Germanic World*, 10 & 37; Simek, "Continental Germanic Religion," 294 & *Dictionary of Northern Mythology*, 204–208 & 230 & 309 & 279–280 & 356–357

9 Equivalent to the OHG: *mittilagart* or OE: *middangeard*. See Cathey, *Heliand*, 336; Gallee, *Old-Saxon Texts*, XXIV; Woolf, *Ancient Civilizations*, 462; Rauch, *The Old Saxon Language*, 300 & 345 & 365 & Tiefenbach, *Altsächsisches Handwörterbuch*, 272

10 Green, "Three Aspects of the Old Saxon Biblical Epic," 255; Barney, *Word-Hoard*, 10; Augustyn, "Thor's Hammer and the Power of God," 37; Rauch, *The Old Saxon Language*, 314 & Tiefenbach, *Altsächsisches Handwörterbuch*, 481

11 Grimm, *Teutonic Mythology V.II*, 856–857

12 Grimm, *Teutonic Mythology V.I*, 26; Barney, *Word-Hoard*, 34–35; Tiefenbach, *Altsächsisches Handwörterbuch*, 310 & Green, *Language and History in the Early Germanic World*, 13 & 384–385

13 Kritsch, *Theophoric Place Names*, 91–92 & Green, *The Carolingian Lord*, xix

14 Bede, *The Reckoning of Time*, 54

15 Augustyn, *The Semiotics of Fate, Death, and the Soul in Germanic Culture*, 120 & Lindenfeld, *World Christianity and Indigenous Experience*, 262–264

16 Cathey, *Heliand*, 13–14

17 Gallee, *Old-Saxon Texts*, 245–247; Karras, "Pagan Survivals," 567 & Springer, *Die Sachsen*, 154

18 Wood, "Religion in Pre-Carolingian Thuringia and Bavaria," 324

19 Gallee, *Old-Saxon Texts*, 248; Kristoffersen, *Pacifying the Saxons*, 20 and I use the term "pidgin" because the formula contains elements of Old High German and Old English, see Springer, *Die Sachsen*, 155

20 Kelly, *The Devil at Baptism*, 10

21 Grimm, *Teutonic Mythology V.I*, 131; Simek, *Dictionary of Northern Mythology*, 240–249 & 373–374 & Lincoln, *Gods and Demons, Priests and Scholars*, 21–22

22 Colum, *Nordic Gods and Heroes*, 82–177; Davidson, *The Lost Beliefs of Northern Europe*, 60 & 76–79; Leeming, *The Oxford Companion to World Mythology*, 296 & 403; Smith, *The Echo of Odin*, 100 & 159–171; Bucholz, *Perspectives for Historical Research in Germanic Religion*, 128 & 132–133: Diaconus, *History of the Langobards*, 16–19 & Somerville & McDonald, *The Viking Age*, 49, 60–61 & 138–141

23 Kahler, *The Germans*, 35 & Kritsch, *Theophoric Place Names*, 81–82

24 Larrington, *The Poetic Edda*, 57–59; Motz, "The Goddess Nerthus," 4; James, "The Northern World in the Dark Ages," 84 & Woolf, *Ancient Civilizations*, 466

25 Northcott, *An Interpretation of the Second Merseburg Charm*, 45; Milis, *The Pagan Middle Ages*, 31; Kritsch, *Theophoric Place Names*, 82 & Fortson, *Indo-European Language and Culture*, 325–326

26 Jeep, *Medieval Germany*, 113

27 Ibid. 112–113 & Kritsch, *Theophoric Place Names*, 90–91
28 Green, *The Carolingian Lord*, 9–17
29 Davidson, *The Lost Beliefs of Northern Europe*, 103; Simek, *Dictionary of Northern Mythology*, 63–64; Leeming, *The Oxford Companion to World Mythology*, 380 & Woolf, *Ancient Civilizations*, 467–469
30 Reinhardt, *Germany 2000 Years V.I*, 14–15
31 Simek, *Dictionary of Northern Mythology*, 322
32 Davidson, *The Lost Beliefs of Northern Europe*, 79–80
33 Wolfram, *The Roman Empire and its Germanic Peoples*, 245; Stenton, *Anglo-Saxon England*, 54. Missionaries used genealogy as a way of humanizing Anglo-Saxon deities, suggesting they were originally people falsely venerated as gods. See Niles, "Pagan Survivals and Popular Belief," 129
34 Davidson, *Gods and Myths of Northern Europe*, 60; Simek, *Dictionary of Northern Mythology*, 276 & Springer, *Die Sachsen*, 156–157
35 Reinhardt, *Germany 2000 Years V.I*, 15 & Kristoffersen, *Pacifying the Saxons*, 20–21
36 Shaw, *Pagan Goddesses in the Early Germanic World*, 96
37 Grimm, *Teutonic Mythology V.I*, 301–305; White, "The Goddess Frig," 288 & 298 & Tiefenbach, *Altsächsisches Handwörterbuch*, 109
38 Davidson, *The Lost Beliefs of Northern Europe*, 105 & 108 & *Myths and Symbols in Pagan Europe*, 119–120; Simek, Dictionary of Northern Mythology, 89–95 & 173 & 378–379; Leeming, *The Oxford Companion to World Mythology*, 140 & D. H. Green has argued that the occurrence of *fro* in Old Saxon is likely used as a title meaning "lord" and not an equivalent of the Scandinavian god Freyr. See Green, *The Carolingian Lord*, 19–32 & 46
39 Fuller, "Pagan Charms in Tenth-Century Saxony?" 162 & 168; Milis, *The Pagan Middle Ages*, 31 & Kritsch, *Theophoric Place Names*, 170
40 Filotas, *Pagan Survivals*, 116
41 Murphy, *The Heliand*, 32 & Augustyn, *The Semiotics of Fate, Death, and the Soul in Germanic Culture*, 30
42 Ibid.
43 Grimm, *Teutonic Mythology V.I*, 312; Simek, *Dictionary of Northern Mythology*, 137–138; Smith, *The Echo of Odin*, 47; Milis, *The Pagan Middle Ages*, 20 & Woolf, *Ancient Civilizations*, 495
44 Bede, *The Reckoning of Time*, 54
45 Ibid.
46 Shaw, *Pagan Goddesses in the Early Germanic World*, 69–70 & 95–96; Sermon, "From Easter to Ostara," 331–342; Simek, *Dictionary of Northern Mythology*, 254–255; Backman, *The Worlds of Medieval Europe*, 109; Reinhardt, *Germany 2000 Years V.I*, 185–186; Leeming, *The Oxford Companion to World Mythology*, 111 & Brooks, "The Social and Political Background," 4
47 Grimm, *Teutonic Mythology V.I*, 291 & White, "The Goddess Frig," 302
48 Lauder, *Legends and Tales of the Harz Mountains*, 155
49 Motz, "The Goddess Nerthus," 8; Jolly, *Popular Religion in Late Saxon England*, 8 & Niles, "Pagan Survivals and Popular Belief," 130
50 Bede, *The Reckoning of Time*, 53; Davidson, *Gods and Myths of Northern Europe*, 112–113; Simek, *Dictionary of Northern Mythology*, 220; Billington, "The Midsummer Solstice," 45; Shaw, *Pagan Goddesses in the Early Germanic World*, 44–45 & Stenton, *Anglo-Saxon England*, 97–98
51 Colum, *Nordic Gods and Heroes*, 175; Barney, *Word-Hoard*, 32; Davidson, *Gods and Myths of Northern Europe*, 61–63 & Davidson, *Myths and Symbols in Pagan Europe*, 93 & 96
52 Krappe, "The Valkyries," 55–57; Simek, *Dictionary of Northern Mythology*, 61 & 84 & 171 & 349; Northcott, *An Interpretation of the Second Merseburg Charm*, 45; Shaw, *Pagan Goddesses in the Early Germanic World*, 61–62 & Grendon, *Anglo-Saxon Charms*, 110–111

53 Jeep, *Medieval Germany*, 112; Rauch, *The Old Saxon Language*, 295 & Tiefenbach, *Altsächsisches Handwörterbuch*, 195

54 Augustyn, *The Semiotics of Fate, Death, and the Soul in Germanic Culture*, 33 & 40–41

55 Reinhardt, *Germany 2000 Years V.I*, 480–481; Thompson, *The Saxons and Germanic Social Origins*, 612; Kahler, *The Germans*, 36; Niles, "Pagan Survivals and Popular Belief," 133–134 & for a survey of north German folklore see Thorpe, *North German and Netherlandish Popular Traditions and Superstitions*, 1–334

56 Grimm, *Teutonic Mythology V.II*, 447 & 519 & Simek, *Dictionary of Northern Mythology*, 67 & 107

57 Cotterell, *The Encyclopedia of Mythology*, 186–187; Costambeys, *The Carolingian World*, 92; Davidson, *The Lost Beliefs of Northern Europe*, 113; Cathay, *Heliand*, 12–14; Tornaghi, *Anglo-Saxon Charms and the Language of Magic*, 439–464; Jolly, *Popular Religion in Late Saxon England*, 11 & 123 & 133–134 & 138–140 & 162–163; Lipscolmb et al., *A History of Magic, Witchcraft and the Occult*, 64 & Niles, "Pagan Survivals and Popular Religion," 126–130

58 Rampton, *European Magic and Witchcraft*, 165–166

59 Ibid. 156–160 & 167; Payne, *English Medicine in the Anglo-Saxon Times*, 139–140. The word "leech" is derived from the Anglo-Saxon *laece*, meaning "healer." See Cosman, *Medieval Wordbook*, 143

60 Milis, *The Pagan Middle Ages*, 125–127; Shinners, *Medieval Popular Religion*, 292–295 & 313–317 & Raiswell & Winter, *The Medieval Devil*, 223–226

61 Murphy, *The Heliand*, 36

62 Ibid. 37

63 Milis, *The Pagan Middle Ages*, 30

64 Tacitus, *The Agricola and The Germania*, 49

65 The English translation is my own; however, it is based on the German edition by Wilhelm Wattenbach. See Wattenbach, *Die Übertragung des hl. Alexander von Rudolf und Meginhart*, 6–8

66 Tschan, *History of the Archbishops of Hamburg-Bremen*, 10

67 Springer, *Die Sachsen*, 70

68 Ehlers, "Between Marklo and Merseburg," 139 & Simek, *Dictionary of Northern Mythology*, 310–311

69 Cathey, *Heliand*, 161; Gallee, *Old-Saxon Texts*, XXI; Rauch, *The Old Saxon Language*, 277 & Tiefenbach, *Altsächsisches Handwörterbuch*, 5

70 Wood, "Christianization and the Dissemination of Christian Teaching," 724–725; Gallee, *Old-Saxon Texts*, 249–255; Kolner, The *Indiculus superstitionum et paganarium*, 4 (for the Latin text see pg. 3) & for a complete English translation see McNeill, *Medieval Handbooks of Penance*, 419–421

71 Kolner, *The Indiculus superstitionum et paganarium*, 3 & Milis, *The Pagan Middle Ages*, 54–55

72 Ibid. 4 & 25–27

73 Rampton, *European Magic and Witchcraft*, 129–130; Karras, "Pagan Survivals," 560–566; Gallee, *Old-Saxon Texts*, 253 & Tiefenbach, *Altsächsisches Handwörterbuch*, 290

74 Ibid. 129–130

75 Tschan, *History of the Archbishops of Hamburg-Bremen*, 87 & Karras, "Pagan Survivals," 560–566

76 Grimm, *Teutonic Mythology VI*, 73 & Fuller, "Pagan Charms in Tenth-Century Saxony?" 165

77 Davidson, *The Lost Beliefs of Northern Europe*, 56–57 & *Myths and Symbols in Pagan Europe*, 24 & 91 & Niles, "Pagan Survivals and Popular Belief," 123–124

78 Grimm, *Teutonic Mythology VI* 111

79 Widukind, *Deeds of the Saxons*, 22. From the *Deeds of the Saxons*, © Catholic University of America Press. 2014. Reproduced with the permission of the Catholic University of America Press through PLS Clear.

80 Simek, *Dictionary of Northern Mythology*, 175–176; Dean, "Felling the Irminsul," 16; Schmidt, *Charlemagne*, 46–47 & Cusack, *Conversion among the Germanic Peoples*, 128

81 Tschan, *History of the Archbishops of Hamburg-Bremen*, 10–11

82 Cusack, "Pagan Resistance to Charlemagne's Mission," 43; Simek, *Dictionary of Northern Mythology*, 375–376; Leeming, *The Oxford Companion to World Mythology*, 407; Smith, *The Echo of Odin*, 116–117 & for a primary source documentation of Yggdrasil see Somerville and McDonald, *The Viking Age*, 50–53

83 Wood, "Pagan Religion and Superstitions East of the Rhine," 257

84 Cusack, "Pagan Resistance to Charlemagne's Mission," 43; Ehlers, *Die Integration Sachsens in das fränkische Reich*, 390 & Springer, *Die Sachsen*, 163

85 Riche, *The Carolingians*, 103 & Grünewald, *Westfalen zwischen Franken und Sachsen*, 22

86 Grimm, *Teutonic Mythology V.I*, 116

87 Kurlander, *Hitler's Monsters*, 7–9; Yenne, *Hitler's Master of the Dark Arts*, 101–130 & Dean, "Felling the Irminsul," 15

88 Ibid. 179; Halle, "Archaeology in the Third Reich," 93–96 & Longerich, *Heinrich Himmler*, 296–297

89 Ibid., 177–178

90 Williams, *Atrocity or Apology?*, 23

91 Davidson, *Myths and Symbols in Pagan Europe*, 88–89 & 174 & Capelle, "Anglische, sächsische und angelsächsische Holzschnitzkunst," 117–132

92 Kurlander, *Hitler's Monsters*, 168; Davidson, *Gods and Myths of Northern Europe*, 83; Leeming, *The Oxford Companion to World Mythology*, 369 & Smith, *The Echo of Odin*, 6

93 Nielsen, "Saxon Art between Interpretation and Imitation," 198; Davidson, *The Lost Beliefs of Northern Europe*, 38–41, & Axboe, "Danish Kings and Dendrochronology," 231

94 Ibid. 206–209. A collection of Germanic bracteate can also be found in Karl Hauck's *Die Goldbrakteaten der Völkerwanderungszeit*, accessible online through the Bayerische StaatsBibliothek (bsb-muenchen.de)

95 Simek, "Continental Germanic Religion," 299

96 Cathey, *Heliand*, 150

97 Reinhardt, *Germany 2000 Years V.I*, 5; Simek, *Dictionary of Northern Mythology*, 268–269 & Freeborn, *From Old English to Standard English*, 21–23

98 Davidson, *The Lost Beliefs of Northern Europe*, 4; Lipscolmb et al., *A History of Magic, Witchcraft and the Occult*, 69; Woolf, *Ancient Civilizations*, 460 & Wallace-Hadrill, *The Frankish Church*, 21

99 Algeo, *The Origins and Development of the English Language*, 44–45; Cathey, *Heliand*, 320; Murphy, *The Heliand*, 3; Fortson, *Indo-European Language and Culture*, 309 & Rauch, *The Old Saxon Language*, 289

100 Green, *Language and History in the Early Germanic World*, 254–255

101 Murphy, "The Old Saxon Heliand," 52

102 Costambeys, *The Carolingian World*, 87

103 Karras, "Pagan Survivals," 560–566

104 Dutton, *Carolingian Civilization*, 3; Palmer, "Defining Paganism in the Carolingian World," 408; Gallee, *Old-Saxon Texts*, 254 & Rampton, *European Magic and Witchcraft*, 129–130

105 Milis, *The Pagan Middle Ages*, 45; Filotas, *Pagan Survivals*, 218–219 & for 'Pyromancy' see Cosman, *Medieval Wordbook*, 195

106 Rampton, *European Magic and Witchcraft*, 129–130 & Dutton, *Carolingian Civilization*, 3

107 Ibid. 91 & 121 & 168–173 & McNeill, *Medieval Handbooks of Penance*, 329–331

108 Filotas, *Pagan Survivals*, 186–187 & 190–191

109 Ibid. 365–366
110 Wattenbach, *Die Übertragung des hl. Alexander von Rudolf und Meginhart*, 6–8
111 Rampton, *European Magic and Witchcraft*, 129–130
112 Filotas, *Pagan Survivals*, 192–193
113 Murphy, "The Old Saxon Heliand," 51
114 Wattenbach, *Die Übertragung des hl. Alexander von Rudolf und Meginhart*, 6–8 & Tschan, *History of the Archbishops of Hamburg-Bremen*, 10–11
115 Karras, "Pagan Survivals," 560–566 & Rampton, *European Magic and Witchcraft*, 129–130. According to Saxon folklore, witchcraft may have been practiced by early Saxons on the *Hexentanzplatz* (witches' dance floor)—a plateau high in the Harz Mtns. of Saxony-Anhalt. At the very least, the area continues to be revered as a sacred site by Germanic neo-pagans. See Lauder, *Legends and Tales of the Harz Mountains*, 2–250; Buse, *The Regions of Germany*, 220 & Von Schnurbein, *Norse Revival*, 316–317
116 Davidson, *Gods and Myths of Northern Europe*, 55–56; Buchholz, "Religious Foundations of Group Identity," 328 & Butt, *Daily Life in the Age of Charlemagne*, 17
117 Tacitus, *The Histories and the Annals*, 347–349 & Davidson, *Myths and Symbols in Pagan Europe*, 59
118 Flierman, *Saxon Identities*, 47
119 Riche, *The Carolingians*, 103
120 Wattenbach, *Die Übertragung des hl. Alexander von Rudolf und Meginhart*, 6–8; Howorth, "The Ethnology of the Germans (IV)," 432; Bucholz, "Perspectives for Historical Research in Germanic Religion," 119–120 & 128; Simek, "Continental Germanic Religion," 292; Abram, *Myths of the Pagan North*, 55 & Lincoln, *Gods and Demons, Priests and Scholars*, 21
121 Bede, *The Reckoning of Time*, 53; Fletcher, *The Conversion of Europe*, 256; Shaw, *Pagan Goddesses in the Early Germanic World*, 49 & Pope Gregory II believed that the Thuringians, neighbors of the Saxons, were still performing animal sacrifices in 724. See Filotas, *Pagan Survivals*, 162
122 Gallee, *Old-Saxon Texts*, XXII; Welch, "Pre-Christian Practices in the Anglo-Saxon World," 863–864 & Tiefenbach, *Altsächsisches Handwörterbuch*, 35
123 Rampton, *European Magic and Witchcraft*, 129–130
124 Karras, "Pagan Survivals," 560–566
125 Simek, *Dictionary of Northern Mythology*, 16 & Niles, "Pagan Survivals and Popular Belief," 124–125
126 Ibid. 19–25
127 Ibid. 35
128 Fuller, "Pagan Charms in Tenth-Century Saxony?" 166
129 Buse, *The Regions of Germany*, 111–112 & 139–140
130 Grimm, *Teutonic Mythology V.I*, 43
131 Milis, *The Pagan Middle Ages*, 45
132 Ibid. 44 & Durant, *The Age of Faith*, 741
133 Ibid. 43 & Halsall, *Barbarian Migrations and the Roman West*, 27–28; Robben, "Veränderungen und Kontinuitäten während des Christianisierungsprozesses in Nordwestdeutschland," 87; Effros, *Merovingian Mortuary Archaeology and the Making of the Early Middle Ages*, 86–87 & Filotas, *Pagan Survivals*, 6
134 Siegmund, "Social Relations among the Old Saxons," 84. Well into the nineteenth century, there was a popular association in folklore of megalithic tombs with heathen places of sacrifice; see Schwikart, *Journey through Lower Saxony*, 63
135 Buse, *The Regions of Germany*, 123;. Similar associations can be seen in England. In Northumbria, a former sixth- to seventh-century Anglo-Saxon temple has been identified within proximity to a Bronze Age tumulus. See Niles, "Pagan Survivals and Popular Belief," 123
136 Halsall, *Barbarian Migrations and the Roman West*, 385–386

137 Effros, *Merovingian Mortuary Archaeology and the Making of the Early Middle Ages*, 118 & 171–172 & Butt, *Daily Life in the Age of Charlemagne*, 72

138 Nicolle, *The Conquest of Saxony*, 38; Grünewald, *Westfalen zwischen Franken und Sachsen*, 21–22 & Bachrach, *Charlemagne's Early Campaigns (768–777)*, 207–208

139 Siegmund, "Social Relations among the Old Saxons," 88 & Grünewald, *Westfalen zwischen Franken und Sachsen*, 20–21

140 Ibid. 107; Davidson, *The Lost Beliefs of Northern Europe*, 134; Both, "Eine sächsische Hofwüstung," 108; Grünewald, *Westfalen zwischen Franken und Sachsen*, 20–23 & Heather, *Christendom*, 287

141 Karras, "Pagan Survivals," 560–566; Laux, "Kleine karolingische und ottonische Scheibenfibeln," 9–12 & Both, "Eine sächsische Hofwüstung," 108

142 Ibid.; Richards, "An Archaeology of Anglo-Saxon England," 58; IJssenneggar, "Between Frankish and Viking," 90 & Fehring, *The Archaeology of Medieval Germany*, 57–58

143 Frank, "Germanic Legend in Old English Literature," 84–85

144 McNeill, *Medieval Handbooks of Penance*, 419 & Rampton, *European Magic and Witchcraft*, 129–130. It may also be relevant that the term *galdor* appears in Old English (ON: *galdr*), which implies songs, incantations, witchcraft, or charms performed in a ritual context. See Algeo, *The Origins and Development of the English Language*, 100; Simek, *Dictionary of Northern Mythology*, 97–98 & Jolly, *Popular Religion in Late Saxon England*, 7 & 75–76 & 93 & 98–99 & 127 & 165

145 Filotas, *Pagan Survivals*, 47 & 223 & Springer, *Die Sachsen*, 159

146 Cathey, *Old Saxon*, 12

147 DeVun, *The Shape of Sex*, 191

148 This sentiment had its origin in the Biblical story of Genesis, where the Serpent's influence on Eve perpetuated the notion that women were especially susceptible to demonic machinations. The writing of Tertullian is notably vitriolic on the subject. See Raiswell and Winter, *The Medieval Devil*, 74–77

5 Confronting Paganism and the Foundations of the Early German Church

To understand the making of the German Church is to understand the birth of the idea of crusade, at least in the sense of armed penetration into a strange world in the name of Christ. It was an idea that as a prerequisite demanded pagans.[1]

—*J. M. Wallace-Hadrill*

The Origins of Christianity among the *Germani*

Incentivized by the imminent End of Days, following the crucifixion of Jesus, his disciples undertook their best efforts to fulfill the Great Commission, whereby Christ instructed them to spread his teachings to peoples of all nations.[2] Thereafter, Christian communities sprouted throughout the Greco-Roman world, coexisting among a milieu of mystery cults.[3] Like members of these other sects, early Christians were often misunderstood and made convenient scapegoats for persecution during troubled times.[4] However, everything changed with Constantine. His conversion (or "coming out") following the Battle of Milvian Bridge in 312 AD ended the persecutions and garnered protection and recognition for the Church and its flock.[5] Suddenly, professing the Christian faith garnered imperial favor and economic investment.[6] The prestige of Christianity benefited enormously, and following decades of growth, imperial patronage, political integration, and the solidification of doctrine, Christianity became the "official religion" of the Roman Empire during the reign of the emperor Theodosius (379–395), after which paganism (in its myriad guises) was declared illegal.[7] From there, persecution, absorption, and evangelism promoted wider Christianization.[8]

This process continued as Germanic tribes began crossing into Roman territory. The acceptance of Christianity was sometimes a stipulation of their settlement or a means of integration into the Roman army.[9] By the fourth century, the missionary Ulfilas ("little wolf") had also translated the Bible into Gothic, which assisted in converting Goths and other "Germans" from east of the Rhine.[10] The bulk of these early converts, due to the influence of the Goths, converted to Homoean Arianism, a competitive heretical Christian sect that rejected the Catholic (Nicene) interpretation of the Trinity (divine union of Father, Son, and Holy Spirit).[11]

By the seventh century, Goths, Vandals, and Lombards had all become Arians.[12] Yet, by the eighth century, Arianism had nearly disappeared. What changed? In

DOI: 10.4324/9781003379157-7

part, the conversion of Clovis to Catholicism broke the trend and set in motion a growing association between the Franks, Roman civilization, and the Papacy. In addition, Justinian's attempted reconquest of the west brought about the collapse of Gothic and Vandal power.[13] As for the Lombards, the Franks (with papal support) would see to their destruction during the reign of Charlemagne. With the collapse of the Arian kingdoms came the collapse of Arianism itself.[14] For the remaining Germanic peoples, their religious transformation was ushered in by the Roman Catholic Church.

For the present study, an essential aspect of this process occurred in England, where ecclesiastical growth ushered in a period of Anglo-Saxon missionary activity aimed toward "Germans," which supplemented an evolving network of Frankish churches. These developments coincided with the collapse or transformation of local paganisms and, from the very beginning, were correlated to the patronage of those in power, including donations of wealth and land, proclamations of support, political coercion, military action, and legal enforcement. In Francia, kings sought to extend their authority alongside the growth of the Church, which could be used to centralize power and ensure collective unity.[15] By the time Charlemagne ascended to the throne, most of his kingdom had been "Christianized."[16] However, not all Frankish subjects had been brought into the Christian fold. Eastern Frisians, for example, stubbornly clung to their pagan traditions despite Frankish military and political pressure against them. Yet, none remained as exhaustingly resistant to religious transformation as the Saxons. For Charlemagne, that resistance would manifest as an intermittent 33-year conflict, leading to a bitter and traumatic crusade. His successes and failures were in no small part determined by the legacy of those who came before him and their own struggles in confronting paganism and forming the foundations of the early "German" Church.

Christianity in Francia after Clovis

In Frankish Christianity, God was a distant figure and had to be reached through the medium of the Virgin Mary (the *Auxilium Christianorum*, "help of Christians") and a myriad of other saints who could act on one's behalf.[17] As a result, saints played an essential function in spiritual life, and their awe-inspiring stories could be found painted on church walls, often accompanied by scenes from the gospels.[18] For an illiterate population, such depictions were "books for poor people" *(Biblia pauperum)* and fundamental for disseminating Christian teachings; as such, they were tolerated (not without protest) by Franks as a means of education.[19]

The power of the saints could also be gleaned from sacred sites, cult centers, and relics seen on pilgrimage.[20] As Ermold the Black reminds us, only a "demented" person would "call into question the efficacy of the relics of the saints."[21] However, people had to be careful not to merely replace pagan idolatry with saintly idolatry, which appears to have been widespread.[22] (Saints may have also taken on the roles of lesser spiritual entities, as can be seen, for example, in much of modern Latin American Catholicism or Haitian Vodun.[23]) Holy people were also appreciated during celebrations, feasts, and holidays.[24] While for the few who could read, that is, nobles and clergy, education came from manuscripts produced by networks of scribes in their scriptoriums.[25]

In Francia, Christianity was also responsible for framing moral expectations. This was especially true concerning marriage, sexual deviance, and childbirth.[26] Social customs and superstitions were observed critically, and the Church expressed annoyance, for example, with musicians and actors who kept alive pagan storytelling traditions.[27] Likewise, while Church scholars saw the forest as a haven of seclusion for dedicating their energies toward God, the wilderness was the abode of trolls, spirits, and enchanted landscapes among ordinary people.[28] As indicated in Chapter 4, in contrast to more "formal religion," these elements of "popular religion" proved difficult to alter.[29] Nevertheless, in the aftermath of Clovis' conversion, pressure was increasing on a legal and political level to root out superstitions deemed "heathen holdovers." For example, in the sixth century, Theuderic I had to calm a crowd of pagans in Cologne who were furious that a missionary had burned their temple and idols.[30] However, the eradication of local paganisms pressed on, and Theuderic's brother, the Frankish king Childebert I, felt it necessary to issue a decree demanding the abandonment and removal of idols from fields, as well as condemned problematic behaviors such as drunkenness, improper songs, and having female dancers present during holiday feasts.[31]

It isn't clear how successful such edicts were in extirpating pagan or "inappropriate" customs; however, the persistent condemnation found in pastoral literature and the need for similar decrees over the following centuries leave room for doubt.[32] For example, as late as the 740s, Carloman (the Austrasian Mayor of the Palace) declared that every bishop should see to it that none of his flock were perpetuating pagan rites such as making sacrifices to the dead, casting lots, divination, using amulets, consulting auguries, or giving animals as offerings in church while invoking the saints. Nor should they sell Christians as slaves to pagans or continue to practice "Niedfeor" (the ritual use of fire we saw mentioned concerning Saxons in Chapter 4).[33]

Given the difficulties of dispelling heathen hang-ups, Christian teachings inevitably fused with pagan customs.[34] Scholars have long debated the processes by which this occurs; however, Marc Baer has succinctly summed up common trends into four categories:

1 Acculturation: changes accompanying socio-political integration.
2 Adhesion (hybridity): adopting new beliefs/customs alongside the old.
3 Syncretism: fusing new and old systems together.
4 Transformation: replacing the old with the new.[35]

Concerning syncretism, it is critical to remember, as Lindenfeld has noted in the Colonial context, that within missionary encounters, translation is a two-way process.[36] Missionaries present a Christian message in a particular manner (based on sectional allegiances); however, at the same time, those on the receiving end interpret what they hear within the parameters of their cultural worldviews. However, regardless of how syncretism occurs, two systems do not typically contribute equally. If one system is accommodating and inclusive, it will be far more vulnera-ble to another that is imperial or exclusive. Oral polytheistic systems are especially vulnerable to monotheistic, proselytizing, and literate systems (see Conclusion).

In Early Medieval Francia, each of these processes is visible. Results varied, but rural people clung to their traditions longer than those in urban centers, the latter of whom were more likely to be exposed to new ideas and experience the direct intervention of Church and government.[37] Indeed, terms used to denote peo-ple clinging to pre-Christian practices, that is, the Latin "pagan" (*pagani*) and the later Germanic/Norse equivalent "heathen," refer to rural people—a connotation that continued well into the modern era.[38]

Given the variability of exposure to Christianity, missionary activity continued to combat local superstitions within Francia long after the conversion of Clovis.[39] One famous example comes from a sixth-century report by Gregory of Langres concerning the people of Dijon. According to Gregory, the Dijon locals continued to express reverence for an obscure pagan tomb, which was seen as an obstacle to proper Christian practice. Gregory's solution to this problem was to declare the tomb the site of the third-century martyr Saint Benignus (who may have been killed in Dijon), allowing him to appropriate the pagan site and commandeer the devotion of its pilgrims.[40] It was a technique missionaries replicated for centuries, and it played a significant role in promoting a "cult of the saints."[41]

A similar example can be seen in the sixth-century account of Columbanus, an Irishman who, while utilizing the patronage of King Childebert II, preached among the Franks.[42] He established the influential Luxeuil Abbey in Burgundy, built on top of Roman ruins near a former pagan site.[43] In addition, Columbanus later found himself in the Austrian village of Bregenz, where, according to his biographer Jonas of Bobbio, in 611, he disrupted a pagan ritual of the Suevi (Suebi).[44] The Suevi had been busy preparing a cask of ale as an offering to the god Woden, but when Columbanus heard what they were doing, he decided to intervene. In a dra-matic episode, Columbanus channeled the power of God and blew mightily on the cask, causing it to burst into pieces.[45] In awe of this miracle, the locals renounced their gods and submitted to Christian baptism.[46]

Such stories are a standard motif in Medieval hagiography, where, in Bachrach's words, the primary purpose is "to glorify the memory of a particular saint" and "display their holiness via various feats."[47] They often used Sulpicius Severus' *Life of St. Martin* as a model, which records the fourth-century missionary exploits of St. Martin of Tours and his wanderings throughout Gaul.[48]

We see further encounters with paganism in Francia during the seventh century. One comes from Eligius of Aquitaine, the "patron saint of goldsmiths and met-alworkers," who preached in a village near Noyon in northern France.[49] Outside Noyon, Eligius sought to disrupt a local pagan festival; however, during his sermon of condemnation, he was interrupted by an annoyed villager who chastised him as a troublesome "Roman" who would never stop his people from preserving their ancestral customs.[50] Nevertheless, Eligius continued teaching, established an epis-copal center at Noyon, and built a nunnery. He was particularly active in Flanders, where he constructed monasteries and churches.[51] From one of his sermons, we get

a sense of what missionaries were trying to root out: sorcery, divination, enchant-
ing herbs, heeding auguries, wearing amulets, and numerous other rituals associated with temples, stones, fountains, and trees. Each was considered infected with
the "poison of the devil" and an affront to God.[52]

Despite confrontational encounters, missionaries pressed on, and Christianity in
Francia increasingly played a critical role in defining what it meant to be a "Frank."
Indeed, in the introduction to the *Lex Salica Karolina*, Franks are described as having been "established by the power of God" and as "rejecting barbarian rites."[53]
That declaration juxtaposed Franks with surrounding heretical and pagan peoples,
whose misguided views justified campaigns against them.[54] Those campaigns were,
in turn, led by rulers who, continuing the ancient custom of "divine kingship," were
considered representatives of God's will.[55]

Missionary Activity in South and Central Germany: Rupert, Corbinian, Killian, and Pirmin

Among southern Germanic peoples, missionary activity was underway throughout
the seventh century, as demonstrated by a few notable examples. In the 690s, a
bishop from the Rhineland, later known as Saint Rupert, was evangelizing near
Salzburg.[56] Before his arrival, Rupert was in Bavaria per the request of Duke
Theodo of the Agilofing family. He accepted Theodo's invitation only after being
rejected, abused, and exiled by the pagan community of Worms. However, by the
time he reached Salzburg, his luck had changed. The new community he founded
(supplemented with Irish missionaries) became an important center for spreading
the faith in Austria and Bavaria. This endeavor continued with the Frankish hermit Corbinian, who established himself at Freising with the support of the Bavarian Duke Grimoald. At Freising, Corbinian founded a Benedictine monastery and
preached from 715 until his death in 730.[57]

Among the Thuringians of Central Germany, the gospel was spread by Killian,
the "Apostle of Franconia." Along with his companions, Killian received papal
instruction in 686 to preach among the "heathens" and eventually found himself
at the castle of Würzburg, where he received hospitality and protection from Duke
Gozbert, the local pagan leader. However, disputes arose, and their relationship
soured. The situation eventually turned violent, and in 689, Killian was put to death
for opposing the duke's marriage to his brother's widow Geilana.[58] (When Geilana,
a pagan, heard of Killian's criticism of her marriage, she had him beheaded.[59])
Despite this unfortunate end, before his martyrdom, Killian succeeded in attaining
the conversion of Gozbert and other notables in East Franconia and Thuringia, pav-
ing the way for a more thoroughly Christianized Central Germany.[60] In addition,
Würzburg became one of the most important German ecclesiastical centers.[61]

In Alamannia, which comprised territory in southwest Germany, missionary
activity in the early eighth century continued with the work of Pirmin, possibly a
Visigoth who fled to Francia following the Arab conquest of Spain. Pirmin gained
the favor of Charles Martel and the support of Franconian and Bavarian nobles,
allowing him to conduct missionary work in the region of Alsace and along the

Upper Rhine and Danube. By 724, Pirmin had established Reichenau Abbey on an island in Lake Constance (at the foot of the Swiss Alps).[62] However, after three years, Pirmin's stay on the island was cut short by the anger of the Alamannian Duke Lantfrid, who believed Pirmin was an agent of Charles Martel (with whom Lantfrid was at odds). Yet, by 730, Lantfrid was dead, and Pirmin had become the "Apostle of Alamannia." Beyond Reichenau Abbey, he established the Church in Alsace, Switzerland, and Bavaria, including the monasteries of Murbach, Pfäffers, Niederaltaich, and Hornbach.[63]

Pirmin's ultimate goal had been to destroy the remnants of paganism in Alamannia and correct misguided perceptions of Christianity. As he noted in a tract dedicated to priests working in the region, they needed to reform those "whose faith was shaky" and whose knowledge of Christianity was "extremely vague and confused."[64] Despite the best efforts of Pirmin and others like him, missionary activity in Alamannia and the development of the Church in the region remained "haphazard," mainly due to political instability and a lack of effective ecclesiastical organization.[65]

Amandus in Frisia

Further north, Amandus, a Neustrian Frank (b. 584), operated among the people of the Low Countries.[66] Throughout the early seventh century, utilizing the patronage of the Frankish king Dagobert, Amandus conducted missionary work among the pagans of Belgium and the Netherlands, during which he supplemented his preaching with the destruction of temples, upon whose rubble he constructed churches and monasteries.[67] To communicate with the pagan Frisians, Amandus purchased English slaves to use as translators. (They could help due to linguistic similarities between Old English and Old Frisian.) As Amandus continued to preach, he gained a reputation for performing miracles, one of which involved him raising a man from the dead near Ghent. We are told this miracle caused the locals to abandon their beliefs and tear down one of their temples.[68] By 647, Amandus was bishop at Maastricht, an influential center for later missionary initiatives in the region.[69]

The Conversion of England

A significant development for the growth of the German Church came with the arrival of Anglo-Saxon missionaries on the continent, which followed decades of religious strife in England. Due to the Roman occupation and presence of early missionaries, Christianity had been in England for centuries. However, a relapse into paganism occurred with the arrival of the Anglo-Saxons.[70] According to Bede, although the Anglo-Saxons arrived as pagans, they were able to conquer the Britons because the Britons made for "bad Christians."[71]

The conversion of Anglo-Saxons began in the sixth century at the behest of Pope Gregory, who, in 597, sent Augustine to convert King Aethelberht of Kent, whose wife was already a Christian from Francia.[72] Aethelberht allowed Augustine to preach within his domain, and on Christmas Day in 597, the king converted and was baptized (alongside thousands of his followers). Augustine then created the first English bishopric at Canterbury.[73] Soon after, the Irish monk Aidan, alongside several others from Iona, formed monastic communities in northern England, some of the earliest being Lindisfarne, Whitby, and Jarrow.[74]

In 601, Pope Gregory sent a letter to King Aethelberht imploring him to put more effort into converting his people by suppressing idol worship and destroying associated shrines.[75] However, by following Gregory's advice, Aethelberht produced a pagan backlash. According to Bede, when Aethelberht died in 616 and was succeeded by his son Eadbald, the people of Kent relapsed into idolatry and "the worship of demons," facilitating war in Kent between pagans and Christians.[76] However, in the mid-seventh century, Eorcenberht succeeded his father Eadbald as king of Kent and set about overthrowing all the *deofelgyld* ("devilish idols") in his kingdom.[77] It was a war the pagans of Kent lost. Nevertheless, Anglo-Saxon resistance to conversion undermines a well-known statement by the nineteenth-century historian John Richard Green that, in England, "Woden yielded without a struggle to Christ."[78]

Around the same time as the Kent conflict, Pope Boniface wrote to King Edwin of Northumbria, urging him to reject idol worship, omens, and absurd customs associated with pagan shrines. Only then could his people be free from the devil's bondage.[79] The Pope further entreated Edwin's wife, Queen Ethelberga, to pressure her husband into fulfilling these endeavors because he was "slow to listen to preachers."[80] Boniface also expressed baffled irritation at the stubborn commitment of the English to their idols, mainly because those idols had been created by the very people who worshiped them.[81]

Edwin heeded Boniface's words, and the destruction of pagan shrines commenced. The king was assisted in that destruction by a reformed pagan priest, Cofi, who helped burn a pagan shrine east of York.[82] The king also permitted the Christian priest Paulinus to preach within his domain, and it wasn't long before the king and his retainers received baptism.[83]

King Penda of Mercia later killed Edwin; however, before his death, he was able to secure the commitment of King Earpwald of East Anglia to Christianity. Earpwald's father, King Redwald (employing a diplomatic strategy), allowed religious pluralism and possessed an altar of Christ and pagan idols within the same sanctuary.[84] Yet, Earpwald was less understanding than his father, and he too was killed by pagans, causing the people of East Anglia to relapse into "heathenism." However, the region was eventually restored to Christian rule by Earpwald's brother Sigbert and the influence of the Burgundian bishop Felix.[85]

Cyclical religious strife was a recurring theme throughout England. To the north in Bernicia, between 634 and 635, King Oswald defeated pagans in battle and began converting the region. By 640, Earconbert of Kent was ordering the destruction of idols in his kingdom, which may have been partially motivated by his devout Christian daughter Earcongata (who was educated in a Frankish nunnery). Earcongata was not alone, and it became increasingly common for members of the English nobility to receive religious instruction in Francia, which tied the Anglo-Saxon Church closer to that of the Franks.[86]

This back-and-forth conversion process continued steadily throughout the seventh century. The Middle Angles became Christian during the reign of King Peada, who was compelled to convert as part of a marriage arrangement between his daughter Alchfled and King Oswy of Northumbria. King Oswy also helped restore East Anglia to the Church and initiated Mercia's conversion following the death of Penda.[87] It wasn't long after the defeat of Mercia that the people of Sussex also saw conversions, particularly following the preaching of Wilfrid and the approval of King Ethelwalh. By the late seventh century, the conversion of England was politically "complete" when the Isle of Wight formally accepted Christianity.[88]

Despite widespread conversions among the English, religious allegiance was fragile. Famine, plague, and drought (among other calamities) caused relapses into paganism, as occurred among the East Saxons in 665. However, these relapses could be countered by political, economic, and military pressure. In addition, miracle stories helped establish sacred places to draw in pilgrims and built up the reputations of Christian missionaries and the power of their God.[89] These were aided by acts of Christian charity and the hopeful message of salvation and paradise beyond death. As the English Church grew, significant monastic settlements were founded in Rochester, London, and York.[90] While there was still much work to be done in England, by the late seventh century, English missionaries were ready to turn toward their heathen cousins across the North Sea, ushering in what C. H. Talbot has called "the great turning point" in "the history of the west."[91]

Anglo-Saxon Arrivals: Wilfrid, Wigbert, and the Two Hewalds

One of the earliest Englishmen to undertake missionary efforts on the continent was Wilfrid of Hexham, a bishop of Northumbria.[92] Wilfrid was part of a growing movement of English ecclesiastics who desired to convert pagans they considered distant kin, namely Frisians, Saxons, and Danes.[93] That sentiment is first evident with the influential Saint Ecgberht, a Northumbrian monk who became bishop at Lindisfarne following his studies in Ireland.[94] Ecgberht also organized some of the Frisian missions that followed in Wilfrid's footsteps.[95]

As for Wilfrid, while he succeeded in bringing about the conversion of Frisian nobles and laid the groundwork for later missions in the area, his efforts to garner wider conversions ultimately failed. Within a few years, Wilfrid was back in England, directing his attention toward the people of Sussex.[96] Wigbert of Wessex (who was sent by Ecgberht) picked up where Wilfrid left off. Wigbert landed in Frisia during the reign of the pagan king Radbod, "the enemy of the Catholic Church," and appears to have been just as unsuccessful as Wilfrid.[97] He, too, returned to England.

Soon after, in the early 690s, Ecgberht directed a new missionary enterprise toward the "Old Saxons" and dispatched the "Two Hewalds": Hewald the Black and Hewald the White.[98] According to Bede, when the Hewalds arrived in the territory of the Old Saxons, they were welcomed by a local "reeve," whom they asked to bring to his lord so that they could speak with him.[99] However, when the Saxons in the reeve's village became aware that the Hewalds were Christian (after observing them singing psalms and making offerings to Christ), they became distraught.[100] Fearful that the Christians might convince their lord to abandon the gods and compel them to convert, the Saxons seized the Hewalds and proceeded to brutally murder them—Hewald the White with a sword and Hewald the Black by having his limbs torn off. Both of their bodies were then flung into the Rhine.

When the villagers' lord heard what happened, he was furious and had the perpetrators of the crime killed and their village burned.[101] Allegedly, the bodies of the Hewalds were also found (via miracles) and handed over to the Franks. However, that claim (alongside the account of revenge enacted upon their murderers) may simply be hagiographical tropes used to display the sanctity of the martyrs and the inevitable justice of God's vengeance.[102] Nevertheless, Pippin II had the martyrs handed over to the missionary Willibrord, who buried them in the church of St. Cunibert in Cologne.[103]

There are several striking features in Bede's account. Not only does it give insight into the decentralized nature of Saxon society, but it also suggests Saxon's awareness of the ramifications of converting to Christianity. Bede readily admits that following the conversion of their leader, the people would be *compelled* to convert. The notion of *cuius regio eius religio* (meaning: "Let the religion of the realm be decided by the ruler") had ancient roots.[104]

Willibrord: The "Apostle of the Frisians"

Missionary work in the Netherlands continued with another Northumbrian, Willibrord, later Bishop of Utrecht, known to posterity as the "Apostle of the Frisians."[105] Willibrord arrived in Frisia in 690, along with several companions, after studying in Ireland and time as a monk in Wilfrid's monastery at Ripon.[106] He landed in Frisia shortly after the Frankish defeat of the pagan king Radbod at the Battle of Dorestad, which provided Willibrord with more security and easier access to potential converts.[107] As the Merovingian period came to a close, Willibrord also gained the protection of Frankish Mayors of the Palace.[108]

The defeat of Radbod was crucial for missionary activity to resume in Frisia, and following his defeat, Radbod was forced to allow missionaries in his territory. Eventually, Radbod himself was nearly baptized by the Frankish missionary Wulfram; the ex-Archbishop of Sens. Wulfram gained the king's respect for intervening in an attempted pagan sacrifice. The Frisians had tied two boys to stakes in water at low tide, where they were to await death and appease the anger of a sea god.[109] Horrified, Wulfram cut the boys loose, an act Radbod deemed courageous. Thereafter, under Wulfram's influence, Radbod agreed to baptism. However, when Wulfram congratulated the king on his decision to convert and escape eternal damnation in Hell, Radbod was dismayed to learn he wouldn't see his pagan ancestors in Heaven.[110] Instead of following through with the ritual, Radbod turned away in disgust, proclaiming he would rather follow his ancestors to Hell than gain Heaven without them.[111] Over the following decades, he resumed his role as the scourge of Franks and Christians.

Returning to Willibrord, in 692, he journeyed to Rome to meet with Pope Sergius, from whom he sought to acquire sacred relics to replace destroyed pagan idols.[112] About the same time Willibrord was in Rome, a little-known tribe called the Boructuarii (located somewhere between the Yssel and Ems) began to convert but were suddenly defeated in war by the Old Saxons, putting a halt to their Christianization.[113] Given the proximity between Boructuarii, Saxons, and Frisians, these developments likely caused some anxiety for Willibrord when he later journeyed back to the region.

By 695, Willibrord was being consecrated in Rome as the "Apostle of the Frisians" by Pope Sergius. Fortune continued to favor Willibrord in 698 when he was granted the estate of Echternach (in Luxembourg) by Irmina of Trier, mother-in-law to Pippin II.[114] Eventually, coming under Pippin's protection, Echternach became a significant monastic center. From Echternach, Willibrord's influence expanded further into Hesse and Thuringia, where he was granted estates and patronage from the Thuringian duke Hetan II.[115]

Within a decade, Willibrord was declared archbishop of his see at Utrecht, which had been under Frankish control since its conquest by King Dagobert I.[116] In Utrecht, Willibrord founded a cathedral alongside several churches and monasteries.[117] However, around 710, after a prolonged period of struggling to gain converts in Frisia, Willibrord redirected his ministry toward the Danes. He journeyed to Denmark during the reign of the "savage" King Ongendus, who (perhaps to Willibrord's surprise) received him hospitably and allowed him to preach.[118] Yet, Willibrord met with failure among the Danes and had to settle for purchasing 30 Danish boys (presumably slaves) who became part of Willibrord's entourage.[119]

On his return home, Willibrord's ship ran aground on the island of Heligoland ("Fositeland"), a hallowed place to pagan Frisians. According to Alcuin of York's *Vita Willibrordi*, the island was dedicated to the Frisian deity Fosite, contained a temple, and was subject to rules that forbade killing animals on the island or taking water from a local spring. Violation merited death. However, believing these superstitions were "silly," Willibrord proceeded to baptize three men in the sacred spring, after which he slaughtered some of the local livestock for food. The locals were horrified by these acts of desecration and confused by the failure of their gods to punish the Christians. Unsure of what to do, they sent word to King Radbod, informing him of the situation.[120]

Willibrord and his companions were eventually taken before Radbod, where lots were cast for three days to determine if they should be killed. Fate was kind toward Willibrord, but one of his companions was less fortunate and "won the martyrs crown."[121] Willibrord scolded Radbod for his worship of devils, reminding him that if he refused to change his ways, eternal torment in "the flames of hell" lay in wait.[122] Radbod was unconvinced and sent Willibrord back to the Franks.

Willibrord got into similar trouble on the island of Walcheren (in Zeeland), where he and his companions destroyed an "idol of the ancient superstition," possibly connected to the goddess Nehalennia.[123] Willibrord, "moved by zeal," smashed the idol, after which the shrine's guardian, "seething with anger," struck Willibrord on the head with a sword.[124] Willibrord was ultimately unharmed, and the situation diffused when he prevented his companions from fighting the guardian.[125] However, Alcuin claimed the guardian was "seized and possessed by the devil three days later," causing him to take his own life.[126] Again, God's vengeance had been inescapable.

Willibrord and his companions eventually arrived safely back in Frisia, where they resumed their missionary endeavors; yet, a significant disruption occurred in 714 when Pippin II died, and Radbod launched another rebellion. The Frisian king inspired fear by destroying churches and murdering missionaries, which motivated Willibrord to flee to his estate at Echternach.[127] Willibrord remained at Echternach until Radbod died in 719, after which he returned to Frisia and established a reputation for providing welfare to beggars.[128] From his base in Frisia, he founded a monastery in Antwerp, which he later granted to an Irish companion.[129] He died in 739 and was buried in the abbey church at Echternach, which became a place of pilgrimage and a conduit for miracles.[130]

Boniface

In the final years of his ministry, Willibrord was assisted by Wynfrith of Devon (later known as St. Boniface), perhaps the most discussed English missionary who operated among Medieval Germans.[131] Born about 675 in the Kingdom of Wessex, Boniface spent his younger days at a monastery in Exeter but was later educated outside of Winchester at the Benedictine monastery of Nursling.[132] At Nursling, he studied until his abbot's death in 716, after which he journeyed to Frisia to preach.[133]

When Boniface landed in Frisia, he traveled to Dorestad to meet with Radbod (who was still living).[134] However, the situation proved difficult because Radbod was leading the Frisians in revolt.[135] Boniface's biographer Willibald writes that, during this conflict, priests in the area were dispersed and many churches destroyed, and further, locals resumed the worship of idols.[136] As a result, Boniface returned to England disappointed at failing to reap a "harvest of souls."[137] However, the tide turned for missionaries in the region following the death of Radbod in 719, the news of which Boniface received "with great joy."[138] That same year, Boniface journeyed to Rome seeking papal endorsement from Pope Gregory II for his missionary ambitions toward "the savage peoples of Germany."[139] Gregory granted Boniface his blessing and charged him with spreading the gospel among Germans "still bound by the shackles of paganism."[140] With papal support secured, Boniface returned to Frisia to join Willibrord and his mission, which he supported until 721 by helping Willibrord preach, build churches, and destroy pagan cult sites.[141]

From Frisia, Boniface made forays into Hesse to deliver locals from "the captivity of the devil."[142] In Hesse, he encountered warlords who were "partial Christians" and, upon securing their support, established a monastic cell beneath the fortress of Amöneburg (from where he preached to Hessians on the Saxon border).[143] Within a year, Boniface returned to Rome, and Gregory II consecrated him "Bishop to the Germans."[144] Significantly, Gregory also helped Boniface acquire the protection of Charles Martel by sending a letter of introduction in December 722.[145] Charles' protection proved critical in the years to come.[146] Indeed, in a later letter written to Daniel of Winchester in the early 740s, Boniface readily admitted that without Charles' support (and the fear he inspired), Boniface would not have been able to organize and defend the Church nor suppress pagan rites.[147]

As many scholars have noted, the Church and Frankish might walked hand in hand as missionaries made their way among pagans.[148] It was a mutually beneficial relationship. Missionaries received protection, funding, and land, while Frankish rulers gained an advantage in disintegrating the social fabric of their enemies while simultaneously centralizing their power.[149] Charles Martel secured Boniface's protection by granting him a letter of safe conduct in 723, which guaranteed support from nobles and magnates within Francia.[150] However, such protection did not make Boniface immune from violence. Both pagans and Christians posed a threat, and Boniface was not well-liked by some influential members of the Church, notably, Bishop Gewilib of Mainz and the Irish Abbot Virgil of Salzburg.[151]

Nevertheless, with the backing of Charles Martel and Pope Gregory II, Boniface returned to Central Germany to work in Hesse and Thuringia.[152] Among the Hessians, Boniface encountered people who continued to heed auguries, practice divination, engage in conjuring, recite incantations, and make sacrifices at trees and springs.[153] Amid these pagans, possibly in 723 or 724, Boniface discovered the "Donar's Oak" at Geismar, a sacred tree of some significance.[154] Accompanied by soldiers sent from Charles Martel, with axes and a "divine wind," Boniface tore down the tree in full view of the pagans. When Donar failed to strike Boniface dead, the locals were bewildered.[155] Boniface then repurposed the remains of the oak to build a chapel dedicated to St. Peter, which became an early part of his monastic settlement of Fritzlar.[156]

The destruction of Donar's Oak must have been an impactful event for those who revered it. As Carole Cusack has noted, "the fall of the Donar Oak symbolically prefigured the collapse of their worldview."[157] The actions of Boniface at Geismar were meant to demonstrate the power of the Christian God over pagan superstitions.[158] He was never one for subtle means of persuasion; as Ian Wood has observed, "Boniface had a more stringent view of Christianity than did many others...evangelization was a more rigorous concept than it was for other missionaries."[159] Adam of Bremen confirmed as much, claiming Boniface "excelled all others in the zeal and assiduity of his preaching."[160]

Often Boniface was heeding the advice of Bishop Daniel of Winchester, who sent him a letter concerning methods of conversion for the Germans in 723/724.[161] In that letter, Daniel advises Boniface to convince pagans to explain the origins of their deities, allowing the missionary to dispel irrational components of their beliefs. In addition, pagans should be shown the futility of worshiping man-made images. Comparisons could then be made between the thriving and civilized state of Christian peoples and the miserable and impoverished circumstances of pagans.[162] The ultimate goal was not to anger pagans but to cause confusion and make them "ashamed of their absurd opinions" and "disgusting rites."[163] Critically, confidence in the power of local deities had to be undermined.[164]

Boniface took this advice further with instructions to his own pupils. According to Boniface, missionaries should end all traces of paganism, including practices being merged with Christianity. Worship of old gods, reverence toward pagan shrines, trust in omens, casting lots, folk healing, pagan symbols, and the use of incantations all needed to be eradicated. Proper respect also needed to be shown to the Church, and the privileges of the clergy should be recognized. Prayer, the fundamentals of Mass, and correct reception of the sacraments should be taught, as well as penance for sin and the obligation to financially support the Church.[165] However, missionaries were also to establish trust with locals through healing, demonstrating mercy, assisting the poor, and practicing the virtues of charity and forgiveness.[166]

By 732, Boniface had been elevated to Archbishop of Mainz, after which his attention centered on Bavaria, where he divided the Church into the four dioceses of Salzburg, Regensburg, Passau, and Freising.[167] Boniface was not laying the foundations of the Bavarian church but utilizing patronage from the ruling Agilofing family, building on ground established by prior missionaries, and initiating much-needed reforms.[168] Boniface had received a concerned letter from Pope Gregory II, who was horrified that Bavarian locals were eating horses and being baptized by priests who offered sacrifices to "Jupiter." Worse still, Christian slaves were being sold to heathens for sacrifices.[169] Boniface was instructed to root these practices out entirely.

While Boniface was addressing pagan survivals and reforming the Church in Bavaria, his original point of operation was being threatened. During the 730s, his benefactor Charles Martel faced revolts from both Frisians and Saxons, which temporarily halted the spread of Christianity among them. The Frisian rebellion, beginning in 734, was led by a Duke named Bubo but was checked by Charles Martel's assault on northern Frisia.[170] Bubo was killed, the region ravaged, and pagan temples were destroyed.[171] Only after this destruction was unleashed could missionaries resume their work. However, as late as 738, Charles Martel was still dealing with the Saxons. That same year Boniface wrote a letter seeking prayers from the English in bringing about the conversion of their Saxon cousins on the continent so that their hearts could be turned away from the "snares of the devil" and gathered "among the Children of Mother Church."[172] Shortly afterward, Boniface received a reply from Bishop Torthelm of Leicester praising him for his efforts and rejoicing at the prospect of the "Old Saxons" coming to believe in "Christ the Almighty God."[173]

It was a year of many letters condemning paganism remnants in "Germania." Gregory II wrote to the nobles of Hesse and Thuringia, admonishing them to abstain from divination, wearing amulets, speaking incantations, sorcery, and fortune-telling by groves and fountains.[174] Shortly after, his successor Pope Gregory III wrote a similar letter to the bishops of Bavaria and Alamannia, as well as a letter to Boniface congratulating him on freeing "a hundred thousand souls" from the "power of the heathen" and bringing them "into the bosom of Mother Church."[175] However, he also sent one to the people of "Old Saxony" in support of Boniface:

> Let no one henceforth deceive you with high-sounding words to seek salvation in the worship of idols made by hands, be they of gold or silver or brass

or stone or any other substance. These lying deities, called gods by the heathen of old, are well known to be the dwelling places of demons. For all the gods of the Gentiles are demons…Depart, my children, from the service of idols and come, worship the Lord our God…our brother and fellow bishop Boniface is sent to you that he may learn the conditions among you and may comfort your hearts with the word of exhortation in Christ Jesus our Lord, so that you may be delivered from the snares of the devil and be found worthy to be counted among the children of adoption and, set free from eternal damnation, may enter into everlasting life.[176]

There is much to digest from the above letter, but who *precisely* was Gregory's audience? We may have a clue from a letter written by Boniface to Gregory in 740/741, in which he hails the success of Saxon conversions, notably four "princes" named Eoba, Rutwic, Wulderic, and Dedda.[177] Boniface's letter is lost; we only know this content from the Pope's reply. However, it suggests that akin to efforts toward noble families of surrounding Germanic peoples, papal appeals were explicitly made to the nobles and magnates of Saxony.

Throughout the 740s, Boniface continued to develop the Church in Germany by organizing the dioceses of Eichstatt, Würzburg, Büraburg, and Erfurt and helping found (alongside his disciple Sturmi) what became the highly influential monastic center of Fulda.[178] Constructed in the "woods of Buchonia" upon the ruins of a destroyed villa, Fulda proved to be an essential base of operations for missionary activity in the region; it was also an incredibly well-landed and economically powerful institution.[179] Fulda was centered on a Frankish royal estate containing 15,000 plowlands used as hunting grounds for nobles and a staging point for launching campaigns against the Saxons.[180] It was granted to Boniface and his companions via Carloman (son of Charles Martel) and, by 779, housed nearly 400 monks.[181]

Not all of Boniface's investments prospered like Fulda. Büraburg and Erfurt disappeared from a lack of support, and Boniface faced opposition from Austrasian nobles and ecclesiastical rivals. Nevertheless, increasingly, Boniface's' work in Mainz and Wurzburg prospered.[182] In the vicinity of Würzburg alone, important nunneries such as Kitzinggen, Ochsenfurt, and Tauberbischofsheim began to form.[183] Ochsenfurt was eventually entrusted to the English nuns Lioba (a relative of Boniface) and Thecla.[184] Lioba, whose biography was written c. 836 by Rudolf of Fulda, later rose to become abbess of Bischofsheim and was a confidante of Charlemagne's wife, Hildegard.[185]

Reforms continued in 747 when Boniface called a synod (an assembly of the clergy) where Thuringian, Frankish, and Bavarian bishops were required to attend and swear allegiance to Rome.[186] A few years later, Boniface further tightened "Germanic" connections to Rome when he anointed Pippin III as King of the Franks. Within a few years, Pippin pledged an oath to Pope Stephen II to protect the Roman Church against any threat posed by the Lombards (Arians), which secured papal support for Carolingian rule.[187]

With his successes multiplying, Boniface made a final attempt at garnering conversions in Frisia. About 754, he resigned as Archbishop of Mainz and, alongside his companions, set off for Frisia to preach, destroy heathen worship, and build churches (some allegedly over pagan temples).[188] Throughout this process, Boniface's entourage offered the rite of baptism to locals. However, one day, as they prepared for baptisms at Dokkum, Boniface and his group were set upon by "a multitude of wild heathen."[189] The situation quickly turned violent. Boniface called for peace but to no avail. Rapidly, the "frenzied mob of heathens" charged and attacked.[190] Boniface tried to defend himself with a gospel book he was carrying, but he and all 52 of his companions were murdered.[191] And so, as Adam of Bremen put it, Boniface was "crowned with glorious martyrdom."[192] His body was taken to Utrecht, Mainz, and finally, Fulda, to be buried in the local crypt.[193] His bones were spread further afield among other churches.[194] At Fulda, which became the center of his cult, Boniface's remains gained a reputation for healing, while his place of death at Dokkum became a memorial mound and a miraculous pilgrimage site.[195] To this day, Fulda harbors a statue in his honor and watches over the book he may have used to defend himself.[196] According to his biographer Willibald, Boniface's murderers were also hunted down by a vengeful militia of Christian Frisians, who, subject to God's wrath, were "slaughtered in great numbers."[197] The families of the pagan raiders were enslaved.[198]

It is hard to estimate the political ramifications of Boniface's death. However, it is possible that his martyrdom exacerbated conflict between Franks and the Frisian-Saxon pagans they were trying to subdue and convert. As Stofferahn has noted, the death of Boniface "seems to have effected a sea of change in prevailing attitudes toward spreading the faith."[199] Put bluntly, his martyrdom may have contributed to a more militarized approach toward conversion because the dangers of missionaries operating in regions not yet pacified were abundantly clear.

The Legacy of Boniface: Willibald, Willehad, and Lebuinus

Following in the footsteps of Boniface was another Englishman of Wessex named Willibald, who, incidentally, was related to Boniface on his mother's side. Willibald spent much of his early life at the monastery of Waldheim in southern England, after which he spent 20 years traveling throughout much of the known world.[200] His wandering ended in 738 when, at the request of Boniface, Willibald was sent by Pope Gregory III to assist the German mission.

Shortly after, Willibald became particularly active in Thuringia and Bavaria. In Thuringia, although Christianity was evident in the region as early as the 530s, the area was still predominantly pagan in the 740s. Willibald reported that the local dukes Theobald and Hetan essentially brought Christianity in the region to an end, and locals worshiped springs and consulted auguries. Other Hessian leaders, such as Dettic and Deorulf, were Christian only in name.[201]

Before his encounters in Thuringia, Willibald had been established in 741 as Bishop of Eichstatt in Bavaria, where he also encountered residual paganism.[202] The continued prominence of paganism in Bavaria is substantiated by Bishop Arbeo of Freising's *Vita Corbiniani* (Life of Corbinian), which mentions the continuation of witchcraft in the region.[203] During the mid-eighth century, Bavaria was under the leadership of the Agilofings, who had been forced to recognize the over-lordship of Charles Martel. However, despite Frankish suzerainty, Bavarian dukes continued to seek their independence. Following the death of Charles Martel, tensions between Bavarians and Franks resurfaced and continued to be a source of friction until the interference of Charlemagne in the 780s.[204] All that is to say, the transition of power likely contributed to the continued practice of paganism in the region, as the enforcement of conversions on a wide scale posed significant challenges (particularly in rural areas missionaries tended to avoid). Furthermore, competition between prominent ecclesiastical figures made operating in the region more difficult.

Discord within the Church and half-hearted conversions were cause for concern. Consequently, Charles Martel summoned a "Germanic Council" (*Concilium Germanicum*) in April 742 to address Church reform and problems of corruption.[205] It is suspected that the *Indiculus Superstitionum* may have been composed there, primarily to target pagan practices in Saxony and Austrasia.[206]

Back in Frisia, Boniface's work continued with Willehad of Northumbria, who arrived in the region in 766 to work around Dokkum.[207] According to Adam of Bremen, he was "inflamed with a desire for martyrdom" and had no trouble challenging pagans directly.[208] In one instance, Willehad became engaged in an argument with locals whom he chided as "silly" for seeking aid from stones and deaf idols.[209] In making such assertions, Willehad was following the precedent set by Boniface and the advice given to him by Daniel of Winchester. Indeed, Willehad eventually grew bolder and (alongside his companions) began destroying Frisian idols. His reward for that behavior was to be beaten with cudgels and threatened with having his throat slit.[210] It was not the only time he faced violent backlashes.[211] However, despite such setbacks, his reputation as a missionary grew, and in time, Willehad would gain the attention of Charlemagne and become a component of the king's conversion strategy for the Saxons.

Another inspired by Boniface was Lebuinus (aka Liafwin), an Anglo-Saxon who was once a monk at Wilfrid's monastery of Ripon. In the early 750s, Lebuinus resolved his life to the conversion of Germans and was soon welcomed at Utrecht, where he was responsible for preaching to Frisians and Saxons.[212] Lebuinus appears to have been a persuasive missionary. From the mid-750s to about 770, he gained the support of Westphalian nobles, one being a man called Folcbert from the village of Suderg near Münster.[213] Further support came from a Saxon matron named Avaerhilda, who assisted Lebuinus in establishing a church at Deventer in the modern Dutch province of Overijssel.[214] Deventer quickly became a significant launching point for missionaries operating among Frisians and Saxons. It remained so until the eruption of the Saxon Wars during the reign of Charlemagne, which is where we will return to Lebuinus in more detail.

Conclusion

Most of our information concerning the establishment of the early Church, methods of conversion, and commentary on paganism comes from hagiography ("writing about the holy"), often written accounts of saints' lives.[215] As a result, much of what we are told is written in an idealist fashion that relies upon formulaic motifs, often with a specific agenda in mind, be it political claims of a bishopric or the enhancement of a saint's cult.[216] Nevertheless, it is somewhat comforting for the historian to follow a point made by Bachrach that, despite their agendas, "writers had to be aware of writing things that would have stood out to readers or audience as blatantly incorrect."[217]

Unfortunately, historical accounts written by those on the receiving end of the conversion process have never been found and likely never existed. Pagans of the Germanic world were inheritors of an oral tradition, and in the Early Middle Ages, control and production of written knowledge was the sole purview of Church scholars.[218] Therefore, as with any historical inquiry, in analyzing the conversion process, we must remember who is telling the story and from what perspective. This holds equally true for historians who have guided subsequent interpretations of these accounts. The conversion of so-called barbarians has often been presented within the framework of linear "providential history," in which the redemption of pagan souls (by whatever means) is seen as part of God's divine plan.[219] Furthermore, the destruction of paganism is often relegated as a necessary phase in positivist notions of inevitable progress.[220] Christian civilization is juxtaposed with pagan barbarism. These views replicate missionary accounts and royal chronicles, which are often riddled with dehumanizing language. For example, in the *Chronicle of Fredegar*, the Merovingian king Dagobert refused an alliance with the Slavic pagan king Samo because it wasn't permissible for Christians to go into an alliance with "dogs."[221] That perspective made violence more palatable, but it was incentivized by how Christians interpreted paganism.[222] The gods of pagans were likened to demons (the interpretation of the apostle Paul, Justin Martyr, St. Augustine, Origen, Tertullian, Eusebius, Caesarius of Arles, Porphyry, Martin of Tours, Martin of Braga, Isidore of Seville, etc.), while their practices were Satanic, or at the very least the superstitions of fools who had been duped.[223] These views were not mutually exclusive.[224]

Such notions made dehumanizing pagans easier. In a letter written to Boniface in December 722, Pope Gregory II compared the pagans of Germany to "brute beasts."[225] Writing over a century later, Rudolf of Fulda recalled, "like all German peoples...Saxons were savage by nature, devoted to the devil's service, and adversaries of the true religion."[226] With pagans relegated to barbaric "devil worshippers," it made their suppression a moral imperative.

Since the Merovingian Age, Frankish kings had considered themselves "the elect of God," endowed with a divine mission as earthly representatives of Christ.[227] There was no separation of church and state. Bishops acted as the king's agents, while monasteries and ecclesiastical positions were frequently given as royal endowments or sold to friends and family to extend the influence of those in power.[228] Conversion itself, at least initially, was often a top-down affair.[229] At the same time, the early Church was highly militarized. Ecclesiastical building projects followed conquest, Church property was fortified, abbeys took part in arms manufacturing and the mustering of troops, and bishops went to war (as did, e.g., Bishop

Gewilib of Mainz and his father against the Saxons in the 740s).[230] Even Benedictine monks called themselves *milites Christi*, that is, "soldiers of Christ."[231] It has been suggested that the employment of this term was used metaphorically, merely to denote the spiritual warfare in which monks were engaged (against demonic forces and the temptations of sin).[232] The connection to *spiritual* warfare is undoubtedly valid and can be rooted in various Biblical passages, perhaps most explicitly in Paul's letter to the Ephesians.[233] However, monastic centers simultaneously participated in physical warfare against earthly enemies of Christ, which was a significant component of the grander cosmic war between good and evil.[234]

Theologically, disseminating the Christian message on the ground level was incredibly complex.[235] When missionaries taught Christian doctrine, the substance was often lost, misinterpreted, or confusing. For example, ideas of original sin or repentance were likely foreign to Germanic pagans who had no precedent for the concept of salvation.[236] To use a Colonial parallel, this same challenge faced missionaries in Mexico, where there were no words in Nahua for "sin" or "divine forgiveness."[237] As a result, missionaries had to find ways of communicating their ideology through language and symbols familiar to those they encountered.[238] Critically, they had to find ways of undermining a "world-centric" and "empirical religiosity" in favor of a transitory and transcendent religious outlook emphasizing the afterlife.[239]

The notion of divine reciprocity was seemingly fundamental to Germanic paganisms. Through the appeasement and placation of deities via sacrifices or other ritual observances, practitioners could expect tangible forms of prosperity such as health, fame, fertility, or wealth.[240] Missionaries, therefore, needed to show pagans the prosperity of Christians in the present world *and* the benefits of salvation in the next. This was typically done by comparing Christian societies' power and technological or economic success to the supposed backwardness and vulnerability of pagan ones.[241]

The Church also offered alienated or vulnerable members of society a place of belonging, the promise of salvation, and equal status before God that ignored class and gender distinctions.[242] Nevertheless, many pagans were unwilling to give up ancestral traditions, and even fewer were prepared to abandon them altogether. Missionaries were forced to allow some accommodations, a strategy that even a hardliner like Boniface supported when other methods failed. The consequence of these accommodations was a dynamic religious syncretism in which pagan and Christian elements fused.[243]

Despite residual paganism and syncretic developments, the foundations of the early German Church were firmly in place by the late eighth century. At that point, an extensive ecclesiastical network had formed across Western Europe. However, while missionaries made substantial progress among Franks, Bavarians, Alamannians, and Thuringians, significant segments in Frisia and most Saxons remained stubbornly pagan. That pagan conservatism was fundamentally coupled with their political independence, an observation readily apparent to Charlemagne in the 770s as he set out to prove himself an empire-builder and defender of the Church.

Contrary to a hypothesis proposed by Yitzhak Hen that Charlemagne's Saxon conversion efforts replicated lessons learned from Islamic expansion (or Jihad), there already existed a long history of "structural violence" associated with Christianization in the west.[244] Charles had no need to look to the successors of the Prophet for guidance.[245] Romans, missionaries, Germanic warlords, and Charles's ancestors provided enough examples to draw from.[246] And if there were still doubts, Charles could always reference the Bible, where stories like Joshua's destruction of Jericho established precedents for "righteous conquest."[247] Encouragement and affirmation of Charlemagne by popes, bishops, and court scholars also served as positive reinforcement.[248] For some of these, Charles was the new king "David," the warlord of the Israelites whose son Solomon was responsible for building the temple in Jerusalem.[249] Charles had no qualms with that comparison, but he was also fond of likening himself to Josiah, another Jewish king known for his reforms and ruthless destruction of idolatry.[250]

Notes

1 Wallace-Hadrill, *The Frankish Church*, 143. From *The Frankish Church*, © J. M. Wallace-Hadrill. 1983. Reproduced with the permission of Oxford Publishing Ltd. through PLS Clear.

2 Matthew 28: 19–20 & Mark 16: 15–16, see Coogan et al., *The New Oxford Annotated Bible with Apocrypha*, 1790; Kee, "From the Jesus Movement toward Institutional Church," 55; Heather, *Christendom*, 47 & Gibbons, *The History of the Decline and Fall of the Roman Empire*, 142

3 Lipscomb et al., *A History of Magic, Witchcraft and the Occult*, 44 & Cusack, *Conversion among the Germanic Peoples*, 30–31

4 Rives, "Human Sacrifice among Pagans and Christians," 65–66; Backman, *The Worlds of Medieval Europe*, 34–36 & Steffen, "Religion and Violence in Christian Traditions," 103

5 Cantor, *The Civilization of the Middle Ages*, 48–49; Armstrong, *Fields of Blood*, 153. Peter Heather has argued that Constantine may have already been Christian or a Solar monotheist before Milvian Bridge and his conversion was a gradual process of coming out when it was politically safe to do so. See Heather, *Christendom*, 10–19

6 Including tax exemptions, land grants, commodity donations, and clerical privileges. See MacMullen, *Christianizing the Roman Empire*, 49; Jacoby, *Strange Gods*, 40 & Heather, *Christendom*, 88

7 Fletcher, *The Conversion of Europe*, 38; Wickham, *The Inheritance of Rome*, 52 & Halsall, *Barbarian Migrations and the Roman West*, 100

8 Pounds, *An Historical Geography of Europe*, 169 & Hillgarth, *Christianity and Paganism*, 45 & 47–49

9 Wood, *The Missionary Life*, 7 & Bachrach, *Warfare in Medieval Europe*, 98

10 Wolfram, *The Roman Empire and Its Germanic Peoples*, 75–76; Gibbs, *Medieval German Literature*, 23; Schäferdiek, "Germanic and Celtic Christianities," 53 & Heather, *Christendom*, 172–178

11 Russell, *The Germanization of Early Medieval Christianity*, 138; Wolfram, *The Roman Empire and its Germanic Peoples*, 309; Brennecke, "Deconstruction of the So-called Germanic Arianism," 121–123 & Heather, Christendom, 26 & 35 & 158

12 Baldoli, *A History of Italy*, 14 & König, *The Germanic Languages*, 20

13 Brown, "The Transformation of the Roman Mediterranean," 8

14 Brennecke, "Deconstruction of the So-called Germanic Arianism," 119; Schäferdiek, "Germanic and Celtic Christianities," 58–59 & Heather, *Christendom*, 198

15 Geary, *Before France and Germany*, 177

16 Wood, "Pagan Religion and Superstitions East of the Rhine," 264

17 Riche, *Daily Life in the World of Charlemagne*, 273–274; Wallace-Hadrill, *The Frankish Church*, 93; Cosman, *Medieval Wordbook*, 20 & Bremmer, "Changing Perspectives of a Saint's Life," 201

18 Noble, "Carolingian Religion," 304–306; Newman, *Daily Life in the Middle Ages*, 60–61; Backman, *The Worlds of Medieval Europe*, 147 & Shinners, *Medieval Popular Religion*, 157

19 Sypeck, *Becoming Charlemagne*, 33–34; Nees, *Early Medieval Art*, 146–147 & 187; Cosman, *Medieval Wordbook*, 29 & McManners, "Introduction," 11–13

20 Reuter, *Germany in the Early Middle Ages*, 41 & Jolly, *Popular Religion in Late Saxon England*, 28

21 Noble, *Charlemagne and Louis the Pious*, 125. Republished with the permission of The Pennsylvania State University Press, from *Charlemagne and Louis the Pious: Lives by Einhard, Notker, Ermoldus, Thegan, and the Astronomer*, Thomas Noble, © 2009; permission conveyed through Copyright Clearance Center, Inc.

22 Filotas, *Pagan Survivals*, 148–149

23 Lindenfeld, *World Christianity and Indigenous Experience*, 39–40 & 100–101

24 Riche, *Daily Life in the World of Charlemagne*, 241–243

25 These illuminated manuscripts became a significant component of why historians designate the period as a "renaissance" and were crucial in preserving our historical knowledge. See Costambeys, *The Carolingian World*, 4; Gallee, *Old-Saxon Texts*, XLVII; Reinhardt, *Germany 2000 Years V.I*, 53; Nees, *Early Medieval Art*, 224 & Cantor, *The Civilization of the Middle Ages*, 190–191

26 Divorce was forbidden unless one could prove adultery. Birth control, abortion, and infanticide were explicitly condemned, although such practices remained common. Likewise, homosexuality, incest, bestiality, and masturbation were all incompatible with Christian life. Rape was also condemned, as protecting women's honor was fundamental to preserving social order. See Riche, *Daily Life in the World of Charlemagne*, 53; Geary, *Before France and Germany*, 107; Goetz, *Life in the Middle Ages*, 51; Butt, *Daily Life in the Age of Charlemagne*, 59; Rampton, *European Magic and Witchcraft*, 142–143; Wemple, *Women in Frankish Society*, 41 & Drew, *The Laws of the Salian Franks*, 80 & 157

27 Ibid. 87

28 Riche, *Daily Life in the World of Charlemagne*, 26–28 & Blair, "Overview," 728–729

29 Noble, "Carolingian Religion," 300–302 & Jolly, *Popular Religion in Late Saxon England*, 9

30 Wallace-Hadrill, *The Frankish Church*, 31

31 Milis, *The Pagan Middle Ages*, 23 & Wallace-Hadrill, *The Frankish Church*, 32–33

32 Wood, "Pre-Christian Religion in Thuringia and Bavaria," 324

33 Emerton, *The Letters of Saint Boniface*, 91–94

34 Geary, *Before France and Germany*, 135 & Backman, *The Worlds of Medieval Europe*, 75

35 Baer, "History and Religious Conversion," 25–27

36 Lindenfeld, *World Christianity and Indigenous Experience*, 22–23

37 Cantor, *The Civilization of the Middle Ages*, 118; Geary, *Before France and Germany*, 32; Backman, *The Worlds of Medieval Europe*, 71–72 & 204–205 & Wallace-Hadrill, *The Frankish Church*, 29

38 Welch, "Pre-Christian Practices in the Anglo-Saxon World," 864 & Filotas, *Pagan Survivals*, 19

39 Cantor, *The Civilization of the Middle Ages*, 145

40 Wood, *The Merovingian Kingdoms*, 74 & Farmer, *The Oxford Dictionary of Saints*, 45
41 Effros, "De Partitiones Saxoniae," 275; Appleby, "Spiritual Progress in Carolingian Saxony," 603–604; Jolly, *Popular Religion in Late Saxon England*, 27 & Lindenfeld, *World Christianity and Indigenous Experience*, 36
42 Farmer, *The Oxford Dictionary of Saints*, 99–100
43 Arblaster, *A History of the Low Countries*, 28–30; Raaijmakers, *The Making of the Monastic Community of Fulda*, 139–140 & Bitel, "Gender and the Initial Christianization of Northern Europe," 418
44 Geary, *Before France and Germany*, 170–171 & Wood, "Religion in Pre-Carolingian Thuringia and Bavaria," 319
45 Davidson, *Myths and Symbols in Pagan Europe*, 44
46 Fletcher, *The Conversion of Europe*, 95–96
47 Bachrach, *Warfare in Medieval Europe*, 19
48 Rampton, *European Magic and Witchcraft*, 61–66 & 110–112 & Raiswell & Winter, *The Medieval Devil*, 110
49 Wickham, *The Inheritance of Rome*, 176 & Farmer, *The Oxford Dictionary of Saints*, 144
50 Russell, *The Germanization of Early Medieval Christianity*, 159
51 Farmer, *The Oxford Dictionary of Saints*, 144
52 Payne, *English Medicine in the Anglo-Saxon Times*, 112–113 & Filotas, *Pagan Survivals*, 254
53 Drew, *The Laws of the Salian Franks*, 171
54 Costambeys, *The Carolingian World*, 80. Similar observations were made earlier by Caesarius of Arles. See Filotas, *Pagan Survivals*, 226–227 & 251–252
55 Green, *The Carolingian Lord*, 224 & Raiswell & Winter, *The Medieval Devil*, 121
56 Farmer, *The Oxford Dictionary of Saints*, 387
57 His body was interred at Freising Cathedral, where he is venerated as a saint.
58 Farmer, *The Oxford Dictionary of Saints*, 255 & Warner, *Ottonian Germany*, 70
59 Oman, *The Dark Ages*, 208
60 Wood, *The Merovingian Kingdoms*, 312
61 Ring, *Northern Europe*, 809
62 Mackay, *Atlas of Medieval Europe*, 44 & Farmer, *The Oxford Dictionary of Saints*, 362
63 Fletcher, *The Conversion of Europe*, 202–203
64 Sullivan, "The Carolingian Missionary and the Pagan," 707–708
65 Reuter, *Germany in the Early Middle Ages*, 60
66 Farmer, *The Oxford Dictionary of Saints*, 16
67 Arblaster, *A History of the Low Countries*, 30; Geary, *Before France and Germany*, 177 & McKitterick, *History and Memory in the Carolingian World*, 210
68 Fletcher, *The Conversion of Europe*, 139
69 Ibid. 152
70 Mackay, *Atlas of Medieval Europe*, 38
71 Brooks, "The Social and Political Background," 5 & Heather, *Christendom*, 263
72 Wells, *Barbarians to Angels*, 39; Durant, *The Age of Faith*, 522 & Heather, *Christendom*, 238
73 Crossley-Holland, *The Anglo-Saxon World*, 156–157
74 Ibid.
75 Bede, *Ecclesiastical History of the English People*, 94
76 Ibid. 113
77 Swanton, *The Anglo-Saxon Chronicle*, 27
78 Algeo, *The Origins and Development of the English Language*, 92
79 Bede, *Ecclesiastical History of the English People*, 120–124
80 Ibid.
81 Ibid. 122

82 Ibid. 129–131
83 Durant, *The Age of Faith*, 534 & James, "The Northern World in the Dark Ages," 78–79
84 Bede, *Ecclesiastical History of the English People*, 132–133. This type of adhesion could be interpreted as cautiously "having one foot on each side"; see Baer, "History and Religious Conversion," 28
85 Ibid.
86 Ibid. 144–155
87 Wickham, *The Inheritance of Rome*, 161
88 Backman, *The Worlds of Medieval Europe*, 109
89 Wickham, *The Inheritance of Rome*, 171
90 Blair, "The Anglo-Saxon Period," 66–72
91 Talbot, *The Anglo-Saxon Missionaries in Germany*, xv
92 Arblaster, *A History of the Low Countries*, 31–33 & Geary, *Before France and Germany*, 214–215
93 Wood, *The Missionary Life*, 43–44; Cantor, *The Civilization of the Middle Ages*, 166–167. The notion of converting people based on ancestral ties has parallels in the Colonial era. For example, when African-Americans settled in Liberia following centuries of being enmeshed in Western cultural and religious ideas, they were horrified by the "heathen" customs of Liberian natives and earnestly attempted to root them out. See Lindenfeld, *World Christianity and Indigenous Experience*, 27
94 Farmer, *The Oxford Dictionary of Saints*, 141 & 447–448 & Palmer, "The 'Vigorous Rule' of Bishop Lull," 269
95 Wallace-Hadrill, *The Frankish Church*, 144–145
96 Bede, *Ecclesiastical History of the English People*, 304
97 Later in life, Wigbert accompanied St. Boniface and had better results. See Talbot, *The Anglo-Saxon Missionaries in Germany*, 69; Emerton, *The Letters of Saint Boniface*, 40 & Farmer, *The Oxford Dictionary of Saints*, 447
98 Although educated in Ireland, the Hewalds were both Northumbrian.
99 Bede, *Ecclesiastical History of the English People*, 281
100 Schäferdiek has noted that, given the proximity of Westphalians to the Franks, it seems unlikely the Saxons would not have quickly recognized the religious affiliation of the Hewalds. See Schäferdiek, "Der Schwarze und der Weiße Hewald," 12
101 Bede, *Ecclesiastical History of the English People*, 281
102 Ibid. 282 & Schäferdiek, "Der Schwarze und der Weiße Hewald," 12
103 Nelson, *King and Emperor*, 39 & Farmer, *The Oxford Dictionary of Saints*, 209
104 This was famously the conclusion of the 1555 Peace of Augsburg and the 1648 Peace of Westphalia. See Nees, *Early Medieval Art*, 217; Reinhardt, *Germany: 2000 Years V.I*, 212 & Armstrong, *Fields of Blood*, 264
105 Talbot, *The Anglo-Saxon Missionaries in Germany*, 7 & Nyberg, *Monasticism in North-Western Europe*, 7–8
106 Durant, *The Age of Faith*, 534 & Wallace-Hadrill, *The Frankish Church*, 145–146
107 Wallace-Hadrill, *The Fourth Book of the Chronicle of Fredegar*, 86
108 Arblaster, *A History of the Low Countries*, 31–33 & Oman, *The Dark Ages*, 208
109 Ibid. 32 & Cusack, "Between Sea and Land," 7–8
110 This fear is common in the global history of missions. For example, natives in the Peruvian Andes tried to persuade missionaries to baptize their dead pagan ancestors so that they would be able to go to Heaven. See Gose, "Converting the Ancestors," 165. Similarly, Huron Indians told Jesuit missionaries that they had no interest in going to Heaven because they didn't know anyone there. See Taylor, *American Colonies*, 111
111 Geary, *Before France and Germany*, 215
112 Bede, *Ecclesiastical History of the English People*, 280–284
113 Ibid. & Farmer, *The Oxford Dictionary of Saints*, 452
114 Wallace-Hadrill has suggested Echternach may have been meant for missionary penetration into Saxony; see Wallace-Hadrill, *The Frankish Church*, 145–146

115 Fletcher, *The Conversion of Europe*, 201–202
116 Ibid.
117 Wood, *The Merovingian Kingdoms*, 161; Nelson, *King and Emperor*, 39 & Jellema, "Frisian Trade in the Dark Ages," 17
118 Talbot, *The Anglo-Saxon Missionaries in Germany*, 9
119 Fletcher, *The Conversion of Europe*, 199–204
120 Sullivan, "The Carolingian Missionary and the Pagan," 721
121 Noble, *Soldiers of Christ*, 200
122 Talbot, *The Anglo-Saxon Missionaries in Germany*, 10–11
123 Ibid. 12–13 & Simek, "Continental Germanic Religion," 293
124 Noble, *Soldiers of Christ*, 201
125 Wood, *The Missionary Life*, 84
126 Noble, *Soldiers of Christ*, 202
127 Nelson, *King and Emperor*, 45
128 Sullivan, "The Carolingian Missionary and the Pagan," 728
129 Arblaster, *A History of the Low Countries*, 32
130 Altet, *The Early Middle Ages*, 140 & Raaijmakers, *The Making of the Monastic Community of Fulda*, 45
131 Durant, *The Age of Faith*, 535
132 Raaijmakers, *The Making of the Monastic Community of Fulda*, 19
133 Cathey, *Heliand*, 7–8
134 Willibald, *The Life of Saint Boniface*, 43–44
135 Fletcher, *The Conversion of Europe*, 205–206
136 Talbot, *The Anglo-Saxon Missionaries in Germany*, 35 & Willibald, *The Life of Saint Boniface*, 44
137 Ibid. 36
138 Ibid. 41 & Willibald, *The Life of Saint Boniface*, 52–53
139 Ibid. 39 & Willibald, *The Life of Saint Boniface*, 51
140 Ibid. 68 & Davis, *The Lives of the Eighth-Century Popes*, 4
141 Ibid. 40–41
142 Ibid. 42
143 Schlesinger, "Early Medieval Fortifications in Hesse," 243–244 & Willibald, *The Life of Saint Boniface*, 57
144 Geary, *Before France and Germany*, 215–216
145 Talbot, *The Anglo-Saxon Missionaries in Germany*, 74–75 & Emerton, *The Letters of Saint Boniface*, 45
146 Raaijmakers, *The Making of the Monastic Community of Fulda*, 23
147 Russell, *The Germanization of Early Medieval Christianity*, 197; Milis, *The Pagan Middle Ages*, 23 & Cantor, *The Civilization of the Middle Ages*, 168
148 Oman, *The Dark Ages*, 373
149 Raaijmakers, *The Making of the Monastic Community of Fulda*, 23–24
150 Emerton, *The Letters of Saint Boniface*, 47
151 Palmer, "The 'Vigorous Rule' of Bishop Lull," 256
152 Murphy, *The Saxon Savior*, 14 & Emerton, *The Letters of Saint Boniface*, 52–53
153 Talbot, *The Anglo-Saxon Missionaries in Germany*, 45 & Willibald, *The Life of Saint Boniface*, 63–64
154 "Donar's Oak" was technically "Jupiter's Oak" (*rubor jovis*); however, Jupiter is generally taken to be the Latin approximation of Donar (Thor). See Simek, *Dictionary of Northern Mythology*, 238; Reuter, *Germany in the Early Middle Ages*, 62 & Cathey, *Old Saxon*, 10
155 Farmer, *The Oxford Dictionary of Saints*, 56–57 & Youngs, "A Transcript of Submission," 4
156 Willibald, *The Life of Saint Boniface*, 63–64
157 Cusack, *Pagan Saxon Resistance to Charlemagne's Mission*, 41 & 44
158 Cathey, *Heliand*, 7–8 & Rambo, *Understanding Religious Conversion*, 77

159 Wood, *The Merovingian Kingdoms*, 310

160 Tschan, *A History of the Archbishops of Hamburg-Bremen*, 12–13

161 Emerton, *The Letters of Saint Boniface*, 48–50

162 Talbot, *The Anglo-Saxon Missionaries in Germany*, 76–78; Sullivan, "Early Medieval Missionary Activity," 24 & 28–29 & Heather, *Christendom*, 255

163 Ibid.

164 Sullivan, "Carolingian Missionary Theories," 273–278 & Riche, *Daily Life in the World of Charlemagne*, 200

165 Ibid.

166 Ibid. 291–292

167 Wood, *The Merovingian Kingdoms*, 305–306

168 Reuter, *Germany in the Early Middle Ages*, 57

169 Emerton, *The Letters of Saint Boniface*, 58–59

170 Costambeys, *The Carolingian World*, 48–49

171 Riche, *The Carolingians*, 20–22 & Oman, *The Dark Ages*, 234

172 Emerton, *The Letters of Saint Boniface*, 74–75

173 Ibid. 75–76

174 Ibid. 69–70

175 Ibid 71–74

176 Ibid. 45–47. From *The Letters of St. Boniface*, Ephraim Emerton, © 1940 Columbia University Press. Reprinted with permission of Columbia University Press.

177 Honselmann, "Die Annahme des Christentums durch die Sachsen," 201–203

178 Fletcher, *The Conversion of Europe*, 205–207 & Raaijmakers, *The Making of the Monastic Community of Fulda*, 26–27

179 Verhulst, *The Carolingian Economy*, 43; Bachrach, *Warfare in Medieval Europe*, 108 & Raaijmakers, *The Making of the Monastic Community of Fulda*, 3 & 27–29 & 204–205

180 Reinhardt, *Germany 2000 Years V.I*, 56 & Durant, *The Age of Faith*, 564

181 Fletcher, *The Conversion of Europe*, 207 & Talbot, *The Anglo-Saxon Missionaries in Germany*, 136

182 Reuter, *Germany in the Early Middle Ages*, 61–63

183 Raaijmakers, *The Making of the Monastic Community of Fulda*, 24 & Parsons, "Some Churches of the Anglo-Saxon missionaries in Southern Germany," 33–34

184 Ibid. 66; Farmer, *The Oxford Dictionary of Saints*, 273; Wemple, *Women in Frankish Society*, 177 & 182 & Thiebaux, *The Writings of Medieval Women*, 142–143

185 Bitel, "Gender and the Initial Christianization of Northern Europe," 425–426 & Thiebaux, *The Writings of Medieval Women*, 143. Another influential Anglo-Saxon woman connected to Boniface was Walpurga, the later abbess of Hildesheim. See Farmer, *The Oxford Dictionary of Saints*, 441

186 Cathey, "The Historical Setting of the *Heliand*," 9

187 Cathey, *Heliand*, 7–8

188 Talbot, *The Anglo-Saxon Missionaries in Germany*, 55 & Willibald, *The Life of Saint Boniface*, 80–81

189 Ibid.

190 Ibid. 56–57

191 Willibald, *The Life of Saint Boniface*, 81–86. The raiders ransacked their goods but were disappointed to find manuscripts instead of gold.

192 Tschan, *A History of the Archbishops of Hamburg-Bremen*, 13 & Scholz, *Carolingian Chronicles*, 40

193 Mackay, *Atlas of Medieval Europe*, 65 & Raaijmakers, *The Making of the Monastic Community of Fulda*, 40

194 Sypeck, *Becoming Charlemagne*, 55 & Riche, *The Carolingians*, 75

195 Arblaster, *A History of the Low Countries*, 31–33; Raaijmakers, *The Making of the Monastic Community of Fulda*, 44–45 & Willibald, *The Life of Saint Boniface*, 90–93

196 Reinhardt, *Germany 2000 Years V.I*, 37; Fletcher, *The Conversion of Europe*, 212 & Thiebaux, *The Writings of Medieval Women*, 145

197 Talbot, *The Anglo-Saxon Missionaries in Germany*, 58

198 Willibald, *The Life of Saint Boniface*, 86–87

199 Stofferahn, "Staying the Royal Sword," 462

200 Talbot, *The Anglo-Saxon Missionaries in Germany*, 153–177 & Farmer, *The Oxford Dictionary of Saints*, 452

201 Wood, *The Merovingian Kingdoms*, 309

202 Sullivan, "The Carolingian Missionary and the Pagan," 707–708

203 Wood, *The Merovingian Kingdoms*, 307–308

204 Ibid.

205 Riche, *The Carolingians*, 54–55 & Raaijmakers, *The Making of the Monastic Community of Fulda*, 36–37

206 Rampton, *European Magic and Witchcraft*, 129

207 Farmer, *The Oxford Dictionary of Saints*, 449

208 Tschan, *History of the Archbishops of Hamburg-Bremen*, 13

209 Sullivan, "The Carolingian Missionary and the Pagan," 718

210 Tschan, *History of the Archbishops of Hamburg-Bremen*, 13–14

211 Wood, *The Missionary Life*, 80–86

212 Talbot, *The Anglo-Saxon Missionaries in Germany*, 229

213 Goldberg, *The Saxons Stellinga Reconsidered*, 474

214 Wood, *The Missionary Life*, 115 & Ring, *Northern Europe*, 207

215 Fletcher, *The Conversion of Europe*, 10 & Halsall, "The Sources and Their Interpretation," 68

216 Palmer, "Defining Paganism in the Carolingian World," 405; Geary, *Before France and Germany*, 176; Kling, *A History of Christian Conversion*, 106; Cantor, *The Civilization of the Middle Ages*, 53 & Lapidge, "The Saintly life in Anglo-Saxon England," 260–261

217 Bachrach, *Warfare in Medieval Europe*, 11

218 Arblaster, *A History of the Low Countries*, 28–30 & Durant, *The Age of Faith*, 94

219 Rundnagel, "Der Mythos vom Herzog Widukind," 498–501; Wolfram, *History of the Goths*, 4; Cantor, *The Civilization of the Middle Ages*, 77–78 & Cusack, *Conversion among the Germanic Peoples*, 2

220 Jolly, *Popular Religion in Late Saxon England*, 38

221 Barford, *The Early Slavs*, 212 & Pohl, *The Avars*, 308

222 Ferguson, *The Vikings*, 51

223 Jolly, *Popular Religion in Late Saxon England*, 73; Chadwick, "The Early Christian Community," 40; Frenschkowski, "Witchcraft, Magic and Demonology in the Bible," 23–24; Lipscolmb et al., *A History of Magic, Witchcraft and the Occult*, 102 & 47–48; Hillgarth, *Christianity and Paganism*, 57–64; Rampton, *European Magic and Witchcraft*, 36–38 & 67–79, & 84 & 89–96 & 98–102 & 113–118; MacMullen, *Christianizing the Roman Empire*, 17–18; Raiswell & Winter, *The Medieval Devil*, 84–87 & 111 & Gibbon, *The History of the Decline and Fall of the Roman Empire*, 134–135

224 These interpretations lasted well into the Colonial era and were utilized against indigenous peoples worldwide. See Kling, *A History of Christian Conversion*, 325, 336–337; Gooren, "Anthropology of Religious Conversion," 92 & Lindenfeld, *World Christianity and Indigenous Experience*, 19

225 Emerton, *The Letters of Saint Boniface*, 42–43 & Talbot, *The Anglo-Saxon Missionaries in Germany*, 71

226 The English translation is my own; however, it is based on the German edition by Wilhelm Wattenbach. See Wattenbach, *Die Übertragung des hl. Alexander von Rudolf und Meginhart*, 8

227 Ibid. 5–6

228 Ibid. 20–22

229 Heather, *Christendom*, 244

230 Fletcher, *The Conversion of Europe*, 190; Parsons, "Some Churches of the Anglo-Saxon Missionaries in Southern Germany," 31; Verhulst, *The Carolingian Economy*, 78; Raaijmakers, *The Making of the Monastic Community of Fulda*, 53 & 266; Milis, *The Pagan Middle Ages*, 26; Emerton, *The Letters of Boniface*, 92–93 & Bachrach, *Charlemagne's Early Campaigns (768–777)*, 224–225 & *Warfare in Medieval Europe*, 107

231 Backman, *The Worlds of Medieval Europe*, 99; Goetz, *Life in the Middle Ages*, 105; Wemple, *Women in Frankish Society*, 166; & Bremmer, "Changing Perspectives on a Saint's Life," 204

232 Green, *The Carolingian Lord*, 323. Occasionally, such as in Cynewulf's heroic Old English *Juliana* poem, conflict between a saint and the devil could involve physical combat. See Bremmer, "Changing Perspectives on a Saint's Life," 210 & Frederick, "Warring with Words," 71

233 Ephesians 6: 11–17. See Coogan et al., *The New Oxford Annotated Bible with Apocrypha*, 2059–2060; Armstrong, *Fields of Blood*, 204–205 & Kelly, *The Devil at Baptism*, 22–23

234 For example, the Frankish civil war of the 830s between Louis the Pious and his sons was sometimes interpreted as the direct result of the devil's machinations. See De Jong, *The Penitential State*, 260

235 Russell, *The Germanization of Early Medieval Christianity*, 197 & 201

236 Ibid. 27 & 33; Sullivan, "Carolingian Missionary Theories," 288 & Cathey, *Old Saxon*, 4

237 Lindenfeld, *World Christianity and Indigenous Experience*, 37

238 Kling, *A History of Christian Conversion*, 109

239 Cathey, *Heliand*, 12–13; Chadwick, "The Early Christian Community," 60; Fletcher, *The Conversion of Europe*, 6–7 & Hefner, "Introduction," 8

240 Ibid.

241 This method was used in subsequent conversion efforts around the globe. For an amusing example in later Saxon folklore, see "The Lost Sketch-Book of the Bergenstein Chapel" in Lauder, *Legends and Tales of the Harz Mountains*, 35–36 & see also Russell, *The Germanization of Early Medieval Christianity*, 23–24 & Lindenfeld, *World Christianity and Indigenous Experience*, 15–16

242 Kling, *A History of Christian Conversion*, 104 & 127; Schäferdiek, "Der Schwarze und der Weiße Hewald,"21 & Cusack, *Conversion among the Germanic Peoples*, 18–20

243 Russell, *The Germanization of Early Medieval Christianity*, 38; Wallace-Hadrill, *The Frankish Church*, 17; Milis, *The Pagan Middle Ages*, 14 & 55; Filotas, *Pagan Survivals*, 9; Cusack, *Conversion among the Germanic Peoples*, 20–21 & Reinhardt, *Germany 2000 Years V.I*, 30–31

244 König, "Charlemagne's 'Jihad' Revisited," 33

245 Nelson, "Religion and Politics in the Reign of Charlemagne," 23–26

246 *The Chronicle of Fredegar* claims Charles Martel conquered by the power of Christ alone, and his son Pippin's conquests were divinely granted; see Wallace-Hadrill, *The Fourth Book of the Chronicle of Fredegar*, 95 & 116

247 Coogan et al., *The New Oxford Annotated Bible with Apocrypha*, 321–354; Kling, *A History of Christian Conversion*, 165; Steffen, "Religion and Violence in Christian Traditions," 104–106 & Armstrong, *Fields of Blood*, 110

248 Dessens, *Res Voluntaria, Non Necessaria*, 3 & 49 & 51

249 Coogan et al., *The New Oxford Annotated Bible with Apocrypha*, 455–456; Butt, *Daily Life in the Age of Charlemagne*, 21; Armstrong, *Fields of Blood*, 118 & see the poem by Theodulf in Godman, *Poetry of the Carolingian Renaissance*, 151

250 Mayr-Harting, "The West," 101 & De Jong, *The Penitential State*, 17

Part II

Charlemagne's Saxon Wars

6 The Makings of a Crusade, 772–777

Historians have long debated the cause of Charlemagne's Saxon Wars, the primary difficulty being that it is challenging to disentangle what we know occurred later in the conflict from the intentions that initiated it.[1] In addition, we have primarily the perspectives of Frankish elites and partisans, making any understanding of the Saxon point of view difficult to surmise.[2] While a *casus belli* could always be conveniently manufactured, there are several possible motivations to consider, including Saxon expansion, a growing impatience with raids on Frankish settlements, the protection of frontier churches, a desire to reimpose tribute upon a treasonous people, the necessity of collecting loot to appease retainers, strategic interest in trade routes (e.g., the *Helweg* and Rhine), and access to natural resources in the Saxony (notably in the Harz Mountains).[3] It may also be that Charlemagne was simply following in the footsteps of his ancestors, who had engaged Saxons in violent clashes for generations.[4] After all, Franco-Saxon feuding, to some degree, had been going on for nearly 300 years.[5]

Some scholars have also portrayed Charlemagne's initial invasion of Saxony as a simple border retaliation. However, there are practical considerations that dispute this. As Bachrach has noted, the scale of Charles' campaign would have required intensive logistical planning, including the mobilization of troops, preparation of food and repair supplies, reconnaissance and scouting of Saxon terrain and strongholds, as well as establishing an invasion route that could be resupplied and provide lodging for the royal entourage.[6] These considerations suggest that planning the invasion of Saxony began in 771, possibly in the Fall, when it became apparent that Charles' brother Carloman was no longer a threat.

The invasion may have also been motivated by a desire to bring the Saxons within Christendom. The Saxon monk, Widukind of Corvey, held this view, stating that Charlemagne, in his wisdom, did not think it right to allow such a noble people (Saxons) to be "bound by vain error [i.e., paganism]."[7] Abbot Egil of Fulda more explicitly voiced the same sentiment:

> After the king reigned prosperously for four years he began to consider how he might gain the Saxon people to Christ…He took counsel with the servants of God and asked them to pray that the Lord would grant his desire. Then he gathered together a mighty army, placed it under the patronage of Christ, and

DOI: 10.4324/9781003379157-9

accompanied by bishops, abbots, and priests and all true believers, set out for Saxony. His purpose was to bring this people, which had been fettered from the beginning with the devil's bonds, to accept the faith and to submit to the mild and sweet yoke of Christ.[8]

However, the most famous primary source account of Charlemagne's motives for the Saxon Wars undoubtedly comes from Charlemagne's biographer Einhard, who demonstrates the multifaceted nature of conflict and its origins:

> No war ever undertaken by the Frank nation was carried on with such persistence and bitterness, or cost so much labor, because the Saxons, like almost all the tribes of Germany, were a fierce people, given to the worship of devils, and hostile to our religion, and did not consider it dishonorable to transgress and violate all law, human and divine. Then there were peculiar circumstances that tended to cause a breach of peace every day. Except in a few places, where large forests or mountain ridges intervened and made the bounds certain, the line between ourselves and the Saxons passed almost in its whole extent through an open country, so that there was no end to the murders, thefts, and arsons on both sides. In this way the Franks became so embittered that they at last resolved to make reprisals no longer, but to come to open war with the Saxons.[9]

It seems highly likely that economic, religious, military, historical, and personal motivations all factored in the king's decision to wage war against the Saxons. In addition, Egil, Widukind, and Einhard's accounts make Charles' conversion impulse seem considerably important. As we saw in the previous chapter, such an impulse was by no means an aberration from prior Frankish policy.[10] Nevertheless, it should be noted that the idea of conversion as an *early* contributor to Charles' campaign has been called into question. Some scholars attribute it to being nothing more than the emphasis of later hagiography.[11] Yet, if that is the case, it is a very repetitive notion, and the religious overtones of the conflict are certainly replicated in several chronicles from a very early date.[12] If the war was not about conversion at the outset, it quickly became a significant factor soon after.

Perhaps Charles also wanted to break the cycles of history. As Oman has noted, the Saxon's "obstinate paganism and unconquerable courage had baffled ten generations of Frankish missionaries and kings."[13] Could such a precedent be challenged? Whatever the motivation, Charles would try. With the benefit of hindsight, it seems all the young king needed was a viable pretext for opening hostilities, and shortly after the death of his brother Carloman, he had one.[14]

An Unusual Assembly: Deventer, Lebuinus, and Marklo

We left Lebuinus in the previous chapter preaching among the Saxons and doing so with support from some of the local nobility.[15] The source material indicates that he was, all things considered, beginning to have success garnering conversions in the region. However, while Lebuinus had cause to rejoice, local pagans were getting worried. As their kin turned away from the old gods and began embracing a new one, resentment festered, resulting in a band of Saxons formulating a plan to be rid of Lebuinus for good.

The attack came in January 772, when a Saxon war-band crossed into the Dutch province of Overijssel and headed toward Deventer. It is unclear if Lebuinus and his companions caught wind of the incoming threat or if they were still in the area when the Saxons arrived. However, we do know that Lebuinus fled and sought refuge in Utrecht.[16] In the meantime, the Saxons were left disappointed that their prey had escaped and settled on sacking and burning his church at Deventer.[17] Christians in the area were driven away; it is unclear if any were killed.

After the attack, the Saxons returned home. It would have been unwise to linger at the scene of the crime for long. Word of their arson would reach Lebuinus, and pagan aggression toward a house of God would not sit well with the Christians of Utrecht. Utrecht was no meager outpost on the fringes of Carolingian civilization. Since the late seventh century, the town had served the Franks as a prosperous tolling center and slave market.[18] Even as late as March 769, cartulary evidence demonstrates that Charlemagne confirmed tithing rights for Utrecht's church of St. Martin, whose wealth came from slaves, tolls, and local markets.[19] Given its position as an economic asset and a spiritual center in the region, we can assume that what happened within the vicinity of Utrecht, especially violence, was bound to have repercussions.

According to the *Lebuini vitae*, back in Saxony, the time had come for the annual assembly. We do not know if any of those who participated in the raid on Deventer attended the assembly at Marklo that (allegedly) followed. However, given the potential ramifications of such an act, it is certainly conceivable that the raid was sanctioned by members of the Saxon nobility who opposed the spread of Christianity in the area. If so, some of the participants may have been among the thousands of Saxons gathered on the banks of the Weser. Indeed, discussion of raids and the possibility of war would have been on the assemblies' agenda, and recent news of Deventer may have been on their minds. We can imagine members of the assembly arguing over what occurred and their infinite surprise when Lebuinus himself showed up in the middle of the discussion to give a scolding lecture.

The stubborn missionary had been warned not to go. Upon returning from Utrecht and not long before he arrived at Marklo, Lebuinus was a guest in the hall of a Saxon nobleman named Folcbert. Folcbert and his son Helco, who looked kindly upon Lebuinus, pleaded with him to avoid the Saxon assembly. It was simply too dangerous. Helco was sure that Lebuinus would be dragged away and killed; Folcbert thought his attending suicidal. Their words fell on deaf ears. Lebuinus could not ignore what he felt divinely called to do. He trusted in God for his protection, and off he went.

When Lebuinus arrived at the assembly, the Saxons were gathered in a circle mid-discussion, having just finished offering up prayers to the gods for the well-being of their people. At that moment, the missionary moved into the center of the circle, armed with a cross in hand and a Gospel book underneath his arm.

He called out to the Saxons that he was a messenger of "Almighty God" and had come to bring the Saxons God's message. The Saxons were shocked, and the assembly went quiet, allowing Lebuinus to continue speaking:

> The God of heaven and Ruler of the world and His Son, Jesus Christ, com-
> mands me to tell you that if you are willing to be and to do what His servants
> tell you He will confer benefits upon you such as you have never heard of
> before. Then he added: As you have never had a king over you before this
> time, so no king will prevail against you and subject you to his domina-
> tion. But if you are unwilling to accept God's commands, a king has been
> prepared nearby who will invade your lands, spoil and lay them waste and
> sap away your strength in war; he will lead you into exile, deprive you of
> your inheritance, slay you with the sword, and hand over your possessions
> to whom he has a mind: and afterwards you will be slaves both to him and
> his successors.[20]

In an alternative version of the story, as related by the ninth-century Frankish monk Hucbald of St. Amand, Lebuinus goes on to chastise the Saxons for foolishly believing in gods (under the influence of the Devil) made of stone, wood, brass, and gold.[21]

The Saxons were displeased with having their gods mocked and their lives threatened. One Saxon derided Lebuinus as a "wandering charlatan" who went about "preaching wild, fantastic nonsense," and therefore, a justifiable candidate for being stoned to death.[22] Others agreed and started gathering rocks and sharpen-ing fence stakes. Before they could unleash their fury, a calmer Saxon named Buto intervened and reprimanded the mob with a lesson in hospitality.[23] In the meantime, Lebuinus disappeared from sight.

What are we to make of this? The tale has all the creativity and tell-tale exag-gerations commonly associated with hagiography. We simply do not know how much of it is true. Certain features stand out. Lebuinus' warning to the Saxons of a king who will bring them Christianity by whatever means necessary (and the consequences of that endeavor) has the ring of prophecy in hindsight. The author may have attributed the historical fate he knew to be true of the Saxons into the mouth of Lebuinus to enhance the missionaries' spiritual credentials.[24] At the same time, Lebuinus could have been in contact with Frankish leadership and counted on their support. It is also possible that, following the destruction of his church, Lebuinus voiced a complaint in Utrecht that fell upon sympathetic ears. As noted in the previous chapters, missionary activity in the region was seldom far from Frankish military enforcement.

It may also seem surprising that Lebuinus could attend such a gathering, say what he did, and hope to make it out unscathed. However, if reports concerning the support he gathered among Westphalian nobles are accurate, he might have counted on some of them to be in attendance at the assembly and to speak on his behalf. Indeed, in Hucbald's account, Folcbert's son Helco was planning on attending the assembly, in which case Lebuinus would have had allies present to offer protection.[25] In addition, other powerful Saxon families in Westphalia, notably the Ekbertines (who controlled settlements along the Ems), are believed to have already been Christian and may have had friendly ties with the Frankish royal family.[26] There is also speculation that other Christian Saxon communities had been founded during the Bonifatian period, which means there may have been other unmentioned Christianized Saxon nobles at the assembly.[27] Regardless, Lebuinus returned to Deventer, where he resumed preaching. From the ashes of his old church, he built a new one.[28] In the meantime, the Saxons were left to ponder the missionaries' words and anxiously await the fulfillment of his prophecy.

A Declaration of War

Word must have reached the young Frankish king of what happened at Deventer. The burning of churches within the realm would not go unnoticed. It is unclear exactly when, but probably sometime in the Spring of 772, after the alleged Saxon gathering at Marklo, Charlemagne called an assembly of his own in the Rhenish city of Worms and gathered support for a formal declaration of war against the Saxons.[29] Burning Lebuinus' church at Deventer certainly *could* have been all the excuse needed for opening further hostilities. No one would object to the king assuming his role as "defender of the faith."[30]

It is improbable that those present at Worms anticipated the ferocity and longevity of what was coming. At the outset of war, illusion and romanticism cloud good judgment. Such adventures also often benefited the nobles, many of whom gained recompense for their participation by acquiring loot and land. Meanwhile, ordinary soldiers could prove their loyalty and worth. Honor demanded reprimanding the Saxons because they had tested Frankish resolve and taken advantage of the transition of power. In particular, they were testing the tenacity of the new Frankish king. In that regard, Saxons were not alone. The Franks would also assess their lord and utilize the campaign to gauge his leadership and generosity.[31] Undoubtedly, Charles was aware of being under such scrutiny as he led his army to war.

The War Begins: The Campaign of 772 and the Destruction of the Irminsul

Charles marched north from Worms, making his way into the southern fringes of the Teutoburg Forest and the Saxon region of Engria. Why initiate his campaign from Worms? Bachrach has shown that Frankfurt, Mainz, or Coblenz would have been more obvious choices, the latter leading conveniently through the Frankish fortified valley of the Lahn.[32] However, that route would have also been obvious to the Saxons, making it difficult to conceal, evaporating any element of surprise. Perhaps, cunningly, Charles chose the less obvious route from Worms, which the Saxons were not expecting. That decision would give the Saxons less time to coordinate a response and increase their stronghold garrisons. This is especially true if Bachrach's hypothesis is correct, and Charles' army took the Main-Kinzig route into the vicinity of Fulda and then north to the fortified Frankish area surrounding

Fritzlar.[33] That path provided concealment with the Taunus Mountains and Vogels Gebirge, as well as a steady supply line from the monastic complex of Fulda.[34] From Fritzlar, it would no longer be possible to conceal an invasion of Saxony, but by then, the Saxons would have only a few days to scramble together their defenses. It was a clever ruse built upon systematic intelligence gathering and, if accurate, demonstrates the degree to which Charlemagne was well-prepared.[35]

Eventually, Charles' army arrived in Engria, the Saxon "heartland." Why choose the Saxon interior rather than the closer and more accessible Westphalia? As Robinson has noted, it may be that Charles wanted to drive a wedge between the various Saxon peoples and prevent them from presenting a united defense.[36] However, it could also be that Charles was trying to make amends for historical grievances. The territory south of the *Teutoburger Wald* was once under Frankish control but lost to Saxon conquest in 695.[37] It may also be that the king's primary strategic interest was taking control of the Eresburg because that's where his army headed first.[38]

The Eresburg was an ancient Saxon stronghold situated on a low mountain overlooking the Diemel (a tributary of the Weser).[39] At the base of the mountain, there was likely a village that provided supplies and whose residents could flee to the stronghold when in danger.[40] "Fortified by nature" and enclosed with tall circular walls and ramparts, the Eresburg had repelled enemies before.[41] It is speculated that the fortress dated back to the Germanic Iron Age and once served as a point of resistance against Roman expansion.[42] The Eresburg is just one of many Saxon hill forts we know of, but our sources indicate its strategic importance for maintaining control of the region.

To what extent the Eresburg maintained a full garrison is unclear; however, Bachrach has estimated it would have taken anywhere from 1,600 to 3,000 ablebodied men to properly defend (based on an estimated perimeter of 2,000 meters).[43] That means an army wanting to take the Eresburg by storm would have required a considerable number of troops (at least three to five times the defending force).[44]

According to the *Royal Frankish Annals* (*RFA*), which chronicles events concerning Francia between the years 741 and 829, despite the stronghold's advantageous position, when Charles arrived at the Eresburg, he quickly captured it from the Saxons.[45] It is unclear how difficult the assault on the fortress was or if the Saxons simply abandoned it. However, a later twelfth-century source (Symeon of Durham's *History of Kings*) reports that during the campaign of 772, Charles was forced to retreat after losing many of his leading noblemen.[46] We don't know if the retreat occurred at the Eresburg (or at all), but if it did, the Eresburg seems the most likely candidate to have caused the king trouble. An assault on the fortress would not have been easy, likely requiring catapults, battering rams, and siege ladders.[47] The later fighting of 772 mainly occurred on open ground, where (unless Saxons utilized an ambush) the Franks had military superiority. It is also notable that the 802 *Annales Nordhumbrani*, in contrast to Frankish sources, paints Charlemagne's campaign of 772 as a failure and claims that the king lost many noblemen.[48]

While most of our sources imply that the Eresburg was the primary Frankish target, some conflicting evidence is worth noting. At the outset of the campaign, there is a possibility the Franks also assaulted the Sigiburg (or Syburg), a Westphalian hillfort overlooking the Ruhr, which would have required a minimum of 1,350 warriors to defend.[49] If true, the Franks may have encountered serious resistance there as well. A Frankish attack on the Sigiburg would also mean that it wasn't only Engrians but also Westphalians who were brought into the war at its genesis.[50] Whatever the more accurate chronology of these initial events might be, it is clear that the Franks had taken control of the Eresburg by July or August 772, after which they garrisoned the fortress and made ready for further operations. As for the Saxons, following the capture of their stronghold, they retreated toward the Weser.

In the meantime, Charlemagne avenged the destruction of Lebuinus' church and, with part of his army, headed toward the Irminsul and what may have been the epicenter of Old Saxon paganism. Thietmar of Merseburg (in the eleventh century) claimed the Irminsul stood inside the Eresburg itself, possibly existing under the Church of St. Peter that Charles later had built.[51] However, the site is more likely to have been located within proximity of the stronghold, possibly in the Teutoburg Forest only a few miles away, in the Ebbe Mountains, on the Priesterberg hill in the valley of the Diemel, or (more broadly) on a hill overlooking the headwaters of the Lippe, which could refer to the western slopes of the *Teutoburger Wald* in what is now Bad Lippspringe.[52] If the latter of these scenarios is true, then it would mean the Irminsul stood only a mere six miles from what would become the site of Paderborn, *the* Frankish stronghold in Saxony believed to have been built over a former Saxon settlement that was burned to the ground.[53] While mere speculation, one wonders if there is a connection between the destroyed Saxon settlement and the Irminsul.

While the site's location remains open for debate, most scholars agree on its importance for Saxon religion. Concerning Saxon cosmology, the Irminsul has been called an "axis mundi" (a "world pillar"), denoting the center of the universe and a point of connection between different planes of existence.[54] This was the view of Rudolf of Fulda.[55] In his *Translatio Sancti Alexandri*, Rudolf states:

> They [Saxons] paid divine reverence to springs and dense leafy forests. Yes, they had erected a wooden block of no small size and worshiped it under the open sky; in their native language they called it Irminsul, the pillar that carries the universe; as it were.[56]

We don't know if the Irminsul was *the* most important Saxon cult site; some scholars doubt this.[57] Nevertheless, no other sites associated with Saxon paganism were mentioned by name during the conflict. This silence is notable because if the Franks encountered other significant pagan sites, chroniclers would have been eager to mention their destruction and demonstrate the power of the Christian God.

When the king and his retinue of soldiers and priests arrived at the Irminsul, they began destroying it. At the same time, they confiscated a treasure deposit of silver and gold (possibly offerings) that had accumulated there.[58] Some scholars, such as Springer, doubt the treasure ever existed. Springer's objections are centered on the fact that Einhard never mentions any treasure in his work and that sources mentioning the Irminsul do not note anyone defending the site, suggesting it was of little importance.[59] However, Einhard's failure to mention events at the Irminsul is not altogether surprising; his commentary on the Saxon wars is notably vague compared to other contemporary chronicles. His work was meant to honor the life of Charlemagne, not give critical commentary on Charles' military campaigns. Indeed, the first 12 years of the Saxon Wars (772–804) only take up a few pages of his work, most of which describe the reasons for and nature of the conflict rather than the conflict itself.[60] As for the lack of resistance, the sources mentioning the Irminsul do not clarify one way or another. In addition, the potential acquisition of loot from the Irminsul would provide another motivation as to why Charles targeted the site: booty could be used to reward his retainers and finance further campaigns.[61]

While we do not know if there was resistance or what happened to the Saxon pagans who were the site's keepers, the scene has been romantically imagined in a nineteenth-century painting by German artist Hermann Wislicenus, whose work shows the submission and sorrow of the Saxons as their great pillar is brought low (see Frontispiece photo).[62] In the painting, Charles sits triumphantly upon a gray steed, while to his left stands a black-robed priest holding forth a tall crucifix. Before the image of Christ, the pagans bow their heads. Wislicenus imagined the scene taking place in a forest near a small body of water and high rock formation, a setting similar to the unsubstantiated Externsteine site advocated by Himmler and Teudt.[63] The artist, and perhaps these later Nazi theorists, may have relied on the *RFA*, which lend further credence to the notion that the Irminsul was located *outside* the Eresburg. After the collection of the Saxon treasure, the chronicle claims there was a terrible drought at the location where the Irminsul stood. This was a problem because Charles needed to stay in the area for two to three days to destroy the "temple" in its entirety, but his army was running out of water. However, the situation eventually resolved itself (miraculously) when water suddenly sprang forth from a nearby "stream."[64]

There are certain clues in the chronicle's report. First, the Irminsul is described as its own place near a stream, where Charles and his army had to travel to and remain for days.[65] It seems odd descriptive language to use if the site was inside the Eresburg, which the king had just taken control of and garrisoned. It is also intriguing that the Irminsul is described as a "temple," and it seems there were other idols nearby and that the Irminsul was simply the focal point of a temple complex (or located within proximity to another cult site).[66] However, the use of "temple" here may simply be referring to a smaller shrine (Old Saxon: *wih/wiha* or *rakude*) that housed images of deities.[67] Alternative reports in the *Moselle* and *Lorsch Annals* merely refer to the Irminsul as a "sanctuary."[68] Nevertheless, if the site took multiple days to destroy, it suggests something more elaborate than we might imagine.

The Irminsul was likely cut down.[69] Upon its destruction, we are told Charles' priests chanted psalms in thanks to God for their triumph.[70] It had undoubtedly been a fruitful endeavor for the king. He successfully demonstrated the powerlessness of Saxon gods and represented himself as "defender of the faith," all while simultaneously acquiring loot for which he could secure the loyalty of his retainers.[71]

Yet, for the Saxons, it must have been a shocking, confusing, and infuriating tragedy, and the religiously motivated violence in the years ahead suggests it was not easily forgotten.[72]

With the Eresburg secure and the Irminsul destroyed, Charles led his army in pursuit of the Saxons who retreated toward the Weser. When the Franks neared the river, the king "parlayed with the Saxons," who offered their surrender.[73] To guarantee their submission, Charles took 12 Saxon hostages, most likely from those responsible for leading Saxons troops.[74] In addition, the king required the Saxons to allow the peaceful operations of missionaries within their territories.[75] The Saxons agreed, and the king began the journey home. He might have pressed further into Saxony, but the onslaught of drought likely discouraged him, as did the fact that territory beyond the Weser was essentially *terra incognita*.[76] To guarantee success, it was wise to wait for better conditions.

The First Saxon Revolt, 772–774

Charlemagne did not remain in Francia long; pressing concerns were calling from the south. By the summer of 773, the time had come for Charles to deal decisively with King Desiderius and the Lombards, and with papal support, he crossed the Alps and laid siege to the north Italian city of Pavia.[77] That campaign was also a success; within a year, the city had fallen.[78] Desiderius surrendered, after which he was banished to the Abbey of Corbie, and Charles could add "King of the Lombards" to his title.[79] Charles then celebrated his victory in Rome during Easter of 774, where he was gratefully received by Pope Hadrian.[80] It was an important development for the slowly rising power of the papacy; yet, for Charles, the celebration was cut short because, while he was in Rome, word arrived that Saxons from every region (except Nordalbingia) had taken advantage of his absence and were in open rebellion. When the king heard the details of the revolt, he knew he couldn't linger. With great haste, he returned across the mountains and prepared for another invasion.

The Saxons had not waited long to unleash their fury once Charles left for Italy, and while the king was away, they undid everything he had achieved during the campaign of 772. As Bachrach has observed, the fact that Saxons made a habit of rebelling while the king was distant suggests they were well informed of his whereabouts.[81] Perhaps intel came from traders, scouts, spies, or informants tasked with keeping tabs on Frankish movements.

The Saxons began by retaking the Eresburg, probably in late 773. At the same time, they occupied the Sigiburg, crediting the idea that the fortress *had* been captured by Franks in 772. Growing bolder, the Saxons turned their attention toward Francia itself and conducted raids into the fortified Hessian region of Franconia.[82] There, they (seemingly) sought revenge for the destruction of the Irminsul by attempting to destroy Boniface's church at Fritzlar.[83] The assault didn't go according to plan. Fritzlar wasn't easy prey. The monastic settlement was located near the Büraburg, an old rectangular Frankish hillfort overlooking the Eder, built of solid stone and mortar.[84] When the Saxons arrived in the vicinity, local inhabitants retreated to the shelter of the Büraburg, bringing with them the relics of St. Wig-bert.[85] The Saxons attacked, but they were unprepared for a serious assault and forced to withdraw. Instead, they set their sights on Boniface's church. According to the *RFA,* the Saxons tried burning the church, but suddenly two young men on white horses (angels?) appeared to defend it. Terrified by these divine guardians, the Saxons panicked and fled. However, the body of one Saxon holding a torch in his hand was later found dead near the church, demonstrating the vengeance of God.[86]

Setting aside the report's embellishment, the general picture we have of these events is a Frankish repulsion of Saxon raiders, the partial destruction of Fritzlar, and possibly the slaughter of civilians and monks who failed to make it to safety.[87] Nevertheless, the Saxons do not appear to have pushed further into Francia. The Frankish garrison in the region may have prevented them, or (very likely) they sus-pected their recent activities would not go unanswered. Scouts would be sending word that Charles was en route. Prudence demanded a tactical withdrawal.

The King Returns to Saxony: 774

By 774, Charles had returned to Francia, stopping in Ingelheim, a Rhenish settle-ment that later became the king's imperial palace. From Ingelheim, Charles dis-patched four armies into Saxony. Three of these detachments fought the Saxons, each bringing the king victory. The fourth didn't engage the enemy but instead took to pillaging.[88] It is unclear how long these campaigns lasted or to what extent they devastated Saxony; however, the implication is that they went into the Winter of 774 and that by the beginning of 775, Saxons either were still in rebellion or had initiated a new one. Charles celebrated Christmas of 774 in the northern Frank-ish village of Quierzy but again cut his festivities short because of the Saxons.[89] In response, the king led one of his characteristic winter campaigns, vowing to "attack the treacherous and treaty-breaking tribe of the Saxons and to persist in this war until they were either defeated and forced to accept the Christian religion or entirely exterminated."[90] The situation must have been dire to merit Charles marching his army through the winter, and his rhetoric certainly implies an angry and vengeful mood. Indeed, again non-Frankish sources give insight into the king's temperament. According to the *Annales Nordhumbrani*, Charles laid waste to Sax-ony because "he was confounded in his mind," that is, because he was insane.[91]

From the Westphalian town of Düren, Charles made preparations for the cam-paign, which included making endowments to the monastery of Hersfeld so that it would be able to give logistical support for the war effort.[92] At Düren, an assembly was held, and once again, Frankish soldiers were called to action from across the realm. The core of these troops likely came from Austrasia, Neustria, Burgundy, and Aquitaine, but conscripts probably also arrived from Frisia, Thuringia, Ale-mannia, and Brittany.[93] These forces were, by all accounts, devastatingly effec-tive.[94] The Syburg (Sigiburg/Hohensyburg) was captured by storm, and soon after, the Eresburg was retaken, restored, and re-garrisoned.[95] The Syburg was also repaired, while simultaneously, Charles had a church built dedicated to St. Peter, which could assist in the conversion of Saxons in the Ruhr valley.[96]

Following these defeats, the Saxons assembled at Brunisberg (Brunesberch/ Brunesberg; possibly Brunsberg near Höxter) to defend their hold on the Weser, which may have included a small stronghold designed to guard the river crossing, but the Franks pushed them back and occupied both banks.[97] Many Saxons were killed in the process.[98] Charles then divided his army, leaving one portion to maintain control of the Weser valley while the other he led personally to the River Oker to parlay with the Eastphalians.

The Eastphalian Saxons were under the leadership of a nobleman called Hessi (or Hassio), who was persuaded to surrender and swear fealty to the Frankish king.[99] His surrender was the beginning of a gradual process by which the Saxon nobility was brought within a system of Frankish patronage, leading to further "class" divisions within Saxony. Hessi and others like him quickly learned the benefits of Frankish generosity and Christian authority.[100] Wealth, land, and titles were paraded as rewards for faithfulness and baptism. Indeed, upon offering his loyalty, Hessi was made a duke and given lavish gifts; he eventually even married into the Carolingian family, beginning an effective strategy of assimilating Saxony through the fusion of Franco-Saxon elites.[101] After the capitulation of the Eastphalian duke, Charles was also met by Engrian Saxons in the Buckegau region, who (under their leader Brun) also surrendered.[102] Both Eastphalians and Engrians, as was customary, were required to give hostages to guarantee their good behavior.[103] Meanwhile, the Westphalians continued the revolt. Their leader, a man called Widukind, needed more convincing.

The Origins of Widukind

Widukind's origins are obscure. His name, which means "child of the forest," may have been something of a metaphor (or kenning).[104] However, it is quoted consistently by separate sources and is the only name repeatedly associated with Saxon resistance. While unique, the name "Widukind" is by no means inconsistent with the nature of early Germanic names, which often have associations with nature, religion, animals, and war.[105] Yet, as one historian has noted, "Widukind" might also be translated as "wolf-like man," which may be an honorary title earned by way of his guerilla-style tactics.[106]

According to Rudolf of Fulda, Widukind stood out among his people "because of his noble family and his many possessions" but added with less praise that he was also "the originator and unrelenting instigator of [Saxon] perfidy and their many disgraces."[107]

While Widukind's ancestry has not been determined with any degree of certainty, that has not stopped centuries of speculation during which family connections were invented for him. These include the idea that he was born in 730 to Duke Warnechin of Engern, that his mother was Kunhilde of Rugen (a West Slavic island in the Baltic), that he had a daughter or sister named Hasela, that the Eastphalian count Hessi was his cousin, or that the Engrian duke Brun was his brother.[108] Each of these are Late Medieval or Colonial inventions, often politically motivated, and as a result, they tend to be (mostly) rejected by modern scholars as unreliable.

Similar examples can be found concerning Widukind's alleged brides. In the thirteenth-century *Chronicle of Brunswick*, he is said to have been married to a woman named Geva, sister to the Danish king Sigfred, by whom he had a son called Wigbert.[109] The Wettins proposed an alternative theory, postulating that Widukind married Suatana, the daughter of a Bohemian prince, a convenient notion for making ancestral territorial claims in the east.[110] The Bohemian connection can be readily rejected; however, the idea that Widukind married a member of the Danish royal family may have some merit, as the Danes were consistently willing to offer Widukind and his companions refuge.[111] In addition, Widukind's son Wigbert is substantiated by several other sources (according to Rudolf of Fulda, Wigbert was married to a woman named Odrada).[112]

Whatever the case concerning his origins, by 775, Widukind had taken on a leadership role in the rebellion (particularly in Westphalia), and by some means, he maintained ties with the Danes.[113] In the years ahead, he would build his reputation by becoming the primary Saxon adversary of Charlemagne.

Westphalia Persists

After Charles received submission from Eastphalians and Engrians, he rejoined his army guarding the Weser valley, which had set up camp in the town of Lübbecke (*hlidbeki*) in the Wiehen Hills.[114] However, according to the revised *RFA,* before the king could arrive and reunite his forces, the Westphalians launched an assault on the town. Intriguingly, this was done by stealth and deception.[115] The Saxons somehow managed to intermix with Frankish foragers as they returned to their camp, all while pretending they belonged. Once inside the camp, they began slaughtering Frankish soldiers as they slept, suggesting these events occurred at night or in the early morning.[116]

Eventually, the Frankish garrison mustered a counter-attack and repelled the Saxon tricksters, but every indication suggests this was a Saxon victory. One of those indicators is the reaction of the king. When Charles finally reunited his army with the remnants of the Lübbecke survivors, he was furious.[117] According to the revised *RFA*, Charles quickly inflicted a "three-fold slaughter" on the Westphalians, gaining him "considerable booty" and hostages.[118] It seemed as though the king wanted to make clear that any Frankish defeat would be met by infinitely wider Saxon devastation. As the *Moselle Annals* confirm, during the campaign of 775, while Charles was in Saxony, he "laid it waste" and unleashed "a great slaughter."[119]

During the Westphalian campaigns, Widukind managed to escape the king's grasp. It is unclear at this juncture how aware Charles was of Widukind or how concerned he was regarding the rebels' influence, but the king couldn't linger long in Saxony to search for him. He had to be content with Westphalia's seeming pacification because the Lombards were also in revolt.[120] Rapidly, Charles headed for Italy.

The Westphalian Revolt of 776

The king's second sojourn to Italy was another Frankish success. Duke Hrodgaud, leader of the Lombard revolt, was killed in 776, and a portion of Lombard territory thereafter became the Frankish "march of Friuli," a militarized frontier zone.[121] Charles stayed in Italy through Easter of 776 before returning to Francia, where, upon arriving in Worms, he was greeted with bad news. The Saxons (predominantly Westphalians) were once again in revolt. According to the *RFA*, they had betrayed their oaths, abandoned their hostages, and (by trickery) convinced the Frankish garrison occupying the Eresburg to abandon the fortress. In addition, Saxons had dismantled the Eresburg by destroying its walls and buildings, which was undoubtedly an attempt to remove any means by which the Franks could establish a fortified foothold in Saxony.[122]

Following the Eresburg's capture, the Saxons tried to convince the Frankish garrison guarding the Syburg to leave; however, they declined, forcing the Saxons to use catapults against the fort. Yet, these malfunctioned and did more damage to the Saxons than the Franks.[123] Scholars have long since taken this event to indicate that Saxons were unfamiliar with siege equipment.[124] The catapults they used may have been captured from the Franks, damaged during transportation from the Eresburg, or poorly made by the Saxons themselves.[125] Regardless, with the catapults ineffective, the Saxons had no choice but to storm the Syburg with ladders. The chronicler then claims that God joined the battle on the side of the Franks, manifesting his power with two red flaming shields over the Syburg church. Once again, the presence of a divine miracle incentivized the Saxons to flee in terror, causing a stampede in which Saxons were trampled or impaled with spears by their own men. While the chaos ensued, the Franks gave pursuit, slaughtering the Saxons as they fled to the Lippe.[126] Outside of divine intervention, what caused the rout is unclear. However, one possibility is a successful flanking maneuver by Frankish reinforcements, concealed by smoke the Saxons were using against the Syburg garrison.[127]

After their retreat, Saxon survivors were forced to regroup and establish fortified positions nearby. There was little time to construct elaborate defenses, so they cut down trees or branches to make roadblocks, which would have been particularly useful in stopping a mounted pursuit by Frankish cavalry.[128] Meanwhile, Charles held a short assembly in Worms before advancing with an army back into Saxony.

When he arrived, the king broke through the rebel fortifications and again forced the Saxons to flee to the Lippe. The Westphalians had no choice but to seek terms of surrender. The *Petau Annals* claim that, after "the pagans" saw that they could no longer resist, terrified men from the leading Saxon families came to the king and begged for peace.[129] Charles' stipulations were simple: their land was forfeit, they were obliged to become Christians (to be "purged with the water of holy baptism"), and, henceforth, they would submit to the rule of the king.[130] The Saxons agreed, and Charles immediately began restoring the Eresburg, which was once again garrisoned. In addition, the Franks constructed a new strategically significant fortress, made of wood and stone, on the Pader (a tributary of the Lippe), which came to be called Karlsburg (*urbs Karoli*; later, Paderborn).[131]

At Karlsburg, the Saxons were called upon to fulfill their oath of conversion. A multitude of Saxons came to the healing mineral waters of the Lippe to be baptized and turn over hostages to the king.[132] Shortly after, in the Spring of 777, Charles held a general assembly (a "Mayfield") of Franks and Saxons at Karlsburg.[133] It was another show of submission, a symbolic spectacle by which Charles could demonstrate his power and religious fervor, notably to the Saracen dignitaries in attendance from Spain.[134] The *Earlier Metz Annals* record the scene. Saxons:

> [i]n accordance with their own law and custom, with their own hands delivered their freedom and property to king Charles as a pledge, so that, should they again change their faith, they should lose their property and fall into permanent servitude.[135]

The *Petau Annals* note further that, following Saxon submission, the Franks built a church in the area (likely that of St. Salvator, the Redeemer).[136]

Conclusion

The surrender of Saxons in 777 ended the first phase of the war, which has accurately been described as a contest for control over Saxon strongholds.[137] Despite some successes on the battlefield, the conflict had gone poorly for the Saxons: they lost key strategic fortifications, suffered devastating military defeats, watched as their pagan shrines were destroyed and replaced with churches, and endured the submission of their nobles to Charles' authority. However, not all of the rebel warlords had capitulated. The *RFA* note specifically that Widukind was not among those who surrendered. Instead, he was still considered to be in open revolt. He was also inaccessible, heading north with his companions into *Nordmannia* to seek refuge with King Sigfrid and the Danes of Hedeby.[138] For Charles, that must have been troublesome news; the Danes could be formidable foes.[139] Were the Saxons seeking more than sanctuary? Was there chance of a "pagan alliance" between Saxons and Danes?

We can speculate on the existence of such questions in the king's mind because of the correlation in the conflict, from the outset, of religious conversion and political submission. The destruction of pagan cult sites, forced baptisms following military defeats, requirements to allow missionaries free reign to preach and build churches, and the conversion and integration of Saxon nobles were all clear signs. Charles was not just looking to punish Saxon treason or aggression but to transform Saxony by dismantling its religious practices and commandeering its political elites. The king would achieve those goals by whatever means necessary, indicating to nearby pagan peoples like the Danes that they should be on their guard as Frankish expansion continued to creep steadily toward their border.

Notes

1 McKitterick, *Charlemagne: The Formation of a European Identity*, 104
2 Springer, *Die Sachsen*, 178

3 Ibid. 179–180; Robinson, *Old English and its Closest Relatives*, 105–109; Sypeck, *Becoming Charlemagne*, 55–56; Fletcher, *The Conversion of Europe*, 195; Durant, *The Age of Faith*, 462; Riche, *Daily Life in the World of Charlemagne*, 149; Reuter, *Germany in the Early Middle Ages*, 68; Mayr-Harting, "Charlemagne, the Saxons, and the Imperial Coronation of 800," 1113–1123 & "The West," 92; Landon, "Economic Incentives for the Frankish Conquest in Saxony," 48; Morrissey, *Charlemagne and France*, 18 & 24; Lübeck, "Das Kloster Fulda und die Sachsenmission," 47; Wallace-Hadrill, *The Frankish Church*, 183; McKitterick, *The Frankish Kingdoms under the Carolingians*, 61; Bachrach, *Charlemagne's Early Campaigns (768–777)*, 194–195; Lintzel, *Untersuchungen zur Geschichte der alten Sachsen*, 50–52 & for an example of the Franks fabricating a *casus belli*, see Dessens, *Res Voluntaria, Non Necessaria*, 40

4 Costambeys, *The Carolingian World*, 73

5 Howorth, "The Early Intercourse of the Danes and the Franks," 157 & Dean, "Felling the Irminsul," 15

6 Bachrach, *Charlemagne's Early Campaigns (768–777)*, 179–182 & 193

7 Widukind, *Deeds of the Saxons*, 26

8 Talbot, *The Anglo-Saxon Missionaries in Germany*, 199–201

9 Einhard, *The Life of Charlemagne*, 30–3. Republished with the permission of The University of Michigan Press, from *The Life of Charlemagne*, Einhard, © 1960; permission conveyed through Copyright Clearance Center, Inc. & this description was copied almost verbatim by Rudolf of Fulda, see Wattenbach, *Die Übertragung des hl. Alexander von Rudolf und Meginhart*, 8–10

10 Dean, "Felling the Irminsul," 16

11 McKitterick, *Charlemagne: The Formation of a European Identity*, 104

12 Scholz, *Carolingian Chronicles*, 14

13 Oman, *The Dark Ages*, 263

14 Williams, *Atrocity or Apology?* 22

15 Wood, *The Missionary Life*, 12

16 Ibid. 115

17 Ferguson, *The Vikings*, 50–51

18 Bachrach, *Charlemagne's Early Campaigns (768–777)*, 514

19 Loyn, *The Reign of Charlemagne*, 137–138

20 Talbot, *The Anglo-Saxon Missionaries in Germany*, 232

21 Sullivan, "The Carolingian Missionary and the Pagan," 716–717

22 Talbot, *The Anglo-Saxon Missionaries in Germany*, 232–233

23 Ibid.

24 Becher, "Non enim habent regem idem Antiqui Saxones," 15–18 & Springer, *Die Sachsen*, 150

25 Talbot, *The Anglo-Saxon Missionaries in Germany*, 231 & Springer, "Was Lebuins Lebensbeschreibung über die Verfassung Sachsens wirklich sagt," 258

26 Leidinger, "Zur Christianisierung des Ostmünsterlandes," 27–29

27 Lübeck, "Das Kloster Fulda und die Sachsenmission," 59–61

28 Wood, *The Missionary Life*, 115

29 McKinney, *The Saxon Poet's Life of Charles the Great*, 11–12

30 Oman, *The Dark Ages*, 271 & Bradbury, *The Routledge Companion to Medieval Warfare*, 115

31 Landon, "Economic Incentives for the Frankish Conquest of Saxony," 55 & Riche, *Daily Life in the World of Charlemagne*, 73

32 Bachrach, *Charlemagne's Early Campaigns (768–777)*, 220–232

33 Ibid.

34 Ibid.

35 Ibid. 197–199 & 218 & Bachrach, *Warfare in Medieval Europe*, 343–344

36 Robinson, *Old English and Its Closest Relatives*, 106

37 Nicolle, *The Conquest of Saxony*, 10
38 King, *Charlemagne*, 150
39 Cichy, "Die Eresburg," 1–2
40 Ibid. 4–7. The land the Eresburg occupied later became the village Obermarsberg. See Bachrach, *Charlemagne's Early Campaigns (768–777)*, 218; Widukind, *Deeds of the Saxons*, 36 & Langen, "Die Bedeutung von Befestigungen in den Sachsenkriegen Karls des Großen," 190–196
41 Ibid. 1–7; Cathey, *Heliand*, 146–147 & McKinney, *The Saxon Poet's Life of Charles the Great*, 13
42 Ibid. 8–12 & Nicolle, *The Conquest of Saxony*, 13–14
43 Bachrach, *Charlemagne's Early Campaigns (768–777)*, 233–234
44 Ibid.
45 Scholz, *Carolingian Chronicles*, 48
46 Rembold, *Conquest and Christianization*, 52
47 Bachrach, *Charlemagne's Early Campaigns (768–777)*, 236–237
48 Landon, *Conquest and Colonization*, 80
49 Schlesinger, "Early Medieval Fortifications in Hesse," 251–256 & Bachrach, *Charlemagne's Early Campaigns (768–777)*, 433–434
50 Oman, *The Dark Ages*, 276
51 Grünewald, *Westfalen zwischen Franken und Sachsen*, 22; Cichy, "Die Eresburg," 2–5 & Warner, *Ottonian Germany*, 91
52 Davidson, *Myths and Symbols in Pagan Europe*, 21–22; Bachrach, *Charlemagne's Early Campaigns*, 237–239; Murphy, *The Saxon Savior*, 15 & *The Heliand*, 129; Simek, *Dictionary of Northern Mythology*, 175; Fouracre, "Frankish Gaul to 814," 102; Oman, *The Dark Ages*, 273; Langen, "Die Bedeutung von Befestigungen in den Sachsenkriegen Karls des Großen," 199; Springer, *Die Sachsen*, 162; Dettmer, *Der Sachsenführer Widukind*, 11–12 & Heather, *Christendom*, 388
53 Honselmann, "Paderborn 777," 400
54 Cusack, *Pagan Saxon Resistance to Charlemagne's Mission*, 39; Smith, *The Echo of Odin*, 27; Schmidt, *Charlemagne*, 46–47; Kritsch, *Theophoric Place Names*, 65–66 & Tiefenbach, *Altsächsisches Handwörterbuch*, 200
55 Cathey, *Heliand*, 12–13
56 The English translation is my own; however, it is based on the German edition by Wilhelm Wattenbach. See Wattenbach, *Die Übertragung des hl. Alexander von Rudolf und Meginhart*, 9–10
57 Springer, *Die Sachsen*, 165
58 Becher, *Charlemagne*, 53 & Collins, *Early Medieval Europe*, 279–280
59 Springer, *Die Sachsen*, 180
60 Einhard, *The Life of Charlemagne*, 30–40
61 Nelson, *King and Emperor*, 116
62 Rembold, *Conquest and Christianization*, 28–29
63 Longerich, *Heinrich Himmler*, 296–297
64 Scholz, *Carolingian Chronicles*, 48–49 & McKinney, *The Saxon Poet's Life of Charles the Great*, 13
65 Howorth, "The Ethnology of Germany (IV)," 419–420
66 Mayr-Harting, "Charlemagne, the Saxons, and the Imperial Coronation of 800," 1113–1115
67 Murphy, *The Heliand*, 9 & 172; Simek, *Dictionary of Northern Mythology*, 355; Rauch, *The Old Saxon Language*, 313 & Tiefenbach, *Altsächsisches Handwörterbuch*, 460
68 King, *Charlemagne*, 132 & Kritsch, *Theophoric Place Names*, 99–100
69 Davies, *Europe*, 281 & Dean, "Felling the Irminsul," 16
70 Nicolle, *The Conquest of Saxony*, 12–13

71 Collins, *Charlemagne*, 47–48 & Morrissey, *Charlemagne and France*, 16
72 Bachrach, *Charlemagne's Early Campaigns (768–777)*, 214–215
73 Scholz, *Carolingian Chronicles*, 49
74 Bachrach, *Charlemagne's Early Campaigns (768–777)*, 241–242
75 Robinson, *Old English and its Closest Relatives*, 105–109
76 Bachrach, *Charlemagne's Early Campaigns (768–777)*, 243–244
77 Einhard, *The Life of Charlemagne*, 28–30
78 Davis, *The Lives of the Eighth-Century Popes*, 139
79 Riche, *The Carolingians*, 98 & Costambeys, *The Carolingian World*, 67
80 Scholz, *Carolingian Chronicles*, 49–50
81 Bachrach, *Warfare in Medieval Europe*, 370
82 King, *Charlemagne*, 44
83 McKinney, *The Saxon Poet's Life of Charles the Great*, 15
84 Fehring, *The Archaeology of Medieval Germany*, 95–97; Dean, "Felling the Irminsul," 17 & Bachrach, *Warfare in Medieval Europe*, 252
85 Farmer, *The Oxford Dictionary of Saints*, 447
86 Scholz, *Carolingian Chronicles*, 50
87 Nicolle, *The Conquest of Saxony*, 11–30
88 Scholz, *Carolingian Chronicles*, 50–51
89 McKinney, *The Saxon Poet's Life of Charles the Great*, 16–17
90 Scholz, *Carolingian Chronicles*, 51. Republished with the permission of The University of Michigan Press, from *Carolingian Chronicles: Royal Frankish Annals and Nithard's Histories*, Bernard Scholz, © 1970; permission conveyed through Copyright Clearance Center, Inc.
91 Landon, *Conquest and Colonization*, 80
92 Bachrach, *Charlemagne's Early Campaigns (768–777)*, 430–431
93 Ibid.
94 Ibid. 431–432
95 Ibid. 435 & Robinson, *Old English and its Closest Relatives*, 105–109
96 Ehlers, *Die Integration Sachsens in das fränkische Reich*, 435
97 Bachrach, *Charlemagne's Early Campaigns (768–777)*, 440–445 & Langen, "Die Bedeutung von Befestigungen in den Sachsenkriegen Karls des Großen," 188–195
98 Scholz, *Carolingian Chronicles*, 51
99 Ibid. & McKinney, *The Saxon Poet's Life of Charles the Great*, 18
100 Effros, "De Partitiones Saxoniae," 268 & Cathey, *Heliand*, 9–11
101 Paxton, *Anchoress & Abbess in Ninth-Century Saxony*, 29
102 Scholz, *Carolingian Chronicles*, 51
103 Cathey, "The Historical Setting of the *Heliand*," 11
104 See the discussion in: Green, *The Continental Saxons*, 322 & Springer, *Die Sachsen*, 195–196
105 Speidel, *Ancient Germanic Warriors*, 26 & 9–50
106 Nicolle, *The Conquest of Saxony*, 11–30
107 The English translation is my own; however, it is based on the German edition by Wilhelm Wattenbach. See Wattenbach, *Die Übertragung des hl. Alexander von Rudolf und Meginhart*, 10–11
108 Rundnagel, "Der Mythos vom Herzog Widukind," 475–477
109 Howorth, "The Early Intercourse of the Danes and the Franks," 157 & 163
110 Rundnagel, "Der Mythos vom Herzog Widukind," 486–488
111 Dettmer, *Der Sachsenführer Widukind*, 96–97
112 Wattenbach, *Die Übertragung des hl. Alexander von Rudolf und Meginhart*, 5
113 Dean, "Felling the Irminsul," 18; Melleno, "Between Borders," 360–361; McKinney, *The Saxon Poet's Life of Charles the Great*, 34 & Dettmer, *Der Sachsenführer Widukind*, 28–30

114 Ibid. 17

115 Bachrach, *Charlemagne's Early Campaigns (768–777)*, 451–452

116 Scholz, *Carolingian Chronicles*, 50–53

117 Bachrach, *Charlemagne's Early Campaigns (768–777)*, 452–453

118 Scholz, *Carolingian Chronicles*, 50–53

119 King, *Charlemagne*, 132

120 Scholz, *Carolingian Chronicles*, 53

121 Ibid. 55

122 King, *Charlemagne*, 151

123 Scholz, *Carolingian Chronicles*, 53

124 Dettmer, *Der Sachsenführer Widukind*, 19

125 Bachrach, *Charlemagne's Early Campaigns (768–777)*, 519 & 539–540

126 Scholz, *Carolingian Chronicles*, 53

127 Bachrach, *Charlemagne's Early Campaigns (768–777)*, 541–548 & Langen, "Die Bedeutung von Befestigungen in den Sachsenkriegen Karls des Großen," 210–211

128 Ibid. 548 & Langen, "Die Bedeutung von Befestigungen in den Sachsenkriegen Karls des Großen," 184–188

129 King, *Charlemagne*, 151

130 Scholz, *Carolingian Chronicles*, 55–56 & McKinney, *The Saxon Poet's Life of Charles the Great*, 20

131 King, *Charlemagne*, 133; Thompson, *The Saxons and Germanic Social Origins*, 604; Langen, "Die Bedeutung von Befestigungen in den Sachsenkriegen Karls des Großen," 205–210; Bachrach, *Charlemagne's Early Campaigns (768–777)*, 557 & Honselmann, "Paderborn 777," 402

132 Scholz, *Carolingian Chronicles*, 55 & King, *Charlemagne*, 151

133 Ibid. & King, *Charlemagne*, 133

134 Nelson, *King and Emperor*, 166

135 King, *Charlemagne*, 15. The translation is from *Charlemagne: Translated Sources*, P.D. King, © 1987.

136 Ibid.; Honselmann, "Paderborn 777," 400 & Ehlers, "Könige, Klöster und der Raum," 207–216

137 Lintzel, *Untersuchungen zur Geschichte der alten Sachsen*, 49–50 & France, *Warfare in the Dark Ages*, 329

138 Scholz, *Carolingian Chronicles*, 55 & McKinney, *The Saxon Poet's Life of Charles the Great*, 21

139 Derry, *A History of Scandinavia*, 18

7 The Rise and Fall of Widukind, 777–785

The Danish emporium of Hedeby was located on the Schlei inlet leading out to the Baltic Sea. In the late 770s, this young market town was of little-known importance, yet within a few decades, Hedeby developed into one of the great trading centers of the north.[1] That transformation was in no small part a later byproduct of the Saxon Wars (see Chapter 9). But what of Hedeby at the arrival of Widukind and the Saxon refugees? We can be sure of a few things. Located in the south of Jutland, Hedeby sat upon flat heathland, surrounded by small stretches of forest and marshland on its outskirts.[2] Situated strategically on a north-to-south route known as the *Heerweg* (or *haervejen*, the "road of warriors"), Hedeby existed at a crossroads among Danes, Saxons, Frisians, and Slavs.[3] As a result, Hedeby developed into a poly-ethnic/religious community, a condition confirmed by archaeological excavations of the town's cemeteries.[4] Within proximity lay the residence of the Danish king Sigfred, a ruler whose origins remain obscure. Indeed, to call him "King of the Danes" is probably an overestimation. In all likelihood, Sigfred's authority was limited to southern Jutland.[5] His dwelling was possibly a hall situated within Hedeby itself.[6] However, archaeological evidence suggests the Hochburg, a hill-fort on the outskirts of the town walls, may have been the royal residence (as well as a place of refuge during troubled times).[7]

Defensive walls that later developed into the famous *Dannevirke* surrounded portions of Hedeby as early as the 730s; these were likely constructed in response to Slavic raids and Frankish expansion.[8] Within those walls, Hedeby came to life. The town bustled with the commotion of merchants and tradesmen plying their wares. Locals drank barley-beer and feasted on cod while perusing the latest supply of furs, reindeer antler, "Frisian" cloth, and ceramics shipped in from the Rhineland.[9] Like their Saxon neighbors, they lived in spacious long-houses and *Grübenhauser*.[10]

Perhaps the town's most unique asset was that it gave traders and travelers an efficient means of transporting ships and goods overland between the Baltic and the North Seas, avoiding the hassle of sailing around the northern Skaw of Jutland.[11] Indeed, from Hedeby, it was only a short ten-mile portage to Hollingstedt and access to the North Sea.[12] In those days, men did not wish to test the wrath of the icy waters if they could avoid it. After all, these people were largely still pagan, and maritime superstitions were widespread in their sea-faring culture.[13] Njord, the

DOI: 10.4324/9781003379157-10

god of the sea, was not easily appeased, and terrors always lurked in the deep.[14] The sea itself was the very blood and sweat of the primeval giant Ymir, and those who perished in its waves risked spending eternity in the underwater realm of the goddess Ran.[15] At least, such is what we are told in later Norse myth.[16]

Our image of Hedeby will expand in due course; however, for the moment, this brief overview will serve to introduce what was becoming a sanctuary for Saxons fleeing Frankish might. This was the case for Widukind and his followers, who, in the late 770s, found in Hedeby royal patronage and sympathetic ears. There the Saxon rebels lingered, biding their time and building support. In the meantime, Charles was implementing significant changes back in Saxony, and missionaries were picking up where Lebuinus had left off.

Early Missionary Activity in Saxony: Fulda, Sturmi, and Liudger

Several ecclesiastical institutions were involved in the initial Saxon mission, including (among others) Mainz, Cologne, Würzburg, Utrecht, and Amorbach.[17] However, in the early years of the conflict, it was the fortified Hessian abbey of Fulda that became a key staging ground for missionary activity (as well as military intervention) within Saxony.[18] Fulda's early development can be traced back to St. Boniface and Sturmi, who fostered the abbey's growth alongside grants of royal patronage from Charles Martel's son Carloman.[19] Patronage continued with Charlemagne, who gifted the monastic community estates (including Hammelburg) and appointed his loyal friend Sturmi to organize the Saxon mission during the Paderborn assembly of 777.[20]

There is some controversy surrounding Sturmi's role in the Franco-Saxon conflict. Some scholars believe he would have been a staunch advocate of Frankish militarism, particularly given the vulnerability of his estates to Saxon raids.[21] However, Sturmi may have also wished to capitalize on the political and economic patronage Fulda would receive as reciprocity for its assistance in the war effort.[22] At Fulda, Sturmi had nearly 400 monks at his disposal, some of whom were appointed to bring about Saxon conversions through baptisms and to eradicate pagan cult sites.[23] We are told that Sturmi and his companions demanded that Saxons abandon their idols, destroy their temples, and cut down their sacred groves so that churches could be built in their place.[24] While such actions could be justified from an evangelical perspective, the enthusiasm with which they were undertaken was likely aided by cultural prejudice.[25] As the contemporary abbot Egil of Fulda proclaimed in his hagiographical account *The Life of Sturmi*, Saxons were a "depraved and perverse people."[26]

Nearby, the eastern Frisians were facing similar perceptions, and one of their own, a man named Liudger, was assigned to bring about their conversion. That instruction initially came from Albericus, Bishop of Utrecht, who tasked Liudger with evangelizing and destroying pagan sites in eastern Frisia. That particular order was then expanded upon by Charlemagne, who instructed Liudger to journey to Heligoland and destroy a local temple.[27] Once complete, Liudger sent a portion of the treasure he found at the cult site back to the king.[28]

Liudger does not appear to have had any qualms about his mission.[29] For one, his visionary experiences solidified his religious convictions.[30] Furthermore, Christianity was a significant component of his heritage. His grandfather, Wrssing, was a staunch opponent of the pagan king Radbod and had assisted in bringing Liudger's family land and wealth (in both Frisia and Westphalia).[31] Liudger's education within the Church was also of some note. Two of his uncles were priests; he was tutored by Gregory of Utrecht (a disciple of Boniface) and was also taught by Alcuin of York (who later became a leading scholar at Charlemagne's court).[32] Therefore, when Liudger began his missionary activity in Frisia, he could do so with some confidence.

Beginning in 777, Liudger made his staging ground Lebuinus' rebuilt church at Deventer, from which he established a reputation as a decent man and convincing teacher (one of his converts was a famous blind Frisian bard named Bernlef).[33] He remained in Frisia for some time, utilizing connections and building his flock near Dokkum.[34] Years later, due to his rising reputation, he would be called to missionary work further east among the Saxons.[35] However, the region would need to endure several more years of turmoil before that could happen. That being said, contemporary views seemed more optimistic. We need to only read the words recited to Charlemagne's court at Douzy in 777 (likely) by the Lombard scholar Paulinus in his *Poem Concerning the Conversion of the Saxons*:

> Prince Charlemagne, girded with gleaming arms,
> Adorned with a plumed helmet,
> Aided by the miraculous power of the eternal judge,
>   Conquered this people through various massacres, through a thousand victories,
> And crushed them through bloodied shields, through bellicose spears,
> And he subjected them to himself with a glittering sword
> And dragged the legions of forest-worshippers to the heavenly kingdom.[36]

However, the poet spoke too soon, and the Saxons were still far from being pacified.[37]

Hostilities Renewed: Roncesvalles and the Return of Widukind

The year 778 would not be remembered by Charles fondly. Of course, he couldn't have known that when he marched his army across the Pyrenees into northern Spain to face Abd al-Rahman I, leader of the Umayyad Emirate of Cordoba.[38] Before his Iberian campaign concluded, there was room for optimism. In cooperation with his Iberian allies, Charles had laid siege to Saragossa and successfully "neutered" the city of Pamplona by destroying its defenses.[39] Satisfied, the king led his army back home through the Pyrenees via the Roncesvalles Pass, which is where the situation took a turn for the worse when a guerilla force of Basque warriors ambushed Charlemagne's rearguard, culminating in a devastating Frankish defeat.[40] Several prominent nobles were killed, including Charlemagne's friend

Roland, the military governor of the Breton March. To make matters worse, the Basques ransacked the Frankish baggage train and made away with Charles' recently acquired loot.[41]

These events were immortalized in *The Song of Roland* (*La Chanson de Roland*), an eleventh-century epic and French romantic literary treasure.[42] Yet, for Charles, there was nothing romantic about what happened, and things would only get worse. News spread quickly of the Frankish defeat, and 1,000 miles away, the Saxons received it with invigorating delight.[43] The actions of missionaries in Saxony, coupled with the Frankish occupation, had continued to breed resentment throughout 777. With the king vulnerable, demoralized, and distant, it didn't take long for Saxons to capitalize on his misfortune.[44] Widukind returned from Hedeby and once again led the Saxons into open rebellion.[45]

Raiding in the Rhineland: The Revolt of 778

The Saxon revolt of 778 was particularly vicious. It included assaults within Saxony as well as throughout Frankish territory in the Rhineland. Our sources indicate that a significant component of these attacks included plundering and destroying churches.[46] The *Moselle Annals* record:

> The perfidious people of the Saxons, betraying the faith of Christ, sallied forth from their lands and came as a hostile army to the river Rhine, burning and wasting everything, sparing nothing whatsoever.[47]

The Saxons initially moved against the recently constructed Karlsburg, which they destroyed. Incidentally, thereafter Karlsburg would be called "Paderborn," perhaps in an attempt to distance a site associated with the king's name from a Saxon victory.[48] (These symbolic notions had to be considered to deflect stains upon the young king's reputation.) Following the Karlsburg's destruction, the Saxons headed toward Deutz (now a borough of Cologne).[49] Deutz was sacked, but a Frankish garrison from Coblenz drove the Saxons away. Nevertheless, Saxon raiding continued, and slaves were captured during their withdrawal. In addition, news of Westphalian victories spread, and Eastphalians joined the revolt.

In the meantime, Franks from Coblenz pursued the Saxons but were lured into an ambush ending with a Saxon victory that opened up the region to Saxon predations. The *Royal Frankish Annals* (*RFA*) report that the rebels "plundered along the river [Rhine], and committed many atrocities, such as burning the churches of God in the monasteries and other acts too loathsome to enumerate."[50] Egil adds that the Saxons went about "laying everything waste and slaughtering all the inhabitants... they put to the sword everyone they met with savage ferocity."[51]

During this phase, the Saxons made their way toward the Abbey of Fulda, which had become the epicenter of missionary endeavors in Saxony. When the monks at the abbey (including Sturmi) received word of an incoming Saxon war-band, they gathered up the relics of St. Boniface and made a hasty retreat over the Rhon

Mountains to Hammelburg, leaving the Saxons to face more formidable opponents upon their arrival.[52] Coming to the aid of the abbey was a Frankish army of Alamans and Eastern Franconians who successfully held the Saxons back.[53]

By this time, Charlemagne had received news of what was happening, which he learned upon arriving in the Burgundian city of Auxerre.[54] The king wasted no time sending a response, and a Frankish army was quickly mustered (possibly from the Christenberg fortress) to restore order.[55] The Saxons caught wind of the incoming host and decided it was time to return home, making their way back to Saxony via the Lahn River valley. However, the Franks caught up with the Saxons near Leisa on the River Eder (the "Saxon Poet" claims at Baddanfeldun), where "the Saxons turned to give them battle."[56] The contest went poorly for the rebels, and according to the *RFA*, many were slaughtered or forced to retreat.[57]

Despite setbacks for the Saxons, hostilities continued into 779 when Charles returned to Saxony to burn and decimate the land as far as the Weser.[58] Both the *Moselle* and *Petau Annals* record Saxons (likely Engrians and Eastphalians) handing over hostages.[59] The campaign would have continued, but famine in Francia necessitated the king's return to Worms.

Nevertheless, in 780, Charles was back in Saxony, only this time he marched as far as the Elbe, where he received the surrender of Saxons in the region. Hostages (slaves and freemen) were handed over to the king, and the land was divided up "between bishops, priests, and abbots" so "that they might preach and baptize there."[60] An entry for the same year in the *Petau Annals* celebrates these developments, claiming the Saxons abandoned their idols, "worshipped the true God," and built churches.[61]

In contrast to the 779 campaign, the Frankish advance of 780 was focused on Saxons in Westphalia and some of those in the north. We are given a more thorough account in the *RFA*, which tells us that Charles stopped at the Eresburg before making his way to Lippe to hold an assembly. Following the completion of that assembly, the king marched to the Elbe, making his way to Ohrum on the west bank of the River Oker, where Nordliundi and Saxons from the Bardengau were baptized.[62] The Franks continued north to where the Ohre flows into the Elbe, at which point the king resolved everything "pertaining to Saxons and Slavs" before returning home.[63] The mention of simultaneous dealings with Slavs (specifically Wends) and Frisians also occurs in the *Petau* and *Moselle Annals*, suggesting these peoples may have been in revolt at the same time as the Saxons.[64]

If there was cooperation among Saxons, Frisians, and Slavs, it certainly wouldn't be the last time Saxons tried to coordinate collective resistance against the Franks. Yet, their efforts were crushed, and Charles could use a few years of quiet on the Saxon front to concentrate on other endeavors. However, during 780–782, Saxony was by no means neglected. At some point between 778 and 780, Widukind once again sought refuge among the Danes, but it was only a matter of time before he might return. Charles would utilize that time by stepping up his efforts to transform Saxon society and, as the chronicles allude to, that began in large part with the Church.

The Continuation of Missionary Efforts: Willehad and Lull

By 776, the missionary Lebuinus was dead, his body having been buried in his rebuilt church at Deventer.[65] Lebuinus' death is estimated based on the fact that Liudger was sent in 775 to restore his church and secure relics associated with his name.[66] According to Egil, following Lebuinus' demise, "the wicked Saxons" wasted and burned Deventer and then spent three days unsuccessfully searching for Lebuinus' body.[67] With Lebuinus gone, Sturmi and his companions at Fulda became primarily responsible for the Saxon mission. Moreover, due to Frankish military success in Saxony during 778 and 779, Sturmi was tasked by Charles with stepping up his efforts. However, by that time, Sturmi was in his early 70s, "weak and weary with age."[68] Still, Sturmi followed the king's orders, but it was ultimately too much for his body to bear, and he became gravely ill. Despite the best efforts of Charlemagne's physician (Wintar), Sturmi died shortly after. He was replaced as abbot of Fulda by Baugulf, an east Frankish noble, but the task of converting the Saxons fell to Willehad, who had been preaching among the Frisians since the early 760s.[69]

In 780, Charles summoned Willehad to court and tasked him with directing his efforts toward the Saxons.[70] Willehad obeyed, and that same year he began missionary efforts in the region of Wigmodia, a "province" between the Elbe and the Weser near Bremen. In Wigmodia, Willehad preached, baptized, and began building churches.[71] For several years, the region would remain Willehad's center of operations. However, his work was not without significant interruptions (to which we will return).

Willehad was not alone in directing missionary work among the Saxons. Further south, in Thuringia, Charles had also instructed Lull, Archbishop of Mainz, to assist the Saxon mission from his abbey of Hersfeld.[72] Alongside Fulda, Hersfeld was a significant component in initiating religious reforms and conversions in the region. While not as well-endowed as Fulda, Hersfeld was by no means a meager institution. Indeed, in January 775, Charles granted Hersfeld royal patronage and a charter for mineral rights and the collection of tithes.[73] Until the death of Lull in 786, Carolingian support for Hersfeld continued with additional land grants and support for relic transitions.[74] (After Lull's death, imperial favor for Hersfeld declined, suggesting it was Lull in particular that was deemed a valuable asset by Charlemagne.[75])

From his correspondence, Lull was a stern, authoritative, unforgiving, and ambitious man, which is probably why he was not well-liked.[76] Lull was a hardliner in the Bonifatian tradition and exhausted much effort in promoting the cult of his idol Boniface.[77] Nevertheless, despite his problematic personality, imperial favor and ambition combined to extend his influence, notably in Thuringia and Hesse, where he gained a hold over the Bonifatian foundations of Büraburg and Fritzlar.[78] However, it is unclear how involved Lull was in the Saxon mission.[79] The Saxons were no doubt a troublesome nuisance whose raids came too close to Lull's areas of operation.[80] He had every reason to promote their Christianization, even if by conquest, but he does not seem to have been *personally* involved in missionary activity in Saxony. That task likely fell to Hersfeld's monks, although Lull may have acted as their overseer or as an advisor to the king on the matter.

In addition to Charles mobilizing influential missionaries in the field, in 780, a church dedicated to St. Peter was founded in the Westphalian village of Soest.[81] Charles also established other monastic cells in Westphalia, notably Meppen priory and the Abbey of Visbek, which were called upon to contribute to the region's conversion.[82] This was part of a grander strategy, noted in the *Moselle and Lorsch Annals*, whereby Charles divided up Saxony into ecclesiastical administrative regions to help facilitate Church organization and wider spread conversions.[83] It is unclear how effective these early strategies were. The source material raises some doubts. However, it was only the beginning. During the brief interlude of peace, Charles (alongside his advisors) also worked on legal statutes to help solidify a new status quo for Saxon society. These were revealed in the form of capitularies (legislative acts), and their draconian measures all but guaranteed a renewal of violence.[84]

The *Capitulatio de partibus Saxoniae*

In 782 (possibly 785, see note 85), Charles held an assembly with his army at Lippspringe (Paderborn), where he took steps to begin restructuring Saxon society.[85] According to the *RFA*, all Saxons were in attendance except for Widukind.[86] However, the same source also notes that the Danish king Sigfred sent emissaries (led by his relative Halfdan) to the assembly, presumably to assure Charles that, despite harboring Saxon rebels, he had peaceful intentions.[87] It served its purpose, and there is no indication of serious discord between Franks and Danes at the time.

The first measure addressed at the assembly was the appointment of Frankish and Saxon nobles as counts who, working on behalf of Charles, would assist in the administration of Saxony to remodel it on Frankish standards.[88] Again it seems members of the Saxon nobility were cozying up to the king, and it would be surprising if such behavior didn't exacerbate hostilities or "class" divisions within Saxony itself.

The second development was implementing what has come to be known as the "First Saxon Capitulary," or the "Capitulary for the parts of Saxony" (*capitulatio de partibus Saxoniae*).[89] In a list of 34 statutes, it is here that, to quote Janet Nelson, Charles' agenda for "suppressing Saxon identity" has gained particular renown.[90] Indeed, Oxford medievalist Richard Fletcher has gone so far as to characterize them as a "blueprint" for "the comprehensive and ruthless Christianization of a conquered society."[91]

Before analyzing the capitularies, it should be remembered that while their introduction was likely announced at the Paderborn assembly, after their unveiling, it was the responsibility of the king's *missi dominici* to spread word of the edicts throughout Saxony at *local* assemblies.[92] However, it is unlikely that many Saxons would have attended assemblies where they could hear the message of the *missi*. Therefore, the dissemination of information would have been slow and confusing.[93] Adherence to new laws would have been particularly challenging to enforce under these circumstances, especially given the society's overwhelmingly rural nature. In addition, despite the harshness of the capitularies, for example, their over-reliance on the death penalty, Saxon law could be quite cruel. Capital punishment was by no means unknown. However, if capital punishment would not have been surprising, the capitularies assuredly deviated from the norm in their attempt to eradicate Saxon paganism, a theme that echoes throughout the edicts.[94]

The assault on pagan religious customs begins in the first capitulary, where new churches built in the region must be given "more illustrious honor" than the "shrines of the idols had."[95] Churches were also to be places of sanctuary where those seeking refuge would be immune from violence (c.2 & 14).[96] For anyone who dared to enter a church violently or stole from a House of God, the price was death (c.3).[97] Murdering a member of the Church, such as a priest, bishop, or deacon, would also result in death (c.5).[98] Similar crimes mentioned in the *Lex Salica Karolina* (Carolingian Frankish law) could be rectified through paying fines, albeit exorbitantly large ones (200–600 solidi).[99]

If out of "contempt for Christianity," one ate meat during lent, the price was death (c.4).[100] However, there was a caveat here that if an individual ate meat out of necessity, it would be considered. The lent requirement was part of a strategy to integrate Saxons into Christian customs, as seen in several other capitularies. For example, except during times of war or under exceptional circumstances, individuals were required to be in church on the Lord's Day (c.18).[101] In addition, all newborns were to be baptized within a year after birth, or else their parents faced hefty fines (c.19).[102]

Witches believed to practice cannibalism "after the manner of the pagans" were to be killed (c.6). We can compare this to a similar statute in the *Lex Salica Karolina*, where cannibalistic witchcraft was met with a fine of 200 solidi.[103] While popular belief in such occurrences is likely, cannibalism as a "pagan practice" among Saxons has not been validated. However, a general distinction between "light" and "dark" forms of witchcraft (*maleficium*) seems to have been relatively common in Early Medieval Europe.[104] Ritualistic cannibalism may have belonged to the latter and could be interpreted in myriad ways. For example, in the seventh-century *Edict of Rothair* for the Lombards, some believed witches could "eat a living man from within."[105] It is also worth remembering that early Christians were accused of practicing cannibalism due to a misunderstanding of the Eucharist, that is, the ritual ingestion of the body and blood of Christ.[106] Could a similar misunderstanding of rituals concerning Germanic pagans have occurred? Regardless, associations between witchcraft and cannibalism lingered in Europe for centuries, well into the later era of the witch craze.[107]

Beyond targeting witches, there was also a proscription against "diviners" and "soothsayers," who were to be handed over to the Church (c.23).[108] What was done with these individuals is not altogether clear. They may have faced persecution or were targeted for the influence they might wield if converted. Attempts to root out such individuals were by no means isolated to the Saxons. As late as 789, in his *Admonitio Generalis* (General Admonition), Charlemagne issued a decree condemning "sorcerers and enchanters" to death.[109]

Human sacrifice, for which we do have historical evidence among early Saxons, was also banned on pain of death (c.9).[110] However, while evidence indicates the continued presence of animal sacrifices in Saxony, it is unclear how common human sacrifice remained in the late eighth century.[111] That being said, Pope Gregory III wrote a letter to Boniface in 732 condemning the sale of Christian slaves to pagans in Germany and Frisia for the purpose of sacrifices, so the possibility should be considered.[112]

The seventh capitulary is historically notable due to its criminalization of cremation, again for which the price of violation was death.[113] While burning the dead appears to have been in a general decline across Western Europe, it remained in practice among the Saxons (at least in part).[114] Indeed, despite its criminalization, there is evidence of cremation being practiced in Saxony as late as the twelfth century.[115] While we can't be sure, its criminalization may have actually facilitated its survival as a cultural marker or point of resistance. Even with confusion in the archaeological record, the capitulary demonstrates that Charlemagne interpreted cremation as a pagan practice to be rooted out.[116] Furthermore, the seventh capitulary is not the only one that deals with funerary customs. In capitulary 22, related legislation required the bodies of Saxon Christians to be buried in church cemeteries and not "the mounds of pagans."[117] Incidentally, we have evidence of mound graves continuing to be used in the Netherlands and Westphalia into the early ninth century, typically in connection with individuals of higher social status.[118]

Saxons attempting to hide from baptism were also suspect. A refusal to accept baptism equated to a continued dedication to paganism and, therefore, was punishable by death (c.8).[119] Intriguingly, "if one shall have made a vow at springs or trees or groves, or shall have made any offering after the manner of the heathen or shall have taken of a repast in honor of the demons," he will pay a fine, or if unable to pay, "shall be given into the service of the church" until his debt is paid (c.21).[120] This capitulary is especially surprising when compared to the edict concerning lent (c.4). A continuation of pagan practice is met with a fine, while a failure to integrate Christian practice is met with death. This may say something about where the priorities of the capitularies lay. However, it may also be that such practices were relatively common and deemed somewhat harmless, as they tend to show up frequently in Early Medieval pastoral literature, where the resulting punishment is performing extended periods of penance.[121] However, even in official policy outside of Saxony, condemnation of nature reverence continued, and in the 794 Council of Frankfurt, there was a call for "the destruction of trees and groves."[122] This followed in the wake of Charlemagne's General Admonition, in which he condemned the "observances which stupid people make at trees, rocks, and springs."[123]

Conspiracies or collective action against Christians by pagans was, again, a capital offense (c.10).[124] That capitulary went alongside a general requirement of loyalty to the king, the violation of which also merited death (c.11).[125] Loyalty and obligations in early medieval society were made public by swearing oaths, which the capitularies mandated would subsequently take place in churches (c.32). This last stipulation was not unusual for the Carolingian Empire. In the later 803 additions to the *Lex Ribuaria,* it was decreed that all oaths were to be sworn in churches over relics.[126]

Saxons were also expected to contribute economically to the local development of the Church. Those contributions were in the form of land: a house and two *mansi* (which averaged about 60–96 acres) and labor: one male and female servant per every 120 Saxons (c.15).[127] Given that this stipulation was not up for debate, it is hard to see it as anything other than a systematic form of slavery. However, it is unclear how long these servants remained obligated to the Church or what the conditions of their lives entailed. Indeed, those given over to the Church may have already been slaves within Saxony.

Saxons were also required to donate a portion of their wealth to local priests and churches via tithes (c.16 & 17).[128] Because Saxons operated outside of a currency-based economy, tithes would have been in the form of land, labor, vital resources, domesticated animals, or material goods.

A survey of capitularies discussed thus far has displayed the prominent position of religious transformation in Charlemagne's Saxon agenda. However, other components of the capitularies are worth noting. For one, enforcing rigid class structures (which already existed in Saxon society) is visible. Prohibitions against illegal marriage (c.20) essentially re-emphasized the status quo, which required marrying within one's class.[129] A violation of marriage customs was met with fines, and both upper- and lower-class individuals were held accountable. However, nobles faced lighter punishments when it came to violence or rape. Sexual assault of a nobleman's daughter was met with death, while nothing is said concerning the rape of lower-class women (c.12).[130] In like manner, proscriptions are made against killing high-born "lords" and "ladies" but not against "commoners" (c.13).[131] If anyone aided in causing the death of a count, their property was forfeit, and they were to be given over into serfdom (c.30).[132]

In addition to status-related mandates, there are more general legal concerns: accepting bribes or concealing criminals was to be met with fines or loss of office (c.24 & 28), individuals were not to be hindered from seeking justice (c.26), and perjurers were to be held accountable according to Saxon law, harkening back to earlier traditions (c.33).[133] These later edicts are relatively standard legal jargon for the period and find much in common with other Germanic law codes. However, in the last capitulary (c.34), there is a more fundamental assault on Saxon society in that it forbids independent public assemblies. Instead, assemblies could only be held if the king's *missi* called for one, while local judicial assemblies had to be administered by a count alongside Christian priests.[134] In this final capitulary, we witness an undermining of the traditional form of representation in Saxony, which served at least three functions: (1) it lessened the means of generating collective resistance, (2) it eradicated a collective political component of Saxon society (as well as its possible religious functions), and (3) it transferred authority to counts and the Church and away from freeborn Saxons, especially those who had not yet committed themselves to Frankish rule.[135]

Mutual Devastation: The Saxon Revolt of 782

The culminating effect of the capitularies was *not* the peaceful integration of Saxony into the Carolingian Empire. Instead, the disruption of political and religious practices, restructuring of power, increased economic obligations, and the deepening of class divisions generated widespread animosity.[136] Peace came to an end, and hostilities were renewed.

Following the Paderborn assembly, Charles returned to Francia, and Widukind returned to Saxony.[137] The capitularies likely drew the rebel leader back, and he appears to have galvanized support throughout Saxony quickly. There is also an indication in the *RFA* that he did so quietly, as Charles was unaware of the renewed Saxon revolt until it was reported by his commanders (Frankish and Saxon), whom he sent east to fight Sorbian raiders.[138] However, if the revolt began quietly, it soon expanded in scope and violence. Franks, Saxon counts, and Christian institutions were all targeted. The recent Christian communities founded by Willehad and Liudger were put to flight or put to the sword.[139] According to Adam of Bremen, Willehad and Liudger were among those who fled. Liudger made for Rome, from where he journeyed to the abbey of Monte Cassino (he resided there for the next two years).[140] Willehad also fled to Rome; however, he eventually rejoined his flock (which had fled to Echternach) in 785.[141]

When Charlemagne's commanders (Adalgis, Gailo, and Worad) heard Widukind was back leading a revolt, they abruptly stopped pursuing the Sorbs and directed their campaign toward the Saxon rebels.[142] During this period, in the Süntel Mountains, the Franks suffered their most devastating defeat of the conflict.[143] The complete narrative, which the original *RFA* almost ignores, is given in the revised *RFA*. Adalgis, Gailo, and Worad led their East Frankish army into Saxony to unite with Count Theodoric's quickly assembled army of Ripuarians. Together these forces advanced into the Süntel Mountains, where the Saxons had set up a fortified position. Once they were close to the Saxon position, Theodoric pitched camp, while the East Frankish host crossed a nearby river and encamped on the opposite bank. However, while they were encamped, the East Frankish commanders began to fear that if they went into battle with Theodoric, he would receive all the honor for the victory rather than them. So instead, they attacked without him, leading a hasty and disorganized charge against the Saxons' well-situated position. It was a strategic blunder of monumental proportions. The Franks were quickly surrounded and slaughtered "almost to a man."[144] Adalgis, Gailo, and several other nobles were among the dead.

The account is striking, especially when compared to those reported by other sources. The original *RFA* merely state that the Franks waged war against the Saxons and fought bravely and (somewhat dismissively) that Adalgis and Gailo died in the Süntel Mountains,[145] while the *Moselle Annals* only note that some of Charles' men "met their deaths in that insurrection."[146] The implication is that chroniclers were not particularly keen to elaborate on a serious Frankish blunder. It is also telling that the battle was significant enough to merit recording in the *Anglo-Saxon Chronicle*, although it is inaccurately dated to 779.[147]

How the battle was fought, its location, and the routes each army took to get there have all been subject to scholarly fascination. Klocke has proposed that Adalgis, Gailo, and Worad took the Kassel-Hersteller road to the Weser or started further west and took the Eresburger road along the Teutoburg forest, while Theodoric approached from the Rhineland, possibly from Cologne.[148] After their arrival within proximity of the Saxon position, Theodoric's troops stayed on the left bank of the Weser near Rehem, while the other commanders crossed over to find a suitable route around the mountains.[149]

As for the Saxons, they appear to have established their primary fortified position on the Hohenstein, a mountain in the Weser Hills (southeast of Langenfeld), which contained the Amelungsburg (an iron-age ring fort) as well as a possible cult site dedicated to Donar.[150] However, archaeological evidence suggests that the nearby Barenburg (located 16 miles to the east in the Osterwald near Eldagsen) may have also been a mustering point for Saxon reinforcements, including mounted troops, which could have been used to ambush unsuspecting Frankish forces and assist in trapping them in a pincer movement.[151]

The exact battlefield location has not been determined with certainty. Cosack has suggested somewhere in the valley of the Deisterpforte (the "Deister Gate," located between the two Deister hill ridges), possibly close to the village of Hachmühlen.[152] However, another tradition suggests the battle occurred on the Dachtelfeld plateau, a forested area containing several springs near the Hohenstein, including the so-called *Blutbach* (Blood Stream), which *supposedly* acquired its name from the Frankish slaughter that turned the waters red with blood.[153]

Wherever the battle took place, the severity of the Frankish loss is evident by the king's reaction.[154] If the deaths of Frankish nobles were as significant as the revised *RFA* claim, then Charles almost certainly would have faced pressure from elite Frankish families to seek revenge. However, there is little indication that the king needed prodding. The source material makes clear that Charles was angry, and he acted with characteristic speed and severity in making amends.

Shortly after the defeat, the king led his army into Saxony, where he "wasted it with cruel sword" and slaughtered an "immense multitude of Saxons."[155] War was supplemented with the acquisition of people, and according to the *Petavian Annals*, Saxon hostages were led into Francia.[156] The thoroughness of Charles' armies temporarily halted resistance, and Widukind fled again to the Danes. However, this time the king was not so easily appeased. Following Widukind's retreat, Charles and his army made their way to the Verden on the Aller, a village where loyal Saxons (presumably nobles) were tasked with gathering up rebels who participated in the revolt.[157] Why Verden was chosen is not altogether clear. Perhaps it was due to the village's proximity to the Süntel Mountains, or maybe the area surrounding Verden had become a hotspot for rebels. Regardless, in Verden, the king made a decision that would forever stain his legacy: on a single day, near the banks of the River Aller, Charles had 4,500 Saxon prisoners beheaded.[158] This event, later known as "the Blood-Bath of Verden," even if exaggerated, in all likelihood, happened. Multiple sources indicate the slaughter of Saxons in 782 (though some of these, admittedly, may refer to battles rather than executions).[159]

The hypotheses proposed by some scholars that the number of victims reported is merely a scribal error or refers to deportations seem unfounded.[160] As is the notion that because Einhard does not mention the event, it didn't occur. Medieval manuscripts underwent an editing process, and a scribal error of that magnitude almost surely would have been noticed. In addition, deportations of 4,500 people would have taken multiple days, weeks, or even months and could not have occurred in a single day.[161] Nor does the idea of deportations make sense in the context of individuals being taken to Verden (for processing?). In addition, as discussed concerning the destruction of the Irminsul, Einhard's failure to mention an event should not be taken as proof that it didn't occur. Einhard was writing to glorify Charlemagne's image, and what happened at Verden detracted from that goal.[162] It was also not the first time a Frankish massacre of rebels had been concealed or ignored. In 746, Charlemagne's uncle Carloman massacred several Alamannic rebels at Cannstatt, which the *RFA* failed to report.[163] There are also reports of massacres from the Merovingian age, for example, in the 630s when Dagobert slaughtered families of Bulgar refugees fleeing the Avars during the night.[164] The point here is that a Frankish king performing massacres is by no means an anomaly. Despite Charlemagne's otherwise praiseworthy attributes, there are no indications that such an act was outside his character. In addition, the binding obligations of the 782 capitularies likely gave Charles all the legal backing he needed for dispensing "justice" in its most brutal form.[165]

While the massacre was probably met with approval by contemporary enemies of the Saxons, modern historians have been more ready to condemn the king's actions.[166] Rosamond McKitterick has called what happened at Verden a "horrifying reprisal" for the Frankish defeat in the Süntel Mountains, while others have been quick to characterize the event as nothing short of genocide.[167] The Verden massacre even garnered sympathy among Nazis, notably Heinrich Himmler. In 1934/1935, the SS Reichsführer went so far as to commission a "Saxon's grove" (*Sachsenhain*) near Verden, containing 4,500 monument stones for the dead (which are still standing).[168] While Hitler saw Charles as a model Germanic ruler promoting tribal unification, for Himmler (among others), Verden had transformed the Frankish king into a Romanized *Sachsenschlachter* ("slaughterer of Saxons").[169]

The Aftermath of Verden, 783–785

Just like the capitularies, the massacre at Verden did little to pacify Saxon resistance. Indeed, once again, harsh measures stoked defiance.[170] A renewed revolt seems to have begun in the spring of 783, possibly following the death of Charles' wife, Queen Hildegard. Here the *RFA* state that, upon hearing news of the rebellion, Charles again journeyed into Saxony with a small Frankish army. The Saxons had been assembling in a plain outside of Detmold (*Theotmalli*), which is where the king led his forces. When he arrived, the Franks engaged the Saxons "vigorously" on the Mount Osning hill ridge in the *Teutoburger Wald*, slaughtering many and causing others to flee.[171] The *Moselle Annals* claim thousands of Saxons were killed.[172]

Following his victory, the king returned to Paderborn to assemble a larger army. Less than a month later, he led that force to the River Hase, where the Saxons were gathered. They fought, and again the Saxons were decisively defeated.[173] Yet, the campaign continued, and Charles led his army raiding north across the Weser as far as the Elbe, after which he returned to Francia.[174] The king may have gained a few months of peace, but again in 784, the Saxons were in a state of rebellion, and this time they had help. Our sources claim the Saxons allied with the Frisians, who were also trying to rid themselves of Frankish suzerainty. This is likely what the monk Altfrid of Hildesheim referred to when he wrote that Widukind, the "root of wickedness," rose up alongside the Frisians to burn churches, expel priests, and cause folks as far as the Fleo River to abandon Christianity.[175]

Charles met this new challenge again in person, leading his army across the Rhine at Lippenham to "terrify the people into submission."[176] Upon arriving in Saxony, the king "went here and there devastating the countryside" and "destroying everything" until he came to Hockeleve (Petershagen).[177] Charles may have been trying to put a wedge between the Saxons and the Frisians to prevent them from unifying. However, flooding halted the king's advance, so he headed south into Thuringia, from where he made his way into Eastphalia.[178] At the same time, he sent his son Charles the Younger (who was only 12 years old) with a detachment against the Westphalians.[179] The targeted Saxons capitulated after having their villages burned, allowing father and son to regroup at Schöningen.[180]

From Schöningen, the elder Charles returned to Francia, while his son lingered in Saxony to deal with continued resistance in Westphalia. Saxon rebels were gathering on the River Lippe, so Charles the Younger rode to meet them. His forces eventually found the Saxons, engaged them in the Dreingau region (possibly in a cavalry battle), and again the Franks won the day.[181] Satisfied with his success, the victorious son returned to Francia and rejoined his father at Worms.

Upon his arrival, the king took counsel with his son and made plans to continue the Saxon campaign through the Winter. That decision suggests that Saxon resistance continued to be significant or that Charles hoped to deal a decisive blow by devastating the Saxons during a season in which war was not typically waged. The details of the winter campaign are lacking; however, the *RFA* suggest it proved more difficult than anticipated. The king did not simply lead a raid into Saxony before returning to the comforts of a Frankish villa. Instead, he spent part of the Winter of 784 encamped in Saxony at Lügde (in the Weissgau region near the River Emmer) and the rest of the Winter into June of the following year at the Eresburg (where he oversaw repairs and built a church).[182]

Throughout this period, the king continued to raid and pillage the Saxons, unleashing relentless devastation on the local population.[183] However, early on, he was stifled by flooding of the River Werre (a tributary of the Weser) and so spent more time at the Eresburg with his family. Yet, even though the king lingered for longer periods at the stronghold, he still sent out regular detachments of Frankish raiders, some of whom he continued to join. These were particularly brutal.[184] The *RFA* claim that, after Charles routed the Saxon rebels and captured their strongholds, the roads throughout Saxony were cleared so effectively that no one offered resistance, and the king could travel freely wherever he liked.[185]

These final campaigns of 785 were decisive in dealing a demoralizing blow to the Saxons (particularly in Westphalia). Following the Paderborn assembly, which included Franks and Saxons, Charles traveled to the Bardengau and sent word to Widukind requesting a parley.[186] After giving assurances of safe passage through an exchange of hostages, Widukind agreed to meet.[187] Charles returned to Francia and sent his emissary Amalwin to negotiate the exchange and lead Widukind (along with Abbio, his son or brother-in-law) to meet the king at the villa of Attigny.[188] It was there, in the presence of the king, that the rebel finally succumbed.

The Surrender of Widukind

If Widukind was involved in the Saxon rebellion beginning in 772, he had been fighting intermittently by the time he surrendered for nearly 13 years. Repeated defeats, the devastation of Saxony, a failure of the Saxon gods to defend their people, and general exhaustion and hopelessness with the war could have all contributed to his surrender.[189] There may have also been popular sentiments in Saxony to desist from further hostilities after such prolonged devastation. At the same time, Charles offered Widukind an honorable "out," one that many Franks likely didn't think he deserved.

Later legends attributed Widukind's surrender to his legitimate conversion to Christianity. Indeed, one story went so far as to claim he experienced a vision of Christ while sneaking into the Eresburg during Easter disguised as a beggar.[190] Although the story is unlikely, Widukind did eventually join the Christian fold. The *RFA* inform us that upon arriving in Attigny, Widukind and Abbio were baptized alongside their companions, after which "the whole of Saxony" was considered subjugated.[191] However, the *Moselle Annals* are more telling. They claim that when Widukind, "author of so many evils and inciter of perfidy," came to Attigny, Charles himself baptized the rebel as well as honored Widukind with "magnificent gifts."[192]

Charles' direct involvement with the baptism ceremony demonstrates the event's significance. Indeed, the indication is that the king went so far as to become Widukind's godfather, establishing spiritual kinship between them and mutual obligations of loyalty and friendship.[193] Coupled with the lavish gifts, Charlemagne essentially offered Widukind a pathway to surrender that allowed him to avoid humiliation.[194]

Given the protracted length of the war, Charles was undoubtedly relieved to have pacified his long-term nemesis. After all, according to the eighth-century Bavarian dignitary Creontius, Widukind had done the king "great damage."[195] Yet, the baptism of Widukind also served the dual function of enhancing the king's image. On the one hand, Charles publicly displayed his victory over a defiant pagan; on the other, he exemplified the Christ-like virtue of mercy.[196]

Practical measures aside, following Widukind's baptism, Charles was elated. Indeed, the king sent a letter to Pope Hadrian informing him of the defeat of the Saxons (as well as gifts from Saxony). The Pope replied by congratulating the king and ordering three days of prayer and celebration during vigils in June.[197] How the Saxons received the news is less understood, although one can imagine many were bitterly disheartened by it. Symbolically, Widukind may have been an icon of hope and resistance in the face of an overwhelming onslaught on their way of life. Therefore, Widukind's conversion, at least partially, might have seemed definitive in ending any chance of restoring Saxon life to the norms of pre-Frankish rule.

It is also possible that Widukind may have been seen as a kind of "prophetic" figure, perhaps similar to the Lakota leader Sitting Bull, whose leadership had come about during a state of tribal crisis.[198] However, that interpretation has not gone without criticism. Some scholars (utilizing the depiction of Widukind as a tyrant in the *Lorsch Annals* and the later commentary of Thietmar of Merseburg) have seen Widukind as a greedy and power-hungry man, asserting he may have wanted to become the "King of Saxony."[199] We are given virtually no insight into the personal motivations behind Widukind's revolts, but the lack of kingship as an institution within Saxony makes that assumption hard to swallow. Another scholar has suggested Widukind may have been the head of an "anti-noble" populist movement, akin to what occurred with Julius Caesar in the last days of the Roman republic.[200] However, this also seems unlikely, especially since Widukind was tied to various noble clans. P. D. King has also suggested that Widukind's reputation "remains inflated to a degree wholly unjustified by the sources."[201] Nevertheless, Widukind is the only consistent name associated with the Saxon rebellion. The king's involvement with his baptism and letter to the Pope indicate his significance in the conflict. Indeed, Widukind's surrender, for Charlemagne, was synonymous with the surrender of Saxony itself.[202]

The Fate of Widukind in History, Legend, and Myth

Widukind's submission was not the end of his story. However, what became of him has been subject to legend, disparate historical clues, and contradictory reports. One attractive and popular scenario is that Widukind was exiled to the Bavarian monastery of Reichenau on an island in Lake Constance (*Bodensee*). There is undoubtedly historical precedent for monasteries being used as "prisons" for individuals needing to be tucked away from public life.[203] However, if monastic exile occurred with Widukind, certain factors make it difficult to confirm. Yet, what evidence is there even to suggest Reichenau?

Primarily, this theory is built upon a reference in the Reichenau Fraternity Book to a monk named Uiituchind, who entered the monastery in 786 and died in 825.[204] As Schmid observed, in the same source, Uiituchind is called *dominator*, which had associations with tyranny and Christian persecution, a view the monks of Reichenau could easily attribute to Widukind.[205] There is also some indication that Charles may have journeyed to Reichenau in 786 to deal with a succession dispute, in which case he could have brought Widukind with him.[206] Doing so would have been seen by contemporaries as an act of mercy, and it would be hard for Widukind to cause trouble from such an isolated locale. Further, there would have been symbolic and triumphalist value in Widukind being "humbled" into spending his remaining days undergoing penance.

As for the problems with the Reichenau scenario, for one, contemporary sources are eerily silent on Widukind's fate after his baptism. If an adversary of Widukind's caliber had been exiled to monastic imprisonment, it seems likely one of the chronicles would have mentioned it (as they tended to do when this occurred with other Frankish political opponents).[207] As for the Reichenau Fraternity Book entry, the primary concern is Widukind's age. If Schmid's analysis is correct, Widukind would have lived at Reichenau for 40 years, and assuming he was baptized at around age 30, that would make him roughly 70 years old when he died.[208] Seventy is undoubtedly an unusual (though not necessarily problematic) age to live to in the Early Middle Ages. However, this is based on an assumption about Widukind's age at his baptism, which we simply do not know. An estimate of Widukind being 30 at his baptism also seems relatively young. That would place his birth in c. 755, making him only 17 at the initial invasion of Saxony and 19 in 774 when he had a military leadership role in Westphalia. None of that is impossible within the context of the Early Middle Ages; however, it does seem unlikely. Yet, if the Widukind mentioned at Reichenau is not "Widukind the rebel," it could plausibly be one of his sons, perhaps a son who also participated in the rebellion.[209] The name "Widu-kind" is incredibly rare and seems only to be associated with the rebel's clan. If this is the case, then the chronology of events would make more sense.

It is also possible that Charles utilized Widukind for his own ends, possibly as a count in southern Saxony.[210] There are a few reasons worth considering that possibility. The first is precedent. We saw in the previous chapter that when Saxon leaders surrendered, Charlemagne made a habit of rewarding them with gifts and titles of authority. This allowed Saxon elites to maintain or even expand their power. Despite Widukind being a more persistent adversary, there is no reason Charlemagne would not have considered making him the same offer. Indeed, a Widukind-turned-Frankish asset could be beneficial for the king, symbolically and practically. If Widukind could be persuaded, he could bring over other nobles or "commoners" who remained hostile to Frankish rule.

Another reason for considering this scenario comes from Altfrid's *Second Life of St. Liudger*, which mentions a ninth-century encounter with Widukind. In that source, Liudger traveled through Hesse, where he saw a horse thief tied to a stake. The thief had been put there by a duke Widukind, who, after having the thief stoned, left him for dead. However, the thief was also Christian, so Liudger appealed to Widukind to allow him to bury the man. Widukind agreed, and Liudger had a pit dug where the body was placed when, suddenly, the corpse miraculously showed signs of life.[211] (Thereafter, the burial spot was called Buddenfeld after the name of the condemned thief Buddo.[212])

If the story contains any truth, it may prove that Widukind continued to hold authority in Saxony after his surrender. However, many scholars doubt its authenticity.[213] For one, the notion of Widukind having a man stoned to death is unusual, given that stoning was not typically a form of punishment in Early Medieval Europe (but does occur in the Bible). Furthermore, the miracle narrative is a common motif employed in hagiography to bolster the reputation of saints, and this seems the most likely motivation for writing the story of Liudger's encounter. However, why the author chose to depict Widukind is another matter entirely. Altfrid's account was written in the mid- to late ninth century when knowledge of what happened to Widukind among Franco-Saxon elites might still have been commonly known. Widukind as a count was then, at the very least, considered a plausible scenario less than a century (or earlier) after Widukind was dead.

There are additional historical reasons why the notion of Widukind continuing to hold authority in Saxony should be taken seriously. These include the Enger connection, the position of Widukind's descendants, and the 922 synod of Koblenz. From the Koblenz synod, we are not told much, but a few details indicate the status of Widukind following his surrender, as well as the continued prestige of his family. Bishops at the synod were entitled to collect tithes from the inheritance of "the old duke Widukind" and his descendants, indicating that the Widukind clan held hereditary estates.[214]

However, the most enduring tradition concerning Widukind's fate is his connection to Enger, where he is said to have built churches (some claim even over the former Irminsul site).[215] Further, in the tenth-century Ottonian *Life of Mathilda*, Widukind is recorded engaging Charlemagne in a duel.[216] He is ultimately defeated but survives to aid in the conversion of Saxony by founding churches in Enger. From the same period, Widukind was reportedly buried in the Dionysius Church in Enger (alongside his wife Geva), which he supposedly founded; a local reliquary (depicting the Virgin holding Jesus) is thought to be one of the gifts given to him by Charlemagne at his baptism.[217]

It is unclear to what extent the Ottonian sources can be trusted, but for some time, Enger continued to honor the death of Widukind, which was said to have occurred on January 7 (year unknown).[218] Due to this association, the site later became a place of pilgrimage for upper-class Germans, romantics, and nationalists.[219]

While Widukind's connection to Enger remains unclear, the positions held by his descendants are better known. His son, Wigbert (Wibreht), and grandson, Waldbert, continued to be involved in Carolingian political life as high-ranking nobles and acted as patrons of the Church in Saxony and beyond.[220] We will return to some of these accounts in later chapters, but suffice it to say, for now, the Widukind clan was wealthy enough that they were able to donate estates to the Church in Utrecht while also possessing several properties in and around Wildeshausen.[221] Furthermore, Widukind's grandson Waldbert was educated in the court of Charlemagne's grandson Lothar, eventually becoming a Westfalen count, and Waldbert's son (Wigbert the Younger) was later made Bishop of Verden, while his daughter (or sister?) became Abbess of Vreden.[222] Even as late as 890, following the collapse of Carolingian rule in East Frankia (which included Saxony), Arnulf of Carinthia is recorded granting estates to Widukind's great-grandson.[223] These details demonstrate that Widukind's family did not suffer a significant loss of prestige after Widukind's surrender; instead, they continued to hold positions of authority and possessed considerable landed wealth. All that makes it more likely that Widukind continued to hold power, or at the very least, that he brokered a deal with Charlemagne ensuring his family's status was not diminished due to his submission.

In later myth and folklore, Widukind was subject to various interpretations. He was simultaneously demonized as a barbarous pagan *and* hailed as a champion of Christianity.[224] Many Widukind legends center on his baptism and conversion. One famous example is that, following his christening, Widukind's black steed turned white, symbolizing his spiritual transformation and newfound purity.[225]

(In 1946, the white steed was made the official symbol of Lower Saxony's coat of arms.[226])

Other stories spoke of Widukind going off to fight Saracens or pursuing (and slaughtering) the murderers of St. Boniface in Frisia.[227] Similarly, a strange twelfth-century invention (replicated in various guises up through the seventeenth) depicted a crusading Widukind being killed in a duel with Gerold of Vinzgau, who ruled over the pagans of Swabia.[228] The tale is particularly odd because Gerold's daughter Hildegard was married to Charlemagne, and Gerold was presumably a fully Christianized Frankish magnate. Of course, historical minutiae are hardly the goal of legend, and by the seventeenth century, Widukind's Christian exploits had become such that he was venerated as the "saint of Westphalia."[229] German Catholics and Protestants both vied for control of Widukind's bones, sometimes rather dramatically. When they fell into Protestant hands at Herford Abbey in 1673, Bishop Christoph Galen von Münster brought 8,000 armed men to forcibly retrieve them (although he was required to give them back when he failed to convince Abbess Elizabeth of the Palatinate that his actions were justified).[230]

The eighteenth and nineteenth centuries were fruitful in propagating Widukind legends via poems, plays, paintings, and novels. Many present a romanticized chivalric Widukind as an exemplar of virtue, bravery, and cunning.[231] In some, he was an incarnation of the "Saxon folk-soul" and a defender of the German people against imperialism.[232] During this period, monuments of Widukind began to crop up, for example, in Herford (depicting Widukind receiving a sign from God) and Enger (honoring the fallen dead from the German wars of unification).[233]

Noble houses across Europe were also eager to claim Widukind as an ancestor, including the Ottonians, Capetians, Wettins, Guelphs, Billungers, Schwarzburgers, Ascanians, Hohenzollerns, Counts of Waldeck, Counts of Oldenburg, Dukes of Savoy, Marquises of Ferrara, Counts of Montferrat, and the Marquises of Friuli.[234] One historian has placed him (alongside Arminius) in "the nationalist pantheon of immortal Germans," a sentiment that has undoubtedly been replicated by others and continued to manifest in German legends.[235] Indeed, as early as the sixteenth century, nationalist commentators were exalting Widukind's "Germanicity," which was often used in contrast to the French during periods of conflict such as the Thirty Years War.[236] That same sentiment lingered over the following centuries, making notable appearances during the conquests of Napoleon and the eruption of the First World War.[237] In these later conflicts, legends spoke of Widukind riding his mighty steed out of the Babilonie (a hillfort in the Wiehen Hills near Lübbecke) to fight for the German people.[238]

Widukind also received praise among the upper echelons of the Third Reich. In a 1934/1935 publication in the Nazi magazine *Der Schulungsbrief,* Walter Gebhardt wrote of Widukind:

> The figure of the Saxon leader is unforgettably imprinted on the German folk. A white steed carries him, in front of his folk, into battle; he has entered saga as the most faithful preserver of his tribe, as passionate enemy of the new faith and the new custom, as protector of freedom and ancestral legacy.[239]

Such were undoubtedly the sentiments of Himmler and Rosenberg, both of whom sought to promote the "cult of Widukind" and Saxon resistance as propaganda exemplifying the strength and resilience of the *Deutscher Geist*.[240] This was supplemented with anti-French representations of Charlemagne and notions of Saxon (i.e., German) racial purity.[241] In 1939, Rosenberg and Himmler went so far as to promote the opening of a Widukind memorial in Enger, which, as Krull has discussed, contained a "consecration room" that "guests would enter via a door decorated with runes."[242] Following the end of the Second World War, the memorial was turned into a museum. After a few awkward decades of "de-Nazification," it was reborn in 2007 as a more historical and insightful cultural exhibit.[243]

Conclusion

Between 777 and 785, Charles implemented several strategies intended to facilitate the submission, political integration, and conversion of the Saxons. Ecclesiastical institutions were at the front of these endeavors by promoting missionary activity, destroying or appropriating pagan cult sites, supporting the war effort, and constructing new religious structures and settlements. The Church was also increasingly entangled in Saxon legal affairs, including settling disputes and oversight of assemblies. Simultaneously, in addition to criminalizing paganism, capitularies legally required Saxons to support the Church (via resources and slaves) and engage in Christian rituals. Failure to comply could be met with the death penalty. However, the threat of violence extended beyond legal mandates. It was also used in scorched earth campaigns to promote fear via massacres, slavery, and the destruction of property. In addition, Charles continued his courtship of the Saxon nobility, whose influence could be wielded against incalcitrant Saxons who continued to resist Frankish rule. Eventually, even the rebel Widukind fell into this category. His submission was demonstrated the same way it had been by previous Saxon nobles, that is, via baptism and conversion.

Notes

1 Khamnueva-Wendt et al., "Classification of Buried Soils," 3
2 Almgren, *The Viking*, 55–62 & Kaufmann, *The Medieval Fortress*, 85
3 Hamerow, *Early Medieval Settlements*, 170; Sindbaek, "The Lands of 'Denemearce'," 176 & Nyberg, *Monasticism in North-West Europe*, 17
4 Pulisano, *Medieval Scandinavia: An Encyclopedia*, 275
5 Wickham, *The Inheritance of Rome*, 474
6 For the role of halls see Hedeager, "Scandinavia," 517–519
7 Dobat, "Danevirke Revisited," 36–56 & Pounds, *An Historical Geography of Europe*, 219
8 Ibid. & Fehring, *The Archaeology of Medieval Germany*, 140–142
9 Jørgensen, "Rural Economy," 136–137; Verhulst, *The Carolingian Economy*, 103 & 109–110 & Goetz, *Life in the Middle Ages*, 21
10 Ibid. 19
11 Derry, *A History of Scandinavia*, 22
12 Almgren, *The Viking*, 55–62 & Jellema, "Frisian Trade in the Dark Ages," 28

13 Davidson, *Myths and Symbols in Pagan Europe*, 37

14 Simek, *Dictionary of Northern Mythology*, 233–234

15 Larrington, *The Poetic Edda*, 48–59; Simek, *Dictionary of Northern Mythology*, 1–2 & 260; Leeming, T*he Oxford Companion to World Mythology*, 407–408; Campbell, *The Masks of God*, 107; Andren, "Old Norse and Germanic Religion," 848–849 & Somerville & McDonald, *The Viking Age*, 48

16 Davidson, *Myths and Symbols in Pagan Europe*, 210–211

17 Lübeck, "Das Kloster Fulda und die Sachsenmission," 63–64 & McKitterick, *The Frankish Kingdoms under the Carolingians*, 60

18 Paxton, *Anchoress & Abbess in Ninth-Century Saxony*, 8; Innes, *State and Society in the Early Middle Ages*, 29 & 150; Bachrach, *Charlemagne's Early Campaigns (768–777)*, 529–530. Raaijmakers has argued that we should not overestimate Fulda's involvement with the Saxon mission and has demonstrated that Saxon nobles did not start sending their sons to the abbey until the early ninth century. However, a lack of close relations between Saxon noble families and Fulda until the ninth century does not negate Fulda's direct involvement in the eighth. See Raaijmakers, *The Making of the Monastic Community of Fulda*, 77–78

19 Costambeys, *The Carolingian World*, 103

20 Hammelburg had been granted originally to the missionary Willibrord in 716 by the Thuringian duke Hetan II. For Charlemagne's patronage of Fulda, see: Riche, *The Carolingians*, 104; Talbot, *The Anglo-Saxon Missionaries in Germany*, 199–201; Nelson, *King and Emperor*, 162; Verhulst, *The Carolingian Economy*, 56 & In September 774, Charles sent a letter to Sturmi granting Fulda the right to choose its own abbot; see Percival, *The Reign of Charlemagne*, 141–142 & Raaijmakers, *The Making of the Monastic Community of Fulda*, 29

21 Bachrach, *Charlemagne's Early Campaigns (768–777)*, 111 & 226

22 Ibid. & 184–186

23 Ibid. 184–186; De Jong, "Carolingian Monasticism," 624–625; Lübeck, "Das Kloster Fulda und die Sachsenmission," 53–54 & Raaijmakers, *The Making of the Monastic Community of Fulda*, 53

24 Talbot, *The Anglo-Saxon Missionaries in Germany*, 200

25 Faulkner, *Law and Authority in the Early Middle Ages*, 66 & Gillis, *Heresy and Dissent in the Carolingian Empire*, 42

26 Talbot, *The Anglo-Saxon Missionaries in Germany*, 200

27 Sullivan, "The Carolingian Missionary and the Pagan," 716–718

28 Wood, *The Missionary Life*, 109–110 & Farmer, *The Oxford Dictionary of Saints*, 273

29 Leidinger, "Zur Christianisierung des Ostmünsterlandes," 35–37

30 Wood, *The Missionary Life*, 128

31 Ibid. 101 & Bachrach, *Charlemagne's Early Campaigns (768–777)*, 619

32 Arblaster, *A History of the Low Countries*, 33; Palmer, "The 'Vigorous Rule' of Bishop Lull," 273; Knibbs, *Ansgar, Rimbert and the Forged Foundations of Hamburg-Bremen*, 42 & Barlow, *The Letters of Alcuin*, 9–17

33 Landon, *Conquest and Colonization*, 47 & Milis, *The Pagan Middle Ages*, 32

34 Talbot, *The Anglo-Saxon Missionaries in Germany*, 233

35 Costambeys, *The Carolingian World*, 105

36 Rembold, *Conquest and Christianization*, 78. From *Conquest and Christianization: Saxony and the Carolingian World, 772–888*, © Ingrid Rembold, 2018. Reproduced with the permission of Cambridge University Press through PLS Clear.

37 Authorship of the poem is disputed; other candidates have included Lull as well as Angilbert. See Landon, *Conquest and Colonization*, 60

38 Bachrach, *Charlemagne's Early Campaigns (768–777)*, 629–630

39 Nelson, *King and Emperor*, 168–169

40 McKinney, *The Saxon Poet's Life of Charles the Great*, 22–23

41 Scholz, *Carolingian Chronicles*, 56
42 Morrissey, *Charlemagne and France*, 45–51 & Gibbs, *Medieval German Literature*, 93–94
43 Fletcher, *The Conversion of Europe*, 195–197
44 McKinney, *The Saxon Poet's Life of Charles the Great*, 23
45 Scholz, *Carolingian Chronicles*, 56–58
46 McKinney, *The Saxon Poet's Life of Charles the Great*, 24
47 King, *Charlemagne*, 133. The translation is from *Charlemagne: Translated Sources*, P.D. King, © 1987.
48 Landon, *Conquest and Colonization*, 106–107 & Knibbs, *Ansgar, Rimbert and the Forged Foundations of Hamburg-Bremen*, 52
49 Ibid. 152
50 Scholz, *Carolingian Chronicles*, 56. Republished with the permission of The University of Michigan Press, from *Carolingian Chronicles: Royal Frankish Annals and Nithard's Histories*, Bernard Scholz, © 1970; permission conveyed through Copyright Clearance Center, Inc.
51 Talbot, *The Anglo-Saxon Missionaries in Germany*, 200
52 Henderson, *A History of Germany in the Middle Ages*, 72 & Lübeck, "Das Kloster Fulda und die Sachsenmission," 55–57
53 Robinson, *Old English and Its Closest Relatives*, 105–109 & McKinney, *The Saxon Poet's Life of Charles the Great*, 24
54 Scholz, *Carolingian Chronicles*, 56
55 Schlesinger, "Early Medieval Fortifications in Hesse," 248
56 King, *Charlemagne*, 152 & McKinney, *The Saxon Poet's Life of Charles the Great*, 24
57 Scholz, *Carolingian Chronicles*, 56–58
58 King, *Charlemagne*, 152
59 Ibid. 132
60 Ibid. 133
61 Ibid. 152–153
62 Scholz, *Carolingian Chronicles*, 58
63 Ibid.
64 King, *Charlemagne*, 133 & 152–153
65 Effros, "De Partitiones Saxoniae," 275–285
66 Talbot, *The Anglo-Saxon Missionaries in Germany*, 233
67 Ibid. 233
68 Ibid. 201
69 Lübeck, "Das Kloster Fulda und die Sachsenmission," 57–59; Raaijmakers, *The Making of the Monastic Community of Fulda*, 72 & Knibbs, *Ansgar, Rimbert and the Forged Foundations of Hamburg-Bremen*, 43
70 Farmer, *The Oxford Dictionary of Saints*, 449
71 Sullivan, "The Carolingian Missionary and the Pagan," 708 & 730–731
72 Farmer, *The Oxford Dictionary of Saints*, 277 & Lübeck, "Das Kloster Fulda und die Sachsenmission," 51–52
73 Nelson, *King and Emperor*, 157–158 & 192
74 Palmer, "The 'Vigorous Rule' of Bishop Lull," 266 & Raaijmakers, *The Making of the Monastic Community of Fulda*, 45
75 Ibid.
76 Ibid. 261–266 & 273–274 & Raaijmakers, *The Making of the Monastic Community of Fulda*, 42–43
77 Ibid. 249–255 & Wemple, *Women in Frankish Society*, 166
78 Ibid. 267
79 Lull was mostly preoccupied with his ambitions in Thuringia, Hesse, and Bavaria.
80 Palmer, "The 'Vigorous Rule' of Bishop Lull," 270–271
81 Jeep, *Medieval Germany*, 724

82 Flierman, *Saxon Identities*, 130–132 & Gallee, *Old-Saxon Texts*, XIII

83 Ibid. 92; Leidinger, "Zur Christianisierung des Ostmünsterlandes," 27–29 & Lübeck, "Das Kloster Fulda und die Sachsenmission," 49–51

84 Reuter, *Germany in the Early Middle Ages*, 29; Pounds, *An Historical Geography of Europe*, 172 & Wamers, *Carolingian Pfalzen and Law*, 154 4

85 There is a debate concerning the date here. Some scholars (including myself) are in favor of 782 due to the uprising that followed soon after. The renewal of violence seems to be a response to these edicts. However, others have been more in favor of 785 following the surrender of Widukind and see the capitularies as solidifying Saxon pacification. There is also debate as to whether or not the capitularies were issued in a single piece of legislation or combined from two. See Nelson, *King and Emperor*, 196; Wallace-Hadrill, *The Frankish Church*, 413; Dessens, *Res Voluntaria, Non Necessaria*, 42; Bauer, "Die Quellen für das sog. Blutbad von Verden," 59–60 & Springer, *Die Sachsen*, 221

86 Scholz, *Carolingian Chronicles*, 59

87 Ibid. & Note: Other emissaries were also in attendance, including representatives of the Avars.

88 King, *Charlemagne*, 134 & 153

89 Costambeys, *The Carolingian World*, 74–75 & for the Latin text see Von Schwerin, *Leges Saxonum und Lex Thuringorum*, 37–44 & for a German translation, see Eckhardt, *Die Gesetze Des Karolingerreiches III*, 2–10 & for an English translation see Rampton, *European Magic and Witchcraft*, 131–132

90 Nelson, *King and Emperor*, 197; Carroll, "The Bishoprics of Saxony," 221 & Oman, *The Dark Ages*, 279

91 Fletcher, *The Conversion of Europe*, 215

92 Jones, *Cambridge Illustrated History of France*, 65–66; Davies, *Europe*, 302 & Riche, *Daily Life in the World of Charlemagne*, 16

93 It is not entirely understood to what extent capitularies were *actually* put into effect or how successfully they were enforced. See Davis, *Charlemagne's Practice of Empire*, 4–5

94 For English translations of the capitularies, see Boretius, *Translations and Reprints from the Original Sources of European History*, 2–5; King, *Charlemagne*, 205–208; Dutton, *Carolingian Civilization*, 66–69 & Loyn et al., *The Reign of Charlemagne*, 51–54

95 Dutton, *Carolingian Civilization*, 66–69

96 Ibid.

97 Ibid.

98 Ibid.

99 Drew, *The Laws of the Salian Franks*, 177–178

100 Dutton, *Carolingian Civilization*, 66–69

101 Ibid.

102 Ibid.

103 Drew, *The Laws of the Salian Franks*, 199

104 Bailey, "Witchcraft and Demonology in the Middle Ages," 48–49; Wolfram, *History of the Goths*, 106–108 & Rampton, *European Magic and Witchcraft*, 3 & 86–87 & 139

105 Ibid. 48

106 Chadwick, "The Early Christian Community," 43

107 Lipscolmb et al., *A History of Magic, Witchcraft and the Occult*, 115

108 Dutton, *Carolingian Civilization*, 66–69

109 Lipscolmb et al., *A History of Magic, Witchcraft and the Occult*, 62

110 Dutton, *Carolingian Civilization*, 66–69

111 Karras, "Pagan Survivals", 560–562

112 Effros, "De Partitiones Saxoniae," 284–285

113 Dutton, *Carolingian Civilization*, 66–69
114 Simek, *Dictionary of Northern Mythology*, 49
115 See the discussion in: Green, *The Continental Saxons*, 98–99
116 Effros, "De Partitiones Saxoniae," 277 & 281–283
117 Dutton, *Carolingian Civilization*, 66–69
118 Effros, "De Partitiones Saxoniae," 268–285
119 Dutton, *Carolingian Civilization*, 66–69
120 Ibid.
121 McNeill, *Medieval Handbooks of Penance*, 274–277
122 Filotas, *Pagan Survivals*, 282
123 Ibid. 300
124 Dutton, *Carolingian Civilization*, 66–69
125 Ibid.
126 Loyn, *The Reign of Charlemagne*, 85–86
127 For the size of *mansi* see the footnotes of: Noble, *Charlemagne and Louis the Pious*, 255
128 Dutton, *Carolingian Civilization*, 66–69
129 Ibid.
130 Ibid.
131 Ibid.
132 Ibid.
133 Ibid. & Elsakkers, "Raptus Ultra Rhenum," 30
134 Ibid.
135 Goldberg, "Popular Revolt," 476
136 Henderson, *A History of Germany in the Middle Ages*, 73
137 McKinney, *The Saxon Poet's Life of Charles the Great*, 29
138 Scholz, *Carolingian Chronicles*, 59–61
139 Flierman, *Saxon Identities*, 126 & Knibbs, *Ansgar, Rimbert and the Forged Foundations of Hamburg-Bremen*, 36
140 Tschan, *History of the Archbishops of Hamburg-Bremen*, 13–14, & Arblaster, *A History of the Low Countries*, 33
141 Wood, *The Missionary Life*, 110–111; Sullivan, "The Carolingian Missionary and the Pagan," 708 & Knibbs, *Ansgar, Rimbert and the Forged Foundations of Hamburg-Bremen*, 36
142 McKinney, *The Saxon Poet's Life of Charles the Great*, 30
143 In the Middle Ages the Süntel referred to the entire Weser and Wiehen Mtn. range, see Klocke, "Um das Blutbad von Verden und die Schlacht am Süntel 782," 169–180
144 Scholz, *Carolingian Chronicles*, 60
145 Ibid.
146 King, *Charlemagne*, 134
147 Swanton, *The Anglo-Saxon Chronicle*, 52–53
148 Klocke, "Um das Blutbad von Verden und die Schlacht am Süntel 782," 169–180
149 Ibid.
150 Nicolle, *The Conquest of Saxony*, 52–55
151 Cosack, "Neue Spuren sächsischer Krieger in der Barenburg," 234–245
152 Ibid. 245–246
153 Nicolle, *The Conquest of Saxony*, 52–60
154 One possible indication of his displeasure is that Charlemagne may have removed Worad from office due to his role in the Frankish defeat. See: Davis, *Charlemagne's Practice of Empire*, 109
155 King, *Charlemagne*, 134
156 Rembold, *Conquest and Christianization*, 54
157 Reinhardt, *Germany: 2000 Years V.I*, 43

158 Scholz, *Carolingian Chronicles*, 61; McKinney, *The Saxon Poet's Life of Charles the Great*, 31; Stofferahn, "Resonance and Discord," 10; Becher, *Charlemagne*, 144 & Kahler, *The Germans*, 48

159 Nelson, *King and Emperor*, 195–196 & Bauer, "Die Quellen für das sog. Blutbad von Verden," 55–57

160 Bradbury, *The Routledge Companion to Medieval Warfare*, 118 & Klocke, "Um das Blutbad von Verden und die Schlacht am Süntel 782," 151–157 & for those in favor of these see arguments see Springer, *Die Sachsen*, 191–192

161 Bauer, "Die Quellen für das sog. Blutbad von Verden," 41–43

162 Klocke, "Um das Blutbad von Verden und die Schlacht am Süntel 782," 161–165

163 Ibid. 165–168

164 Wallace-Hadrill, *The Fourth Book of the Chronicle of Fredegar*, 61

165 Heather, *Christendom*, 390

166 Williams, *Atrocity or Apology?* 21

167 McKitterick, *Charlemagne*, 104; Jones, *Cambridge Illustrated History of France*, 63; Kristoffersen, *Pacifying the Saxons*, 26 & Davis, *Charlemagne's Practice of Empire*, 157

168 Longerich, *Heinrich Himmler*, 297–298; Rembold, *Conquest and Christianization*, 30–33; Kurlander, *Hitler's Monsters*, 181 & Rundnagel, "Der Mythos vom Herzog Widukind," 503–505

169 Lambert, "Heroisation and Demonisation in the Third Reich," 534–536; Rembold, "Quasi una gens," 5 & *Conquest and Christianization*, 30–31; Becher, *Charlemagne*, 148; Sypeck, *Becoming Charlemagne*, 201–202 & Lambert, "How the Past was Used," 1–15

170 Henderson, *A History of Germany in the Middle Ages*, 74 & Dean, "Felling the Irminsul," 20

171 Scholz, *Carolingian Chronicles*, 61

172 King, *Charlemagne*, 134

173 McKinney, *The Saxon Poet's Life of Charles the Great*, 32

174 Scholz, *Carolingian Chronicles*, 61

175 The English translation is Ingrid Rembold's, see Rembold, *Conquest and Christianization*, 43

176 Holland, *Germany*, 31

177 Scholz, *Carolingian Chronicles*, 61–62 & King, *Charlemagne*, 153

178 Ibid. & King, *Charlemagne*, 134

179 McKitterick, *Charlemagne*, 52

180 Scholz, *Carolingian Chronicles*, 62 & McKinney, *The Saxon Poet's Life of Charles the Great*, 33

181 Ibid. & McKinney, *The Saxon Poet's Life of Charles the Great*, 33

182 Ibid.& King, *Charlemagne*, 153 & 134

183 McKinney, *The Saxon Poet's Life of Charles the Great*, 33–34

184 King, *Charlemagne*, 154

185 Scholz, *Carolingian Chronicles*, 62

186 King, *Charlemagne*, 134

187 Kosto, "Hostages in the Carolingian World," 135–136 & Freise, "Widukind in Attigny," 25–27

188 Scholz, *Carolingian Chronicles*, 62–63 & it is suspected that Abbio was either a brother or son-in law of Widukind. He may have been sent to St. Wandrille after his surrender. See: Schmid, "Die Nachfahren Widukinds," 19 & "Der Sachsenherzog Widukind als Monich auf der Reichenau," 257

189 Dettmer, *Der Sachsenführer Widukind*, 31–32

190 Nicolle, *The Conquest of Saxony*, 42–83

191 Scholz, *Carolingian Chronicles*, 63

192 King, *Charlemagne*, 134
193 Henderson, *A History of Germany in the Middle Ages*, 72–74; Freise, "Widukind in Attigny," 27–30 & Springer doubts that this occurred, because it is not mentioned in the *RFA*, nor is there any proof that after Widukind's baptism Charlemagne had any interest in maintaining this role, see Springer, *Die Sachsen*, 194
194 McKinney, *The Saxon Poet's Life of Charles the Great*, 34
195 King, *Charlemagne*, 342
196 Rembold, *Conquest and Christianization*, 66–69
197 Nelson, *King and Emperor*, 209; Riche, *The Carolingians*, 104–107 & Sullivan, "Carolingian Missionary Theories," 278
198 Wood, "Pagan Religion and Superstitions East of the Rhine," 263
199 Becher, "Non enim habent regem idem Antiqui Saxones," 28–31; Warner, *Ottonian Germany*, 74; Springer, *Die Sachsen*, 109 & Rundnagel, "Der Mythos vom Herzog Widukind," 483–485
200 Arnold, *Medieval Germany*, 43
201 King, *Charlemagne*, 50
202 Schmid, "Der Sachsenherzog Widukind als Monich auf der Reichenau," 256 & Freise, "Widukind in Attigny," 12–13
203 Henderson, *A History of Germany in the Early Middle Ages*, 76; Fletcher, *The Conversion of Europe*, 191 & Dessens, *Res Voluntaria, Non Necessaria*, 40
204 Schmid, "Der Sachsenherzog Widukind als Monich auf der Reichenau," 260–266
205 Ibid. 268–269
206 Ibid.
207 Freise, "Widukind in Attigny," 33–36 & Krull, "Das Widukind Museum Enger," 1–2
208 Schmid, "Der Sachsenherzog Widukind als Monich auf der Reichenau," 272–273
209 Springer, *Die Sachsen*, 198
210 Dettmer, *Der Sachsenführer Widukind*, 48–50
211 Freise, "Widukind in Attigny," 38–43
212 Dettmer, *Der Sachsenführer Widukind*, 47–48
213 Schmid, "Der Sachsenherzog Widukind als Monich auf der Reichenau," 256–257 & Springer, *Die Sachsen*, 197
214 Ibid. & Freise, "Widukind in Attigny," 38–43
215 Ibid. 53–58 & Rundnagel, "Der Mythos vom Herzog Widukind," 501–503
216 Freise, "Widukind in Attigny," 17–18; Dettmer, *Der Sachsenführer Widukind*, 115–116 & Behr, "Die Sachsenkriege Karls des Großen," 226–227
217 Ibid. 33–36; Krull, "Das Widukind Museum Enger," 1–2 & 16–17; Schmid, "Der Sachsenherzog Widukind als Monich auf der Reichenau," 257 & Wemple, *Women in Frankish Society*, 103
218 Dettmer, *Der Sachsenführer Widukind*, 74–76 & Schmid, "Der Sachsenherzog Widukind als Monich auf der Reichenau," 275–276
219 Rundnagel, "Der Mythos vom Herzog Widukind," 492–494
220 Faulkner, *Law and Authority in the Early Middle Ages*, 39; Schmid, "Der Sachsenherzog Widukind als Monich auf der Reichenau," 257–259 & Honselmann, "Die Annahme des Christentums durch die Sachsen," 212–214
221 Dettmer, *Der Sachsenführer Widukind*, 98–107
222 Ibid. 98–107; Freise, "Widukind in Attigny," 38–43 & Schmid, "Der Sachsenherzog Widukind als Monich auf der Reichenau," 271–272
223 Ibid. 109–111
224 Hines, "The Conversion of the Old Saxons," 305; Riche, *The Carolingians*, 106–107; Morrissey, *Charlemagne and France*, 110 & 131; Reuter, *Germany in the Early Middle Ages*, 138 & Krull, "Das Widukind Museum Enger," 16
225 Rundnagel, "Der Mythos vom Herzog Widukind," 486–488
226 Schwikart, *Journey through Lower Saxony*, 14

227 Rundnagel, "Der Mythos vom Herzog Widukind," 477–479 & Dettmer, *Der Sachsenführer Widukind*, 53–55

228 Ibid. 488–489 & Dettmer, *Der Sachsenführer Widukind*, 73–76

229 Ibid. 494–496

230 Ibid.

231 Ibid. 496–505 & Dettmer, *Der Sachsenführer Widukind*, 116–155

232 Ibid.

233 Krull, "Das Widukind Museum Enger," 18–20

234 Rundnagel, "Der Mythos vom Herzog Widukind," 476–477 & 479–480 & 480–482; Freise, "Widukind in Attigny," 17–18; Dettmer, *Der Sachsenführer Widukind*, 102; Springer, *Die Sachsen*, 200 & Behr, "Die Sachsenkriege Karls des Großen," 225

235 Rundnagel, "Der Mythos vom Herzog Widukind," 491; Pinson, *Modern Germany*, 4 & 9; Krull, "Das Widukind Museum Enger," 17–18 & Dettmer, *Der Sachsenführer Widukind*, 6–7

236 Ibid. 491–494

237 Ibid. 498–501

238 Ibid. 501–503

239 Gebhardt, *Karl und Widukind*, 39

240 Lambert, "Heroisation and Demonisation in the Third Reich," 534–536; Rembold, "Quasi una gens," 3 & Ruehl, "German Horror Stories", 138

241 Nicolle, *The Conquest of Saxony*, 29–30; Lambert, "How the Past was Used," 1 & Dettmer, *Der Sachsenführer Widukind*, 503–505

242 Krull, "Das Widukind Museum Enger," 3–6

243 Ibid. 7–24

8 The Northern Campaigns, 786–804

Following Widukind's surrender in 785, Charlemagne likely believed the Saxon Wars were over. Indeed, for several years, the Saxon front *was* relatively peaceful.[1] However, that peace rested uneasily, and in hindsight, chroniclers recalled its ending bitterly. Take, for example, the *Royal Frankish Annals* (*RFA*) account for the period immediately following Widukind's surrender in 785, which laments how the "stubborn treachery of the Saxons" remained quiet for a few years only because they were unable to find "convenient opportunities" to revolt.[2]

If the Saxons were waiting to rebel, others were not. According to the *RFA* and the *Annals of St. Nazarius*, in 786, a plot was formed among East Frankish and Thuringian nobles (led by Count Hardrad) to capture and kill the king. However, the conspiracy was discovered, and those responsible were punished with blinding, banishment, or confiscation of lands.[3] While the motivations for the Thuringian revolt have been debated, some scholars think it may be rooted in how well Widukind was treated following his surrender.[4] After all, it was primarily Eastern Franks in the Rhineland who had borne the brunt of Saxon incursions. Many of their kin had died in the conflict, compliments of Widukind, and it is certainly feasible that a desire for vengeance would have been prominent. However, admittedly, this is mere speculation and goes unspecified in our sources.

Whatever their motivation, the Thuringians were dealt with, freeing up the king to pacify the Bretons (who had stopped paying tribute) and further cement his authority over the Lombards.[5] The following two years (787 and 788) were spent solidifying loyalty in Bavaria, during which Saxons were called upon to make up part of an army that included Eastern Franconians and Thuringians.[6] However, this force was never required to engage in combat. The Agilofing duke Tassilo III, whom Charles had long considered a rival, was simply imprisoned alongside his son.[7]

Saxons were gradually becoming integrated within the Empire as one of its constituent peoples. In addition to making up a contingent in the Frankish army, Saxons attended the 788 Ingelheim assembly, which included Franks, Bavarians, and Lombards.[8] The records for the Ingelheim assembly suggest events in Bavaria were taking center stage—in particular, concerns over Tassilo's role in stirring up the Pannonian Avars.[9] Throughout the remainder of 788, the Franks engaged the Avars in battles throughout Italy and Bavaria, but despite Frankish victories, conflict with the Avars continued to escalate. The Avars directly correlated to the

DOI: 10.4324/9781003379157-11

continuation of the Saxon Wars. Therefore, it is worth pausing to note something about who they were.

The Avars

By the late eighth century, the Avars had become a multi-ethnic people situated along the Danube in the former Roman province of Pannonia, which correlated roughly to western Hungary, Austria, and parts of southeastern Europe. However, their origins lay further east. While their ethnogenesis is hotly debated, the Avars were likely of Turkic and Mongolic origin, possibly descended from the Juan-Juan (Rouran) people who were displaced in the late sixth century.[10] What followed their exile was a period of nomadic wandering in which they were stuck between hostile Turkish and Byzantine neighbors.[11] However, this same period saw their rise to power. Throughout the late sixth century, Byzantines employed the Avars in dealing with their peripheral foes, allowing them to amass wealth and consolidate their hold on the Carpathians and the middle Danube.

During their raiding, the Avars eventually reached as far as Thuringia, culminating in conflict with the Franks in the 560s. As the Avars expanded their domain, they continually absorbed new peoples, adding a significant Slavic element to their society.[12] Eventually, they were able to extract tribute from the Byzantines themselves, but increasingly their attention was drawn west and away from the Eastern Empire.[13]

When the Lombards left for Italy in 568, they left a vacuum in Pannonia, which the Avars filled.[14] Their hold on the region was demonstrated in 582 when their khagan (or *jugur,* i.e., "king of kings") named Baian conquered Sirmium.[15] Avar power continued to expand into the early seventh century, during which their proclivity for long-ranged raiding established their reputation as the "new Huns."[16] By the reign of Charlemagne, their power had long been in decline. Still, during its golden period, the Avar khaganate could boast itself as one of the strongest political entities in central Europe.[17]

Culturally, the Avars must have seemed exotic to Franks of the late eighth century. These were people who, utilizing stirrups decorated with griffins and plants, had mastered the use of cavalry warfare.[18] They were expert wielders of lances and skillfully crafted composite bows.[19] The Avars were also pagans, many of whom fused animist customs with a belief in Turkic and steppe deities. They utilized magic, ritually buried horses, held sacred the open air and water, and paid homage to the great sky god Tengri.[20] It was, therefore, easy for Franks to "otherize" the Avars when the need arose. Their historical reputation, warrior prowess, and paganism were evidence enough for being a threat. That evidence was demonstrated throughout the eighth century as Avars continued to raid Frankish territory.[21]

Charles' patience ended in 787/788 with Avar incursions into Bavaria.[22] From then on, he was determined to be rid of the Avar threat for good. The year 788 proved devastating for the Avars, and Frankish forces in Italy and Bavaria won repeated victories against them.[23] However, despite such losses, the Avars resisted Frankish rule for several years. Indeed, Einhard claimed that, except for the Saxon war, for Charles, the Avar conflict "was the greatest that he waged."[24]

Obodrites

The Avars were not the only peripheral people of note regarding this phase of the Saxon Wars. More directly involved were a West Slavic people known as the Obodrites (Abodrites), who had recently become allies (or clients) of the Franks. Throughout the later course of the conflict, they became increasingly involved in military campaigns against the Saxons. Like the Avars, it is necessary to know something about them to understand the full scope of the war.

By the eighth century, the Obodrites had emerged as a confederation of Polabian Slavic peoples situated between the Elbe and the Baltic.[25] Their primary territory included areas in Schleswig-Holstein and western Mecklenburg, one of their chief settlements being Schwerin (*Zuarin*).[26] They also controlled the key Baltic trading port of Reric.[27] Overall, Obodrite territory was a land of lakes, valleys, and waterways.[28] Dotting the landscape, from at least the early eighth century, were moderately sized earth and timber strongholds.[29] These were likely in the so-called *grod* style, in which settlements were surrounded by circular wooden walls.[30]

Like their Saxon neighbors, Obodrites lived in a patriarchal world of fishermen, herders, hunters, farmers, merchants, and warriors.[31] At Reric, craftsmen worked antler bone, molded pottery, and forged materials from iron and bronze.[32] These items might then be exchanged for Frankish or Scandinavian goods.[33] Trade could also be supplemented by raiding, for which Obodrite warriors had a reputation.[34] Like Saxons, they fought primarily with spears and bows and relied little on cavalry.[35]

The Obodrites were also predominantly pagan. They could be identified by their partially shaved heads, which they wore to honor their gods.[36] Among those deities were Perun (Perkuno), a storm god, and Sventovit, the four-headed god of fertility, fire, and war.[37] Ancestors were also venerated, and the dead (typically cremated) always needed appeasement.[38] Nature was feared and respected, and fickle spirits lurked among bogs, trees, and stones.[39]

To the south of the Obodrites lay the Wiltzi (Veleti/Wends), another Slavic people in Pomerania.[40] These were the traditional enemies of the Obodrites, and it was because of threats from the Wiltzi that the Obodrite chieftain Witzan allied himself with the Franks sometime in the early 780s.[41] The Franks had no qualms about lending their aid against the Wends. After all, going back to the early seventh century, they too had been enemies after the Frankish adventurer Samo made himself a "Slavic" king and stirred up the Wends against them.[42] In exchange for their aid, Franks could also utilize the Obodrites as a check on the Saxons or other less amicable peoples in the east.[43]

Trouble in the East, 789–792

In 789, Charlemagne was called upon to defend the Obodrites against the Wiltzi, after which he led an army to deal with their leader Dragowit. His forces crossed the Rhine at Cologne, after which they passed into Saxony and constructed bridges across the Elbe (one of which was fortified to guard the river crossing).[44] Simultaneously, as they were now deemed part of the Empire, Saxons were called upon to commit troops to the campaign. While the Saxons complied with the requirement, Einhard notes bitterly that "their obedience lacked sincerity and devotion."[45]

Charles' forces were supplemented by a Franco-Frisian navy, Witzan's Obodrites, and a Sorbian contingent.[46] Together these marched against the Wiltzi, "a most pagan people," who were unable to put up much resistance.[47] The Frankish king then ordered the land of the Wiltzi "to be laid waste with fire and sword."[48] Dragowit was forced to come to terms, which required handing over hostages and surrendering his people's land.[49] The *RFA* celebrated the outcome, exclaiming that Charles "by the gift of God" established his authority over the Slavs.[50]

Before the year ended, Charlemagne's court scholar Alcuin wrote a letter to the missionary Willehad. In that letter, he asked how well the Saxons were responding to Willehad's preaching. At the same time, he wondered if there was any hope of converting their Danish neighbors. Yet, more pressing was his concern for the recently conquered Wiltzi and if they were "accepting the Christian faith."[51] What is noteworthy in Alcuin's letter is that just like the Frisians and Saxons before them, peripheral pagan peoples to the north and east of the Empire were now coming into focus as potential converts. For the Wiltzi, like their neighbors, emphasis on conversion followed in the wake of conquest.[52]

In many ways, this was the beginning of a long and troubled trajectory in which the crusading zeal of the Germanic-Christian world targeted peoples of Eastern Europe as souls to be gained.[53] We will return to Saxon missionary endeavors among the Slavs in subsequent chapters. At present, it is merely worth noting the stirring interest that gave birth to later pursuits.

To return to 790, it appears (in rare form) to have been a relatively peaceful year for Charles. Much of it was spent at Worms, where he received emissaries from the Avars seeking to reconcile border disputes.[54] The Saxon front was calm as well. Indeed, another of Alcuin's letters demonstrates the optimism of the time. That correspondence, written to his Irish friend Colcu at the monastery of Clonmacnoise, boasted:

> By God's mercy His holy church in Europe enjoys peace, gains ground and grows greater. For the Old Saxons and all the peoples of the Frisians have been converted to the faith of Christ under pressure from king Charles, who has won some over by rewards, others by threats.[55]

The coming years would demonstrate the extent to which Alcuin's words represented "wishful thinking." Still, they tell us something of what may have been believed by the upper echelons of Frankish society at the time.

The following year returned the realm to a state of war. Attempts to settle matters diplomatically with the Avars had failed, leading Charles to officially declare war in 791. The *RFA* states the reason for this failure as being the "excessive and intolerable outrage" Avars committed against the Church and its people.[56]

Once more, Franks, Frisians, and Saxons were called upon to commit troops to the campaign and seek revenge against the "Huns." The *Lorsch Annals* paint the scene: Charles assembled a large host against "the most arrogant" Avars.[57] His army was then divided into three parts, one of which he led through Bavaria into Avar territory along the southern shore of the Danube. While on the northern side followed the second contingent, composed of Ripuarian Franks, Frisians, Thuringians, and Saxons. Meanwhile, a Frankish navy supported both forces.[58]

After pausing for three days of prayer and fasting, these armies were led deeper into Avar lands, where they spent 52 days decimating the region.[59] Frankish sources conclude that the campaign was successful, but not all went according to plan. Prominent members of the Church accompanying the army (Angilram of Metz and Bishop Sindpert) were killed.[60] Simultaneously, a devastating equine pestilence virtually wiped out the Frankish horse supply.[61] That catastrophe must have left the king feeling particularly vulnerable, and because he was unable to travel far quickly, Charles spent the Winter at the old Roman fortress of Regensburg in Bavaria.[62]

The king resided in Regensburg well into 792, during which he was forced to address an attempted coup led by his bastard son Pippin "the Hunchback" and a band of Frankish nobles.[63] After it failed, many of the perpetrators were executed.[64] According to Notger, Pippin was also "whipped, tonsured, and sent away...to St. Gall."[65] Charles was deeply saddened by familial betrayal, but worse news was coming. The Saxons, tired of being used for Frankish campaigns in the east, had revolted.[66]

The Northern Revolts, 792–798

The significance of the 792 Saxon revolt is attested by its repeated mention in multiple sources. These suggest not only the seriousness of the threat but also the surprise at its outbreak. Its coverage is taken up most fully in the *Lorsch Annals*:

> The Saxons, believing that the people of the Avars was bound to avenge itself on the Christians, made most fully manifest what had long previously been luring concealed in their hearts; as a dog returns to his vomit, so they returned to the paganism which they had long since spewed forth, again abandoning Christianity, breaking faith with God as well as the lord king, who conferred many benefits upon them, and binding themselves to the pagan peoples living round about them. Sending their *missi* also to the Avars, they presumed to rebel, first against God, next against the king and the Christians: they ravaged all the churches in their lands, destroying and burning them; they drove out the bishops and priests who held authority over them, seizing some and killing others; and they reverted in all fullness to the worship of idols.[67]

The same sentiment is recorded in the *Petau Annals*:

> The Saxons betrayed the faith they had long since pledged to the lord king Charles, fell into error, deviated from the path and were overtaken by darkness.[68]

The account found in the *Lorsch Annals* is the only source suggesting the Saxons tried to ally with the Avars, and perhaps this was done by Saxons who had become familiar with the Avars during their campaigns against them. P. D. King has speculated that Saxons returning from the Avar front would have been aware of the decimation of the Frankish horse supply and capitalized on the king's vulnerability.[69] That seems probable, given the Saxons' history of utilizing their enemy's misfortunes to their advantage. However, other sources suggest Saxons were trying to orchestrate a wider conspiracy against the Franks. According to the *Wolfenbuttel Annals* (and indicated in the above report from the *Lorsch Annals*), Slavs (Wiltzi) and Frisians revolted at the same time as the Saxons.[70] Charles was then truly facing a "pagan alliance," and King has suggested that (coupled with the horse blight and famine) it was arguably the "grimmest" period of his entire reign.[71]

Circumstances did look dire for the king. We learn from the *Moselle Annals* that part of a Frankish army coming to the king via ship was betrayed by Frisians and Saxons and "in a large part destroyed."[72] This is perhaps the same event noted in the *St. Amand Annals*, which mention Saxons killing Franks where the Elbe meets the sea on Friday, July 6, 792.[73] The revised *RFA* add that, while the Frankish count Theodoric was leading troops through the Frisian *gau* of Rustringen, his army was intercepted by Saxons near the Weser and destroyed.[74] Theodoric, a relative of the king, had been given the undesirable task of conscripting Saxons to fight the Avars, and it is conceivable that he may have stoked personal animosity against himself because of his efforts.

Charles was wrapping up his Pannonia campaign when he heard what was happening in Saxony. News of devastating and unexpected Frankish defeats at the hands of Saxons must have been infuriating, and the revised *RFA* state explicitly that Charles immediately halted his Avar campaign and "concealed the magnitude of the loss" concerning the Saxons.[75] As horses were unavailable for transporting troops and supplies to deal with the rebels, Charles needed an alternative solution. After consulting with his advisors, the king commissioned a canal-building project to make transportation between the Danube and the Rhine more convenient (the idea was to connect the Rednitz and Altmühl to facilitate travel between the Danube and the Main). This was a massive undertaking, one that required intense labor throughout the entirety of the Fall. However, it was ultimately undone by continuous rain, which made conditions on the ground impossible to work with.[76]

The canal project was ambitious, but its failure added to a mounting list of woes.[77] To make matters worse, while the king was busying himself with construction oversight, he received more news of treacherous Saxons and disturbing reports of Saracens raiding Septimania, "slaying many Franks," and returning home victorious.[78] With Winter approaching, Charles decided to journey to Würzburg for the holidays, where he received word that the famine from the previous year was only getting worse.[79] Indeed, the *Moselle Annals* claim hunger was so bad that it "drove men to eat men, brothers brothers, mothers sons."[80]

By 794, the canal project was abandoned, and Charles could finally respond to the Saxon revolt that had begun two years earlier. The king traveled to Frankfurt

(*Franconfurt,* i.e., "ford of the Franks"), where he held a council of bishops from across the realm and received emissaries from Pope Hadrian.[81] From Frankfurt, Charles dispatched two Frankish armies into Saxony: one he led personally and the other Charles the Younger brought through Cologne.

When the Saxons heard the Franks were marching against them, they gathered together to muster a defense on the plain of Sindfeld. However, when the Saxons realized they were surrounded by armies on two sides, they swore, "with no such thing in mind," to convert to Christianity and remain faithful to the king.[82] The *Lorsch Annals* add that Saxons also met Charles at the Eresburg, where they promised to become Christians and swore oaths of loyalty; in reply, Charles sent them priests and accepted their surrender before returning to Aachen.[83] Yet, the revised *RFA* note that the king remained skeptical of Saxon sincerity and would "not forget their treachery."[84]

The king's doubts proved correct when he received word in the Spring of 795 that the Saxons failed to comply with their obligations. The *Lorsch Annals* record in an exhausted note: "infidelity arose from its customary source, the Saxons."[85]

Charles received the news while holding an assembly outside Mainz, where he was informed that the Saxons were refusing to commit to Christianity and had also neglected to send troops to support the king.[86] Another campaign was required, which Charles again led personally. However, he also sent word to his Obodrite allies, ordering them to invade Saxony from the east. The Obodrites obeyed, and their chieftain Witzan led his warriors to meet the Saxons at Lüne, but they were ambushed while crossing the Elbe, and Witzan was killed.[87] Enraged, Charles vowed to "beat down the Saxons," and the death of his ally "made him hate the treacherous people [Saxons] even more."[88]

The king's army marched north to ravage Saxon lands and eradicate the rebels. He was accompanied by loyal Saxon subjects, some of whom marched with him to the Elbe to set up camp at Bardowick. According to the *RFA*, it was within the vicinity of Bardowick that Charles had more Saxon hostages taken than ever before. In response, more Saxons came to be converted and forgiven, except for those dwelling in the Elbe marshlands and Wigmodia, because they were worried Charles would not forgive their involvement in Witzan's death.[89]

Charles stayed in Saxony through much of 796, during which he was joined by his sons Louis and Charles the Younger. In the Summer, he also sent an army to respond to the "Saracen" raiders of Spain, which succeeded.[90] In the meantime, the king moved throughout Saxony, devastating it with fire and sword while simultaneously continuing to take increasing numbers of hostages. These hostages were not select political exchanges associated with the nobility but freemen who were part of the king's developing program of systematic deportations.

The *St. Maximin Annals* confirm this new strategy, claiming "a third" of the males were taken out of the region.[91] The *Alemannic Annals* estimate the number of hostages as equaling 7,070 people.[92] The same language of devastation occurs in the *Petau Annals,* which also mentions raiding and hostage-taking in Wigmodia and the Dreingau.[93]

The simultaneous devastation of the Saxons and the successful response of his army in Spain must have restored the king's mood after the unfortunate events of previous years. Fortune continued to show favor later in 796 when the Franks gained extensive treasure from the Avar campaign, which the king distributed among his retainers and members of the Church (however, some of the treasure was used to finance construction of new buildings at Aachen).[94] Einhard boasted of this newfound wealth that "no war in which the Franks have ever engaged within living memory of man brought them such riches and booty."[95] Notger adds that much of this wealth was distributed "among the bishoprics and monasteries."[96]

The Avars had been embroiled in a civil war during which their khagan was killed, leaving his people weakened enough to be defeated by the Franks and their Slavic allies. The Frankish duke Eric of Friuli and Charlemagne's son Pippin ultimately sealed the Avar's fate by taking their famous stronghold, the so-called Ring.[97] Afterward, the new Avar *tudun* came to Aachen to be baptized and "subjected" his people "to the dominion of the lord Charles."[98] The revised *RFA* note his lack of sincerity.[99] However, any chance of resisting Frankish designs had ended; for all intents and purposes, the Avars were conquered.[100] Pockets of resistance continued over the coming years, but they would all fail.

Following their submission, the Avars became targets for missionaries looking to spread the gospel east.[101] For Charles' court scholar Alcuin, the Avar situation presented an opportunity to avoid replicating a critical mistake made with the Saxons, that is, implementing a tithing system.[102] Indeed, for Alcuin, tithing had been the primary impetus for Saxon resistance.[103] In correspondence with Bishop Arn of Salzburg in 796, Alcuin wrote:

> Tithes…have destroyed the faith of the Saxons. Why should a yoke be imposed on the necks of the recently converted which neither we nor our brothers have been able to sustain?[104]

He lamented further:

> It is because the wretched people of the Saxons has never had the fundament of faith in its heart that it has so often abandoned the baptismal oath.[105]

That same year, Alcuin utilized his *Konigsnahe* ("closeness to the king") to diplomatically offer Charles advice on the Saxons, which also had immediate relevance for the Avars:

> Behold the great devotion and benevolence with which you have toiled to soften the harshness of the unhappy people of the Saxons through the counsel of true health, that the name of Christ might have been spread! But since divine election seems not as yet to have been among them, many remain still now in the filth of most evil customs, to be damned with the devil… consider with wise judgement whether it would be right to impose the yoke

of tithes upon ignorant people who are novices in the faith…We ourselves, born, brought up and thoroughly schooled in the catholic faith, find it hard to consent to a full tithing of our goods: how much more unwilling to give are those of tender faith, child-like will and grasping disposition![106]

Alcuin then advises Charles that it would be better to establish an understanding of the fundamentals of faith via preaching *before* baptism so that the conversion of the Saxons would not be ruined at the outset by a lack of comprehension.[107] There is some evidence that Charles may have utilized Alcuin's advice, but that would come later. Despite large-scale deportations, Saxon resistance had not been entirely quelled, and more measures were needed to deal with rebellions in 797.

Once again, resistance came primarily from the north, particularly in the "intractable region" of Wigmodia.[108] Events that year must have been significant, as they were recorded in several sources. According to the *RFA*, Charlemagne led an army north "beyond swamps and pathless places" to the ocean, eventually arriving at Hadeln.[109] The *RFA* indicate that the campaign was a success and that the king was given hostages and received "the submission of the whole Saxon people" before returning to Aachen.[110] However, the same account mentions that Charles was back in Saxony with his army in November, setting up camp on the Weser at Herstelle ("army-place").[111] He resided there for the Winter of 797 and into the Spring of 798.[112]

The use of deportations during this period is also attested, and the *Lorsch Chronicle* claims Charles took away "every third man, with wife and children," after which the area was settled by Franks.[113] The devastation of Wigmodia is also evident in the *Lorsch Annals*, adding that hostages were also taken from the Frisians.[114]

There are several key features to be gained from these reports. First, deportations continued to be deployed, but notably, Franks were being brought in to resettle land left vacant by the Saxons. Colonization was coupled with conquest.[115] In addition, despite the sweeping victories presented in the chronicles, the fact that Charles wintered in Saxony suggests he was not confident in his enemies' supposed pacification. Further, the mention of Frisians indicates they were again in revolt alongside the Saxons. Indeed, their co-involvement is indicated in other sources, some of which report attacks on Franks in Frisia, possibly led by the Frisian warlords Unno and Eilrat.[116] Yet, how long Frisians had been in rebellion alongside the Saxons is unclear. Regardless, the defeat of 797 was the final blow to their participation. From then on, any Saxons who resisted Charlemagne would do so alone.

The *Capitulare Saxonicum* of 797

In the Fall of 797, Charles returned to Aachen, where on October 20, in the presence of Frankish magnates, ecclesiastical officials, and Saxons, he issued a new set of capitularies for Saxony, the so-called *Capitulare Saxonicum*.[117] The general scholarly consensus has been that these were markedly less cruel than the capitularies issued in 782.[118] Notably, the newer legislation failed to mention tithes, suggesting *perhaps* that Charles had listened to Alcuin's advice.[119] Furthermore, all Saxon peoples (except for the still rebellious Nordalbingians) were given roughly the same status in criminal law as other groups within the Frankish Empire.[120] This can be seen in the opening lines of the capitularies and in a list of provisions Saxons were expected to observe, the violation of which required Saxons to "pay sixty *solidi* in composition just like the Franks."[121]

Noticeably different from the older capitularies was the decreasing reliance upon capital punishment and a preference for fines. While the price for criminal action varied according to status, it is surprising that, even in the case of violence toward members of the Church, compensation could be used to make restitution. Indeed, there seems to be an explicit desire to avoid violence almost entirely (with some notable exceptions). This may reflect a motivation to stop cycles of violence, particularly blood-feuds.[122] It could also be that Charles was trying to demonstrate goodwill toward Saxons who remained loyal, which can be gleaned from the recognition of Saxon rights to hold assemblies, which the capitularies allow.[123]

The 797 capitularies also acknowledge regional currency variations. Saxons existed outside a coin-based commerce system and used material goods to barter. Charles recognized this aspect of Saxon society, and after considering local environments and means of subsistence, he determined what made sense for Saxons to use in place of *solidi*. For example, Bortrini (Westphalians) could use "forty measures of oats" and "twenty measures of rye," 15 measures of "winnowed barley," or "half a measure of honey" to represent a *solidus*, while northern Saxons could use "thirty measures of oats" and "fifteen measures of rye."[124]

Altogether, the 797 capitularies furthered Saxons' integration within the Empire and reinforced their obligations to the king, but they also included forms of accommodation.[125] The lack of violence or persecutory measures, guarantees of legal status, representation in matters of criminal justice, and the recognition of regional forms of subsistence were all positive developments. However, not all Saxons were satisfied. Despite improvements, capitularies from 816 show that even 20 years later, Saxons (and Frisians) were still not considered *entirely* equal within the Empire regarding laws concerning economic compensation.[126]

The Decimation of the North, 798–802

Resistance continued in the north, and in the summer of 798, Charles left Herstelle to deal with the northern Saxons.[127] Troubling news had arrived that "the Nordliudi" living beyond the Elbe had rebelled, as well as executed and ransomed Frankish envoys sent to engage with them.[128] One of those executed was an emissary named Godescal, whom the king had sent to meet with Sigfred in Denmark. When Godescal was returning from his mission, he was captured by Saxons and killed. The revised *RFA* claim the northern Saxons were then "carried away with their own insolence" because they had managed to kill the king's envoys without consequence.[129] Hearing that, Charles became "savagely aroused."[130]

After summoning his army, the king journeyed to Minden, simultaneously sending word to the Obodrites, instructing them to invade from the east. Their chieftain

Thrasco (Drozko), whose father (Witzan) was killed by the Saxons, happily complied.[131] Charles then "laid waste" the area between the Elbe and the Weser.[132]

Eventually, a Franco-Obodrite army arrived from the east, which the Saxons marched out to engage. According to the *Lorsch Annals,* these forces met up near the village of Bornhöved, where a great battle ensued. The contest went poorly for the Saxons, and just under 3,000 were killed.[133]

Virtually all of our sources confirm that, following these northern campaigns, the king took vast numbers of hostages from the Saxons. The *Alemannic Annals* note "countless hostages taken away," the *Petau Annals* "a multitude," while the *St. Amand Annals* mention specifically 1,600 "leading men" taken as hostages and redistributed in Francia.[134] The *RFA* add that many of these hostages had been hand-picked by Saxon nobles as those who were considered "the most treacherous."[135] Deportations and resettlement continued to be used as effective strategies to quell the rebellion, and again Saxon nobles are mentioned as betraying their people. Yet, even with these measures going into full force, the revolt continued.

In 799, Charles stayed in Saxony, setting up residence at Paderborn, where he began constructing a new cathedral.[136] He also dispatched his son Charles the Younger to deal with *infideles* (unfaithful) Saxons along the Weser.[137] His son was successful, and more hostages were taken. The *Lorsch Annals* record for the same year that many of the hostages taken (including women and children) were resettled throughout Francia, after which their vacant lands were granted to bishops, priests, counts, and other loyal magnates.[138]

While his son was dealing with rebels, Charlemagne stayed at Paderborn to await the arrival of Pope Leo, who was fleeing Rome and the virulent anger of his flock.[139] Leo was eventually met by Frankish emissaries and brought to the king, who was undoubtedly annoyed with the holy father. Nevertheless, he consoled the Pope, gave him gifts and due honors, and sent him back to Rome to reclaim his position.[140] This is not the place to explore the intricacies of the papal drama, but what is noteworthy for our purposes is that the Pope could travel through Saxony unscathed. As Rosamond McKitterick has observed, this was "a dramatic symbol of the new status of Saxony as a fully integrated part of the Frankish empire with Paderborn as its principal palace."[141] A decade or two prior, it would have been unthinkable for the heir of St. Peter to travel through such hostile pagan territory. That he did so suggests much of Saxony was considered relatively stable, and Charles wanted to demonstrate his successes in the region (particularly its Christianization).[142]

However, "stability" was not the right word to describe what was happening in the north, and two letters from Alcuin written to the king in the Summer of 799 demonstrate that "the Saxon problem" had yet to be fully reconciled. In one of these, written in June, Alcuin's exhausted tone is unmistakable:

> Let a peace be arranged with that abominable people [the Saxons], if that is possible. Let threats be dispensed with for a while, that they may not be made obdurate and flee but may be kept in hope, until such time as they may be recalled to peace by salutary counsels. You should hold what you have lest,

for the sake of a minor gain, what is greater should be lost. Your own sheep-fold should be protected lest the ravening wolf lay it waste…I addressed your most holy piety on the matter of the exaction of tithes some time ago, saying that it is perhaps better that governmental coercion should be relaxed, for a brief period at least, until such time as the roots of faith become implanted in men's hearts—if, that is, that land is considered worthy of divine election. Those who have abandoned it for other regions were the best Christians, as is widely known, while those who have remained in the country have persisted in the dregs of their wickedness.[143]

Essentially the same message is replicated in a letter from July:

I pray that divine grace one day grant you deliverance from the abominable people of the Saxons, to travel, to govern your dominions, to do justice, to restore churches, to correct the people, to determine what is proper for each authority and order, to defend the oppressed, to establish laws, to give solace to *peregrini* and to show everybody, everywhere, the path of righteousness and heavenly life.[144]

Alcuin makes a case for peace in these letters, gently nudging the king to dispense with "coercion" and allow time to develop goodwill. It is also noteworthy that Alcuin claims Saxons sent to Francia made for better Christians, undoubtedly due to their deeper integration within Frankish culture (and better treatment).[145] He also readdresses the problem of tithing, suggesting Charles had *not* taken his previous advice and that the absence of tithing in the 797 capitularies does not indicate the tithing system was suspended, merely that it never changed.[146]

Following the dismissal of Pope Leo, Charles returned to Aachen, where he could reflect on the year's events. However, he didn't linger there long. Instead, the king traversed the realm, during which (early-mid 800), he solidified coastal defenses, including commissioning a navy to combat the growing threat of piracy (in 799, the Norse raided the monastery of Noirmoutier in Aquitaine).[147] Charles then spent Easter at the northern French abbey of St. Riquier, from where he made for Rouen, Tours, Mainz, Ravenna, and finally, Rome to visit the restored Pope Leo.[148]

Charles stayed in Rome for the Winter, and on Christmas Day, he was declared Emperor of the Roman West (or, in the words of the *Liber Pontificalis,* "pious Augustus crowned by God").[149] Charles thereby established himself as a "successor to the Caesars."[150] The motivations and foreknowledge of the king's ascent to the imperial title have been debated for centuries.[151] However, given the timing of events, it seems highly likely that plans for Charles' coronation were discussed during Leo's visit to Paderborn.[152] Perhaps this was done in a *quid pro quo* arrangement whereby Charles' declaration was the price for Leo's restoration.[153]

Mayr-Harting has hypothesized that one of Charles' motivations for becoming emperor may have been specifically related to the Saxons, suggesting that, while kingship was not a recognized institution in Saxony, the notion of "emperorship" would have been more acceptable based on imperial iconography found on early Saxon bracteate.[154] However, this view remains subject to skepticism and is difficult to prove. Yet, from a broader perspective, the symbol of the imperial title may have been used by Charles to integrate all "Frankish" peoples into a newly restored (and Christian) Roman empire; a *Pax Christiana*.[155]

On the Saxon front, we are not told much about what happened the following year (801). According to the *RFA*, earthquakes and pestilence erupted in Germany along the Rhine, but nothing is said of the troubles north of the Elbe.[156] However, that turmoil *was* still underway is evidenced by an entry for the following year in which the king sent an army of loyal Saxons to deal with rebels on the far side of the Elbe.[157] The Franco-Saxon Wars had become as much a civil war as it had a conflict to resist Frankish rule.[158]

How successful the campaign of these loyal Saxons was is unclear. However, that same year some faithful Saxon nobles were given lands in Francia.[159] The 802 Special Capitularies for the missi (*Capitularia missorum Specialia*) also mentions Saxons who held benefices in Francia.[160] Such gifts would have been given in reciprocity for acts of loyalty, and campaigning against Saxon rebels would certainly qualify.

The "Peace of Salz"

Saxon gifts may be connected to the so-called Peace of Salz, an alleged peace treaty between Charlemagne and Saxon nobles mentioned by the Poeta Saxo for the year 803. The Poet cites Einhard's *Life of Charlemagne* as his source, but Einhard never actually mentions the event. The Poet is our only authority, and his account is generally disbelieved.[161] Nevertheless, the narrative surrounding the Peace of Salz remains relevant because it gives insight into the perspective of an upper-class Saxon who lived relatively close to the events he describes. While the author copies much from Einhard's account, he independently confirms the top-down conversion strategy used by Charlemagne (which he praises) and condemns the heathenism of his ancestors (see Chapter 9). However, the problem with the Poet's account stems from his claim that, as a result of the treaty, Saxons were no longer obliged to pay taxes or tribute to Frankish kings but rather "only the tithe… determined by divine law," that is, that belonging to the Church.[162] This reference to tithes is likely the primary purpose of his writing, which was intended to emphasize Saxons' autonomy and their equal footing with the Franks of the Poet's own time (the late ninth century), which saw a rapid expansion of Saxon power under the Ottonians (see Chapter 12). As a result, it is doubtful the Peace of Salz ever occurred but was instead an opportunistic political fabrication.

The *Lex Saxonum*

To bring legal uniformity to the Empire (likely) in 802/803, Charlemagne codified and reformed laws across the realm.[163] These included the *Lex-Francorum Chamavorum, Thuringorum, Frisionum*, and *Saxonum*.[164] The Saxon Law code

(*Lex Saxonum*, or as it was originally titled, *Incipit liber legis Saxonum*) included 66 chapters on standard legal topics for the period, such as *wergelds*, commerce, theft, marriage, women, property inheritance, slavery, sexual behavior, religion, and punishment.[165] We know the contents provided in the *Lex Saxonum* due to the survival of two manuscripts dated to the late ninth or early tenth century (found in the *Codex Spangenbergianus* and *Codex Corbeiensis*).[166] Ultimately, the laws presented in the Saxon code represent a fusion of Saxon and Frankish customs, with notable deference given to Christianity and the lucrative status of the nobility.[167] However, parceling which legal customs belonged to the Saxons before the Frankish conquest remains problematic, especially given that much of the *Lex Saxonum* seems to be based on the older Frankish *Lex Ribuaria* and tied to earlier Saxon capitularies.[168] Nevertheless, the *Lex Saxonum* should not be seen as a direct copy of these earlier sources. The fact that separate law codes were being created for sub-regions of the empire, each with somewhat different laws, as well as the fact that local variances within Saxony are acknowledged in the *Lex Saxonum*, all suggest the law codes *did* preserve some of the customs for the peoples to whom they are ascribed.[169]

A complete survey of all 66 chapters of the *Lex Saxonum* would take us too far off course; however, a brief overview of notable themes and attributes provides beneficial insight into the priorities of Saxon society and the transformations ushered in by Charlemagne. From the start, any reader of the text will notice its emphasis on violence. Fines, in the form of schillings or *solidi*, are issued for causing accidental or intentional harm in which bruising, bleeding, exposure of bone, disfigurement, mutilation, blinding, or loss of limbs/digits occurs.[170] Violence toward pregnant women was punished doubly.[171] Harming any man coming to or from the army leaving a royal palace (Pfalz) was fined triply.[172] In each of these instances, payment could be avoided if enough "oath-men" swore on one's behalf; however, other instances (e.g., the theft of land) could be settled by duel.[173]

For murder, there was an extraordinary difference in punishment depending on status. Killing a nobleman required payment of 1,440 shillings, a freeman 120 shillings, and a slave 36 shillings.[174] However, killing anyone in a church or anyone leaving a church on a feast day was punished with death.[175] To conspire against the king's life or the Kingdom of the Franks merited the same fate.[176]

The punishment was also death for anyone who killed his master or his master's son or raped his master's wife or daughter.[177] In other instances of rape, or "bride theft," punishment was in the form of hefty fines, that is, twice that of the standard bride price (300 schillings) to the family (600 shillings in total) and 240 shillings to the girl.[178] If the girl was married, 300 shillings would be paid to her father, husband, (sometimes) mother, and herself.[179]

Akin to other Germanic law codes, the *Lex Saxonum* is explicitly patriarchal (although the wergeld for an unmarried woman was twice that of a man).[180] Women could not inherit paternal land unless they lacked brothers, but even then, they were placed under the guardianship of a male relative.[181] Among Eastphalians and Engrians, women were allowed to keep their dowry, but for Westphalians, as soon as a son was born, the marriage gift went to him.[182] However, in Westphalia, any wealth acquired by man and wife was split equally, while among the Eastphalians and Engrians, the wife was to be satisfied with her marriage gift alone.[183]

Some forms of thievery, fraud, or selling individuals into slavery were met with fines, yet the death penalty was issued for stealing horses, beehives, children, items from weaving huts, or anything worth more than 3 schillings.[184] The same was true for burning down another's house.[185] In each instance where the death penalty is used, the code explicitly states that sanctuary will not be given to anyone who flees to a church.[186] These instances demonstrate the extent to which the disruption of critical forms of subsistence was deemed unforgivable.

Later Church Developments in Saxony

At the same time legal reforms were underway, religious institutions in Saxony continued to develop. As early as 787, the missionary Willehad was installed as bishop of the first Saxon bishopric of Bremen.[187] Before dying two years later, Willehad spent his time at Bremen constructing a new cathedral (dedicated to St. Peter) and overseeing evangelical endeavors among Saxons along the Weser and the Elbe.[188] Similarly, a few years later, in 792, a Fulda-trained Frankish aristocrat named Ercanbert was appointed as the first bishop of Minden.[189] Ercanbert's brother was Abbot Baugulf of Fulda, and their family, it seems, had come to acquire extensive lands in Saxony during the Saxon Wars.[190]

By 799, Charlemagne's church at Paderborn (dedicated to St. Mary and St. Kilian) had also been consecrated. However, it would not receive its first bishop until the 806–807 appointment of a Saxon named Hathumar.[191] In addition, between 798 and 800, the Frisian missionary Liudger founded the south Westphalian abbey of Werden on the Ruhr (dedicated to St. Salvator, Mary, and Peter). At the same time, Walther, a Saxon nobleman, established the abbey of Herford north of Paderborn.[192] Herford was likely the earliest all-female religious community in Saxony, of which Walther's daughter (Suala) became the first abbess.[193]

Between 802 and 805, Liudger was also installed as bishop of Münster (*Mimigernaford*), likely a small mission station at the time, where he built further churches in the area (he had already built a church in Münster back in 793).[194] At the same time, Liudger was granted Leuze in Brabant as a refuge in case danger arose, and he was forced to flee again.[195] However, Münster would remain his base of operations for organizing missionary efforts in Westphalia, and it was there that he worked until his death in 809.[196]

Liudger's appointment as bishop coincided with Charles' General Capitulary for the *Missi*, which forbade counts from harboring "magicians, wizards, or witches," suggesting this was a problem among aristocrats of the realm.[197] Indeed, the struggle with pagan hang-ups appears to have been a persistent problem on the king's mind. Back in 786, Charles received a letter from Pope Hadrian in response to *missi* he sent asking what sort of penance Saxon Christians who reverted to paganism should undertake.[198] Hadrian replied that only after purgation by penance could apostates be received again "into the bosom of the church."[199] The correspondence between Charles and the Pope demonstrates that conversion was not a superficial matter for the emperor. He wanted to understand precedent and find a path back for those who wandered astray.[200] That concern lingered with Charles till the end of his life, and even as late as 811, he was asking of his own people during an assembly, "Are we really Christians?"[201] Orthodoxy was critical, and there was little room in the emperor's worldview for heretics, mystics, or "wandering monastic vagabonds."[202]

In 804, a few years prior to the above assembly, we are also given a rare insight into the fate of a leading Saxon who was involved in the Saxon Wars at its genesis, that is, the Eastphalian duke Hessi. Hessi had been made a count and given gifts upon his surrender in 775 but, in his old age, opted to become a monk.[203] After granting lands to his daughters, Hessi joined the monastic community of Fulda, where he passed away.[204] Over the following decades, Hessi's descendants continued to be of some importance in the religious and political life of Saxony (see Chapter 11).[205]

It was also in 804 that Charlemagne and Archbishop Hildebald of Cologne organized the Saxon mission on a broader level by establishing the four bishoprics responsible for it. As Nyberg has helpfully summarized, these included:

- Osnabrück: for land east of the Ems around its tributary, the River Hase.
- Bremen: for the main Saxon settlement area around the estuary of the Weser.
- Minden: for further up the Weser. Except the region around the upper course of the Ems.
- Münster: for Saxons west of the Ems and administration of the Frisian coastland.[206]

Paderborn was also involved in the Saxon mission; however, it was a suffragan of Mainz, not Cologne.[207] These regional divisions served as organizational structures for promoting Christianization and as a means of enhancing the power of local bishops, who were gradually becoming more directly involved in Saxon religious life.

The Capitulation of the North, 804

It is unclear what was happening on the Saxon front in 803. Back in Francia, we have reports of a Winter earthquake reaping havoc, but nothing is said of campaigns.[208] However, by 804, this dearth of information is no longer an issue. According to the *RFA*, after wintering in Aachen, Charles led an army into Saxony, where he deported all the Saxons north of the Elbe and those in Wigmodia (men, women, and children).[209] These deportations are also mentioned in the *Moissac Chronicle*, the *St. Amand Annals*, the so-called *Greatest Salzburg Annals*, and the *Earlier Metz Annals*.[210] Some deportees may have been captured by Charles' elite *scarae* troops, whom the king dispatched to conduct raids throughout the region.[211]

The impression given by our sources is that the scale of these final deportations was substantial. According to Einhard, as many as 10,000 Saxons were removed from north of the Elbe.[212] Their resettlement in Francia changed local landscapes in Bavaria, Hesse, and Thuringia, the remnants of which can be seen in place names such as Sachsenberg, Sachsenried, Hohensachsen, Sachsenhausen, Sachsendorf, Sachsenfllur, and Gross-Sachsenheim.[213] The homes they left behind were also transformed when Charles permitted the Obodrites to occupy their lands.[214]

What was the purpose of these deportations? Ultimately, the king seems to have concluded that Nordalbingia had become a haven for rebels, a frontier of outlaws situated too close to the Danes for comfort.[215] By resettling troublesome Saxons in Francia, particularly in the more densely populated Frankish strongholds along the Rhine, they could be better monitored and integrated. Furthermore, by separating Saxons into isolated pockets, they would be unable to organize resistance easily.[216]

In discussing Medieval Kyiv, historian P. M. Barford has observed that resettlement of populations was often used "to break down old social ties based on kinship and territorial bonds...preventing effective opposition to new social conditions."[217] That observation can be readily applied to Charlemagne's Saxon policy, which was incredibly effective.[218] The year 804, following prolonged periods of "coolly calculated" devastation, put a halt to Saxon resistance for a generation.[219] What Charles Oman described as "the last throes of Saxon despair" had failed.[220] The "unconquerable Saxons" finally succumbed, and, in the words of the so-called Astronomer (Louis the Pious' biographer), "the long and extremely cruel Saxon war" was over.[221] The next time Saxons revolted, Charles would be dead.

Conclusion

The last phase of Charlemagne's Saxon Wars was spent dealing primarily with northern rebels, most of whom were situated on the far side of the Elbe. Many of the prior policies Charles used to convert and pacify the Saxons continued to be employed, including ruthless violence, courtship of the Saxon nobility, and conversion as a price of military surrender. In addition, numerous new ecclesiastical foundations and the establishment of Saxon bishoprics were used to assist in conversion efforts and establish the Church as a more prominent presence. Each of these developments operated alongside the continued political integration of Saxony into the Frankish Empire, which can be seen gradually occurring via the inclusion of Saxons in Frankish campaigns and assemblies, in the reforms of Saxon law, and in building goodwill with loyal Saxons by lessening the harshness of Saxon capitularies. However, Saxons continuing to resist in the north were not beneficiaries of that goodwill, and rather than allow an already protracted war to continue, Charles ordered massive deportations of Saxon families in the region to break their resolve. These were followed by Frankish and Obodrite colonization of northern Saxony, which ended Saxon resistance. Yet, while the conquest of Saxony was over, the consequences of that 33-year endeavor had only just begun.

Notes

1 Lintzel, *Untersuchungen zur Geschichte der alten Sachsen*, 31–32
2 Scholz, *Carolingian Chronicles*, 63
3 Ibid. & King, *Charlemagne*, 154–155

4 Nicolle, *The Conquest of Saxony*, 75

5 Scholz, *Carolingian Chronicles*, 63–64

6 Ibid. 63–69 & McKinney, *The Saxon Poet's Life of Charles the Great*, 38–39

7 Goldberg, *Struggle for Empire*, 48

8 Scholz, *Carolingian Chronicles*, 63–64

9 Musset, *The Germanic Invasions*, 84 & Riche, *The Carolingians*, 101

10 Wolfram, *The Roman Empire and its Germanic Peoples*, 304–306 & Pohl, *The Avars*, 33

11 Musset, *The Germanic Invasions*, 94–95

12 Barford, *The Early Slavs*, 54–58; Kobylinski, "The Slavs," 536–538; Mackay, *Atlas of Medieval Europe*, 14 & Stadler, "Avar Chronology Revisited," 47–82

13 Brown, "The Transformation of the Roman Mediterranean," 9–10

14 Musset, *The Germanic Invasions*, 88

15 Wolfram, *The Roman Empire and its Germanic Peoples*, 305 & Wormald, "Kings and kingship," 575

16 Noble, *Charlemagne and Louis the Pious*, 72 & McKinney, *The Saxon Poet's Life of Charles the Great*, 47–48

17 Stofferahn, "Staying the Royal Sword," 468–470

18 Barford, *The Early Slavs*, 79 & 144 & Pohl, *The Avars*, 237

19 Wolfram, *The Roman Empire and its Germanic Peoples*, 305–306 & Bachrach, *Warfare in Medieval Europe*, 231

20 Pohl, *The Avars*, 254–262 & Leeming, *The Oxford Companion to World Mythology*, 376

21 Wolfram, *The Roman Empire and its Germanic Peoples*, 305

22 Oman, *The Dark Ages*, 285

23 Scholz, *Carolingian Chronicles*, 66–68

24 Einhard, *The Life of Charlemagne*, 37–38

25 Widukind, *Deeds of the Saxons*, 51 & Barford, *The Early Slavs*, 104–105

26 Riche, *The Carolingians*, 109–110 & Tschan, *History of the Archbishops of Hamburg-Bremen*, 65

27 Howorth, "The Early Intercourse of the Danes and the Franks," 154 & Melleno, "Between Borders," 366

28 Barford, *The Early Slavs*, 21; Buse, *The Regions of Germany*, 59 & 132–133 & Thompson, *Feudal Germany*, 532

29 Ibid. 104–107 & 131; Melleno, "Between Borders," 371–372 & Pounds, *An Historical Geography of Europe*, 176 & 200

30 Kaufmann, *The Medieval Fortress*, 89–91

31 Dickinson, "Rural Settlements in the German Lands," 252; Barford, *The Early Slavs*, 119–123 & Davies, *Europe*, 225

32 Melleno, "Between Borders," 366–367

33 Barford, *The Early Slavs*, 116–118

34 Ibid. 140

35 Nicolle, *The Age of Charlemagne*, 19

36 Ibid.

37 Barford, *The Early Slavs*, 194–195; Leeming, *The Oxford Companion to World Mythology*, 311–312 & 359 & 369; Davies, *Europe*, 225; Thompson, *Feudal Germany*, 387–388; Helmold, *The Chronicle of the Slavs*, 158–159 & 274–276; Warner, *Ottonian Germany*, 252–254 & Słupecki, "Slavic Religion," 339

38 Barford, *The Early Slavs*, 123 & 189–191 & 200–201 & Sindbaek, *The Land of "Denemearce"*, 177

39 Ibid. 189–195

40 Howorth, "The Early Intercourse of the Danes and the Franks," 154

41 Nicolle, *The Conquest of Saxony*, 25–26

42 Wallace-Hadrill, *The Fourth Book of the Chronicle of Fredegar*, 39–40, & 56–58

43 Barford, *The Early Slavs*, 107

44 Scholz, *Carolingian Chronicles*, 68–69

45 Einhard, *The Life of Charlemagne*, 37. Republished with the permission of The University of Michigan Press, from *The Life of Charlemagne*, Einhard, © 1960; permission conveyed through Copyright Clearance Center, Inc.

46 Scholz, *Carolingian Chronicles*, 66–69

47 King, *Charlemagne*, 135

48 Scholz, *Carolingian Chronicles*, 68

49 King, *Charlemagne*, 138

50 Scholz, *Carolingian Chronicles*, 68

51 King, *Charlemagne*, 308

52 The order of operations was often similar during the Colonial era: missionaries in New England followed in the aftermath of the Puritan conquest; in Mexico they followed Cortes' destruction of the Aztec Empire; in China, they followed the British encroachments of the nineteenth century; and so on. See: Conclusion.

53 Wickham, *The Inheritance of Rome*, 491

54 Scholz, *Carolingian Chronicles*, 68–69

55 King, *Charlemagne*, 308. The translation is from *Charlemagne: Translated Sources*, P.D. King, © 1987.

56 Scholz, *Carolingian Chronicles*, 69

57 King, *Charlemagne*, 139

58 Ibid. & Scholz, *Carolingian Chronicles*, 69–70

59 Ibid.

60 Ibid.

61 Scholz, *Carolingian Chronicles*, 70

62 Flierman, *Saxon Identities*, 100 & Goldberg, *Struggle for Empire*, 51

63 King, *Charlemagne*, 139–140 & Noble, *Charlemagne and Louis the Pious*, 104 & 233

64 Flierman, *Saxon Identities*, 100

65 Noble, *Charlemagne and Louis the Pious*, 105

66 Many of the Saxon rebels were likely younger warriors who had not participated in the earlier revolts. See Mayr-Harting, "Charlemagne, the Saxons, and the Imperial Coronation of 800," 1123–1128

67 King, *Charlemagne*, 139–140. The translation is from *Charlemagne: Translated Sources*, P.D. King, © 1987.

68 Ibid. 158.

69 Ibid. 57–58

70 Ibid. 158

71 Ibid. 60 & 135

72 Ibid. 135

73 Ibid.

74 Scholz, *Carolingian Chronicles*, 71

75 Ibid.

76 Ibid.

77 For the canal project, see Bachrach, *Warfare in Medieval Europe*, 60–61. In sum, Charles was dealing with the adoptionist heresy, assassination attempts, failed construction projects, Saxon revolts, Saracen encroachments, the Avars, and the death of his wife Fastrada, all within a relatively short period of time. See McKinney, *The Saxon Poet's Life of Charles the Great*, 51–53

78 Scholz, *Carolingian Chronicles*, 71–73

79 Ibid. 73 & King, *Charlemagne*, 136

80 King, *Charlemagne*, 136

81 Scholz, *Carolingian Chronicles*, 73; Schlesinger, "Early Medieval Fortifications in Hesse," 255 & for the meaning of "Frankfurt," see Warner, *Ottonian Germany*, 360

82 Ibid.

83 King, *Charlemagne*, 141 & in the Fulda Easter tables, we are told that in the year 795, "Charles stayed near the Eresburg"; see Raaijmakers, *The Making of the Monastic Community of Fulda*, 60

84 Scholz, *Carolingian Chronicles*, 73

85 King, *Charlemagne*, 141–142. The translation is from *Charlemagne: Translated Sources*, P.D. King, © 1987.

86 Ibid. & Scholz, *Carolingian Chronicles*, 74

87 McKinney, *The Saxon Poet's Life of Charles the Great*, 55

88 Scholz, *Carolingian Chronicles*, 74

89 Ibid. & King, *Charlemagne*, 141–142

90 King, *Charlemagne*, 142

91 Ibid. 160

92 Ibid. 159–160

93 Ibid. 160

94 Ibid. 141–142 & Ring, *Northern Europe*, 3

95 Einhard, *The Life of Charlemagne*, 38. Republished with the permission of The University of Michigan Press, from *The Life of Charlemagne*, Einhard, © 1960; permission conveyed through Copyright Clearance Center, Inc.

96 Noble, *Charlemagne and Louis the Pious*, 91

97 King, *Charlemagne*, 142; Scholz, *Carolingian Chronicles*, 74–75 & Noble, *Charlemagne and Louis the Pious*, 91

98 Ibid. 160

99 Scholz, *Carolingian Chronicles*, 75

100 Pounds, *An Historical Geography of Europe*, 173

101 Their conversion was also remembered in an anonymous Carolingian poem; see Godman, *Poetry of the Carolingian Renaissance*, 187–191

102 Fletcher, *The Conversion of Europe*, 220; Sullivan, "Carolingian Missionary Theories," 277–280 & Stofferahn, "Staying the Royal Sword," 464

103 Milis, *The Pagan Middle Ages*, 26 & Gaskoin, *Alcuin*, 96–98

104 King, *Charlemagne*, 314–315. The translation is from *Charlemagne: Translated Sources*, P.D. King, © 1987.

105 Ibid. 317

106 Ibid. 315–316 & for *Konigsnahe*, see Wickham, *The Inheritance of Rome*, 122 & Goldberg, *Struggle for Empire*, 10

107 Dutton, *Carolingian Civilization*, 126

108 Thompson, *Feudal Germany*, 171

109 Scholz, *Carolingian Chronicles*, 75

110 Ibid.

111 King, *Charlemagne*, 59 & 137

112 Ibid. 161

113 Ibid.

114 Ibid. 142

115 Faulkner, *Law and Authority in the Early Middle Ages*, 42 & Cusack, "Between Sea and Land," 9–10

116 Rembold, *Conquest and Christianization*, 43

117 For an English translation see Loyn et al., *The Reign of Charlemagne*, 54–56; King, *Charlemagne*, 230 & see also Elsakkers, "Raptus Ultra Rhenum," 30 & for the Latin text of the *Capitulare Saxonicum* see Von Schwerin, *Leges Saxonum und Lex Thuringorum*, 45–49 & for a German translation: Eckhardt, *Die Gesetze Des Karolingerreiches III*, 10–16

118 Brunner, *Deutsche Rechtsgeschichte*, 466–467

119 Mayr-Harting, "Charlemagne, the Saxons, and the Imperial Coronation of 800," 1131–1132

120 King, *Charlemagne*, 230–232 & Elsakkers, "Raptus Ultra Rhenum," 30
121 Ibid.
122 Ibid.
123 Ibid.
124 King, *Charlemagne*, 230–232
125 Nelson, *King and Emperor*, 331–333
126 Landon, *Conquest and Colonization*, 57 & Faulkner, *Law and Authority in the Early Middle Ages*, 70
127 King, *Charlemagne*, 137
128 Scholz, *Carolingian Chronicles*, 76
129 Ibid.
130 Ibid.
131 McKinney, *The Saxon Poet's Life of Charles the Great*, 59
132 Scholz, *Carolingian Chronicles*, 76 & King, *Charlemagne*, 161
133 Ibid. 143 & Loyn, *The Reign of Charlemagne*, 42–43
134 Ibid. 161–162
135 Scholz, *Carolingian Chronicles*, 76
136 Honselmann, "Paderborn 777," 400
137 King, *Charlemagne*, 162
138 Ibid. 143 & Loyn, *The Reign of Charlemagne*, 43
139 Ibid. & Scholz, *Carolingian Chronicles*, 77; McKinney, *The Saxon Poet's Life of Charles the Great*, 62 & Davis, *The Lives of the Eighth-Century Popes*, 181–184
140 Davis, *The Lives of the Eighth-Century Popes*, 184–186
141 McKitterick, *Charlemagne*, 51
142 Sypeck, *Becoming Charlemagne*, 116–117 & Behr, "Die Sachsenkriege Karls des Großen," 216–218
143 King, *Charlemagne*, 32. The translation is from *Charlemagne: Translated Sources*, P.D. King, © 1987.
144 Ibid. 322
145 Rembold, *Conquest and Christianization*, 58–59
146 Dessens, *Res Voluntaria, Non Necessaria*, 58 & McKitterick, *The Frankish Kingdoms under the Carolingians*, 62–63
147 Ferguson, *The Vikings*, 85
148 Scholz, *Carolingian Chronicles*, 80–81
149 Davis, *The Lives of the Eighth-Century Popes*, 187–189 & McKinney, *The Saxon Poet's Life of Charles the Great*, 69
150 Pounds, *An Historical Geography of Europe*, 170 & Wickham, *The Inheritance of Rome*, 382
151 Cantor, *The Civilization of the Middle Ages*, 181 & Butt, *Daily Life in the Age of Charlemagne*, 22–23
152 Heather, *Christendom*, 379 & Jeep, *Medieval Germany*, 608
153 Ibid. 380
154 Mayr-Harting, "Charlemagne, the Saxons, and the Imperial Coronation of 800," 1127–1128
155 Gonzalez, *The Story of Christianity V.I*, 315; McKitterick, *History and Memory in the Carolingian World*, 115 & Davis, *Charlemagne's Practice of Empire*, 171
156 Scholz, *Carolingian Chronicles*, 81
157 Ibid.
158 Robinson, *Old English and its Closest Relatives*, 108 & Rembold, "The Poeta Saxo at Paderborn," 177–178
159 Landon, *Conquest and Colonization*, 55 & Rembold, *Conquest and Christianization*, 63
160 Loyn, *The Reign of Charlemagne*, 79–80
161 Springer, *Die Sachsen*, 214

162 McKinney, *The Saxon Poet's Life of Charles the Great*, 72–73

163 Bauer, *Buße und Strafe im Frühmittelalter*, 11. Some scholars contest the date because it is based primarily on a line in the *Lorsch Annals*, a general statement by Einhard, and the later commentary of the Poeta Saxo. See also: Faulkner, "Carolingian kings and the leges barbarorum," 445–446

164 Elsakkers, "Raptus Ultra Rhenum," 41; Drew, *The Laws of the Salian Franks*, 9; Grahn-Hoek, "The Thuringi," 294 & for a German translation, see Eckhardt, *Die Gesetze Des Karolingerreiches III*, 16–127

165 Ibid. 53–54; Faulkner, *Law and Authority in the Early Middle Ages*, 74 & 78; Ehlers, "Könige, Klöster und der Raum," 193–195; Wemple, *Women in Frankish Society*, 27 & For the Latin text of the *Lex Saxonum* see Von Schwerin, *Leges Saxonum und Lex Thuringorum*, 9–34 & also Brunner, *Deutsch Rechtsgeschichte*, 465; Bauer, *Buße und Strafe im Frühmittelalter*, 27 & Elsakkers, "Raptus Ultra Rhenum," 333

166 Bauer, *Buße und Strafe im Frühmittelalter*, 25

167 Ibid. 37 & 43 & 49; Nicolle, *The Conquest of Christianity*, 42–83 & Von Heung-Sik Park, "Die Stände der Lex Saxonum," 210

168 Ibid. 26 & 37; Brunner, Deutsch Rechtsgeschichte, 465–469; Springer, *Die Sachsen*, 239 & Arnold, *Medieval Germany*, 44

169 Seebohm, *Tribal Custom in Anglo-Saxon Law*, 216–217 & Becher, "Non enim habent regem idem Antiqui Saxones," 25–26

170 Eckhardt, *Die Gesetze Des Karolingerreiches III*, 16–23 & 28–33

171 Ibid.

172 Ibid. 24–25

173 Ibid. 30–33

174 Ibid. 20–21

175 Ibid. 22–23

176 Ibid. 28–29

177 Ibid.

178 Ibid. 24–29 & Elsakkers, "Raptus Ultra Rhenum," 34–39

179 Ibid. 24–27

180 Seebohm, *Tribal Custom in Anglo-Saxon Law*, 215 & Nelson & Rio, "Women and Laws in Early Medieval Europe," 107

181 Eckhardt, *Die Gesetze Des Karolingerreiches III*, 24–27

182 Ibid. 26–27

183 Ibid. 28–29

184 Ibid. 22–25

185 Ibid.

186 Ibid. 22–23

187 Nyberg, *Monasticism in North-Western Europe*, 18; Flierman, *Saxon Identities*, 92; Wood, *The Missionary Life*, 90; Noble, "Carolingian Religion," 293; Tschan, *History of the Archbishops of Hamburg-Bremen*, 18–20; Farmer, *The Oxford Dictionary of Saints*, 449 & Gallee, *Old-Saxon Texts*, X

188 Ibid. 20; Knibbs, *Ansgar, Rimbert and the Forged Foundations of Hamburg-Bremen*, 37 & 50; Tschan, *History of the Archbishops of Hamburg Bremen*, xiii & Ehlers, "Könige, Klöster und der Raum," 207–216

189 Ibid. 53 & McKitterick, *The Frankish Kingdoms under the Carolingians*, 62

190 Schieffer, "Die Anfänge der westfälischen Domstifte," 182–184 & Lübeck, "Das Kloster Fulda und die Sachsenmission," 61–62

191 Ehlers, "Könige, Klöster und der Raum," 207–216; McKitterick, *Charlemagne*, 251–253; Flierman, *Saxon Identities*, 130–137; Rembold, "The Poeta Saxo at Paderborn," 188–196 & Schieffer, "Die Anfänge der westfälischen Domstifte," 182

192 Ibid. 207–216; Fletcher, *The Conversion of Europe*, 218–219; Isenberg, "Nach den Sachsenkriegen Karls des Großen," 14–15 & Goetz, *Life in the Middle Ages*, 66–67

193 Ibid. & Flierman, *Saxon Identities*, 137 & Greer, *Commemorating Power in Early Medieval Saxony*, 30

194 Isenberg, "Nach den Sachsenkriegen Karls des Großen," 14–15; Schieffer, "Die Anfänge der westfälischen Domstifte," 176–178; Talbot, *The Anglo-Saxon Missionaries in Germany*, 233; Wood, *The Missionary Life*, 110–111 & Leidinger, "Zur Christianisierung des Ostmünsterlandes," 35

195 Wood, *The Missionary Life*, 110–111

196 Fletcher, *The Conversion of Europe*, 219; Landon, *Conquest and Colonization*, 48 & Isenberg, "Nach den Sachsenkriegen Karls des Großen," 21–22

197 Dutton, *Carolingian Civilization*, 75

198 Dessens, *Res Voluntaria, Non Necessaria*, 50

199 King, *Charlemagne*, 294–295

200 Riche, *Daily Life in the World of Charlemagne*, 191 & Henderson, *A History of Germany in the Early Middle Ages*, 79

201 Noble, "Carolingian Religion," 287; Butt, *Daily Life in the Age of Charlemagne*, 54 & Davis, *Charlemagne's Practice of Empire*, 8–9

202 Riche, *The Carolingians*, 315

203 Flierman, *Saxon Identities*, 147–149

204 Paxton, *Anchoress and Abbess in Ninth Century Saxony*, 30–31 & 83

205 Ibid. 40

206 Nyberg, *Monasticism in North-Western Europe*, 5–6

207 Knibbs, *Ansgar, Rimbert and the Forged Foundations of Hamburg-Bremen*, 59

208 Scholz, *Carolingian Chronicles*, 83

209 Ibid.

210 King, *Charlemagne*, 146 & 164–165

211 Ibid. 146

212 Einhard, *The Life of Charlemagne*, 30–37 & this is repeated by Rudolf of Fulda, see Wattenbach, *Die Übertragung des hl. Alexander von Rudolf und Meginhart*, 10–11

213 Henderson, *A History of Germany in the Middle Ages*, 74; Rembold, *Conquest and Christianization*, 57; Landon, "Economic Incentives for the Frankish Conquest of Saxony," 35 & Bauer, "Die Quellen für das sog. Blutbad von Verden," 51–53

214 Oman, *The Dark Ages*, 289

215 Howorth, "The Ethnology of the Germans (IV)," 428 & Mayr-Harting, "Charlemagne, the Saxons, and the Imperial Coronation of 800," 1131–1132

216 Nelson, *King and Emperor*, 330–331

217 Barford, *The Early Slavs*, 148

218 Barraclough, *The Origins of Modern Germany*, 8

219 Nelson, *King and Emperor*, 322–323

220 Oman, *The Dark Ages*, 280

221 The description given by Notger the Stammerer, see Noble, *Charlemagne and Louis the Pious*, 103, 231 & 236 & King, *Charlemagne*, 173

9   Turbulent Frontiers

The completion of Charlemagne's conquest of Saxony in 804 was not the end of him dealing with the consequences of the conflict. Challenges with conversion, cultural transformation, and political integration remained. At the same time, northern Saxony continued to be a contested frontier zone, while borders in the east were subject to Slavic raiding. Yet, most pressing, was the need to manage tensions with the rising power of the Danes.

Shifting Danish Dynamics

By 804, the Danish king Sigfred was dead. He was succeeded by his presumed relative, Godfred, whom the Danish historian Saxo Grammaticus described as "remarkable" for his "military prowess" and "generosity."[1] Unlike Sigfrid, who (despite giving refuge to Saxon rebels) tried to maintain peace with the Franks, Godfred was willing to engage in hostilities, a characteristic defining many Danish rulers over the following century.[2] A key impetus for that change was the Frankish conquest of Saxony.[3] The removal of culturally similar Saxons from Danish borderlands and their replacement by hostile Frankish, Obodrite, and Frankish-allied Saxons could not have been taken well by the Danes. Trepidation caused by this development is likely (in part) what spawned the wearing of Thor's Hammer amulets, an identity statement by Nordic pagans who felt their way of life was under threat.[4] Afterall, the Danes had heard troubling tales from Saxon refugees and witnessed firsthand what happened to pagans resisting the Franks; their anxieties toward the growing Frankish Empire would hardly be surprising.[5]

During the final phase of Saxon deportations, there is every indication that refugees continued fleeing to Denmark, and Godfred maintained his predecessor's policy of granting them sanctuary.[6] This might have been the opposite of what was intended by the deportations, which Charlemagne partially ordered to keep Saxons from acquiring Danish support.[7] Archaeological evidence near Hedeby confirms the presence of Saxon *Grübenhauser* and artifacts dating from the mid-eighth to the early ninth century.[8] However, if Saxon settlement in the region is confirmed, at what price were Saxons granted hospitality? Was it given freely, or were refugees required to declare loyalty to the new Danish king? Regardless, Godfred didn't wait long to make a show of force, letting the emperor know that moving further

DOI: 10.4324/9781003379157-12

north to procure Saxon exiles would not be tolerated. According to the *Royal Frankish Annals* (*RFA*), immediately after the Frankish settlement of Obodrites in northern Saxony, Godfred made that message clear in dramatic fashion by bringing a fleet and his entire cavalry to a meeting with the emperor on the Saxon border near Hollenstedt. Envoys were then exchanged to discuss the return of Saxon fugitives.[9] However, there is no indication that Godfred had any interest in returning them. The *RFA* account also indicates that he and Charles were wary of each other, and their initial communications ended in an uneasy stalemate. With little accomplished, both sides withdrew. Godfred returned home, and Charles disbanded his army to go hunting in the Ardennes.[10]

Saxons in the East

The following year, Charles found himself busy with other concerns. One pressing issue was the smuggling of Frankish weapons to hostile areas. This prompted the emperor to announce, via the Capitulary of Thionville, that the sale of arms would be forbidden in certain regions, including Bardowick and Scheessel in Saxony. Anyone caught violating that edict would suffer confiscation of their goods.[11] Arms control was especially important as tensions escalated with Danes and Slavs, who might illegally obtain Frankish weapons in Saxony and use them against the Franks. As a result, fostering the goodwill of Saxon elites responsible for defending the frontier and enforcing arms prohibitions may have been a priority.[12]

Regarding the Slavs, Frankish problems with the Wends were ongoing, and in 805, the emperor dispatched three armies into their territory under the leadership of his son Charles the Younger, one of which included a contingent of Saxons. During the campaign, Franco-Saxon forces spent several weeks ravaging the region, leading to the death of Semela, a Bohemia king of the Daleminzi.[13] Meanwhile, a Frankish naval force was sent up the Elbe to Magdeburg, which pillaged the region of Werinofeld (*Hwerenofelda*).[14] The following year, Charles the Younger was back in Slavic lands with his *scarae* troops campaigning against Sorbs along the Elbe. Their leader Miliduoch was killed while Charles's army of Bavarians, Alamannians, and Burgundians decimated Bohemia.[15] A critical component of these campaigns was the construction of two new Frankish strongholds on the Elbe and Saale, creating a militarized march on the eastern borders of Saxony known as the *Limes Saxoniae*, a territorial boundary marked by the Elbe.[16]

Saxons played an increasingly important role in Frankish eastern campaigns and defending the eastern frontier.[17] In 806, following their participation in the Bohemian campaign, Saxons were also required to contribute one warrior out of every six to march against the Avars.[18] That same year, a letter was sent to Abbot Fulrad of St. Quentin announcing a summer assembly at Strassfurt (on the River Bode) in Eastphalia.[19] This is particularly unusual in hindsight, as most assemblies held in Saxony were in Westphalia, closer to the Frankish heartland. The fact that an assembly was taking place in Eastern Saxony is a testament to its growing significance.

In February 806, an announcement (the *Divisio Regnorum*) was also made to formally divide the kingdom upon the emperor's death between his sons.[20] In that plan, Saxony, Frisia, Thuringia, and much of what later became East Francia would be given to Charles the Younger.[21] While the *Divisio* never came to fruition, it might explain why Charles the Younger took a more active role in eastern campaigns. It was a sure way to solidify loyalty in the region through the distribution of loot, and it familiarized its future ruler with his domain. However, Charles the Younger died prematurely in 811, following the death of his brother Pippin in 810.[22] That left the emperor's remaining son Louis as the sole inheritor of the realm.

The Mad King

By 808, war between the Danes and Franks seemed imminent. Indeed, one could argue that a proxy war was already being fought via their Slavic allies and vassals. Each sought tribute, trade access, and buffer zones to ensure prosperity and security, all factors that incentivized Godfred to lead an army into the territory of the Obodrites. In response, the emperor sent his son Charles the Younger with an army of Franks and Saxons to the Elbe "with orders to resist the mad king" if he attacked the Saxon borderlands.[23]

Meanwhile, Godfred took control of several Obodrite strongholds.[24] He was assisted by the Wiltzi, allies of the Danes, who were happy to aid in fighting their traditional Obodrite enemies.[25] Both sides suffered significant casualties, and many Danish nobles were killed, yet, overall, the campaign was a Danish success with "much booty" gained.[26] The Danes also established tributary status partially over Obodrite territory, and their coalition had the satisfaction of expelling the Obodrite chieftain Thrasco and hanging another named Godelaib.[27]

However, the Danes' greatest prize came when they raided the Obodrite coastal emporium of Reric, which Godfred destroyed. However, while the town was upended, many of its people were spared. To commandeer trading tolls in the Baltic and enhance local prestige, the Danish king made the unusual decision to relocate the merchants of Reric back to Hedeby. It was a clever and transformative moment. In the coming years, Hedeby became one of the most successful trading centers in northern Europe, enhancing the wealth and power of its Danish rulers.[28] Archaeological excavations have confirmed its ninth-century role as an international center of commerce and craftsmanship: boat building, glass and metalworking, pottery manufacturing, minting coinage, and slave trading are all attested.[29]

While the enhancement of Hedeby and decimation of the Obodrites were good news for the Danes, the Franks were none too pleased. Yet, they were not standing idly by while Godfred caused disruptions. Upon reaching the Elbe with his army, Charles the Younger constructed a bridge over the river, which allowed his forces to cross easily into the territory of the Linones and Smeldingi, Slavic peoples who had declared their loyalty to Godfred. Charles then proceeded to unleash the necessary devastation of their lands.[30] Upon completing this retaliatory measure, in which many of his men were killed, Charles returned to Saxony.

The Franks and Danes began rapidly preparing for what seemed like an inevitable war. For the remainder of the year, both sides undertook fortifying measures to secure their borders. For the Danes, those actions centered around the expansion and repair of the *Danevirke* ("Danish work"), an extensive series of walls and defensive outposts.[31] Construction on the *Danevirke* was undertaken intermittently since at least the early eighth century, possibly originating in response to Charles Martel's invasion of Saxony or to defend against Slavic and Saxon incursions.[32] Stretching across the Jutland peninsula, the *Danevirke* was a genuinely ambitious architectural undertaking requiring substantial manpower, authority, and resource management to construct.[33] Godfred was responsible for repairing and expanding the *Danevirke* and connecting it to defensive walls surrounding Hedeby.[34] While the Danes were still vulnerable to naval assaults (although they had fleets patrolling the coast), and while the *Danevirke* would have taken somewhere between 7,000 and 10,000 warriors to *actually* man, the defensive barrier was still a significant deterrent to a land invasion.[35] It was also a symbolic testament to what the Danes were capable of doing.[36]

The Franco-Saxon defensive projects of 808–810 were less grand but still significant for securing their eastern and northern borders. Initially, these came in the form of two strongholds built along the Elbe, which the emperor had garrisoned.[37] While these initial strongholds were meant to stand against unfriendly Slavic tribes, others were soon built to defend against the Danes. However, those would have to wait for another series of diplomatic failures between Franks and Danes, as well as Saxon and Obodrite raids on Danish allies, which took place over the following year. At that point, the emperor appointed one of his counts (Egbert) to construct a castle on the Stör, a tributary of the Elbe north of Hamburg.[38] The castle came to be called *Eselfelth* (Itzehoe), and after its completion in the Spring, it was occupied by Franks and Saxons to guard the mouth of the Elbe.[39] The surrounding region was thereafter known as the "Danish March."[40]

That same year, the emperor journeyed with Charles the Younger to hold an assembly at Verden, the village where, decades prior, he had thousands of Saxon captives massacred.[41] Why Verden was chosen is not altogether clear. Perhaps, as Janet Nelson has speculated, it was "an act of remembrance," and after all those years, his conscience was getting the better of him.[42] If so, perhaps it was also part of Charlemagne's attempt to maintain Saxon goodwill.

Whatever the motivation concerning Verden, Franco-Danish tensions continued to escalate. Saxons and Obodrites would not have attacked Godfred's Slavic allies without the emperor's sanction, which the Danes were well aware of. Godfred was also furious with the defection of his tributaries to the Obodrites, but rather than cut his losses and seek diplomatic resolutions, he devised a plan to revenge himself on the Obodrite chieftain Thrasco. According to the *Moissac Chronicle*:

> Godfrid...laid a plot and sent one of his vassals, as if in peace, to kill Thrasco, king of the Obodrites, by treachery; and this he did. And he secretly sent pirates with ships to Frisia who inflicted great injury on the Christian people there.[43]

The assassination of Thrasco happened at Reric, which suggests the Obodrites were in the process of rebuilding their emporium.[44] While killing an allied king was undoubtedly outrageous to Charles, the raiding in Frisia, long considered Frankish territory, proved the tipping point. As far as the emperor was concerned, the Danes and Franks were at war.

This development is shown clearly in the *RFA*, where we learn that Godfred's fleet of 200 ships had not only ravaged Frisia but also fought three land battles against the Frisians, after which they demanded substantial tribute from the locals.[45] Einhard adds:

> King Godfred was so puffed with vain aspirations that he counted on gaining empire over all Germany, and looked upon Saxony and Frisia as his provinces. He had already subdued his neighbors the Abodriti, and made them tributary, and boasted that he would shortly appear with a great army before Aix-la-Chapelle [Aachen], where the King held his court.[46]

Charles immediately sent messengers throughout the realm with orders to gather an army, after which he crossed the Rhine at Lippenham to await the arrival of his forces. Sadly, while waiting, his elephant (Abul-Abbas), a gift from Caliph Harun al-Rashid of Baghdad, fell ill and died.[47] The loss of an exotic gift was one thing, yet Charles likely hoped the elephant could be a useful and intimidating spectacle that demonstrated his prestige and sparked fear in his Danish foes.

The rest of Charles' army eventually arrived at Lippenham, which the emperor led north to where the Aller flows into the Weser (south of Bremen), and set up camp. Charles waited to see if Godfred would follow through with his recent threats, including a boast that he wanted to "fight the emperor in open battle."[48] While a duel between Charles and Godfred would have been the thrilling stuff of legend, it wasn't to be. The reason being that, while Charles was waiting with his army, Godfred was conveniently assassinated.

The murder of Godfred has been subject to much conjecture, some of which ponders the role of elaborate schemes and intrigue. The *Moissac Chronicle* simply states that Godfred "was killed by one of his vassals," which is the same conclusion replicated in the *RFA*.[49] Einhard says more specifically that the assassin was one of Godfred's bodyguards.[50] Other sources claim he was murdered by kin. According to Notger, "the Stammerer" (one of Charles' ninth-century biographers), Godfred was killed during a hunting trip by a son of his through a recently abandoned wife.[51] However, as some scholars have noted, the possibility that the emperor played a role in Godfred's killing can by no means be excluded.[52] Indeed, it may have been a reprisal for the assassination of Thrasco or an attempt to remove what was becoming a particularly troublesome foe. According to *Saxo Grammaticus*, when Charles learned of Godfred's death, he "skipped for joy."[53]

With Godfred dead, his nephew Hemming ascended to the Danish throne, and what had nearly become a full-blown Dano-Frankish war was abruptly stopped in its place. Hemming had no apparent desire for war with the Franks, and envoys were dispatched to secure peace in the Spring of 811, following a Winter of severe cold and blight that decimated the emperor's cattle supply. According to the *RFA*, 12 delegates were sent from the Franks and Danes to Heligen on the River Eider, and together these representatives came to terms (which were "sworn on arms").[54] In addition, the boundary between Denmark and Francia was formally established along the Eider.[55] However, despite these positive measures, the future didn't bode well for Franco-Danish relations. The conquest of Saxony had ushered in an age of uncertainty in the north, and the Viking Age was already underway.[56]

In the meantime, from 810 through 811, Saxons situated on the eastern frontier were still encountering trouble. The castle of Hoohbuoki [Hohbeck] on the Elbe, which had been garrisoned by Charles' envoy Odo and a contingent of eastern Saxons, was attacked by the Wiltzi. In response, after settling affairs with the Danes, Charles returned to Aachen and dispatched three armies. One of these (composed of Franks and Saxons) marched against the Linones, ravaged their lands, and restored the stronghold the Wiltzi had recently destroyed.[57] Another army was sent into Pannonia to deal with Avar-Slavic disputes, while the third was sent west against the Bretons, who were in revolt. Each of these armies was victorious.

For the remainder of the year, the emperor was either at Aachen or inspecting coastal defenses. In November, emissaries named Aowin and Hebbi came from Hemming in Denmark to offer gifts and declarations of peace.[58] Slavic and Avar emissaries also came, apparently by force, from the Pannonia front. However, the year ended sadly for the emperor with the death of his eldest son Charles on December 4.[59] Likewise, the year ended badly for the Danish royal family with the sudden death of Hemming. Soon after, sometime between late 811 and the beginning of 812, a civil war erupted in Denmark as kin competed for the throne. Two factions emerged, one led by Anulo and another by Sigfrid, both nephews of Godfred. Each of these contenders ultimately died in the conflict, which, according to the *RFA*, claimed the lives of 10,940 Danes.[60] The *Moissac Chronicle* confirmed the calamity, claiming there was "a great slaughter of Northmen."[61] In the end, Anulo's faction came out ahead, and his brothers Harald [Klak] and Reginfrid were chosen to rule as joint-kings.[62]

The new joint-kings "officially" replicated their predecessor's peace policy with the Franks, and emissaries were sent to the emperor declaring as much in late 812. The Danish envoys also requested the return of their brother Hemming (Halfdansson), who had previously been given over to the Franks as a hostage.[63] The emperor was receptive to these delegates, and in the Spring of 813, he dispatched Franco-Saxon nobles beyond the Elbe to the Danish border to return Hemming.[64] However, Hemming's brothers could not meet him in person because they were preoccupied with fighting in the northwest of their kingdom (near Westarfolda). In addition, when the brothers (Harald and Reginfred) finally did return home to receive Hemming, they were greeted by their enemies (the sons of Godfred), who chased them from Denmark with a sizable army they had recently amassed.[65] Harald, Reginfred, and Hemming were then forced to seek refuge with the Obodrites. At the same time, Hemming became a vassal of Charlemagne (who granted the Danish exile support for reclaiming the throne).[66] The following decades for Danes and Franks would mirror each other well, each plagued by civil war, political scheming, and instability.[67]

Conclusion

On January 28, 814, while wintering in Aachen, Charlemagne's life ended.[68] His exact age at the time of death remains subject to debate, but generally, he is thought to have been in his late 60s or between 70 and 72.[69] He was buried in the Aachen chapel, entombed in a sarcophagus depicting Pluto's rape of Proserpina, oddly pagan imagery for the leader of a Christian empire.[70]

It is fortunate for Charlemagne that Voltaire was not around to deliver the emperor's eulogy. Nevertheless, writing nearly a thousand later, in an age when the "cult of Charlemagne" was still widespread in France, the philosopher was happy to offer his views on the emperor's legacy in his *Annales de L'Empire*:

> This monarch, like all other conquerors, was basically an usurper: his father had been nothing but a rebel...He usurped half of France from his brother Carloman, who died suddenly enough to warrant suspicions of a violent death; he usurped his nephew's inheritance and their mother's subsistence; he usurped the kingdom of Lombardy from his brother-in-law. We know of his bastards, his bigamy, his divorces, his concubines; we know he had thousands of Saxons murdered; and we made a saint out of him.[71]

Voltaire was writing from an "enlightened" perspective in an age where intellectuals were eager to be rid of the "Dark Ages."[72] Nevertheless, his critique of the emperor is an appropriate point at which we might pause to consider: what was the legacy of Charles the Great, specifically regarding the Saxons at the time of his demise? While the consequences of his conquest were still unfolding, certain trends were already apparent.

On a macro level, Saxony had begun its integration within the Frankish Empire, a process that politically altered the structure of Saxon society. This had been a difficult task. Indeed, for Charlemagne, the Saxons' decentralized, rural, and "backward" nature proved his most persistent challenge.[73] Contrary to chroniclers' oversimplifications, the Saxons had never been one unified people (a *gens Saxonum*).[74] Instead, Saxons were more akin to a "many-headed hydra," each needing to be addressed independently.[75] It was an arduous task to undertake across challenging terrain in a land with few roads.[76] As the Poeta Saxo remembered, the Saxons were so divided that "they had almost as many leaders as they had districts" and were like a "body" whose members had to be "torn away here and there separately."[77]

As a result, an essential strategy for undermining Saxon fragmentation was to control Saxony from within. Charles learned to use Saxon nobles (through intermarriage, gifts, and coercion), as well as counts and clergy, as catalysts for change.[78] The clergy followed in the wake of aggressive missionary activity and the construction of ecclesiastical (often fortified) centers of power, some of which facilitated the beginnings of urban development.[79] These new religious centers were supported financially by local Saxons through tithing, possibly because of a lack of endowments from the royal fisc.[80]

From these new religious centers, the role of the bishop became increasingly influential in Saxon affairs.[81] Indeed, during his reign, Charles founded six bishoprics in Saxony, including Paderborn, Verden, Bremen, Osnabrück, Minden, and Münster.[82] As an appendage of the state, the Church in Saxony could only be seen (at least initially) as a colonial enterprise, and early Church officials in Saxony were seldom Saxon.[83] However, as conversions became more widespread and Saxon nobles declared their loyalty to Charles, that began to change. One component assisting this process was the conversion of Saxon hostages and oblates who might assist in converting their kin.[84] The effectiveness of forced "re-education" and the devastation it can bring should not be underestimated (see Conclusion). Yet, within only a few generations, Saxon Christians could look upon the means of their conversion fondly. The Poeta Saxo, referencing the fate of his people, praised Charlemagne for assembling all the forces of his kingdom to draw the Saxons away from paganism, indicating that the Saxons could not have been convinced to do so by any other means.[85] The Poet then goes on to celebrate:

Who can say how many souls Charles returned to the Lord, when he caused the Saxons to believe in Him? As many as are the churches that now shine where the ancients used to worship pagan temples…so many will be the rewards, O Christ, which Thou shall give to Charles![86]

The conquest of Saxony, presented as an unavoidable obstacle in the path of progress, continued to be replicated by numerous writers over the following centuries.[87] As one nineteenth-century historian noted: "The subjugation of Saxony had been a horrible necessity, without it the unity of Germany could not have been accomplished either in Medieval or modern times."[88] Justifications for the Saxon conquest are often represented in terms of empire, religious unity, or the creation of nation-states. Yet, positivist historians often fail to address the core changes undergone by the Saxon people. This is especially true when we set aside the dominant narrative centered on the Church and nobility, which fundamentally ignores the general population. What changed for them?

The suppression of Saxon spiritual beliefs and customs was one significant development. Religion is a critical feature of how people construct their worldviews, and when those worldviews are "ruptured," it can have profound social and psychological implications.[89] Of course, the Church offered something new to fill the void it helped create. The promise of salvation was perhaps the greatest gift the Church had on hand. However, Charlemagne, local missionaries, and mindful bishops understood that Saxons needed tangible representations of the sacred to assist in their daily lives. These were brought to Saxon society by building churches, encouraging devotion to the saints, importing relics, and replacing indigenous art with Christian ornamental art.[90]

Beyond religious changes, Charlemagne had also transformed the structure of Saxon assemblies, reformed Saxon law (fusing Saxon, Frankish, and Roman customs); redefined Saxon geography through district restructuring, depopulation, and colonization; economically exploited locals and their resources; exacerbated the disparity between "peasants" and nobles; decimated villages; and commandeered countless slaves.[91] According to the ninth-century abbot Hrabanus Maurus of Fulda, these were all done in the spirit of "paternal affection."[92] Nevertheless, it can hardly be denied that what the emperor ultimately left in Saxony was a legacy of trauma, attested in the artifacts of war found hidden beneath the soil across the region.[93] Moreover, even though Saxony had become more fully part of the Frankish Empire, that trauma continued manifesting in the decades following the emperor's death. It was up to Charles' son Louis, and his quarrelsome grandsons, to finish what he started.

Notes

1 Davidson, *Saxo Grammaticus The History of the Danes*, 270–271
2 Haywood, *The Penguin Historical Atlas of the Vikings*, 31
3 Oman, *The Dark Ages*, 325
4 Derry, *A History of Scandinavia*, 27; Almgren, *The Viking*, 59; Simek, *Dictionary of Northern Mythology*, 320–322; Bucholz, *Perspectives for Historical Research in Germanic Religion*, 133; Milis, *The Pagan Middle Ages*, 21 & Heather, *Christendom*, 404. Similar reactions have been seen in a variety of Colonial conversion contexts; see McManners, "The Expansion of Christianity," 318 & Ballhatchet, "Asia," 491 & 510
5 Clements, *The Vikings*, 59–61; Backman, *The Worlds of Medieval Europe*, 175–176; Neill, *A History of Christian Missions*, 69 & Oman, *The Dark Ages*, 289–290
6 King, *Charlemagne*, 70
7 Hooper, *The Cambridge Illustrated Atlas of Warfare*, 15
8 Dobat, "Danevirke Revisited," 44–56
9 Scholz, *Carolingian Chronicles*, 83–84
10 Ibid. 82–88
11 Dutton, *Carolingian Civilization*, 80
12 In the Spring of 805, several high-ranking Saxon hostages who were handed over at earlier points in the war (possibly in the 790s) were released in Mainz. Many of these had been given to Alamannic or ecclesiastical "handlers," and the hostages mentioned in our source (a list possibly composed at the monastery of Reichenau) includes Saxons from every region except Nordalbingia. Having been indoctrinated into the Church, these Saxon hostages were counted on to reintegrate into Saxon society and assist in bringing about wider conversions. Expressions of clemency and rewards for Saxon loyalty also continued over the following years, and as late as 813, Charles granted a Saxon count (Bennit) rights to a Hessian forest on behalf of his father's loyalty to the Franks during the revolts. See IJssennagger, "Between Frankish and Viking," 76; Rembold, *Conquest and Christianization*, 56–59; Nelson, *King and Emperor*, 407–408; Kosto, "Hostages in the Carolingian World," 145; Flierman, *Saxon Identities*, 125 & McKitterick, *Charlemagne*, 256
13 King, *Charlemagne*, 165 & Scholz, *Carolingian Chronicles*, 84–85
14 Ibid. 146–147
15 Scholz, *Carolingian Chronicles*, 85–86
16 Ibid.; Barford, *The Early Slavs*, 250 & Barraclough, *The Origins of Modern Germany*, 7; Barford, *The Early Slavs*, 258; Dobat, "Danevirke Revisited," 42–56 & Dutton, *Carolingian Civilization*, 82
17 Dutton, *Carolingian Civilization*, 81
18 Riche, *Daily Life in the World of Charlemagne*, 17 & Rembold, *Conquest and Christianization*, 89
19 Landon, *Conquest and Colonization*, 56 & Riche, *The Carolingians*, 89–90

20 Loyn, *The Reign of Charlemagne*, 91–92

21 Dutton, *Carolingian Civilization*, 152

22 Henderson, *A History of Germany in the Middle Ages*, 82–83

23 Scholz, *Carolingian Chronicles*, 88

24 Ibid.

25 Ibid.

26 Ibid. & King, *Charlemagne*, 147

27 Ibid.

28 For two centuries, Hedeby maintained its vibrancy, that is, until the raids of Slavs and the Norwegian king Harald Hardrada in the 1050s/1060s. Thereafter, the folk of Hedeby began anew across the Schlei at Schleswig (*Slesvig*). See Riche, *Daily Life in the World of Charlemagne*, 115; Derry, *A History of Scandinavia*, 18 & 22; Bannister, *Finding the Vikings*, 24–25 & Delvaux, "Colors of the Viking Age," 42–43

29 Haywood, *The Penguin Historical Atlas of the Vikings*, 42–43; Almgren, *The Viking*, 55–62; Derry, *A History of Scandinavia*, 22; Melleno, "Between Borders," 364–365; Raffield, "Slave Markets of the Viking World," 688–689 & 696 & Muller-Wille et al., "The Transformation of Rural Society," 62

30 Scholz, *Carolingian Chronicles*, 88 & King, *Charlemagne*, 147

31 Ibid.

32 Clements, *The Vikings*, 61; Ferguson, *The Vikings*, 85; Bannister, *Finding the Vikings*, 24–25; Kaufmann, *The Medieval Fortress*, 85; Hamerow, *Early Medieval Settlements*, 112; James, "The Northern World in the Dark Ages," 72: Ring, *Northern Europe*, 672 & see the discussion in: Green, *The Continental Saxons*, 149

33 Dobat, "Danevirke Revisited," 27, Derry, *A History of Scandinavia*, 50; Squatriti, "Digging Ditches in Early Medieval Europe," 43 & Cunliffe, *Europe between the Oceans*, 459

34 Ibid. 27–41 & Buse, *The Regions of Germany*, 226

35 Squatriti, "Digging Ditches in Early Medieval Europe," 24; Kaufmann, *The Medieval Fortress*, 85 & Bachrach, *Warfare in Medieval Europe*, 27

36 A thousand years later, after having stood as a bulwark of defence for generations, the *Danevirke* remained a symbol of Danish national pride. See Dobat, "Danevirke Revisited," 27–41 & Axboe, "Danish Kings and Dendrochronology," 221–222

37 Scholz, *Carolingian Chronicles*, 88–89

38 Ibid., 90–91

39 King, *Charlemagne*, 147–148

40 Riche, *The Carolingians*, 114

41 King, *Charlemagne*, & 166

42 Nelson, *King and Emperor*, 424–425

43 King, *Charlemagne*, 147–148. The translation is from *Charlemagne: Translated Sources*, P. D. King, © 1987.

44 Scholz, *Carolingian Chronicles*, 91

45 Ibid. 91–94

46 Einhard, *The Life of Charlemagne*, 39–40. Republished with the permission of The University of Michigan Press, from *The Life of Charlemagne*, Einhard, © 1960; permission conveyed through Copyright Clearance Center, Inc.

47 Sypeck, *Becoming Charlemagne*, 188–189

48 Scholz, *Carolingian Chronicles*, 92

49 Ibid. & King, *Charlemagne*, 147–148

50 Einhard, *The Life of Charlemagne*, 40

51 Melleno, "Between Borders," 374 & for Notger, see Noble, *Charlemagne and Louis the Pious*, 107 & Gibbs, *Medieval German Literature*, 31–32

52 Lund, "Scandinavia," 207

53 Davidson, *Saxo Grammaticus The History of the Danes*, 273

54 Scholz, *Carolingian Chronicles*, 93
55 Tschan, *History of the Archbishops of Hamburg Bremen*, 18–22
56 Costambeys, *The Carolingian World*, 171
57 Scholz, *Carolingian Chronicles*, 93–94 & King, *Charlemagne*, 148
58 Ibid. 94
59 Ibid.
60 Ibid. 94–97
61 King, *Charlemagne*, 148
62 Haywood, *The Penguin Historical Atlas of the Vikings*, 31
63 Scholz, *Carolingian Chronicles*, 95
64 Ibid. 96
65 Ibid.
66 King, *Charlemagne*, 149
67 The Danish civil war led to further destabilization of the region and contributed to the acceleration of the Viking Age. With royal authority weakened, it is not difficult to imagine a power vacuum inviting rogues to go a-Viking without fear of consequences back home.
68 Noble, *Charlemagne and Louis the Pious*, 246
69 Ibid. 198
70 Nelson, *King and Emperor*, 484–485
71 Morrissey, *Charlemagne and France*, 205. Reprinted by permission of the University of Notre Dame Press from *Charlemagne and France: A Thousand Years of Mythology*, Robert Morrissey, University of Notre Dame, © 2003.
72 Bartlett, *The Medieval World Complete*, 12
73 Becher, *Charlemagne*, 77; Mayr-Harting, "Charlemagne, the Saxons, and the Imperial Coronation of 800," 1113–1128 & Hooper, *The Cambridge Illustrated Atlas of Warfare*, 12
74 Flierman, *Saxon Identities*, 100 & Springer, *Die Sachsen*, 260
75 Costambeys, *The Carolingian World*, 74 & Lintzel, *Untersuchungen zur Geschichte der alten Sachsen*, 54–56
76 Wickham, *The Inheritance of Rome*, 387 & Collins, *Early Medieval Europe*, 281
77 McKinney, *The Saxon Poet's Life of Charles the Great*, 12
78 Rembold, *Conquest and Christianization*, 89; Landon, "Economic Incentives for the Frankish Conquest of Saxony," 44; Karras, "Pagan Survivals," 556; Gillis, *Heresy and Dissent in the Carolingian Empire*, 35 & Davis, *Charlemagne's Practice of Empire*, 101–102
79 Steur, "The Beginnings of Urban Economies among the Saxons," 171–173
80 Landon, "Economic Incentives for the Frankish Conquest of Saxony," 47; Rembold, "The Poeta Saxo at Paderborn," 182–189 & McKitterick, *Charlemagne*, 251–253
81 Reuter, *Germany in the Early Middle Ages*, 37–38
82 Flierman, *Saxon Identities*, 130–132; McKitterick, *Charlemagne*, 251–253 & Oman, *The Dark Ages*, 289
83 Ibid.; Cusack, *Pagan Saxon Resistance to Charlemagne's Mission*, 40 & Collins, *Charlemagne*, 53
84 Ibid. 137; Holland, *Germany*, 32 & Dessens, *Res Voluntaria, Non Necessaria*, 22
85 Dutton, *Carolingian Civilization*, 535–536 & McKinney, *The Saxon Poet's Life of Charles the Great*, 86–87
86 McKinney, *The Saxon Poet's Life of Charles the Great*, 103. The translation is from *The Saxon Poet's Life of Charles the Great*, Mary E. McKinney, © 1956.
87 Dessens, *Res Voluntaria, None Necessaria,* 5
88 Henderson, *A History of Germany in the Middle Ages*, 74
89 Lindenfeld, *World Christianity and Indigenous Experience*, 9–10

90   Riche, *Daily Life in the World of Charlemagne*, 279; Karras, "Pagan Survivals," 567–571; McKitterick, *Charlemagne*, 329 & Nielsen, "Saxon Art between Interpretation and Imitation," 226–229

91   Reuter, *Germany in the Early Middle Ages*, 67; Landon, "Economic Incentives for the Frankish Conquest of Saxony," 27–31; Wickham, *The Inheritance of Rome*, 378 & 515; Fuller, "Pagan Charms in Tenth-Century Saxony?" 164–165 & Lintzel, *Untersuchungen zur Geschichte der alten Sachsen*, 56–63

92   Faulkner, *Law and Authority in the Early Middle Ages*, 65

93   Landon, "Economic Incentives for the Frankish Conquest of Saxony," 105–106

Part III

Consequences

10 Saxons in the Age of Louis the Pious

Louis was in Aquitaine when he received word of Charles' death, after which he journeyed to Aachen to be acknowledged as his father's successor.[1] Yet, as many commentators have been eager to point out, Louis was not his father.[2] Historians have described him as a "hapless failure," prone to weakness, and better suited for a monastery than political leadership.[3] There is truth in assertions of Louis' religious preoccupations.[4] He disdained the old heroic (presumably pagan) songs and poems his father held dear.[5] He also sought to cleanse Aachen of its debauch-erous festivities, corrupt influencers, and "loose" women, which included send-ing his sisters off to monasteries.[6] However, despite his piety, assertions of Louis' "weakness" or "martial ineptness" go too far.[7] Akin to his father, Louis loved to hunt, grew up learning the art of war, and was forced to address military threats across the realm from the very outset of his reign. In each of these endeavors, Louis made few decisions that would call into question his martial prowess.[8] (Perhaps it is telling that his name, *Hludovig*, translates from Old High German (OHG) to something like "famous" or "loud in battle.")[9] Louis differed from his father in that, rather than prioritizing conquest, he hoped to secure the Empire's frontiers and maintain stability.[10] As part of that broader goal, Louis often called upon Saxons for support, a people with whom he immediately sought to establish goodwill. As for the Saxons, their fate continued to be tied to the political intrigues of the Franks, Slavs, and Danes.

Gaining Saxon Support

Louis' attempt to gain his Saxon subjects' support began soon after he ascended the throne. The earliest case in which this can be seen was in 814 when Louis evicted Obodrite settlers who took over properties belonging to Saxons unjustly removed from their homes.[11] Likewise, during the Paderborn assembly of 815, the emperor set aside time to address Saxon grievances. Part of that process entailed offer-ing clemency to Saxons and Frisians who were "unfaithful" to his father, which included (in some cases) restoration of lands.[12] According to the Astronomer:

> Some attributed this to generosity and some to a lack of foresight, because those peoples, accustomed as they were to natural savagery, ought to have

DOI: 10.4324/9781003379157-14

been held sufficiently in restraint that, unbridled, they could not rush head-
long into treachery. The emperor, however, thought that he could bind them
more effectively to himself if he bestowed desirable benefits upon them, and
his hope was not deceived, for after this he always kept those very same peoples in the greatest devotion to himself.[13]

Louis' generosity toward the Saxons continued in 819 when he restored lands confiscated from several Saxons in the region of Wigmodia. A charter issued by the
emperor that same year demonstrates these Saxons were removed from their lands
toward the end of Charlemagne's Saxon Wars (during the northern deportations).[14]
Louis also courted the Saxon nobility through patronage and by establishing family ties with Saxon families. For example, in the early 830s, he granted the Saxon
count Ricdag important lands along the *Hellweg* as well as enhanced the power
of the influential Saxo-Bavarian Hattonid family.[15] At the same time, following
the death of his beloved wife Irmengardis (in 818), Louis married a woman with
considerable Saxon connections. The bride in question was the ambitious and
intelligent Judith, a daughter of the powerful Count Welf.[16] The Welf connection
brought significant assets, including vast domains and support from Bavaria and
Alamannia.[17] However, Judith was also the daughter of Heilwig (Eigilwi), a woman
"from the most noble Saxon lineage," that is, the powerful Ecbertiner clan.[18] While
Louis' union with Judith was undoubtedly strategic, he was also genuinely fond
of her. Over the coming years, her influence on the emperor (much to the dismay
of contemporaries) was significant. Nevertheless, through his marriage and acts
of generosity, Louis maintained the loyalty of (most) of his Saxon subjects until
the end of his reign. That was no small feat, given recent Franco-Saxon troubles.
As one crisis after another unfolded across the Empire, the Saxons proved to be
a reliable asset, and their positive relationship with the emperor further solidified
their integration within the Frankish Empire, which was significant not only for
geo-political concerns but also as a prerequisite for continuing the conversion of
Louis' Saxon subjects.

Troubles with the Northmen

Following their expulsion from Denmark, Harald Klak and Reginfrid recruited an
army and attempted to regain their thrones. However, their plan ultimately failed,
and in the process, Reginfrid was killed.[19] With little hope of success, Harald fled
to Francia to seek support from the new emperor, who, wanting to steer events in
the north, agreed to lend Harald aid.[20] Louis spent the next 22 years (815–837)
meddling in Danish affairs by promoting their Christianization and lending Harald
Klak assistance in his dynastic disputes with the sons of Godfred. Initially, that
included military support, which Saxons and Obodrites were obligated to partici-
pate in. However, resistance by the sons of Godfred ultimately necessitated an
awkward and unstable co-rule situation between them and Harald.[21]

Despite raiding by both Danish factions and the predations of rogue Vikings,
emissaries managed to contain the situation until 826, when Harald Klak journeyed

to Ingelheim to convert to Christianity. Perhaps he would have noticed the paintings on Ingelheim's walls, which, according to Ermold the Black, depicted scenes of Charles Martel conquering the Frisians and Charlemagne subjugating the Saxons:

> Wise Charlemagne's frank expression is clear to see, his head is crowned…A band of Saxons stand opposite of him, waging battle, he subdues, vanquishes and reduces them to subjection.[22]

After the initial meeting in Ingelheim, Harald was baptized by the emperor at St. Albans in Mainz, alongside his wife (baptized by Judith) and their companions.[23] Just as Charlemagne had become godfather to Widukind, Louis did likewise with Harald, who thereafter became a "subordinate" to the royal family.[24] The emperor also gave Harald gifts and granted him land ownership in Frisia (in the county of Rustringen).[25] It was a place of refuge if his co-rulers should ever cause him trouble. Harald then made his way home through Frisia, accompanied by the Frankish missionary Anskar, who was tasked with explaining to Harald and his retinue the details of their newly adopted faith.[26]

Following Harald's conversion, tensions escalated with the sons of Godfred. One of these sons, Horik, was summoned by Louis but failed to appear at the appointed time, likely because Horik had no intention of continuing co-rule. Indeed, Harald was soon ousted from power and forced to flee Denmark.[27]

By 829, rumors spread across Francia that the Danes were preparing to invade Saxony, and their army had already reached the border. These rumors may have been spread by Harald Klak himself. In a panic, the emperor sent messengers across the realm to muster forces and march as quickly as possible to Saxony. However, before this could happen, Louis received intel that the rumors were false and no such Danish invasion was happening.[28]

Shortly after the fake invasion debacle, the Franks and Danes were able to come to terms, negotiated through leading men (counts and margraves) of Saxony. However, the resolutions failed to appease Harald, who returned to raiding villages in Denmark. Believing these raids were sanctioned by the Franks, the sons of Godfred gathered an army and attacked a Franco-Saxon garrison stationed in a stronghold on the Eider, which (not expecting battle) was surprised and put to flight.[29] Eventually, the confusion was sorted via envoys and restitution, a pattern continuously replicated over the following years.

By 834, Danish Vikings were raiding Frisia, where they sacked Dorestad, slaughtered locals, captured slaves, and burned villages.[30] They returned in 835, prompting the emperor to develop coastal defenses.[31] Yet, despite these measures, Vikings returned to Dorestad in 836 and 837, simultaneously demanding tribute and plundering the island of Walcheren.[32] In response, Louis marched an army to Nijmegen to confront the Vikings. However, the pirates caught wind of his approach and fled.[33] Thereafter, undoubtedly enraged, Louis held an assembly to scold those in charge of coastal defenses and ordered the construction of a new fleet.[34]

Two years later, Frisia was devastated by severe flooding leading to the deaths of thousands in the region.[35] This was followed by more Viking raids, which once again necessitated an exchange of envoys to restore "peace."[36] By the end of Louis' reign, the tenuous relationship between Franks and Danes was nowhere near resolved. Indeed, it would become far worse over the following decades (see Conclusion). The primary problem was that the destabilization of the Frankish Empire coincided with the advent of the Viking Age, which had been incentivized by several factors (some of which we will return to).[37] Yet, the Viking threat was only one of many significant problems facing the Frankish Empire in which Saxons were periodically involved. Just as pressing were the rebellions of nearby Slavic peoples, who were simultaneously dealing with their own crises.

Continued Problems in the East

From 815 to 822, Louis had to contend with multiple challenges along the Slavic frontier. Saxons were involved in resolving each of these. For example, in 816, Louis sent an army of Saxons and Franks to fight the Sorbs, who refused to submit to Frankish rule.[38] In addition, two years later, the Obodrite warlord Sclaomir led a revolt against the Franks because he was disgruntled that Louis demanded he share power with Ceadrag (son of the former Obodrite chieftain, Thrasco).[39] However, Sclaomir was eventually taken by Saxons and East Frankish border commanders to Aachen, whereafter he became a hostage in Francia. Yet, Obodrite leadership problems continued over the following years, during which Sclaomir died in Saxony (in 821).[40]

Simultaneously, a Slavic rebel named Ljudovit launched a rebellion in Upper Pannonia, requiring Louis to send three armies against him.[41] These forces included Saxons, some of whom built and garrisoned a stronghold on the far side of the Elbe (at Delbande) to guard the river crossing.[42] Ljudovit's revolt failed, but just as he became less of a threat, the Saxons encountered a resurgence of confrontations with Wiltzi and Sorbs, who continued raiding their eastern frontier. In response, the Saxons marched against the Sorbs, killed their king Czimislav, and captured 11 of their fortresses.[43] This continued militarization of Saxon borderlands was both defensive and expansionist in nature, however; it foreshadowed a significant expansion of Saxon power. That power was, in turn, demonstrated repeatedly against nearby Slavic tribes over the following three centuries (see Chapter 12).

Family Disputes, 829–840

The raiding of Northmen and Slavic rebellions were serious challenges, but they were hardly the only threats facing Louis the Pious and his subjects. Italic pirates, Basque raiders, and Breton rebels also needed sorting.[44] In the latter's case, Saxons were again called upon, and in the Fall of 824, they joined an army of Thuringians led by Louis and his sons in ravaging Brittany.[45]

Environmental catastrophes also plagued the Empire. In 816, the Rhine flooded due to heavy rain in the Alps.[46] The rains continued to be an issue into the early 820s when excess humidity brought pestilence and crop failure.[47] Shortly after, Thuringia and Saxony were struck by an earthquake, which almost universally

would have been seen as an ominous omen.[48] Within a year, similar signs mani-
fested when another earthquake struck Aachen, hailstorms decimated crops across
the realm (leading to famine-related deaths), and 23 villages in the Saxon county
of Firihsazi were burned due to lightning.[49] For many, the realm appeared to be in
chaos; God's warning signs were everywhere.[50] However, the situation continued
to deteriorate. Peripheral revolts and environmental calamities were problematic,
but they paled compared to the internal crises unleashed by the royal family.

Fractures in Carolingian rule can be observed as early as April 817, when, in his
Ordinatio imperii, Louis declared his wish for the Empire to be divided between
his sons upon his death.[51] Contrary to many surrounding peoples, the Franks did
not practice primogeniture.[52] Instead, inheritance was divided among all heirs.[53] In
the *Ordinatio*, Louis made his firstborn son Lothar co-emperor, while his other sons
were appointed as kings over Aquitaine (which went to Pepin) and Bavaria (which
went to the cunning young Louis "the German").[54] However, the arrangement sub-
ordinated each brother to Lothar, a situation that pleased no one.[55]

Other family members were also displeased. Shortly after the division announcement, news came informing the emperor that his nephew Bernard, King of Italy,
was leading a coup to undermine him. Worse, he had gathered support from several
nobles and high-ranking members of the Church. However, Louis quickly marched
south against Bernard and crushed his rebellion. Several conspirators were executed, some were exiled after having their lands confiscated, and Bernard was
blinded. However, the trauma of the blinding procedure was too trying, and Bernard died a few days later (much to Louis' regret).[56] Bernard's kingdom was thereafter absorbed into the Frankish Empire, coming eventually under Lothar's rule.

To prevent further dynastic challenges, sometime during the Bernard affair (817
to the Spring of 818), Louis had his half-brothers Drogo, Hugo, and Theodoric tonsured and sent away to monasteries.[57] However, these measures were insufficient
to ensure stability, primarily because Louis' greatest threat did not come from his
cousin or half-brothers but from his sons. When Judith gave birth to a new child
(provocatively named Charles, b. June 13, 823), tensions between the brothers over
their future inheritance reached a tipping point.[58] According to the *Histories* written by Charles' advocate and cousin Nithard, Lothar, in particular, saw Charles as
a potential threat.[59] As a result, he tried his best to keep Charles from infringing on
his inheritance, leading to discord with his brothers, father, and Empress Judith.

However, the emperor did his best to secure protection for Charles, and in August
829, he was granted the region of Alamannia "by royal decree." [60] That declaration went too far for Lothar, who rallied his brothers against their father with a cry
to "restore authority and order" to the empire."[61] The brothers answered Lothar's
call, and in the Spring of 830, they moved against Louis at Compiegne, where they
humiliated their father by placing him in confinement and chastened Judith by
making her "take the veil."[62] Judith's brothers (Conrad and Rudolf), whom she had
sought to empower with her influence, were also targeted. On Lothar's orders, they
were tonsured and sent to Aquitaine to be held by Pepin.

Chamberlain Bernard, entrusted with the protection of Charles, fled quickly to
his domain in Septimania. However, Lothar captured Bernard's brother Herbert

and had him blinded and imprisoned in Italy. Having orchestrated a successful coup, Lothar took complete control of the government, simultaneously holding Charles and his father hostage. He then had Charles "surrounded by monks," who were instructed to convince Charles that it would be wise to dedicate himself to monastic life.[63]

Lothar's actions threw the Empire into a state of confusion.[64] That instability prompted members of the Church (and some nobles) to collude with Louis the Pious and his sons Pepin and Louis the German to have the emperor restored. However, there were stipulations. The promotion of the Church was to continue to be a priority for the emperor, and his sons were to receive more land for backing him. All parties agreed to the terms, and in October 830, an assembly was held at Nijmegen, where Louis was restored, and the empress Judith (along with her brothers) returned.

Nijmegen was a strategically chosen location where Louis knew he could count on the nearby support of Saxons and Eastern Franks.[65] It was a successful calculation. Folk from across the realm came forward to renew their support for Louis. In another assembly at Aachen in February 831, some of the supporters of Lothar were also executed or exiled, and Lothar was punished by having his kingdom reduced to Italy, which he was granted only after swearing an oath never to betray his father again.[66]

Although Lothar was chastised, he had no intention of abandoning his ambitions. Already in 832, he was scheming again with Pepin to enlist their younger brother Louis to support a new revolt. Louis the German was already frustrated because he was promised part of the domain his father granted to Charles (Alamannia) and so was easily "convinced" to join Lothar in moving against their father.[67]

Soon after, Saxons were summoned to Mainz to support the emperor in facing this new challenge.[68] Together they journeyed across the Rhine in pursuit of Louis the German, who was forced to flee with his forces back to Bavaria.[69] However, further discord erupted in 833 when Louis took Aquitaine from Pepin and granted it to Charles. That move deeply angered Lothar, Pepin, and some high-ranking exiles who previously supported Lothar in 830. As a result, Lothar *again* moved to seize power, only this time, he had the legitimizing support of Pope Gregory IV.[70]

According to Nithard, the emperor led all his forces against his sons and the Pope's entourage, which met up in Alsace at Mt. Siegwald. However, in what must have been an excruciating experience for the emperor, his sons convinced most of his army to defect or flee, leaving Louis the Pious essentially abandoned. Ultimately, the emperor was captured (alongside Charles), while Empress Judith was exiled to Lombardy.[71]

Following this debacle, on what came to be known as the "Field of Lies" (*Lügenfeld*), Lothar was back in charge. However, Pope Gregory returned to Rome, "filled with regret" over having lent his support.[72] At the same time, upon realizing the extent of Lothar's ambitions, his brothers soon also regretted lending him aid.[73] Thereafter, discord and factionalism continued to undermine stability, and mixed emotions spread among the conspirators when Lothar proceeded to humiliate his father by having him publicly proclaim his ineptitude.[74] Filled with "shame and regret" for having betrayed and humiliated their father twice, Louis the German and Pepin resolved to restore him to the throne (again).[75]

Lothar had been holding Charles and his father hostage in St. Denis, but when he realized the tide was turning against him, he released his prisoners and hastily fled for Vienne.[76] Despite calls for revenge by Louis' supporters, the emperor refused to chase Lothar south.[77] He opted instead to send messengers on his behalf so that he could tend to the logistics of his restoration. His loyal retainers Lothar chased out were brought back, while his sons Pepin and Louis the German returned to his good graces. In the meantime, Empress Judith was seized by those guarding her in Italy and brought to the emperor in Aachen. She then had the pleasure of defending herself against accusations of adultery (with Bernard of Septimania) and witchcraft, which she successfully managed to do in the absence of her accuser (Paschasius Radbertus, abbot of Corbie).[78] The accusations were dismissed, and Judith resumed her role as empress.

By June 834, the emperor was ready to deal more decisively with Lothar. As noted in the *Annals of St. Bertin*, Louis had the Saxons' support.[79]

Louis' army moved into the Breton March to root out Lothar's loyalists. However, it met with serious resistance, leading to the death of Louis' commander (Wido). In response, Lothar laid siege to the city of Chalon, which was ransacked and burned for three days. Some of those resisting at Chalon were beheaded, and Lothar supposedly had Bernard of Septimannia's sister Gerberga, a nun, "drowned in the Saone like a witch."[80]

Feeling confident after Chalons and the success of his supporters in the Breton March, Lothar marched on Orleans. In response, Louis gathered an army and summoned Louis the German to bring his forces from across the Rhine to assist in marching against Lothar. These forces eventually met near the village of Couzy, and despite attempts by Lothar to encourage defectors, they remained steadfast in their support for the emperor.

With few alternatives, in August 834, Lothar surrendered. Fortunately, his father was still in a forgiving mood. Rather than having his son executed or tonsured, Lothar was sent back to Italy, where he was told never to leave without his father's permission.[81] That arrangement held for two years until Louis made further (vast) land grants to Charles during an assembly at Aachen in the Winter of 837.[82] Thereafter, several nobles and high-ranking members of the Church began swearing fealty to Charles, which dismayed both Lothar and Louis the German. The two disappointed brothers expressed their concerns to the emperor, but they were dismissed. Indeed, in September of the following year, Charles' domain was further enhanced, and while Charles managed to reconcile with his brother Pepin, by 839, Louis the German was angry enough to launch a rebellion of his own.

In response, the emperor crossed the Rhine with his army and made for Mainz. The emperor was supported by a significant contingent of Saxons, some of whom came only in response to threats and others by the persuasion of Count Adalbert of Metz.[83] (The influence of Adalbert was enhanced by the reputation of his brother

Banzleibs a powerful margrave in Saxony.)[84] Ultimately, Louis the German's forces were no match for his father's, and so he once again fled back to Bavaria. It should be emphasized that with a few exceptions, Louis the German's support during the 830s came almost exclusively from Bavaria. Most Eastern Franks, Thuringians, and Saxons remained loyal to his father.[85] However, loyalties during the period frequently shifted among noble and ecclesiastical magnates, each of whom sought to secure favor with the faction they believed most likely to succeed.[86]

Louis the German's retreat satisfied the emperor enough to return to Aachen, but the future didn't bode well. According to Nithard, because the emperor was getting old, he and Judith began to fear what would become of Charles and the realm when Louis died. Therefore, they thought it best to gain the support of one son on behalf of Charles so that together they might resist any ill machinations of the others.[87] Somewhat surprisingly, Judith chose Lothar, whom she and the emperor did their best to guilt into protecting Charles and his inheritance. In return, Lothar would receive much of the eastern part of the Empire (excluding Bavaria). Unsurprisingly, given that Lothar's domain was isolated to Italy, he agreed to the proposal.[88]

The arrangement was made official on May 30, 839, in an assembly at Worms, during which Lothar had to "prostrate himself before his father" in a public spectacle of penance. The emperor made a show of forgiveness, after which he and Lothar set about dividing the kingdom. Charles would get the bulk of the Latin "French" west and Lothar the "German" east.[89] Lothar was then sent back to Italy with a reminder not to break his oath as he had in the past.

Around this time, Louis' son Pepin died in Aquitaine, resulting in a dispute over his lands. In response, the emperor journeyed to the region alongside Judith and Charles to extract new oaths from the inhabitants (in support of Charles). With Pepin dead, Charles' hold over the west became more secure. However, back east, trouble was again being stirred up by Louis the German.

While the emperor was in Aquitaine, Louis the German gathered an army of Bavarians, Thuringians, and Saxons to invade Alamannia.[90] When the emperor received the news, he left Charles behind at Poitier and led an army into Thuringia to push back his son's forces, which were forced to retreat beyond the borders of the Empire. Indeed, to make it safely back to Bavaria, Louis the German was forced to buy safe passage through "the land of the Slav," which was no doubt a painful exercise in humility.[91]

Following the rebels' retreat, Louis dispatched instructions for an assembly to be held at Worms on July 1. Word was also sent to Lothar in Italy, who was summoned to help sort out affairs with Louis the German. However, the meeting never came to pass. The emperor suddenly became gravely ill, and sensing the end was near, Louis sent Lothar the imperial insignia, crown, and sword and begged him to protect Judith and his brother Charles.[92] Shortly thereafter, on June 20, 840, Louis the Pious died on his beloved hunting island in the Rhine, located near Ingelheim, downstream from the trading hub of Mainz.[93] According to the Astronomer, his last act was a frantic shoeing away of demons he saw coming for his soul.[94] It was a tragic end to a toilsome life lived by an unfairly remembered man who spent his final years navigating the discord caused by his endlessly scheming sons.

Conclusion

Louis was buried by his half-brother Drogo in the Carolingian ancestral church of St. Arnulf (in Metz) before the magnates of the realm.[95] Few attendees at the burial would have looked back fondly over the emperor's reign, and nearly all would be dreading the inevitable period of uncertainty that awaited. However, among those mourning Louis' demise, we might imagine they included many of his Saxon retainers and subjects. Except those sworn to Louis the German, most Saxon notables had steadfastly supported the emperor through all his troubles with rebels, Danes, and treacherous kin. The gamble Louis took in the early 810s by granting Saxons clemency and attempting to right historical grievances paid off. There were no Saxon rebellions during his reign. That was a success neither his father nor his son Louis could ever claim.

In addition to fostering Saxon support through demonstrations of goodwill, Louis facilitated Saxony's continued integration within the Empire by utilizing Saxon warriors against Slavic and Danish enemies. Saxons were no longer fearful of Frankish (Christian) invasions from the west but, instead, wary of northern and eastern (mostly pagan) foes, whom they now faced *with* Frankish support. As a result, Saxon borderlands were increasingly militarized to defend against Slavic and Viking raiders, the latter of which were (in part) reacting to the Frankish conquest of Saxony and the emperor meddling in Danish affairs.[96] Louis had not only intervened in Danish dynastic disputes but also continued to promote Danish Christianization via missionaries and the conversion of Harald Klak (see Chapter 11). These processes were intimately connected, as Louis hoped to garner more influence over the Danes by installing a subordinate Christianized vassal on the throne. Conversion continued to be coupled with violence and coercion, each used to ensure submission and political allegiance. Despite their political integration, those processes also continued to be applied to the Saxons as various forces conspired to promote their Christianization under the late Carolingians.

Notes

1 Scholz, *Carolingian Chronicles*, 97
2 Morrissey, *Charlemagne and France*, 37; Backman, *The Worlds of Medieval Europe*, 168; Dutton, *Carolingian Civilization*, 164–165 & Noble, *Charlemagne and Louis the Pious*, 203 & 224
3 Costambeys, *The Carolingian World*, 155; Henderson, *A History of Germany in the Middle Ages*, 88–89 & Oman, *The Dark Ages*, 302
4 Wickham, *The Inheritance of Rome*, 392
5 Dutton, *Carolingian Civilization*, 164 & Noble, *Charlemagne and Louis the Pious*, 202–203
6 Riche, *The Carolingians*, 134; Oman, *The Dark Ages*, 303–304; Wemple, *Women in Frankish Society*, 79–80 & 105 & De Jong, *The Penitential State*, 21
7 For the notion that Louis was inept as a soldier, see Cantor, *The Civilization of the Middle Ages*, 193
8 De Jong, *The Penitential State*, 16
9 Goldberg, *Struggle for Empire*, 26; Noble, *Charlemagne and Louis the Pious*, 129 & Fortson, *Indo-European Language and Culture*, 35

10 Riche, *The Carolingians*, 158 & Butt, *Daily Life in the Age of Charlemagne*, 7
11 Melleno, "Between Borders," 376–377 & 383
12 Rembold, *Conquest and Christianization*, 90–92 & Gillis, *Heresy and Dissent in the Carolingian Empire*, 36–37
13 Noble, *Charlemagne and Louis the Pious*, 249. Republished with the permission of The Pennsylvania State University Press, from *Charlemagne and Louis the Pious: Lives by Einhard, Notker, Ermoldus, Thegan, and the Astronomer*, Thomas Noble, © 2009; permission conveyed through Copyright Clearance Center, Inc.
14 Flierman, *Saxon Identities*, 125–126
15 Goldberg, "Popular Revolt," 483–484
16 Henderson, *A History of Germany in the Middle Ages*, 92; Ozment, *A Mighty Fortress*, 45 & Noble, *Charlemagne and Louis the Pious*, 259
17 Sypeck, *Becoming Charlemagne*, 194 & De Jong, *The Penitential State*, 30
18 Dutton, *Carolingian Civilization*, 167; Goldberg, *Struggle for Empire*, 54 & Noble, *Charlemagne and Louis the Pious*, 207
19 Haywood, *The Penguin Historical Atlas of the Vikings*, 31
20 Scholz, *Carolingian Chronicles*, 97–98 & Noble, *Charlemagne and Louis the Pious*, 249
21 Ibid. 97–117 & Noble, *Charlemagne and Louis the Pious*, 250–273 & Dutton, *Carolingian Civilization*, 163 & Haywood, *The Penguin Historical Atlas of the Vikings*, 31
22 The English translation is based on those found in: Godman, *Poetry of the Carolingian Renaissance*, 209; Dutton, *Carolingian Civilization*, 254 & Noble, *Charlemagne and Louis the Pious*, 176
23 Scholz, *Carolingian Chronicles*, 119; Dutton, *Carolingian Civilization*, 168 & Noble, *Charlemagne and Louis the Pious*, 177–178 & 208 & 269
24 Ibid.; Fletcher, *The Conversion of Europe*, 223–225 & Riche, *The Carolingians*, 159
25 Wamers, *Carolingian Pfalzen and Law*, 149–150
26 Dutton, *Carolingian Civilization*, 407–410
27 Scholz, *Carolingian Chronicles*, 122
28 Ibid. 112–117
29 Scholz, *Carolingian Chronicles*, 123 & Noble, *Charlemagne and Louis the Pious*, 274
30 Nelson, *The Annals of St. Bertin*, 30
31 Ibid. 33 & Haywood, *The Penguin Historical Atlas of the Vikings*, 56–57
32 Nelson, *The Annals of St. Bertin* 35 & Howorth, "The Early Intercourse of the Danes and Franks (II)," 22
33 Oman, *The Dark Ages*, 315
34 Nelson, *The Annals of St. Bertin*, 37–40
35 Ibid. 42
36 Ibid. 47
37 Archer, *World History of Warfare*, 133; Wickham, *The Inheritance of Rome*, 478 & Heather, *Christendom*, 404
38 Scholz, *Carolingian Chronicles*, 97–101 & Noble, *Charlemagne and Louis the Pious*, 201 & 251
39 Ibid. 102–103
40 Ibid. 105–117 & Noble, *Charlemagne and Louis the Pious*, 258–259
41 Ibid. 105–107 & Noble, *Charlemagne and Louis the Pious*, 207 & 259–261
42 Ibid. 108–112 & Goldberg, *Struggle for Empire*, 43
43 Ibid. 48
44 Ibid. 101–104 & Noble, *Charlemagne and Louis the Pious*, 130 & 163 & 166 & 206 & 266–267
45 Noble, *Charlemagne and Louis the Pious*, 161 & 208 & Dutton, *Carolingian Civilization*, 168
46 Scholz, *Carolingian Chronicles*, 108

47 Ibid.
48 Ibid.
49 Ibid. 112–117
50 De Jong, *The Penitential State*, 157
51 Jones, *Cambridge Illustrated History of France*, 67
52 Ozment, *A Mighty Fortress*, 44
53 Arblaster, *A History of the Low Countries*, 35
54 Goldberg, *Struggle for Empire*, 6 & 44–46 & Noble, *Charlemagne and Louis the Pious*, 205
55 Ibid. 31
56 Noble, *Charlemagne and Louis the Pious*, 206
57 Scholz, *Carolingian Chronicles*, 130 & Noble, *Charlemagne and Louis the Pious*, 206
58 Naming the boy "Charles" indicated Louis and Judith's ambitions for the boy's future rulership. See De Jong, *The Penitential State*, 32 & Nelson, *Charles the Bald*, 13
59 Ibid. 22–23; Riche, *The Carolingians*, 149; Screen, "The Importance of the Emperor," 27–30; Wickham, *The Inheritance of Rome*, 395 & Noble, *Charlemagne and Louis the Pious*, 266
60 Scholz, *Carolingian Chronicles*, 131
61 Ibid.
62 Ibid. & Goldberg, *Struggle for Empire*, 60
63 Ibid.
64 Ibid.
65 Flierman, *Saxon Identities*, 125–126; Nelson, *The Annals of St. Bertin*, 22 & Noble, *Charlemagne and Louis the Pious*, 209 & 276
66 Ibid.
67 Goldberg, *Struggle for Empire*, 64
68 Nelson, *The Annals of St. Bertin*, 24–26
69 Goldberg, *Struggle for Empire*, 67
70 Noble, *Charlemagne and Louis the Pious*, 279–280
71 Scholz, *Carolingian Chronicles*, 133–134
72 Ibid. 134 & Noble, *Charlemagne and Louis the Pious*, 210–211 & 280–281
73 Charter evidence seems to support the idea that Lothar genuinely wanted to be the emperor of all Francia; see Screen, "The Importance of the Emperor," 39
74 Goldberg, *Struggle for Empire*, 70–71
75 Scholz, *Carolingian Chronicles*, 134
76 Ibid.
77 Noble, *Charlemagne and Louis the Pious*, 284
78 Ibid. 209; Wickham, *The Inheritance of Rome*, 408; Wemple, *Women in Frankish Society*, 80–81 & 95 & Rampton, *European Magic and Witchcraft*, 146–148
79 Nelson, *The Annals of St. Bertin*, 28
80 Scholz, *Carolingian Chronicles*, 135; Nelson, *The Annals of St. Bertin*, 30–31 & Noble, *Charlemagne and Louis the Pious*, 215 & 286
81 Noble, *Charlemagne and Louis the Pious*, 217
82 Scholz, *Carolingian Chronicles*, 136 & Noble, *Charlemagne and Louis the Pious*, 293–294
83 Nelson, *The Annals of St. Bertin*, 41 & Reuter, *The Annals of Fulda*, 16
84 Goldberg, *Struggle for Empire*, 88
85 Barraclough, *The Origins of Modern Germany*, 13; Rembold, *Conquest and Christianization*, 85–86 & Metzenthin, "The 'Heliand': A New Approach," 503
86 Goldberg, *Struggle for Empire*, 58
87 Scholz, *Carolingian Chronicles*, 138
88 Ibid.
89 Oman, *The Dark Ages*, 316

90 Reuter, *The Annals of Fulda*, 17 & & Noble, *Charlemagne and Louis the Pious*, 298
91 Scholz, *Carolingian Chronicles*, 140
92 Henderson, *A History of Germany in the Middle Ages*, 101
93 Nelson, *The Annals of St. Bertin*, 49
94 Noble, *Charlemagne and Louis the Pious*, 302
95 Scholz, *Carolingian Chronicles*, 140 & Noble, *Charlemagne and Louis the Pious*, 195
96 These were in addition to other "push and pull" factors that incentivized warbands to go Viking, including general instability, climate change, the search for wealth, land, resources, and slaves, as well as the desire to enhance warlord's reputations.

11 Christianization in Saxony under the Late Carolingians

Despite facing several crises, Louis the Pious continued his father's agenda for the Christianization of Saxony. That agenda was reinforced in several ways: by integrating Saxon nobles into the Church, through the creation and endowment of religious centers, by dispatching missionaries to pagan frontiers, through the collection and distribution of relics, and by presenting Christian ideas in the vernacular, most visibly in the *Heliand*—the so-called Saxon Gospel.

Ecclesiastical Foundations, Missions, and Relics

In the early ninth century, Saxony was far from being a fully Christianized society. Paganism remained widespread, Christian teachings were misunderstood, church organization was tenuous, and pious converts ran the risk of being taken advantage of by charlatans and "false prophets," as is attested in the *Xanten Annals*.[1] There was also the ever-present danger of heresy, such as with the "predestination controversy" of the Saxon monk Gottschalk (an oblate of Fulda) in the 830s–840s.[2] To remedy such challenges, more structure was needed. As a result, very soon after Louis the Pious ascended the throne, he established new bishoprics in Saxony. The first of these, Halberstadt, was founded in 814, followed soon after by Hildesheim in 815.[3] These were supplemented by additional ecclesiastical centers over the following two decades.[4] The most important of these later foundations was undoubtedly the monastic house of Corvey ("new Corbie"), formed in Höxter by Saxon monks from Corbie (in Picardy) in 822.[5] According to Adam of Bremen, Louis filled Corvey with Frankish monks, including the later influential Anskar.[6] However, these were soon supplemented by Saxon Christians as well.[7] Corvey also benefited from imperial patronage, including royal immunity (in 823), the right to elect abbots, a small collection of relics, and a mission to contribute to the conversion of Saxony and Scandinavia.[8]

The growth of the Scandinavian mission was just as (if not more) important to the emperor than that of Saxony. Those who dwelt beyond the Elbe amid the wild "north wind" desperately needed civilizing.[9] In addition, as DuBois has noted, "Christianization represented a key means of controlling and potentially subjugating pagan populations to the north."[10] In 822, Louis gained papal approval for a Danish mission, after which he dispatched his friend Ebbo of Rheims to the Danes

DOI: 10.4324/9781003379157-15

in 823 (alongside Bishop Willeric of Bremen, who had been preaching among the Nordalbingians).[11] Before departing, the emperor offered Ebbo instructions on what he should communicate to Danish pagans. According to Ermold the Black, Louis advised that Danes should cease giving reverence to statues or images made with their own hands and desist from sacrificing to demons. Too much time had already been devoted to such things, and the time had come to "cut away the condemned religions."[12] Ebbo was also to portray the Christian God as a mighty ruler in heaven, as the creator of all things, and to explain the story of Adam and Eve and the Fall into sin, as well as God's solution in the sacrifice of Jesus.[13] It was also necessary to explain the importance of baptism and gaining eternal salvation. The Old and New Testaments were to be presented as infallible guides to life.[14]

Even with attempts to "buy converts," Ebbo does not appear to have been particularly successful in presenting this message; however, he may have played a role in the conversion of Harald Klak.[15] Indeed, the entire function of his mission may have been to establish a Christian base in Denmark upon which Harald (as a Frankish vassal) could build support.[16] However, ultimately, Harald turned out to be a lackluster tool for assisting the Carolingians in achieving their northern ambitions (see Chapter 12).[17]

After Ebbo returned home, another attempt was made to acquire Danish souls by sending Anskar to Hedeby in 826.[18] Anskar, "desirous of obtaining martyrdom," proved more useful, almost certainly because he gained the favor of the Danish royal family.[19] That being said, he also built rapport among Danish "commoners."[20] According to his biographer Rimbert, beyond his reputation as a learned man, Anskar was known to have vivid (almost mystical) visions, was respected for his bravery, and was trusted for his moral convictions, some of which saw him advocating for escaped slaves in Nordalbingia and seeking care for the poor.[21] Perhaps for these qualities and not his political support, he has become known to posterity as the "Apostle of the North." Nevertheless, Anskar's missions continued to be supported by Frankish and Danish patrons, as well as Christian institutions in Saxony.[22] Indeed, by 829, the bishop of Hamburg in Saxony was assisting in creating a missionary school in Flanders at Tourhout, the primary purpose of which was the conversion of the Northmen.[23] Tourhout was then granted to Anskar by the emperor in 831 as a refuge if he ever found himself in trouble.[24]

Meanwhile, Saxon ecclesiastical institutions continued developing elsewhere. By 833, the abbey of Corvey acquired minting rights, allowing Saxony to contribute to the production of coin-based currency for the first time in its history.[25] Corvey's power continued to grow by gaining the right to tithe, through land grants (such as the villages of Hemeln and Sülbeck) and by acquiring access to vital resources, including a salt work on the Weser.[26] Around the same time Corvey was beginning to prosper, Hamburg was raised to the status of bishopric to provide a base of operations for Anskar's missions.[27] Alongside Bremen, over the following decades, Hamburg played a vital role in conversion efforts among Saxons, Danes, and Slavs.[28] Hamburg was also the beneficiary of royal patronage and, like Corvey, in 834, was granted minting rights.[29] A few years later, Bremen received similar treatment when Louis' son Charles gave its local "Church of the Savior" a hundred *mansi*.[30]

Simultaneously, sometime between 820 and 830, the convent of Wendhausen was founded in Eastphalia on the northern fringes of the Harz Mountains by Gisela, daughter of the Eastphalian count Hessi, who died in 804.[31] The convent was put under the direction of Gisela's daughter Biliheld, who became Wendhausen's first abbess.[32] While Wendhausen is fascinating enough as an early example of a female religious house in Saxony, its reputation was enhanced by the presence of a renowned holy woman and prophetess named Liutbirga (a friend of Anskar), whose cult-following brought the convent and its supporting Saxon family prestige.[33]

It didn't take long for other noble families to catch on to the benefits surrounding monastic foundations. As a result, over the following two centuries, monastic houses (many of them female convents) were founded in Saxony by local aristocratic families to enhance their reputations.[34] In many ways, this phenomenon replicates what occurred among Frankish nobles during the seventh century.[35] Regarding the reasons behind Saxon noblewomen's high level of involvement, scholars have suggested it may be partially rooted in widowed women attempting to avoid being dispossessed of wealth they inherited from dead male relatives.[36] However, with landed wealth invested in ecclesiastical foundations, Saxon women could also command extensive authority by electing abbesses, solidifying familial legacies, enhancing noble kin networks, establishing territorial political claims, and promoting cultural innovations in art and literature.[37]

Supplementing ecclesiastical foundations by noble patrons was an increase in the importation of relics (OS: *wihetha*).[38] This must have occurred more widely than recorded; however, our source examples are not necessarily lacking. Bishops, missionaries, and monks knew full well the value relics had in establishing sacred space, spreading miracle stories, and garnering pilgrims (who brought offerings to support the Church and increase the power of bishops).[39] In addition, relics served as political gifts, bribes, and rewards. As a result, acquiring relics could become competitive or even dangerous.[40] For example, Charlemagne's biographer Einhard was involved in an episode in which relics of the bodies of Sts. Marcellinus and Peter were stolen from outside Rome and brought back to his church at Seligenstadt (Seligenstadt was granted to Einhard by Louis the Pious in 815).[41]

Less than a decade later, the remains of St. Severo were stolen from Ravenna and transported back to Germany. Simultaneously, discord erupted in the Frankish town of Le Mans when a Saxon delegation (sanctioned by the emperor) showed up with a mission to confiscate the remains of their former bishop Liborius. The new bishop, Aldrich, assisted the Saxons in their quest by procuring Liborius' bones from the local Church of the Apostles. After which, Aldrich transported the remains to the Le Mans cathedral and prepared them for departure with the Saxons. However, when the locals learned that Saxons had come to take away their revered relics, they began to riot. Eventually, Aldrich calmed the mob by advocating for Saxony's dire need for saints and reminding them that defying the emperor's order was unwise. That did the trick, and the Saxons left in peace. They spent the next month transferring the relics to their new home at Paderborn, where they were stored away in a local church.[42]

The transfer of relics was not always so dramatic, but the process continued to increase in Saxony in the coming decades. For example, in the 840s, abbess Hathumoda (daughter of the East Saxon count Liudolf) procured relics from Pope Sergius II in Rome, which later wound up in the Saxon abbey of Gandersheim.[43] Again, in 860, nuns from Herford acquired the relics of St. Pusinna from Soissons, which were brought to Westphalia in order "to increase the presence of female saints in the region."[44] Some of these were later transferred to Wendhausen, while the relics of Pusinna's sister (Liutrude) were sent to Corvey.[45]

Even the descendants of the rebel Widukind aided in these endeavors. In 851, his grandson Waltbraht transferred the bones of St. Alexander from Rome back to the Westphalian monastery of Wildeshausen (where a statue in the town square honoring Waltbraht can still be seen).[46] This was done according to a letter of introduction written on Waltbraht's behalf:

> [S]o that by...[the relics'] signs and miracles his countrymen [the Saxons] would be converted from pagan service and superstition to the true religion. For they were even more enmeshed in the heritage of paganism than in the Christian religion.[47]

Our primary source for the story of St. Alexander's relic transfer comes from Rudolf of Fulda and Meginhart's *Translatio Sancti Alexandri*; the first section was written in 863 by Rudolf, and the latter finished by Meginhart in 865. From the above excerpt, it is clear that contemporaries by no means believed Saxony in the mid- to late ninth century had been fully Christianized. Indeed, the opposite sentiment seems more prominent. In the same source, in a letter sent to Pope Leo by Lothar, he implores the holy father to grant Waltbraht relics so that:

> by their signs and miraculous power the majesty and greatness of the Almighty God...may shine forth manifestly to all men...For we find in the territories of our empire a people, Saxons and Frisians intermingled, fettered on the border of the Northmen and Obodrites, which had heard and accepted the teaching of the Gospel for a long time, but because of its neighborhood with the pagans is only partly firm in the true religion, and in part has almost already fallen away, unless God's help and the assistance of Your Holiness gives strength to our weakness. Therefore, we prostrate ourselves before you and humbly implore your goodness...to give us a miraculous remedy, so that this wild people, entangled in the snares of error, will not fall away completely from the true religion and thus perish, but rather, enlightened by doctrine and empowered by miracles, will remain more firmly in the service of the true God.[48]

With the importation of relics, the Church could alter or create sacred space and endow Saxons with acceptable intermediaries for interacting with the divine. The stories of saints' lives were imbued with awe-inspiring power, which served as a means of replacing or assimilating the lore of pagan cults.[49] Yet, the greatest story of all concerned Christ himself, of which one contemporary telling survives in the Old Saxon *Heliand*.

The *Heliand*

In Old Saxon, the term *Heliand* denotes "Savior" (derived from *helian*, "to heal" or "save"), and the work in question is a retelling of "Christ the Savior" through a peculiar lens, that is, that of ninth-century Saxon society.[50] It is a fusion of sorts, combining the essential themes of the gospel alongside elements of a Germanic and pagan worldview.[51] In addition, it is the main primary source for reconstructing the Old Saxon language (alongside the contemporaneous Old Saxon *Genesis*), each of which has been useful in helping us understand early Saxon society and its Christianization.[52]

The "Saxon Gospel" contains roughly 6,000 lines of alliterative verse written in the style of a Germanic epic, very likely with the intention of being read aloud, sung, or chanted.[53] It is the oldest epic in German literature.[54] The original text was composed sometime in the mid-ninth century, likely between 830 and 850, and is historically validated by multiple (slightly) younger manuscripts and fragments currently housed in Britain, Germany, and the Vatican.[55]

The *Heliand*'s composition likely took place at the behest of Louis the Pious; however, it remains possible that its production was instigated by Louis the German.[56] The confusion lies in a reference from the *Praefatio* (an independent preface text), the oldest of which dates to the sixteenth century but is believed to be an authentic copy of an original from the period of the *Heliand*'s composition.[57] This preface references a *Ludduicus pijssimus Augustus*, which is problematic because both Louis the Pious and Louis the German were sometimes called *augustus*.[58] However, the Louis in question is said to have commissioned a Saxon poet to make the gospels intelligible in the vernacular of his Germanic-speaking (*Theudisca loquens lingua*) subjects, both literate and illiterate.[59] This need to reference Germanic-speaking subjects may be one component in favor of Louis the Pious. Louis the German's stronghold was in Bavaria, his rulership eventually extending to East Francia as a whole, the bulk of which was Germanic-speaking. For Louis the German, calling out his Germanic-speaking subjects seems somewhat redundant. However, for Louis the Pious, whose subjects included the Latin-based speakers of the west, the need to single out Germanic-speaking subjects is more fitting. Nevertheless, while most scholars lean in favor of Louis the Pious, if the *Heliand*'s origins lay with his son, perhaps it was a response to the tumultuous period of the Saxon *Stellinga* revolt of the 840s (see Chapter 12).[60]

Confusion also clouds the identity of the text's author; however, it was likely a Saxon of some significance.[61] Scholars have tried isolating the individual based on a mixture of Ingvaeonic and Franconian linguistic features in the text, leading to suggestions such as Gottschalk of Orbais, the Frisian poet Bernlef, Hrabanus Maurus, or the Saxon monks Edelfrid and Haterich.[62] Yet these suggestions remain unprovable, and the presence of multiple copies, varying scribal conventions, and the use of learned dialectical quirks make this linguistic detective work incredibly complicated.[63] In addition, the author did not copy directly from the gospel, commentaries, or paraphrases. The *Heliand* utilizes such works, but the author doesn't balk at rearranging, shortening, expanding, or changing gospel scenes to emphasize particular themes or facilitate a better "narrative flow" (mainly geared toward live and dramatic recitation).[64] The author even goes so far as to change the words of Christ himself, something not done lightly.[65] Similar observations can be seen in the *Old Saxon Genesis*, which some scholars argue may be the product of the same author.[66]

As for where the *Heliand* was written, that, too, is unclear; however, northwest Germany seems likely, and the monastic center of Fulda is undoubtedly the favored choice among scholars due to linguistic features in the text and the presence at the monastery of Hrabanus Maurus' commentary on Matthew and Tatian's *Diatessaron* (a harmony gospel), which the author utilized.[67] However, Essen, Corvey, Werden on the Ruhr, and even southern England have been proposed as potential composition sites.[68]

How the text was used during the later course of the Middle Ages also remains a mystery, yet Martin Luther eventually acquired a copy he was fond of.[69] The first printed version only became available in 1830 following the work of Johann Andreas Schmeller, who gave it the name *Heliand* and dedicated it to the German ethnolinguist Jacob Grimm.[70] However, since the late nineteenth century, Eduard Sievers' German translation of the *Heliand* (published in 1878) has been the standard reference text for subsequent scholars. There have since been numerous English translations.

So much for the text's origins, what of the *Heliand*'s purpose and content? In broad terms, the work is a tool by which the author (and his patrons) tries to bring about (or solidify) the conversion of Saxons to Christianity. This is done not by displacing the old (pagan) with the new (Christian) but by tactfully blending Saxon traditions with Christian teachings.[71] By employing this methodology, the audience is not forced into the awkward position of choosing *entirely* between the two.[72] At the same time, framing the gospel story within a "Germanic" cultural context makes the message more palatable.[73] For example, the setting of the *Heliand* reflects *not* the Biblical Levant but rather the plains and marshes of the north German coast.[74] Christ wanders *not* in a desert but in a dark forest-wilderness (OS: *uuostunnea* or *sinuueldi*).[75] We are also given images of "high horned" ships reminiscent of North Sea vessels sailing the waters of Galilee.[76] While at the marriage at Cana, people drink apple wine and at other times cider or mead.[77] Shepherds also tend horses, while the apostles are described as "fair-skinned."[78] Herod's palace and other important abodes are painted as great mead-halls (OS: *uuinseli*).[79] Others are described as hill-forts or *burgen*.[80] All these occur within the Saxon *middilgard* ("middle-earth" or "mid-world").[81]

Accentuating the *Heliand*'s northern landscape is a myriad of hybrid spiritual phenomena. At the top, we see an awe-inspiring God, the "All-ruler," whose words are mighty spells and runes that harness the power of creation.[82] Christ is called *uuarsago*, a "soothsayer" or "truth-speaker."[83] His birth, through prophecy, is foretold to Mary by the "bright fates" (*thiu berthun giscapu*) and the "fair host of god" (angels).[84] When Christ speaks, His words are acts of "soothsaying," and during the sermon on the mount, the crowd implores him to teach them "the secret runes."[85] Indeed, the *Our Father* prayer is likened to a spell, and through the gift of God, Christ's followers are granted knowledge of "the secret mystery" and "the runes of heaven."[86] These runic comparisons are also made elsewhere, such as when Christ turns water into wine, a performative act of "manifestation through words" (which he refuses to reveal to the apostles due to their immense power).[87]

The personality of Christ is also presented in a multifaceted way, with specific traits emphasized over others. His intelligence, wisdom, strength, cultivation of loyalty, and forgiveness of enemies are all at the forefront.[88] Christ is *leriand*, "the teaching one."[89] Yet, he is also a mighty *drohtin*, a divine (and good) lord of high reputation.[90]

There has been much controversy over the translation and meaning of the term *drohtin*.[91] In Ronald Murphy's work, it becomes "chieftain"; however, this is somewhat misleading.[92] The technical translation is "lord" or "ruler," but the debate centers around to what extent that term implied militaristic functions rooted in the older Germanic comitatus institution and how it was intended to be interpreted by the author of the *Heliand*.[93] Was it merely used to indicate that Christ was a new master, ruler, or authority to which one proclaimed loyalty? Or meant to signify a heroic lord in a political sense, as one who commands men at arms? Perhaps it is telling that in the *Heliand*, Christ is also called a *Siegdrohtin*, a "Victory Lord" or "Lord of Victories."[94] The term may imply victory over death, sin, Satan, or evil. Yet, it may also signify victory over earthly enemies through war.

None of these interpretations are mutually exclusive, nor do they detract from Biblical representations of Christ or Yahweh.[95] At the same time, interpretations of Christ from Antiquity up through the Central Middle Ages (and beyond) often portray or invoke Christ as a God of war.[96] The conversions of Constantine and Clovis followed victories in battle in which Christ was said to have helped them win, and similar justifications followed Frankish conquests in a number of the chronicles.[97] Invocations of "Christ for conquest" certainly lingered into the era of the Crusades, Inquisition, European sectional wars of religion, and European Colonialism.[98]

At the same time, artistic depictions of Christ (e.g., the seventh-century funerary plaque from Gresin, Puy-de-Domehave, or the early ninth-century Utrecht Psalter) show him dressed in the guise of a soldier.[99] Further, in Anglo-Saxon literature, such as the eighth-century poem "The Dream of the Rood," Jesus is represented heroically as a Mighty Warrior King and Lord of Victories, notably in his "harrowing of hell."[100] The same applies to representations of Christ in the Old English/Old Saxon *Genesis*.[101]

Similar examples could be drawn from several Colonial contexts, for example, when Jesuit missionaries in China referred to the Christian God as "Shangdi," that is, "Emperor on High."[102] It should also be remembered that one of the central premises of Christianity is the notion that all humanity is engaged in a cosmic war stretching back to Satan's rebellion.[103] Allegiance to Christ was, therefore, far more than a declaration of subservience to a ruler; it was a commitment to fight against His enemies.[104] Furthermore, in the *Heliand*, like a generous warlord, Christ is called a "jewel" and "ring-giver" (OS: *Boggebo*).[105] With the image of Christ formulated as such, his followers become *druhtfolc*, that is, retainers and "word-wise warriors" deeply devoted to their lord.[106] The apostle Peter is the ideal warrior (the best of thanes/a keen sword thane) and obedient follower, while John the Baptist is a "warrior companion" of the King of Heaven (*gesith hebancuninges*).[107] When Romans and Pharisees come to seize Christ in the garden of Gethsemane, in the spirit of *gefolgschaft* (absolute loyalty), His followers rally to his defense, ready to fight.[108]

Why do Jesus' followers display such fierce devotion? The answer presented in the *Heliand* is undoubtedly a multilayered one. However, the fundamental motivation stems from the demonstrated power of the "Might-Wielding Christ."[109] At a basic level, this is the key theme of the text, which the author goes to great lengths to make apparent to the listener (presumably a potential or recent convert). The power of Christ had not only to equal but also to *surpass* that of the Saxons' pagan gods.[110]

To emphasize His power, in the *Heliand,* Christ becomes the great light-bringer, a healer, miracle worker, and protector of the people who came to bring peace and dispel the dark forces that lurk throughout *middilgard*.[111] Neither demonic "loathsome wights" (*letha uuithi*) nor the crafty "spear-fiend" Devil (*gerfiund*) with his magic helmet (*helidhelm*) could stand before him.[112] Even death held no sway, for this "necromancer" could not only resurrect others but could Himself rise from the grave as well.[113] With such power, taken alongside his gift of prophecy (as when he foretells His death and betrayal), Christ demonstrates His ability to control the very powers of Fate itself.[114] This last point cannot be overemphasized, as "fatalism" appears to have been a significant component of the Saxon worldview.[115] We may hazard that notion because references to "the fates" (*thea uurdi*) or the "workings of fate" appear persistently throughout the text.[116] In much of "Germanic" or Norse myth, all beings, even the gods, were subject to the weaving of the web of Fate (*wyrd*). If this same interpretation held for the Saxons, Christ may have represented something new, a being whose power lay *beyond* Fate. Indeed, in the *Heliand,* Fate itself is ultimately transformed into a tool of the Christian God, becoming, by default, a representation of His will (*gotes uuillen*).[117]

Replicating the Gospel narrative, in the *Heliand,* the Savior came to dispel the darkness of the present world and that of the next.[118] Such was made possible by His great sacrifice on the cross.[119] Only through devotion to Christ and acknowledging that sacrifice could one avoid "the region of *Hel*" and the fiery cataclysm (*Muspell, Mudspel, Muspilli, Mutspelli*) that would bring the end of all things. [120] For those who remained steadfast and loyal, such terrors could be avoided.[121] When they traveled to the next world and sat before God's assembly (*Thing*) on the Day of Judgment, they would not be found wanting.[122] Instead, they would receive a "great treasure hoard" and roam free among the sunny green meadows of paradise.[123] Such were the rewards of the great *Friðubarn*, the "Peace Child."[124]

However, for those who rejected, betrayed, or failed to commit to Christ, "fiery Hell awaits."[125] This message is seen most clearly in the unfortunate and persistently negative portrayal of Jews (as deceitful, loathsome, and murderous), whom the author fashions as "the archetype of all who doubt the divinity of Christ."[126] The fate of Judas (the "troth breaker") is also telling. After he betrays Christ, Judas is attacked by fiends and evil wights, agents of God's fury, who lead him to commit suicide.[127] By describing such a horrific episode, the author forces those who remain heathen (OS: *hethina liudi*, "heath-dwellers") to contemplate whether or not such a fate lay in wait for themselves.[128] Instead, the goal is for the listener to cultivate a visceral "hatred of Jesus' enemies," be they human or demonic.[129] More important, the listener should open their eyes to the light of Christ's message and reject the blindness of past heathen customs that led them astray.[130] Fear of God, hatred of His enemies, and severing the past were then, essentially, evocative emotional tools utilized "to win souls for Christ."[131]

Conclusion

There is much to be considered in how the *Heliand*'s message (combining devotion to Christ, hatred of His enemies, absolute loyalty, and a commission to go forth and win souls in the great cosmic war between Heaven and Hell) contributed to developing a "crusading ethos" among Germanic Christians. However, that message would need time to ferment.[132] In mid-ninth-century Saxony, it had only just begun to germinate. A receptive audience, not crusaders, was what the *Heliand* initially sought.

From a theological perspective, the Old Saxon *Genesis* offered the problem, that is, Satan's rebellion, the Fall, sin, death, and the need for atonement, while the *Heliand* offered the answer: belief in Christ's sacrifice as the salvation of humanity. Armed with these texts, missionaries in the field were well-equipped to present a basic overview of Christian themes.[133] Yet, underlying the *Heliand*'s theological message was also a multifaceted political one. The portrayal of the Jews may have been intended to represent the rebellious and oath-breaking Saxons of the past. However, there are also representations of the Franks as analogous to Romans, positive representations of the nobility and priest class, and the novel (but critical) message of learning to forgive one's enemies.[134] Therefore, alongside the desire to garner conversions, the *Heliand* was a work of "political theology" arguing for Saxons to be content with their lot, that is, their integration within Franco-Christian civilization.[135] Beyond merely accepting this, it was also desirable to give deference to the upper echelons of that civilization, namely, the king, nobles, and representatives of the Church.[136] However, it must have been comforting for marginalized individuals to hear that the heavenly rewards promised in the *Heliand* were dealt out equally, regardless of social status.[137]

To what extent the "Saxon Gospel" was successful in commandeering the loyalty of early converts is difficult to surmise. However, it seems likely that by incorporating elements of Saxon culture within the Gospel narrative, Saxons would have been far more capable of comprehending and accommodating Christian teachings.[138] Indeed, many comparisons could be made to Colonial contexts that illustrate the success of utilizing syncretic or "indigenizing" conversion strategies (see Conclusion).[139] However, if the *Heliand*'s message was well-received by its audience, many Saxons were still dissatisfied with their situation. Resentment toward the Frankish conquest, exploitation by the nobility, and the criminalization of ancestral customs continued to breed hostility. With the death of Louis the Pious, and the eruption of another Frankish civil war, those resentments resurfaced one final time.

Notes

1 Rembold, *Conquest and Christianization*, 234
2 Dutton, *Carolingian Civilization*, 360–364; Wickham, *The Inheritance of Rome*, 417–418 & for an overview of Gottschalk's story, see Gillis, *Heresy and Dissent in the Carolingian Empire*; McKitterick, *History and Memory in the Carolingian World*, 218–220 & Nelson, *Charles the Bald*, 168
3 Flierman, *Saxon Identities*, 130; McKitterick, *Charlemagne*, 251–253; Lübeck, "Das Kloster Fulda und die Sachsenmission," 66–67; Rimbert, *Anskar*, 50; Ehlers, *Die Integration Sachsens in das fränkische Reich*, 65–66 & Knibbs, *Ansgar, Rimbert and the Forged Foundations of Hamburg-Bremen*, 62–63
4 Reuter, *Germany in the Early Middle Ages*, 107
5 Steuer, "The Beginnings of Urban Economies among the Saxons," 172 & Gallee, *Old-Saxon Texts*, XV
6 Tschan, *History of the Archbishops of Hamburg-Bremen*, 21 & Derry, *A History of Scandinavia*, 34
7 Gillis, *Heresy and Dissent in the Carolingian Empire*, 43–44
8 Ibid.; Flierman, *Saxon Identities*, 137–138; Isenberg, "Nach den Sachsenkriegen Karls des Großen," 22–24 & Knibbs, *Ansgar, Rimbert and the Forged Foundations of Hamburg-Bremen*, 64–65
9 For the "North Wind" see Fraesdorff, "The Power of Imagination," 310 & 313 & Notgers' reference in Noble, *Charlemagne and Louis the Pious*, 112
10 DuBois, *Nordic Religions in the Viking Age*, 155
11 Tschan, *History of the Archbishops of Hamburg-Bremen*, 19–24; Rimbert, *Anskar*, 54 & Knibbs, *Ansgar, Rimbert and the Forged Foundations of Hamburg-Bremen*, 10–11
12 Sullivan, "The Carolingian Missionary and the Pagan," 718
13 Noble, *Charlemagne and Louis the Pious*, 170–171
14 Sullivan, "Carolingian Missionary Theories," 285
15 Noble, *Charlemagne and Louis the Pious*, 172–174
16 Knibbs, *Ansgar, Rimbert and the Forged Foundations of Hamburg-Bremen*, 67–68
17 Ibid. 221
18 Sullivan, "The Carolingian Missionary and the Pagan," 726 & Clements, *The Vikings*, 61–62
19 Fletcher, *The Conversion of Europe*, 226–227; Tschan, *History of the Archbishops of Hamburg-Bremen*, 22–23 & Dutton, *Carolingian Civilization*, 429–430
20 Rimbert, *Anskar*, 82–84
21 Ibid. 7, & 28 & 56 & 118–120; Wood, *The Missionary Life*, 123–134; Dutton, *Carolingian Civilization*, 402–408 & 446 & Tschan, *History of the Archbishops of Hamburg-Bremen*, 32–33
22 Farmer, *The Oxford Dictionary of Saints*, 22
23 Arblaster, *A History of the Low Countries*, 36 & Dutton, *Carolingian Civilization*, 413–415
24 Wood, *The Missionary Life*, 124 and the same year Hamburg began constructing a cathedral inside the fort's walls. See Goetz, *Life in the Middle Ages*, 204
25 Riche, *Daily Life in the World of Charlemagne*, 124 & Landon, "Economic Incentives for the Frankish Conquest of Saxony," 47

26 Reuter, *Germany in the Early Middle Ages*, 68; Rembold, *Conquest and Christianization*, 163–164 & Knibbs, *Ansgar, Rimbert, and the Forged Foundations of Hamburg-Bremen*, 65–66

27 Tschan, *History of the Archbishops of Hamburg-Bremen*, xiii & Lund, "Scandinavia," 210

28 Buse, *The Regions of Germany*, 75 & 86–87; Nyberg, *Monasticism in North-Western Europe*, 7 & Rimbert, *Anskar*, 50–52

29 Riche, *Daily Life in the World of Charlemagne*, 124. The emperor also donated a library to Ansgar for his personal use. See Wood, *The Missionary Life*, 259–263

30 Rembold, *Conquest and Christianization*, 164

31 Flierman, *Saxon Identities*, 147–148; Paxton, *Anchoress and Abbess in Ninth-Century Saxony*, 5 & Wemple, *Women in Frankish Society*, 99

32 Ibid. & Ehlers, *Die Integration Sachsens in das fränkische Reich*, 166

33 Ibid.; Backman, *The Worlds of Medieval Europe*, 154–155; Wemple, *Women in Frankish Society*, 100 & 145 & 173 & Greer, *Commemorating Power in Early Medieval Saxony*, 17–18

34 Rembold, *Conquest and Christianization*, 224–225; Paxton, *Anchoress and Abbess in Ninth-Century Saxony*, 4 & 9 & 115–116; Reuter, *Germany in the Early Middle Ages*, 108; Fletcher, *The Conversion of Europe*, 219–221; Carroll, "The Bishoprics of Saxony," 225–226 & Goetz, *Life in the Middle Ages*, 74

35 Greer, *Commemorating Power in Early Medieval Saxony*, 26 & Geary, *Before France and Germany*, 176

36 Ibid. 21–25 & 175

37 Ibid. 22–23 & 29–30 & Wemple, *Women in Frankish Society*, 123

38 Reuter, *Germany in the Early Middle Ages*, 165; Goldberg, *Struggle for Empire*, 173–174; Gallee, *Old-Saxon Texts*, XXI & Ehlers, "Könige, Klöster und der Raum," 200–201

39 Raaijmakers, *The Making of the Monastic Community of Fulda*, 48–49; Shuler, "The Saxons within Carolingian Christendom," 40–45; Wood, *The Missionary Life*, 262–263; Newman, *Daily Life in the Middle Ages*, 81; Wickham, *The Inheritance of Rome*, 54–55 & 178; Milis, *The Pagan Middle Ages*, 68 & Isenberg, "Nach den Sachsenkriegen Karls des Großen," 18–19

40 Raaijmakers, *The Making of the Monastic Community of Fulda*, 41 & Mayr-Harting, "The West," 119

41 For an English translation of Einhard's *Translation of the Relics of Sts. Marcellinus and Peter*, see Head, *Medieval Hagiography*, 205–224 & see also: Farmer, *The Oxford Dictionary of Saints*, 289; Noble, *Charlemagne and Louis the Pious*, 8 & 272; Stone, "Carolingian Domesticities," 229 & De Jong, *The Penitential State*, 22

42 Flierman, *Saxon Identities*, 119–120

43 Paxton, *Anchoress and Abbess in Ninth-Century Saxony*, 3 & 42–45

44 Ibid. 74

45 Ibid. & Isenberg, "Nach den Sachsenkriegen Karls des Großen," 22–24

46 Honselmann, "Die Annahme des Christentums durch die Sachsen," 212–214; Mackay, *Atlas of Medieval Europe*, 50 & Schmid, "Die Nachfahren Widukinds," 3

47 The English translation is my own; however, it is based on the German edition by Wilhelm Wattenbach. See Wattenbach, *Die Übertragung des hl. Alexander von Rudolf und Meginhart*, 11–13

48 Ibid. 14

49 Hutton, *How Pagan Were Medieval English Peasants?* 242

50 Bosman, "Teach us the Secret Runes," 40; Cathay, *Heliand*, 159–160; Kristoffersen, *Pacifying the Saxons*, 45 & for the Old Saxon text, see Sievers, *Heliand*, 7–388; Rauch, *The Old Saxon Language*, 292 & Tiefenbach, *Altsächsisches Handwörterbuch*, 156

51 Angerer, "Beyond 'Germanic' and 'Christian' Monoliths," 73–78; Murphy, *The Saxon Savior*, vii & ix; Haferland, "The Hatred of Enemies," 214 & Dewey, *An Annotated English Translation of the Old Saxon Heliand*, vii

52 Ibid. 86–87; Bosman, "Teach us the Secret Runes," 40 & Robinson, *Old English and Its Closest Relatives*, 109–111 & "A Note on the Sources of the Old Saxon 'Genesis'," 389–396; Gibbs, *Medieval German Literature*, 41; Rauch, *The Old Saxon Language*, 1; Fortson, *Indo-European Language and Culture*, 326 & Kennedy, *The Caedmon Poems*, xxiv–xxv

53 Cathey, *Heliand*, 16; Robinson, *Old English and Its Closest Relatives*, 109–111; Murphy, *The Heliand*, xvi; Goldberg, *Struggle for Empire*, 183; Gibbs, *Medieval German Literature*, 39; Harrison, "Historical Infanticide," 203; Metzenthin, "The 'Heliand': A New Approach," 510 & Scott, *The Heliand*, vii

54 Murphy, "The Old Saxon Heliand," 34

55 Cathey, *Heliand*, 1 & 3; Landon, *Conquest and Colonization*, 201–202; Gibbs, *Medieval German Literature*, 39; Rauch, *The Old Saxon Language*, 100–101; Dewey, *An Annotated English Translation of the Old Saxon Heliand*, iv

56 Ibid. & Gillis, *Heresy and Dissent in the Carolingian Empire*, 44–45

57 Rauch, *The Old Saxon Language*, 101 & for the Latin texts, see 253–256 & see also Sievers, *Heliand*, xxiv–xxvi & 3–4 & Dewey, *An Annotated English Translation of the Old Saxon Heliand*, vi

58 Cathey, "The Historical Setting of the *Heliand*," 25 & *Old Saxon*, 19 & Notger refers to Louis the German as "emperor", see Noble, *Charlemagne and Louis the Pious*, 102

59 Rauch, *The Old Saxon Language*, 101–102 & 253 & Gillis, *Heresy and Dissent in the Carolingian Empire*, 46

60 Goldberg, *Struggle for Empire*, 183

61 Bosman, "Teach us the Secret Runes," 40 & Metzenthin, "The 'Heliand': A New Approach," 509 & 517

62 Landon, *Conquest and Colonization*, 201–202; Augustyn, "Thor's Hammer and the Power of God," 35–36; Metzenthin, "The 'Heliand': A New Approach," 510–511; Gillis, *Heresy and Dissent in the Carolingian Empire*, 45–46 & Sievers, *Heliand*, xxvi

63 Gibbs, *Medieval German Literature*, 3 & 26; Gallee, *Old-Saxon Texts*, 8 & Augustyn, *The Semiotics of Fate, Death, and the Soul in Germanic Culture*, 1

64 Sievers, *Heliand*, xli; Harrison, "Historical Infanticide," 204–207; Dewey, *An Annotated English Translation of the Old Saxon Heliand*, viii–ix & x & Youngs, "A Transcript of Submission," 1–2

65 Metzenthin, "The 'Heliand': A New Approach," 520

66 Sievers, *Heliand*, xxxiii & xxxiv

67 Cathey, *Heliand*, 17; Bosman, "Teach us the Secret Runes," 41; Goldberg, *Struggle for Empire*, 183; Gibbs, *Medieval German Literature*, 30; Gallee, *Old-Saxon Texts*, 28; Harrison, "Historical Infanticide," 204; Wright, *An Old High German Primer*, 85 & Sievers, *Heliand*, XLI

68 Landon, *Conquest and Colonization*, 201–202; Augustyn, "Thor's Hammer and the Power of God," 34; Robinson, *Old English and Its Closest Relatives*, 109–111; Gallee, *Old-Saxon Texts*, XXXVIII; Rauch, *The Old Saxon Language*, 106 & Wallace-Hadrill, *The Frankish Church*, 384–385

69 Pierce, "An Overview of Old Saxon Linguistics," 66–67

70 Murphy, *The Saxon Savior*, 12; Bosman, "Teach us the Secret Runes," 40; Gibbs, *Medieval German Literature*, 39 & Gallee, *Old-Saxon Texts*, XXXVIII

71 Karras, "Pagan Survivals," 570; Augustyn, *The Semiotics of Fate, Death, and the Soul in Germanic Culture*, 2 & Cathey, *Old Saxon*, 7

72 Bosman, "Teach us the Secret Runes," 39

73 Cathey, *Heliand*, ix–x

74 Robinson, *Old English and Its Closest Relatives*, 109

75 Murphy, *The Heliand*, 36 & 39 & Cathey, *Heliand*, 171–172

76 Ibid. 41 & 75; Scott, *The Heliand*, 78 & Dewey, *An Annotated English Translation of the Old Saxon Heliand*, 74 & 94

77 Ibid.; Cathay, *Heliand*, 187; Murphy, *The Heliand*, 7 & 67 & Scott, *The Heliand*, 5 & 68–70

78 Murphy, *The Heliand*, 10 & Landon, *Conquest and Colonization*, 212

79 Ibid. 11, 20, & 149 & Riche, *Daily Life in the World of Charlemagne*, 228–229

80 Murphy, *The Heliand*, 136; Gibbs, *Medieval German Literature*, 40 & Scott, *The Heliand*, 5 & 9 & 11 & 13

81 Ibid. 5 & 24 & 56 & 93 & 118; Scott, *The Heliand*, 2 & 19–20 & 28 & 30 & 143 & Dewey, *An Annotated English Translation of the Old Saxon Heliand*, 2,

82 Murphy, *The Heliand*, 7 & 87; Cathay, *Heliand*, 136–137 & Dewey, *An Annotated English Translation of the Old Saxon Heliand*, 1 & 42 & 65 & 88 & 90 & 182

83 Ibid. 73 & 93 & 98–99; Scott, *The Heliand*, 127 & Rauch, *The Old Saxon Language*, 312

84 Cathey, *Heliand*, 159–160 & Scott, *The Heliand*, 14

85 Murphy, *The Heliand*, 45 & 54 & 87 & Scott, *The Heliand*, 54

86 Ibid. 54–55 & 81; Bosman, "Teach us the Secret Runes," 48 and concerning other deviations of the Lord's Prayer in the Heliand see Metzenthin, "The 'Heliand': A New Approach," 536–537

87 Cathey, *Heliand*, 191

88 Ibid. 142–143; Kristoffersen, *Pacifying the Saxons*, 33–37; Scott, *The Heliand*, 17 & Dewey, *An Annotated English Translation of the Old Saxon Heliand*, 1 & 10 & 19 & 21 & 27 & 127–128

89 Murphy, *The Heliand*, 60 & 62 & 93 & 107 & 151–152 & 165; Gallee, *Old-Saxon Texts*, XXIV; Dewey, *An Annotated English Translation of the Old Saxon Heliand*, 129; Rauch, *The Old Saxon Language*, 297 & Tiefenbach, *Altsächsisches Handwörterbuch*, 237

90 Cathey, *Heliand*, 135; Bosman, "Teach us the Secret Runes," 41 & 50; Murphy, *The Heliand*, 36 & 157; Goldberg, *Struggle for Empire*, 183; Gibbs, *Medieval German Literature*, 40 & Dewey, *An Annotated English Translation of the Old Saxon Heliand*, 3–4 & 9–12 & 14–16 & 19 & 22 & 28 & 33

91 Green, *The Carolingian Lord*, 59

92 Kristoffersen, *Pacifying the Saxons*, 28–29

93 Ibid.; Angerer, "Beyond 'Germanic' and 'Christian' Monoliths", 87; Rauch, *The Old Saxon Language*, 282 & Tiefenbach, *Altsächsisches Handwörterbuch*, 60

94 Dewey, *An Annotated English Translation of the Old Saxon Heliand*, 52, 130 & Cusack, *Conversion among the Germanic Peoples*, 129–130

95 Aslan, "Cosmic War in Religious Traditions," 262–263; Armstrong, *Fields of Blood*, 109 & Lundburg, *Christian Martyrdom and Christian Violence*, 115–116

96 For example, this occurs in the earliest Old High German poem, *Hildebrandslied*, written in the 830s. See Bremmer, "Old English Heroic Poetry," 87

97 Schäferdiek, "Germanic and Celtic Christianities," 64; Jolly, *Popular Religion in Late Saxon England*, 28–29 & Warren, *Violence in Medieval Europe*, 42 & 70 & 88–89

98 Kling, *A History of Christian Conversion*, 468–469; McManners, "The Expansion of Christianity," 304–310 & Ballhatchet, "Asia," 490

99 Wallace-Hadrill, *The Frankish Church*, 99 & Markus, "From Rome to the Barbarian Kingdoms," 88

100 Crossley-Holland, *The Anglo-Saxon World*, 200–204; Marsden, "Biblical Literature: The New Testament," 243–245; Johnson, "Old English Religious Poetry, 176; Keefer, "Old English Religious Poetry," 25 & Heather, *Christendom*, 267. The story of Christ liberating souls from Hell, originating in the Gospel of Nicodemus, continued to be popular throughout the Middle Ages. See Raiswell & Winter, *The Medieval Devil*, 167

101 Kennedy, *The Caedmon Poems*, xxvi–xxvii

102 This was a common occurrence in Colonial missionary encounters: for example, the Sioux equated the Christian God with *Wakan Tanka*, the Cherokee did the same with

the Great Spirit, the Yoruba did likewise with the deity Olorun, and so forth. See Kling, *A History of Christian Conversion*, 464; Lindenfeld, *World Christianity and Indigenous Experience*, 73 & 81 & 226 & Cusack, *Conversion among the Germanic Peoples*, 12

103　Satan's rebellion, and the reasons for it, is described vividly in the Old English/Old Saxon *Genesis* as well as in the Old English *Christ and Satan*; see Kennedy, *The Caedmon Poems*, 8–33; Godden, "Biblical Literature: The Old Testament," 219–222; Johnson, "Old English Religious Poetry," 163 & see also: Aslan, "Cosmic War in Religious Traditions," 260–266; & MacMullen, *Christianizing the Roman Empire*, 18

104　This same theme of opposing loyalties and cosmic conflict is also found in the Old English *Christ and Satan*. See Johnson, "Old English Religious Poetry," 167–168

105　Murphy, *The Heliand*, 42, 90; Kristoffersen, *Pacifying the Saxons*, 51; Scott, *The Heliand*, 39; Dewey, *An Annotated English Translation of the Old Saxon Heliand*, 21, 39; Rauch, *The Old Saxon Language*, 281 & Tiefenbach, *Altsächsisches Handwörterbuch*, 36

106　Murphy, *The Heliand*, 40 & 80; Scott, *The Heliand*, 1 & 83; Dewey, *An Annotated English Translation of the Old Saxon Heliand*, 5 & 26 & 37 & 46 and the Latin equivalent of this term would be *comitatus*. See Cosman, *Medieval Wordbook*, 58 & Cantor, *The Civilization of the Middle Ages*, 197

107　Ibid. 40–41; Cathay, *Heliand*, 223 & 349; Dewey, *An Annotated English Translation of the Old Saxon Heliand*, 100 & 154–155. The Old Saxon words for "thane" (*thegan*, *thegn*) seem to have simultaneously denoted: follower or servant, in addition to military functions. See Green, *The Carolingian Lord*, 103 & 222–223

108　Murphy, *The Heliand*, 160 & Kahler, *The Germans*, 32–33

109　Scott, *The Heliand*, 1 & Dewey, *An Annotated English Translation of the Old Saxon Heliand*, 1–4 & 11–13 & 16 & 20

110　Murphy, *The Saxon Savior*, 76

111　Cathey, *Heliand*, 140 & 152; Scott, *The Heliand*, 16 & 40 & 42 & 98–100 & 102 & 107–108; Kristoffersen, *Pacifying the Saxons*, 18 & 22 & Dewey, *An Annotated English Translation of the Old Saxon Heliand*, 2 & 9 & 13 & 16 & 21 & 32 & 45 & 71 & 73 & 94

112　The Devil plays a disproportionately active role in the *Heliand*, and his appearance is far more frequent than what occurs in the Gospels or the *Diatessaron*. His depiction as the Foe, use of magical armor, and the elf-like characteristics of demons all appear in Anglo-Saxon literature, as well as in the Old Saxon *Genesis*. See Ibid. 171–172 & 181–182; Murphy, *The Heliand*, 36& 55 & 152 & 180; Kristoffersen, *Pacifying the Saxons*, 47; Klaeber, *The Later Genesis and Other Old English and Old Saxon Texts Relating to the Fall of Man*, 51; Scott, *The Heliand*, 2 & 33–37 & 78 & 84–85 & 102–104 & 118 & 123 & 140 & 159–160 & 186–187; Emmerton, *The Letters of Saint Boniface*, 59–60; Payne, *English Medicine in the Anglo-Saxon Times*, 46; Jolly, *Popular Religion in Late Saxon England*, 144–147 & 155–159; Kennedy, *The Caedmon Poems*, xxix–xxx & Dewey, *An Annotated English Translation of the Old Saxon Heliand*, 1–2 & 34–35 & 40 & 53 & 96 & 172–173

113　Ibid. 192; Murphy, *The Heliand*, 186 & 191 & Dewey, *An Annotated English Translation of the Old Saxon Heliand*, 131

114　Ibid. 142–143 & 204; Scott, *The Heliand*, 158 & Dewey, *An Annotated English Translation of the Old Saxon Heliand*, 113

115　Haferland, "The Hatred of Enemies," 215

116　Murphy, *The Heliand*, 7 & 14 & 118 & 151–152; Gallee, *Old-Saxon Texts*, XXIV; Scott, *The Heliand*, 7 & 11 & 25 & 75 & 115 & 157 & 158 & 164 & 185 & Dewey, *An Annotated English Translation of the Old Saxon Heliand*, 7 & 12 & 17 & 71–72 & 108 & 114 & 117 & 171

117　Kristoffersen, *Pacifying the Saxons*, 35; Dewey, *An Annotated English Translation of the Old Saxon Heliand*, 4 & 11 & 18 & 26; Youngs, "A Transcript of Submission,"

     10 & Augustyn, *The Semiotics of Fate, Death, and the Soul in Germanic Culture*, 41–42

118 Ibid. 32 & Dewey, *An Annotated English Translation of the Old Saxon Heliand*, 9 & 29 & 33 & 42

119 Murphy, *The Heliand*, 182 & 187

120 Ibid. 32 & 34 & 39 & 61 & 78 & 85 & 100 & 142 & 146 & 170 & 179 & 191; Simek, *Dictionary of Northern Mythology*, 222–223. Note: This is similar to the Norse Ragnarök ("twilight of the gods"), when all of life is engulfed Sutr's fire. See Leeming, *The Oxford Companion to World Mythology*, 334–335; Gibbs, *Medieval German Literature*, 37; Scott, *The Heliand*, 146; Wright, *An Old High-German Primer*, 140; Dewey, *An Annotated English Translation of the Old Saxon Heliand*, 84& 129 & 136–139; Rauch, *The Old Saxon Language*, 300; Tiefenbach, *Altsächsisches Handwörterbuch*, 280 & Somerville & McDonald, *The Viking Age*, 45–47 & 53–58

121 Ibid. 43; Kristoffersen, *Pacifying the Saxons*, 52 & Dewey, *An Annotated English Translation of the Old Saxon Heliand*, 10 & 18

122 Cathey, *Heliand*, 217

123 Ibid. 205; Murphy, *The Heliand*, 56–57 & 103; Scott, *The Heliand*, 13–14 & 31 & 33 & 43–44 & 55 & 106 & 108 & 168 & Dewey, *An Annotated English Translation of the Old Saxon Heliand*, 9 & 11 & 14 & 54 & 58–59 & 106–107

124 Kristoffersen, *Pacifying the Saxons*, 15; Dewey, *An Annotated English Translation of the Old Saxon Heliand*, 22; Rauch, *The Old Saxon Language*, 286 & Tiefenbach, *Altsächsisches Handwörterbuch*, 108

125 Gillis, *Heresy and Dissent in the Carolingian Empire*, 46–47. The torments of Hell, akin to references to Satan and demons, come up frequently and are described in vivid detail. The same is true for depictions of Hell in the Old Saxon *Genesis*. See Scott, *The Heliand*, 29 & 31 & 60 & 73 & 86 & 88–90 & 106 & 115–116 & 151 & 152; Kennedy, *The Caedmon Poems*, xxx–xxxi; Dewey, *An Annotated English Translation of the Old Saxon Heliand*, 48–49 & 70 & 81 & 84 & 108–109 & 141–142 & Raiswell & Winter, *The Medieval Devil*, 146–149

126 Friedrich, "Jesus Christ between Jews and Heathens," 271–272; Kristoffersen, *Pacifying the Saxons*, 57–58; Scott, *The Heliand*, 80–81 & 132–134 & 141 & 144–145 & 165 & 169–170 & 173 & 175 & 179–182 & 188–191 & 194–195 & 197 & Dewey, *An Annotated English Translation of the Old Saxon Heliand*, 40–41 & 142 & 153–154 & 156

127 Cathey, *Heliand*, 236; Scott, *The Heliand*, 176–177

128 Murphy, *The Heliand*, 106 & Gallee, *Old-Saxon Texts*, XX

129 Haferland, "The Hatred of Enemies," 215 & 219 & Youngs, "A Transcript of Submission," 12–13

130 Kristoffersen, *Pacifying the Saxons*, 59

131 Metzenthin, "The 'Heliand': A New Approach," 534–535

132 Murphy, "The Old Saxon Heliand," 34–35

133 Jeep, *Medieval Germany*, 56

134 Kristoffersen, *Pacifying the Saxons*, 43; Scott, *The Heliand*, 2 & 15 & 20 & 51; Dewey, *An Annotated English Translation of the Old Saxon Heliand*, 8 & 10 & 12 & 16–18 & 20 & Youngs, "A Transcript of Submission," 9–10

135 Youngs, "A Transcript of Submission," 2 & 15–16

136 Metzenthin, "The 'Heliand': A New Approach," 523 & 530 & 538

137 Kristoffersen, *Pacifying the Saxons*, 44

138 Bachrach, *Warfare in Medieval Europe*, 21

139 Kling, *A History of Christian Conversion*, 328 & 450–451; Ballhatchet, "Asia," 500–501; Baer, "History and Religions Conversion," 29–35; Milis, *The Pagan Middle Ages*, 10–11 & Mendoza, "Converted Christians, Shamans, and the House of God," 205

12   *Stellinga* and Beyond

Lothar had no intention of honoring his oath to protect Charles' inheritance, and following his father's death, fraternal discord erupted between him and his equally ambitious brothers. For several years, chaos and shifting loyalties reigned supreme, ultimately leading to a fragmentation of the realm. Within that confusion, a particular element of Saxon society, the so-called *Stellinga*, asserted themselves in a quest to restore their ancestral rights. It was the last Saxon revolt stemming from the Frankish conquest, and its widespread popular support among the "peasantry" against their lords was a unique aberration for the period.[1] However, to fully understand its development, the *Stellinga* must be seen within the broader context of the renewed Frankish civil war.

The Road to Fontenoy

Trouble began again, according to Nithard, due to the greed and ambitions of Lothar, who rapidly set about securing the loyalty of his subjects and scheming to achieve his goal of complete rule over the Empire. Consequently, from the Summer of 840 to June 841, Lothar, Charles, and Louis the German became ensnared in a strategic game of calculation and deception.[2] The brothers chased one another's armies, but, for the most part, serious engagements were avoided. Instead, each faction prioritized securing alliances and prying away the partisans of their rivals. Only after an awkward and a time-consuming dance of feints, withdrawals, and maneuvering did a definitive moment arrive determining the outcome of the conflict. On June 25, 841, at Fontenoy, the brothers and their respective allies finally fought, and bitterly so. Lothar led his army of Austrasians (and Saxons) against Louis' Bavarians and Saxons, while Pepin of Aquitaine led his warriors against Charles.[3] Some fought to a draw; many were butchered. The gruesome scene was remembered hauntingly by the poet Angelbert, who described a terrible massacre where "Christian law" was violated, blood flowed in waves, and the mouth of Cerberus opened with glee in hell to receive the dead (who were "stripped naked" while crows, vultures, and wolves devoured them).[4] In the end, Lothar and his army were forced to retreat.[5]

DOI: 10.4324/9781003379157-16

Desperate Times

The Battle of Fontenoy may have been a defeat for Lothar, but he was still unready to concede, and, in the aftermath of the carnage, Charles and Louis allowed Lothar to get away without giving pursuit. Perhaps, they reasoned, their immense victory would motivate Lothar to have a change of heart. With that hope in mind, on June 30, Charles and Louis went their separate ways.[6] For Charles, necessity returned him to Aquitaine to pursue Pepin (who fled in that direction). Over the next month, Charles tried to restore stability in the region while simultaneously attempting to dispel rumors (spread by Lothar) that he had been killed at Fontenoy.[7] As for Louis, he took his army and headed back toward the Rhine.

Meanwhile, Lothar, now in dire straits, renewed strategizing how best to overcome his brothers. In addition to the propaganda he spread concerning Charles' death, which was intended to inspire defectors and encourage instability, Lothar tried to rally support wherever he could. Given his desperation, it didn't matter where that support came from as long as he could use it. Consequently, Lothar decided to turn to an unlikely place, that is, a brewing movement of discontented Saxon "peasants."[8] These were the *Stellinga*, an Old Saxon term meaning "companions," "comrades," or "restorers."[9]

Courting the Saxons

Lothar acquired support among the Saxons long before the disaster at Fontenoy, most of which came from the nobility. According to the *Translation of Saint Alexander*, that assistance included Widukind's grandson Waltbraht, who had been entrusted to Lothar by his father Wigbert as a child (and had since grown up to become one of his loyal followers).[10] In like manner, during the Frankish civil war, Lothar entrusted his own son (Lothar II) to the temporary care of his partisans among the Saxons.[11]

Saxon elites were a politically divided group. Factionalism among the Saxon nobility can be seen as early as 838 when Louis the Pious revoked the lands of Saxons remaining loyal to his son Louis the German. After that, the nobility was split between those who supported the emperor and (after his death) Lothar and those who belonged to Louis the German. We can glean from Nithard's account that Lothar was primarily supported by Archbishop Otger of Mainz and Count Adalbert of Metz of the Hattonid family, each of whom loathed Louis the German.[12] Adalbert also brought the support of Bishop Baduard of Paderborn and his brothers Hatto, count of Nassau, and Banzleibs, an influential margrave.[13] In addition, Archbishop Otger could acquire aid from the key mid-Rhenish cities of Worms, Mainz, and Speyer.[14]

Louis the German had powerful Saxon friends too. In June 840, after finding out that Lothar was hunting him, Louis met with several Saxon nobles at Paderborn, likely to renew their support.[15] Among these Saxon allies were families such as the Bardonids and Liudolfings, the latter of which possessed extensive lands in Hesse and supported the Franks during Charlemagne's Saxon Wars.[16] Even more crucial were the Ecbertiner, who controlled the monastery of Corvey, along with its wealth, land, resources, soldiers, and strategic access to the *Hellweg*.[17]

Louis' ties to Corvey and the Ecbertiner family had been made possible partially through his wife, Hemma, a member of the influential Welf clan, who was also a cousin to the Saxon duke Ecbert.[18] Through Ecbert's sons, Abbot Warin of Corvey and Count Cobbo (who held vast lands in Saxony and controlled the bishopric of Osnabrück), Louis could draw considerable support in Saxony.[19] Therefore, it was critical for Louis to maintain those ties, which meant, first and foremost, continuing to show favor to Corvey. As Goldberg has discussed, his continuing to do so is made clear by Louis' confirmation of Corvey's "lands, rights, and immunities," as well as his extension of royal protection and land donations.[20] At the same time, Louis revoked the "marcher lordship" granted to Banzleibs (Lothar's partisan) and gave it to Abbot Warin.[21] Louis thereafter continued to pry away (or remove) Lothar's support among the Saxon nobility, which, coupled with the death of Adalbert at Ries (in May 841) and the defeat at Fontenoy, undercut Lothar's sway among Saxon elites.[22]

If Louis had the upper hand among the Saxon elite, then Lothar would turn the freemen and "peasants" against them.[23] By creating chaos in East Francia, Lothar might undermine the stability of Louis' realm and provide himself with time to improve his situation. With any luck, Louis' position could be weakened by the permanent removal of his partisans, which would drain his coffers and undermine his ability to muster troops. Consequently, according to Nithard, Lothar went to Saxony (or sent messengers) to meet with:

> the immense number of *frilingi* [freemen) and *lazzi* [bondsmen], promising them, if they should side with him, that he would let them have the same law in the future which their ancestors had observed when they were still worshipping idols. Since they desired this law above all, they adopted a new name, "Stellinga."[24]

From Nithard's report, we can surmise clues about who the *Stellinga* were and what they wanted. For one, this was a large organization composed of freemen and bondsmen, ergo, the "middling," and "lower" elements of Saxon society.[25] There is speculation that the movement may have comprised a kind of agricultural "guild" or *conjuratione* (sworn association), a particularly dangerous conclusion, given that such organizations had been outlawed by Charlemagne upon pain of death (via the Capitularies of Herstal and Thionville) as well as condemned by Louis the Pious in 821.[26] Their suppression stemmed from fears that "conspiracy" or independent "collective movements" might subvert royal authority.

We may also conclude that the *Stellinga* were "conservative" in the sense that they sought to restore Saxon laws or traditions as they were before the Frankish conquest. However, what precisely the mention of "Saxon law" is referring to is subject to debate.[27] It may indicate a desire to revive a more collective Saxon assembly, as reported at Marklo, in which a wider representation of society would have influenced political decisions.[28] However, if Marklo never existed, then this is a moot point.[29] Yet, even if Marklo never existed, the Frankish conquest brought about a restructuring of public or legal assemblies that *did* exist, in which case certain elements of the population may have been pushed to the side. That seems particularly feasible given the demographics of the *Stellinga*'s members, who would have been disenfranchised when their representative body was outlawed.[30] This is the same element of Saxon society that had resisted Charlemagne and the Saxon nobility for decades (of course, we do not know if the movement was organized by an older generation that witnessed the conquest or by a younger generation that had grown up discontent with its results).

Outside representation, there may have been economic motivations related to tithing, political restructuring, exploitation by the nobility, or taxes.[31] As Goldberg has pointed out, this argument was prevalent among East German Marxist historians, some of whom sought to demonstrate that the imposition of Frankish protofeudalism had brought about economic servitude for the Saxon peasantry.[32] The resulting loss of land thereafter bred dependency.[33] However, while it is unlikely that the Franks introduced this system, it may have been exacerbated by the Frankish conquest, which saw a bolstering of the local nobility and an extraordinary growth of land acquisition by the Church.[34]

At the same time, Nithard's reference to the law being associated with former days of pagan worship indicates there may have been religious motivations.[35] However, some scholars have been skeptical of the "return to paganism" explanation, suggesting Nithard was merely trying to sully Lothar's reputation by accusing him of supporting a pagan, peasant, and Saxon revolt, all of which would conjure feelings of utter horror among Frankish elites.[36] Alternatively, Springer has suggested that Nithard's account implies a desire to return to localized law, which may have existed before the *Lex Saxonum*.[37]

Springer's suggestion may be correct. However, returning to localized law *and* pre-Christian religious practice is not mutually exclusive. Historians too often approach the Christianization of societies as events based on the writing of elite members of the Church and the conversion of leaders.[38] Alternatively, anthropological studies and observations of Colonial or modern conversion experiences demonstrate that this is seldom the case. More often, conversion is a drawn-out and nebulous process, operating alongside various elements of residual paganism.[39] Perhaps the "return to paganism" argument is invalid because most Saxons, especially those of lower status, had never *really* left it. Between the 840s and the 870s, there were continued groans about the persistence of paganism among Saxon peasants, some of which are even alluded to by Louis the German.[40] In addition, we are given the same sentiment in the *Annals of St. Bertin*, which claims:

[Lothar] went so far as to offer those Saxons called *Stellinga*—there is a very large number of them among that people—the choice between some kind of written law and the customary law of the ancient Saxons, whichever they preferred. Always prone to evil, they chose to imitate pagan usage rather than keep their oaths to the Christian faith.[41]

Even if a substantial portion of Saxon society *had* converted, revivalist, prophetic, or reform movements are widespread in religious conversion history.[42] They are especially likely to occur if the conversion process has been violent or if an indigenous society feels their way of life is threatened.[43] Whatever the primary motivation, discontent with contemporary circumstances hardly seems surprising. Over the past half-century, Saxons had been subject to invasion, economic exploitation, political disenfranchisement, religious persecution, forced conscription, and the never-ending destructive feuds of their nobles and lords.[44] It is likely because of those feuds, and the resulting fractured Frankish Empire, that the *Stellinga* believed it might be capable of addressing their grievances.

The opportunity came in July 841, the first point at which we have clear communications between Lothar and the *Stellinga*.[45] These discussions happened either at or from the city of Aachen, which Lothar had fled to following Fontenoy. With the support of the *Stellinga* secured, Lothar made simultaneous appeals for aid elsewhere, including among "other frontier peoples," that is, Slavs and Danes.[46] Among these periphery folk, Lothar also gained the support of Harald Klak, the former (disappointing) Danish vassal of Louis the Pious. The *Annals of St. Bertin* note bitterly:

> Lothar, to secure the services of Harald, who along with other Danish pirates had for some years been imposing many sufferings on Frisia and the other coastal regions of the Christians, to the damage of Lothar's father's interests and the furtherance of his own, now granted Walcheren [in Zeeland] and the neighboring regions as a benefice. This was surely an utterly detestable crime, that those who had brought evil on Christians should be given power over the lands and people of Christians, and over the very churches of Christ; that the persecutors of the Christian faith should be sent up as lords over Christians, and Christian folk have to serve men who worshipped demons.[47]

With these "non-traditional" sources of aid secured, Lothar led his army to Mainz to press his claims among the Austrasian Franks, Thuringians, Alemans, and Saxon nobility, some of whom he persuaded to join his cause through "terror-tactics" and "conciliation" (i.e., threats and bribes).[48] Lothar was then ready to move against his brothers. However, before doing so, he ordered his partisans among the Saxon nobles to meet him at Speyer, where they returned his son Lothar II.[49] This note, coming from the *Annals of Fulda*, has been subject to some debate. We are not entirely sure if Lothar II was being held as a hostage, as a ward among trusted allies, or if Lothar was having his son groomed for political leadership in Saxony.[50] It is also curious that Lothar was having his son returned at *that* particular moment. Perhaps he feared for his son's life, as Lothar had just stirred up the lower Saxon classes against their lords with the intention of brewing chaos in the region. That may seem mere conjecture influenced by hindsight, but it would also be a perfectly reasonable response given the volatile situation. Lothar's loyalty from the Saxon nobility was by no means secure. Further, it is doubtful that Lothar's dealings with the *Stellinga* would have been popular among Saxon nobles, even among Lothar's partisans. Indeed, we cannot even be sure the nobles were aware of these dealings (although it seems likely those closest to Lothar would have been). Given the uncertainty, it was prudent to remove Lothar II from Saxon hands as soon as possible.

Fraternal Discord Continued

Once his son was returned, Lothar crossed the Rhine to drive his brother Louis into the Slavic frontier. However, the plan failed, and he was forced to break off the chase, after which he journeyed to Thionville to plan how best to attack Charles.[51] By September, it became clear to Charles what his brother was up to, leading him to reach out to Louis again for aid. In a repeat of the prior years, the brothers attempted to unite with their respective allies.

The remaining Fall and Winter of 841 brought a series of disappointments for Lothar. Charles snuck some of his soldiers across the Rhine and hid them in the forest of La Perche, which Lothar failed to ambush. Lothar tried to persuade Charles' allies among the Breton nobility to defect, but they declined. It was during this period of frustration, according to the *Annals of St. Bertin*, that Lothar's army moved into the region of Le Mans and began:

> ravaging everything with such acts of devastation, burning, rape, sacrilege and blasphemy that he could not even restrain his men from damaging those whom he was planning to visit. He lost no time in carrying off whatever treasure he could find deposited in churches or their strong rooms for safe-keeping—and...the priests and clergy of other ranks...bound by God's service, he forced to take oaths to himself.[52]

The situation was so bad that Pepin of Aquitaine, who had loyally followed Lothar throughout the conflict, abandoned the cause and returned home filled with regret.[53]

If Lothar had one hope left, it was Bishop Otger of Mainz, who was put in charge of preventing Louis from crossing the Rhine. However, by February 842, Charles knew what Otger was doing and marched his army into Alsace to relieve Louis. Once word reached Otger that Charles was leading an army in his direction, he abandoned the Rhine and made a hasty retreat.[54] Otger's withdrawal allowed Louis to cross the Rhine, and on February 14, he arrived in the city of Strasbourg for a famous meeting, where he and Charles swore oaths of loyalty to each other, "Louis in the Romance language and Charles in the German."[55] (It was the first time linguistic differences had been explicitly noted between Frankish rulers and the earliest textual attestation of Old French.)[56]

In addition to declaring their support for each other, the two brothers condemned Lothar. They then journeyed to Worms, Louis sailing down the Rhine while Charles braved the snowy Spring passing through the Vosges. Upon their arrival, emissaries were sent to Lothar to secure terms. Simultaneously, they sent word to Louis' eldest son Carloman to come and bolster their forces. Louis also dispatched his emissary Bardo into Saxony to meet with the nobles Lothar was courting and persuade them to think carefully about where they pledged their allegiance.

While they waited for replies, Charles and Louis' friendship grew as they encamped with their armies outside Worms, during which they led jovial mock "war games" to keep their troops fit.[57] Yet, the fun ended in March with the arrival of Carloman's army of Bavarians and Alamanni. At the time, Bardo returned from Saxony and informed Louis that the Saxons (likely certain noble factions) had rejected Lothar and were ready to obey Louis' orders.[58] Lothar, however, had refused to reply. So, with their forces at full strength, Charles, Louis, and Carloman set off to hunt Lothar, who had been hiding out at the Rhenish palace of Sinzig.

The allies led their forces by different routes toward Koblenz, where they boarded a ship and crossed the Moselle after holding Mass at St. Castor's. It was here, again, that Otger proved a disappointment. Lothar had returned Otger (along-side Harald Klak and Count Hatto) to river-guarding duty; however, when Otger and his companions gazed upon the incoming host, his forces retreated in terror. With the Moselle opened up to his enemies, it was Lothar's turn to panic. In what likely seemed to contemporaries a shameful act of cowardice, he abandoned his kingdom and fled with his few remaining retainers toward the Rhone.[59]

With Lothar in retreat, Charles and Louis reconvened at Aachen in March 842 to discuss how best to handle their brother's leaderless realm. An assembly was held where Lothar's defeats were proclaimed "divine vengeance" for having sub-jected Francia to endless strife.[60] With Lothar thoroughly condemned, Charles and Louis (alongside their councilors) set about partitioning the realm between them. When these discussions concluded, they had essentially granted Charles the west and Louis the east, a practical arrangement given the territories already under their control. Charles then returned across the Meuse to his domain, but Louis had other matters to attend to.

The *Stellinga* Unleashed

Back in Saxony, the *Stellinga* hadn't been idle while the royal siblings squabbled, and it was "on account of the Saxons" that Louis the German was required to jour-ney to Cologne following the partition of the realm.[61] As Ingrid Rembold has noted, in Cologne, Louis likely met with Saxon partisans of Lothar (noble or otherwise) whom he thought might be capable of influencing the *Stellinga* diplomatically.[62] But what exactly had the Saxons been up to that garnered such attention?

Nithard explicitly states that developments in Saxony were of utmost impor-tance, claiming the misguided Saxons "rallied to a large host…almost drove their lords from the kingdom" and "lived as their ancestors had done according to the law of his choice."[63] These reports are dramatic; however, as Ehlers has noted, it is incredible that the revolt lacks a sense of place.[64] It cannot be tied to any Saxon region at all. Given the fragmented nature of Saxon society, it seems likely that the revolt would have stemmed from a particular area; however, it could have been more widespread and, therefore, difficult to isolate. Indeed, a general revolt across Saxony may be indicated by the alarm it caused.

From the perspective of Franco-Saxon elites, the situation must have seemed like anarchy. Yet, Saxons weren't the only concern. Louis was also worried the *Stellinga* might ally with Slavs and Norsemen, who would invade the Empire and "revenge themselves" by rooting out Christianity.[65] This line from Nithard suggests the *Stellinga* had reverted to paganism, and the term "revenge" was essentially an acknowledgment that Christianity was not brought to these people peacefully.[66]

Indeed, fear of vengeance brought Louis to Cologne to resolve matters lest a "most horrible disaster befall the Holy Church of God."[67] Louis' anxiety was not unfounded, particularly concerning the Northmen, who at that same moment were ravaging the Frankish emporium of Quentovic.[68] However, despite an increase in Viking raids, there is little evidence of any coordination between Saxon rebels and Scandinavians, let alone the Slavs. If anything, their simultaneous stirrings appear to have resulted from instability in Francia, Lothar's machinations, and local sources of turbulence already underway. That being said, coordination is not beyond the realm of possibility, especially if we remember previous Saxon-coordinated revolts with Frisians, Slavs, and Avars, as well as the cordial relationship existing between Saxons and Danes before the Frankish conquest.

Presumably, after the meeting in Cologne, either messengers of Louis or notable Saxons he spoke with returned to Saxony to try and pacify the *Stellinga* through diplomacy. In the meantime, Louis made for Verdun to reconvene with Charles in May. While all this was happening, Lothar resided along the Rhone, where he benefited from shipping revenues in the area and tried to rally support. However, it is unlikely Lothar had any hopes of challenging his brothers at this point and was instead trying to muster enough leverage to barter for a better position. Indeed, he soon sent word to his brothers, asking for reconciliation, peace, and a three-way partition of the realm. Charles and Louis agreed, perhaps due to exhaustion, a desire for stability, or pressure from influential magnates. It took considerable time and arguing, but by June 842, the brothers came to an arrangement (which Nithard believed was overly generous to Lothar).[69] However, much remained to be worked out over the coming year, so each brother returned to their respective domains. Charles again headed for Aquitaine to deal with Pepin, Lothar sought revenge against those who betrayed him in his territories, and Louis headed for Saxony.[70]

Saxons who supported Lothar probably would have felt disheartened by his defeats and concessions, and therefore, many would have returned home in a state of despair. Perhaps, some of these lent their support to the *Stellinga*. Others, notably the upper echelons of Saxon society, would have been furious at what their kinsmen were up to.[71] According to the *Annals of Xanten*, throughout the entirety of Saxony, the "slaves rose up violently against their lords...perpetrated much madness," and the nobles were "persecuted and humiliated."[72]

The messengers Louis sent into Saxony from Cologne were ineffective, requiring Louis to tend to the matter himself. According to Nithard, Louis "distinguished himself by putting down, not without rightful bloodshed, the rebels in Saxony."[73]

The *Annals of Fulda* elaborate further, noting that in August 842, after attending an assembly at the *villa* of Salz:

> [Louis] set out for Saxony, where there was a very serious conspiracy of freedmen seeking to oppress their lawful lords. He crushed this ruthlessly by sentencing the ringleaders to death.[74]

The fullest account is taken up in the *Annals of St. Bertin*:

> Louis marched throughout Saxony and by force and terror he completely crushed all who still resisted him: having captured all the ringleaders of that dreadful example of insubordination—men who had all but abandoned the Christian faith and had resisted Louis and all his faithful men so fiercely—he punished 140 of them by beheading, hanged fourteen, maimed countless others by chopping off their limbs, and left noone able to carry on any further opposition to him.[75]

Each of these reports indicates the same message: the lower and middle classes composing the *Stellinga* had forgotten their place and were waging war against the nobles and partisans of Louis. They were doing so effectively (likely because many Saxon nobles had been absent on the various fronts of the civil war), and indications are made of their relapse into "heathenism." The situation was so bad that Louis needed to tend to the rebels himself, which he did swiftly and without mercy.[76]

The brutality with which the *Stellinga* was handled indicates the fear they instilled, the chaos they caused, and the dangerous ideas they were perpetuating, notably, the dismissal of Christianity and challenging the social order. As Goldberg has noted, this sentiment was even voiced by Lothar's partisan Gerward, who praised Louis for nobly crushing "the arrogantly risen slaves of the Saxons" and restoring them "to their proper nature."[77]

Despite their suppression, the *Stellinga* had not been fully pacified. Following a partition meeting at Koblenz in October, Louis received word that the *Stellinga* had again rebelled against their lords.[78] This stage of the revolt occurred throughout the Fall of 842 (possibly into early 843) and was once more aimed at the Saxon nobility.[79] However, again, things went poorly for the rebels. Nithard reports (with little sympathy) that in November, the *Stellinga* were "put down in a great bloodbath" and that those "who had dared to rise without lawful power perished by it."[80] With the possible exception of discontent in Eastphalia in 852 (mentioned in the *Annals of Fulda*), there were no more Saxon rebellions for the remainder of Carolingian rule.[81]

Transitions

The bloodbath of 842–843 was undertaken by Saxon nobles, some of whom (including Liudolf of Saxony) enhanced their prestige by participating.[82] In the case of margrave Liudolf, his status was such that, by the 860s, he could marry his daughter Liutgard to Louis the German's second eldest son Louis the Younger.[83] From that union emerged the Ottonian lineage (or "Liudolfings"), an ambitious Saxon dynasty that replaced Carolingian rule.[84] That moment came in August 936 when Otto the Great was crowned King of East Francia in the old imperial center of Aachen.[85] The symbolism would not have been lost on anyone. This new dynasty may have been Saxon, but they were branding themselves as heirs of Charlemagne.[86] Within a few years, that image would become all the more apparent as Otto was crowned emperor at St. Peter's Basilica in Rome.[87] Charlemagne's dream of ushering in a new "Holy Roman Empire" had come to fruition. Perhaps Charles would have found it disappointing that this new entity had been achieved, not by his son or grandsons but by the ruling families of people he spent his life waging war against. Perhaps, but I speculate otherwise. Saxony had been reformed in the likeness of Franco-Christian civilization because of *his* conquest, and it was *his* image that Saxon rulers sought to emulate.[88] No, I imagine he would have beamed with pride.

Regardless, in the immediate aftermath of the *Stellinga* revolt, Saxony passed into the care of Louis the German until his death in 876. That determination was made in August 843 with the famous Treaty of Verdun, by which the civil war between the sons of Louis the Pious finally ended. Charles retained the "Latin" and "French" west, Lothar gained an artificial "middle kingdom" milieu, while Louis the German took hold of the "Germanic" east, including Bavaria, Swabia, Thuringia, east Franconia, and Saxony.[89] In his personality and style of governance, Louis was often said to resemble his grandfather Charlemagne.[90] However, unlike Charlemagne, Louis remained a distant figure in Saxon affairs, preferring to focus more on his Bavarian stronghold and the traditional Frankish centers of power in the Rhineland.[91] It is telling that, following his suppression of the *Stellinga*, Louis only ventured into Saxony a few times during his 36-year reign as King of East Francia: once in 845 for an assembly at Paderborn, again in 850 to hunt with Lothar in the Teutoburg Forest, and lastly in 852 to preside over legal disputes at Minden.[92] It was a detached pattern his Carolingian successors would repeat, resulting in a dearth of royal authority and economic investment.[93] As a result, Saxony retained some degree of particularism, and with rulers so distant, power fell to those wielding influence locally, that is, the nobility and officials of the Church.[94] Each of these groups continued to contribute to Saxony's development, including its militarization, economic growth, and Christianization.

Conclusion: The Fate of "Old Saxony"

In large part, the position of the Saxon nobility (including families such as the Liudolfings, Ekbertines, and Billungs) was bolstered by an increasing militarization of the Saxon borderlands.[95] This was due to ongoing feuds with the Saxons' Slavic enemies, including the Obodrites, Sorbs, and Bohemians.[96] As "defenders of the eastern frontier," Saxons garnered a considerable degree of autonomy, and their magnates wasted little time in utilizing that freedom to increase their authority, fortify their holdings, and train their troops in "the necessary baptism of blood."[97]

While Saxons continued to march east, they also went north or west to deal with the growing onslaught of the Northmen.[98] Any review of contemporary chronicles will demonstrate that East Francia did not suffer to the same degree as the west, where between the 840s and the 880s, Vikings brought "divine vengeance" down upon the domain of Charles the Bald.[99] Nevertheless, East Francia still had to contend with serious threats from their northern neighbors, and Saxons knew to be on their guard as Viking raids mounted closer to home. Dorestad, Utrecht, Nijmegen, and Frisia were continually ravaged, and the high-horned ships of the Northmen could be seen sailing up the Rhine.[100] Not even Cologne or the old imperial center of Aachen was safe.[101] However, it was in 845 that the Viking threat truly made its way into Saxony when a vast fleet of Danes sailed up the Elbe and descended upon the trading center of Hammaburg, which they sacked and burned throughout the night.[102] The missionary Anskar was there to witness the horror, and after his church and library were turned to ash, he "escaped all but naked with the relics of the holy martyrs" and fled to Bremen.[103] In the aftermath of the attack, according to Helmold's *Chronicle*, "Saxony was shaken with a great terror."[104] Rimbert adds, in his *Vita Anskari*, that afterward, there were no priests in Hamburg for seven years.[105]

The Hamburg raid had been directed by the Danish king Horik I, and had he not been forced to make amends by Louis the German a few years later, in all likelihood, East Francia would have gone to war with the Danes.[106] Nevertheless, despite restitution, Viking incursions into Saxony continued, and in 851, Northmen sailed back up the Elbe and plundered eastern Saxony.[107] Danes returned in 858 to attack Bremen, but these were repelled.[108] It wasn't until 880 that another major Viking assault was launched against the Saxons, which led to a great battle on the Lüneburg Heath where two bishops and many Saxon nobles were killed, including Brun of the Liudolfinger clan, ancestor to Otto the Great.[109] The Northmen returned to Saxony again in 884 and 885, but each of these times, they were defeated.[110] The victory of 885 wasn't the end of Viking incursions into Saxony, but the worst had passed. Over the following century (as Saxon power grew), the situation flipped, with "Germans" increasingly sending their armies north in search of plunder, trade, and converts.[111]

With the close of the ninth century, a new enemy emerged as threatening as the Northmen. These new foes, hailing from the plains of Hungary, were the Magyars.[112] Out of the collapse of Moravian power, from the late ninth into the mid-tenth century, these nomad raiders grew in strength and number as they raided throughout Saxony and East Francia.[113] Vikings had been effective due to the clever construction of their longships; however, Magyars were successful because of their skills as mounted archers, which allowed them to strike enemies quickly.[114] Nevertheless, despite the terror they wrought, Magyar assaults were eventually checked by Henry of Saxony in the 930s and by Otto I at the Battle of Lechfeld in 955.[115]

While there were a series of *internal* dynastic disputes and feuds among Franco-Saxon elites from the end of Carolingian rule up through the Ottonian era, these ongoing *external* threats of Northmen, Slavs, and Magyars gave the Saxons a greater sense of themselves as a unified people.[116] The "self" becomes apparent by encountering the "other," and increasingly, the Saxon "self" reflected the image of Franco-Christian civilization, which it "inherited."[117] That image stood against the frightening visage of savage heathens on the periphery, whose gifts of fire and sword contemporaries had too long endured.[118] Protracted periods of danger also incentivized the rapid development of fortified structures, particularly in frontier regions vulnerable to attack (e.g., Quedlinburg, Meissen, Magdeburg).[119] Vikings, Slavs, and Magyars were not particularly keen to engage in siege warfare, and the latter were kept at bay due to the construction of burgen.[120] These strongholds were aided by later reforms (instituted by Henry I of Saxony), including a *fyrd*-like system garrisoning forts with "peasant" levies and the retinues of assigned nobles.[121]

The building of *burgen* was an innovation for defensive (or expansionist) warfare and a critical factor in increasing urbanization throughout Saxony.[122] Although Saxony kept its predominantly rural nature throughout the Ottonian era, the growth of fortified strongholds and estates under the control of the nobility facilitated the rise of towns and (simultaneously) the development of a semi-feudal manorial system of dependent farmers, which, in turn, increased population density and led to the growth of markets.[123] These market centers, which began supplementing bartering with coin-based currency (mined from silver in the Harz Mountains), made wider trade networks possible, funded building projects, and enhanced wealth accumulation among elites and the growing merchant class.[124] These upper echelons of Saxon society benefited from a "flowering of learning," the so-called Ottonian Renaissance, which economic growth made possible.[125]

By contrast, individuals of lower status, although not entirely missing out on the benefits of these developments, continued to be subject to oppression, poverty, and the whims of their lords.[126] As a result, economically fueled violence periodically erupted, always with the same result, that is, the "peasantry" facing crushing defeats.[127] Added to these hardships was the recurrent theme of environmental catastrophes, including plague outbreaks, cattle blights, freezing winters, decimated crops, and horrific famines.[128] Indeed, in 853, Saxony's food shortage was so dire that people ate their horses.[129] When another famine broke out in 874, there were reports of cannibalism, and according to the *Annals of Fulda*, "nearly a third of the population" was wiped out.[130]

Despite such calamities, urbanization continued, especially in eastern Saxony following the Ottonian *Drang nach Osten* and the development of new ecclesiastical centers—the most notable being the Archbishopric of Magdeburg (founded in 968) in Saxony-Anhalt.[131] During the Ottonian period, religious foundations were typically connected to the monarch, whose investment was intended to centralize royal authority (the so-called *Reichskirchensystem*), which differed from the *Adelskirche* ("church of the nobility") that preceded it under the Carolingians.[132] How *exactly* were these different? Ultimately, it came down to the level of monarchal involvement. For Ottonian rulers, ownership and investment in ecclesiastical institutions were reasonably consistent, as was their involvement in determining who would become bishop or abbot, leading to widespread nepotism whereby privileged positions within the Church were divided among the royal family.[133]

By contrast, economic investment in Saxon religious institutions was limited for the remainder of Carolingian rule, at least when considering royal patronage.[134] As a result, ecclesiastical centers in Saxony had to rely on local tithing or endowments from the nobility, but even these may have been initially lacking.[135] Nevertheless, there are notable exceptions. In 852, Duke Liudolf and his wife Oda were responsible for establishing the convent of Brunshausen (later transferred to Gandersheim).[136] In addition, the Liudolfings maintained connections to Corvey and the bishopric of Hildesheim. They also founded the female monastery of Liesborn in the Dreingau (which likely already had a church settlement before 785).[137] Other Saxon notables (including many high-born women) laid the foundations of Freckenhorst, Lammespring, Meschede, and Mollenbeck.[138]

Despite its insular nature, the Saxon Church was not cut off from the wider Carolingian-Christian world. Several Saxon bishops served outside of Saxony, and local bishops attended regional synods in 852 (at Mainz), 870 (at Cologne), and 895 (at Tribur).[139] Furthermore, royal patronage *did* occasionally materialize. For example, Lothar continued to support the monastic community of Fulda and Waltbraht's Westphalian church of Wildeshausen.[140] The descendants of Widukind also received royal support in the 870s via Waltbraht's son Wikbert II, who gained the favor of Louis the German and was made bishop of Verden.[141] Louis the German also granted property to the bishopric of Hildesheim in the early 870s, while his son Louis the Younger made similar grants to Verden.[142] According to evidence found in contemporary charters, Verden also received royal immunity privileges alongside the churches of Paderborn, Halberstadt, Hildesheim, and Bremen.[143]

Bremen had initially been subject to the archbishop of Cologne; however, in the decades following the Viking sack of Hamburg, Bremen and Hamburg were united to form the Archbishopric of Hamburg-Bremen, which Pope Nicholas formally approved in 864.[144] Anskar, arriving in Bremen in the late 840s, was given authority over ecclesiastical affairs and became the sees' first archbishop. In the meantime, Anskar continued to focus on his missionary endeavors in the north. Indeed, he even went to Denmark to gain the friendship of King Horik, the very man responsible for the destruction of his church in Hamburg.[145]

Our sources indicate Anskar had some measure of success gaining Scandinavian converts, but the progress of Christianization was disrupted by a Danish civil war in 854. In that conflict, Horik was killed (alongside much of the Danish royal family), and a pagan backlash made the region temporarily unsafe for Christians.[146] Nevertheless, Anskar eventually established good relations with Horik's heir (Horik II), and the northern missionary efforts of Hamburg-Bremen continued with Anskar's successors.[147]

Missionaries were also continuing to look east, where the combination of militarism, economic incentive, and religious fundamentalism took a particularly dark turn. Conversion efforts among western Slavs had been underway since Charlemagne, but the scope of those efforts was heightened with the ascent of the Ottonians.[148] The military and political history of Ottonian-Slavic relations between the ninth and the eleventh centuries cannot be fully covered here. However, the general course of events was strikingly similar to what occurred among the Saxons during the Frankish conquest. Like the Franks, Saxons brought Christianity east with an iron fist, provoking defiant pagan revolts and ushering in cycles of horrific violence.[149] Saxon bishops marched east, while Saxon ecclesiastical centers committed armed retinues to join imperial campaigns beyond the Elbe.[150] These forces brought fire and sword to the lands of the Slavs to burn their villages, capture slaves, exact tribute and cut down their gods.[151] Over a few generations, the Saxons (at least those in charge) had been reforged from defiant pagans into valiant crusaders.[152] In time, like their Danish neighbors, the Slavs would be remade too.[153] It was a theme that repeated around the globe for the next 1,000 years.[154]

Notes

1 Reuter, *The Annals of Fulda*, 21; Wickham, *The Inheritance of Rome*, 534; Reuter, *Germany in the Early Middle Ages*, 102; Goldberg, *Struggle for Empire*, 110; Goetz, *Life in the Middle Ages*, 118–119 & Springer, *Die Sachsen*, 261

2 Scholz, *Carolingian Chronicles*, 141–154 & Goldberg, "Popular Revolt," 492–498

3 Goldberg, *Struggle for Empire*, 101–102; Oman, *The Dark Ages*, 321 & Springer, *Die Sachsen*, 264

4 Godman, *Poetry of the Carolingian Renaissance*, 263–265.

5 Scholz, *Carolingian Chronicles*, 154

6 Ibid. 155–161

7 Ibid.

8 The term "peasant" was not used during this period. I use it here as an umbrella term to denote the "lower" strata of society. See Goetz, *Life in the Middle Ages*, 130–131 & Oman, *The Dark Ages*, 321

9 Flierman, *Saxon Identities*, 127; Rembold, *Conquest and Christianization*, 101; Goldberg, "Popular Revolt," 478–482 & *Struggle for Empire*, 112 & Springer, *Die Sachsen*, 266

10 Ibid. 151; Rembold, *Conquest and Christianization*, 68–69 & Wattenbach, *Die Übertragung des hl. Alexander von Rudolf und Meginhart*, 11–13

11 Screen, "The Importance of the Emperor," 48

12 Goldberg, "Popular Revolt," 485–491 & *Struggle for Empire*, 94–95

13 Ibid. & Fried, "The Frankish kingdoms," 144

14 Ibid.

15 Ibid. & *Struggle for Empire*, 97

16 Ibid. 491–498

17 Ibid. & Faulkner, *Law and Authority in the Early Middle Ages*, 72

18 Ibid.; *Struggle for Empire*, 97 & Ehlers, *Die Integration Sachsens in das fränkische Reich*, 303

19 Ibid.; Faulkner, *Law and Authority in the Early Middle Ages*, 53 & Ehlers, *Die Integration Sachsens in das fränkische Reich*, 174

20 Ibid.; Rembold, *Conquest and Christianization*, 163–164 & Goldberg, *Struggle for Empire*, 97–98

21 Goldberg, "Popular Revolt," 491–498

22 Goldberg, *Struggle for Empire*, 97 & 100. Adalbert was killed outside of Bavaria during a battle against Louis the German in an attempt to prevent him from uniting with Charles.

23 Ibid. & Barraclough, *The Origins of Modern Germany*, 13

24 Scholz, *Carolingian Chronicles*, 167–169. Republished with the permission of The University of Michigan Press, from *Carolingian Chronicles: Royal Frankish Annals and Nithard's Histories*, Bernard Scholz, © 1970; permission conveyed through Copyright Clearance Center, Inc.

25 Rembold, *Conquest and Christianization*, 102–103; Riche, *Daily Life in the World of Charlemagne*, 7, & Robinson, *Old English and Its Closest Relatives*, 108–109

26 Ibid.; Thompson, *The Saxons and Germanic Social Origins*, 608–609; Goldberg, "Popular Revolt," 468–482; Thompson, *Feudal Germany*, 174–175; Goetz, *Life in the Middle Ages*, 118–119 & Loyn, *The Reign of Charlemagne*, 47–49, 87

27 Karras, "Pagan Survivals," 558

28 Goldberg, "Popular Revolt," 468–482

29 Springer, "Was Lebuins Lebensbeschreibung über die Verfassung Sachsens wirklich sagt," 259

30 Reuter, *The Annals of Fulda*, 21

31 Thompson, *The Saxons and Germanic Social Origins*, 608–609; Springer, *Die Sachsen*, 268 & Ehlers, *Die Integration Sachsens in das fränkische Reich*, 260

32 Goldberg, "Popular Revolt," 468–482; Reuter, *Germany in the Early Middle Ages*, 67 & Bartlett, *The Medieval World Complete*, 24

33 Springer, *Die Sachsen*, 269

34 Faulkner, "Carolingian kings and the leges barbarorum," 450

35 Springer, *Die Sachsen*, 269

36 Mayr-Harting, "Charlemagne, the Saxons, and the Imperial Coronation of 800," 1130; Springer, *Die Sachsen*, 268 & Ehlers, *Die Integration Sachsens in das fränkische Reich*, 188

37 Springer, *Die Sachsen*, 267

38 Kling, *A History of Christian Conversion*, 13

39 Baer, "History and Religious Conversion," 25 & Lindenfeld, *World Christianity and Indigenous Experience*, 34–35

40 Goldberg, *Struggle for Empire*, 176–179

41 Nelson, *The Annals of St. Bertin*, 51. From *The Annals of St. Bertin: Ninth-Century Histories, Vol. 1* © Janet Nelson, 1991. Reproduced with the permission of the University of Manchester through PLS Clear.

42 Gooren, "Anthropology and Religious Conversion," 85

43 This can be seen, for example, in the Ghost Dance movement of the Plains Indians that swept across the American West in the late nineteenth century. See Ibid. 86 & Lindenfeld, *World Christianity and Indigenous Experience*, 64 & 80–82 & La Barre, *The Ghost Dance*, 41 & 287; Butler et al., *Religion in American Life*, 307–308

44 Wickham, *The Inheritance of Rome*, 534; Faulkner, *Law and Authority in the Early Middle Ages*, 47–48; Becher, *Charlemagne*, 78–79; Goldberg, *Struggle for Empire*, 109–110 & Thompson, *Feudal Germany*, 173

45 Nelson, *The Annals of St. Bertin*, 50–51

46 Ibid. 51 & Scholz, *Carolingian Chronicles*, 167

47 Nelson, *The Annals of St. Bertin*, 51. From *The Annals of St. Bertin: Ninth-Century Histories, Vol. 1* © Janet Nelson, 1991. Reproduced with the permission of the University of Manchester through PLS Clear.

48 Ibid.

49 Reuter, *The Annals of Fulda*, 20

50 Goldberg, "Popular Revolt," 492–498 & Screen, "The Importance of the Emperor," 48

51 Reuter, *The Annals of Fulda*, 20 & Nelson, *The Annals of St. Bertin*, 51

52 Nelson, *The Annals of St. Bertin*, 51–52

53 Scholz, *Carolingian Chronicles*, 155–161. Republished with the permission of The University of Michigan Press, from Carolingian Chronicles: Royal Frankish Annals and Nithard's Histories, Bernard Scholz, © 1970; permission conveyed through Copyright Clearance Center, Inc.

54 Ibid.

55 Ibid.

56 Cantor, *The Civilization of the Middle Ages*, 186 & Kapovic, *The Indo European Languages*, 322

57 Nithard's account is a rather unique insight into Early Medieval war-games. See Scholz, *Carolingian Chronicles*, 164

58 Ibid.

59 Ibid.

60 Ibid.

61 Ibid. 166

62 Rembold, *Conquest and Christianization*, 122–130

63 Scholz, *Carolingian Chronicles*, 166–167. Republished with the permission of The University of Michigan Press, from *Carolingian Chronicles: Royal Frankish Annals and Nithard's Histories*, Bernard Scholz, © 1970; permission conveyed through Copyright Clearance Center, Inc.

64 Ehlers, *Die Integration Sachsens in das fränkische Reich*, 195

65 Scholz, *Carolingian Chronicles*, 166–167

66 Cusack, *Pagan Saxon Resistance to Charlemagne's Mission*, 41

67 Scholz, *Carolingian Chronicles*, 166–167

68 Ibid. & Nelson, *The Annals of St. Bertin*, 55

69 Scholz, *Carolingian Chronicles*, 169–170

70 Ibid. 170

71 Goldberg, "Popular Revolt," 492–498

72 The translation is Eric Goldberg's. See Ibid. 468–469 & Goldberg, *Struggle for Empire*, 112

73 Scholz, *Carolingian Chronicles*, 170. Republished with the permission of The University of Michigan Press, from *Carolingian Chronicles: Royal Frankish Annals and Nithard's Histories*, Bernard Scholz, © 1970; permission conveyed through Copyright Clearance Center, Inc.

74 Reuter, *The Annals of Fulda*, 21. From *The Annals of Fulda: Ninth-Century Histories, Vol. 2* © Timothy Reuter, 1992. Reproduced with the permission of the University of Manchester through PLS Clear.

75 Nelson, *The Annals of St. Bertin*, 54. From *The Annals of St. Bertin: Ninth-Century Histories, Vol. 1* © Janet Nelson, 1991. Reproduced with the permission of the University of Manchester through PLS Clear.

76 Von Heung-Sik Park, *Die Ständ der Lex Saxonum*, 201

77 Goldberg, "Popular Revolt," 496–498 & Goldberg, *Struggle for Empire*, 112

78 Scholz, *Carolingian Chronicles*, 173

79 Flierman, *Saxon Identities*, 127

80 Scholz, *Carolingian Chronicles*, 173. Republished with the permission of The University of Michigan Press, from *Carolingian Chronicles: Royal Frankish Annals and Nithard's Histories*, Bernard Scholz, © 1970; permission conveyed through Copyright Clearance Center, Inc.

81 Reuter, *The Annals of Fulda*, 33–34 & Thompson, *Feudal Germany*, 176

82 Ehlers, *Die Integration Sachsens in das fränkische Reich*, 262; Riche, *The Carolingians*, 186 & Arnold, *Medieval Germany*, 45

83 Ibid. 159; Paxton, *Anchoress & Abbess in Ninth-Century Saxony*, 6–7 & Raaijmakers, *The Making of the Monastic Community of Fulda*, 284–285

84 Flierman, *Saxon Identities*, 121; Barraclough, *The Origins of Modern Germany*, 19; Reuter, *Germany in the Early Middle Ages*, 131 & Head, *Medieval Hagiography*, 239

85 Fulbrook, *A Concise History of Germany*, 16–19; Reuter, *Germany in the Early Middle Ages*, 136–138 & Thompson, *Feudal Germany*, 28

86 Fletcher, *The Conversion of Europe*, 418

87 Ibid. & Cantor, *The Civilization of the Middle Ages*, 212–214

88 Sypeck, *Becoming Charlemagne*, 205; Henderson, *A History of Germany in the Middle Ages*, 120; Baldoli, *A History of Italy*, 21; Ozment, *A Mighty Fortress*, 49–50 & Warner, *Ottonian Germany*, 22

89 Barraclough, *The Origins of Modern Germany*, 12 & Henderson, *A History of Germany in the Middle Ages*, 102–104 & 111

90 Goldberg, *Struggle for Empire*, 189–196 & 334

91 Barraclough, *The Origins of Modern Germany*, 13; Carroll, "The Bishoprics of Saxony," 244; Faulkner, *Law and Authority in the Early Middle Ages*, 46–47 & Goldberg, *Struggle for Empire*, 223 & 226

92 Rembold, *Conquest and Christianization*, 95 & 130; Reuter, *The Annals of Fulda*, 24 & 33–34; Fried, "The Frankish Kingdoms," 148; Goldberg, *Struggle for Empire*, 134–135 & 154–155 & 164 & Ehlers, "Könige, Klöster und der Raum," 191–195

93 Barraclough, *The Origins of Modern Germany*, 12–13

94 Goldberg, *Struggle for Empire*, 159

95 Leyser, "Henry I and the Beginnings of the Saxon Empire," 31; Fried, "The Frankish kingdoms," 163–164; Barraclough, *The Origins of Modern Germany*, 18–29 & 37–47; Flierman, *Saxon Identities*, 120–124 & 138; Carroll, "The Bishoprics of Saxony," 242 & Goldberg, *Struggle for Empire*, 217

96 Nelson, *The Annals of St. Bertin*, 59 & 65 & 68 & 77 & 81 & 139; Reuter, *The Annals of Fulda*, 22–23 & 28–29 & 32 & 37–51 & 58–60 & 64–65 & 73 & Dutton, *Carolingian Civilization*, 347–350; Thompson, *Feudal Germany*, 489 & Bachrach, *Warfare in Medieval Europe*, 71

97 Henderson, *A History of Germany in the Middle Ages*, 118–119. This situation reminds us of the arrangement Saxons brokered with the Merovingian king Dagobert in the early seventh century (see Chapter 3).

98 Ferguson, *The Vikings*, 103–104 & Fried, "The Frankish Kingdoms," 146

99 Nelson, *The Annals of St. Bertin*, 50–184; Reuter, *The Annals of Fulda*, 23–24 & 30 & 34–35 & 91 & Tschan, *History of the Archbishops of Hamburg-Bremen*, 38–41

100 Ibid. 62 & 65 & 69 & 73 & 74–75 & 79 & 104; Dutton, *Carolingian Civilization*, 348–349 & Reuter, *The Annals of Fulda*, 23–26 & 65 & 79 & 89–90 & 95

101 Reuter, *The Annals of Fulda*, 90–91 & Tschan, *History of the Archbishops of Hamburg-Bremen*, 37–39

102 Nelson, *The Annals of St. Bertin*, 61; Reuter, *Germany in the Early Middle Ages*, 91; Dutton, *Carolingian Civilization*, 347 & 425–427 & Rimbert, *Anskar*, 57–58

103 Reuter, *The Annals of Fulda*, 23–24 & Tschan, *History of the Archbishops of Hamburg-Bremen*, 26

104 Helmold, *The Chronicle of the Slavs*, 57

105 Rimbert, *Anskar*, 61–62

106 Appleby, "Spiritual Progress in Carolingian Saxony," 613; Lund, "Scandinavia," 210 & Goldberg, *Struggle for Empire*, 134

107 Dutton, *Carolingian Civilization*, 349

108 Nelson, *The Annals of St. Bertin*, 87. Again, between 862 and 863, Danes were attacking East Francia, some led by the Viking chieftain Roric, either a nephew or a brother of Harald Klak (who was killed by Saxons on suspicion of treason in 852). Roric continued to be a nuisance; however, in 873, he was somewhat contained by being brought into Louis' service as a vassal. See Ibid. 80–81 & 102 & 104 & Reuter, *The Annals of Fulda*, 32–33 & 70

109 Nelson, *The Annals of St. Bertin*, 220; Reuter, *The Annals of Fulda*, 88–89 & Henderson, *A History of Germany in the Middle Ages*, 110–111

110 Reuter, *The Annals of Fulda*, 95–98 & Asser, *The Life of King Alfred*, 87

111 Ibid. 100; Widukind, *Deeds of the Saxons*, 58; Bachrach, "The Military Organization of Ottonian Germany," 1061; Barraclough, *The Origins of Modern Germany*, 37–43 & Clements, *The Vikings*, 120–122

112 Nelson, *The Annals of St. Bertin*, 102; Backman, *The Worlds of Medieval Europe*, 178 & Hooper, *The Cambridge Illustrated Atlas of Warfare*, 11

113 Reuter, *Germany in the Early Middle Ages*, 128–130; Barraclough, *The Origins of Modern Germany*, 16–18 & Mackay, *Atlas of Medieval Europe*, 25–26

114 Bachrach, *Warfare in Medieval Europe*, 263; Hooper, *The Cambridge Illustrated Atlas of Warfare*, 30; Woolf, *Ancient Civilizations*, 474–476 & Isenberg, "Nach den Sachsenkriegen Karls des Großen," 10

115 Barraclough, *The Origins of Modern Germany*, 37; Cantor, *The Civilization of the Middle Ages*, 214; Hooper, *The Cambridge Illustrated Atlas of Warfare*, 32

116 For "internal" or dynastic disputes, see Riche, *The Carolingians*, 242–244 & 259; Reuter, *Germany in the Middle Ages*, 72–77 & 119–123 & 136–137 & 152–156 & *The Annals of Fulda*, 55–56 & 76 & 81 & 106 & Barraclough, *The Origins of Modern Germany*, 18–29

117 Raaijmakers, *The Making of the Monastic Community of Fulda*, 9

118 Tschan, *History of the Archbishops of Hamburg-Bremen*, 48–50 & Goldberg, *Struggle for Empire*, 131

119 Reuter, *Germany in the Early Middle Ages*, 142–146; Mackay, *Atlas of Medieval Europe*, 35–37; Barraclough, *The Origins of Modern Germany*, 145 & Carroll, "The Bishoprics of Saxony," 241

120 Kaufmann, *The Medieval Fortress*, 94; Thompson, *Feudal Germany*, 191 & Hooper, *The Cambridge Illustrated Atlas of Warfare*, 30

121 Mackay, *Atlas of Medieval Europe*, 25–26 & Bachrach, "Saxon Military Revolution," 219 & "The Military Organization of Ottonian Germany," 1071 & 1084 & Thompson, *Feudal Germany*, 179

122 Heather, *Christendom*, 392

123 Reuter, *Germany in the Early Middle Ages*, 99–101; Mackay, *Atlas of Medieval Europe*, 35–37; Barraclough, *The Origins of Modern Germany*, 137–140; Henderson, *A History of Germany in the Middle Ages*, 146; Thompson, *Feudal Germany*, 172–173 & 179–182 & 304–305 & Whitton, "The Society of Northern Europe," 128

124 Reuter, *Germany in the Early Middle Ages*, 230–231 & 236; Thompson, *Feudal Germany*, 193; Leyser, "The German Aristocracy," 28 & Backman, *The Worlds of Medieval Europe*, 179

125 Reuter, *Germany in the Early Middle Ages*, 246–247 & Backman, *The Worlds of Medieval Europe*, 231

126 Barraclough, *The Origins of Modern Germany*, 85–97 & Thompson, *Feudal Germany*, 309

127 Fulbrook, *A Concise History of Germany*, 16–19 & Thompson, *Feudal Germany*, 196–202 & 208–216

128 Dutton, *Carolingian Civilization*, 350 & Reuter, *The Annals of Fulda*, 31 & 71 & 75 & 85 & 90

129 Ibid. 349

130 Reuter, *The Annals of Fulda*, 75

131 Magdeburg was a Frankish border fort situated on the Elbe from at least 805. See Ausenda, "Jural Relations Among the Saxons," 118; Henderson, *A History of Germany in the Middle Ages*, 133; Barraclough, *The Origins of Modern Germany*, 41 & Warner, *Ottonian Germany*, 6–7 & 36. *Drang nach Osten* is a German term denoting a "drive towards the east," which originated with Charlemagne's conquest of the Avars and campaigns against the Slavs. It was continued by his Carolingian and Ottonian successors and later used for propaganda by the Nazis in their quest for *lebensraum* ("living space") in Eastern Europe. See Goldberg, *Struggle for Empire*, 233; Kurlander, *Hitler's Monsters*, 202. For a more thorough list of major and minor ecclesiastical foundations from the ninth and the eleventh centuries, see Ehlers, "Könige, Klöster und der Raum," 195–216 & *Die Integration Sachsens in das fränkische Reich*, 193–585 (the appendices are notably useful)

132 Barraclough, *The Origins of Modern Germany*, 31–34 & 85–88; Wangerin, "The Governance of Ottonian Germany," 5; Mackay, *Atlas of Medieval Europe*, 35–37; Fletcher, *The Conversion of Europe*, 154; Goldberg, *Struggle for Empire*, 207; Thompson, *Feudal Germany*, 33–42; Warner, *Ottonian Germany*, 43 & Nyberg, *Monasticism in North-Western Europe*, 7

133   Cantor, *The Civilization of the Middle Ages*, 213–214
134   Carroll, "The Bishoprics of Saxony," 219 & 223 & 236–238; Reuter, *Germany in the Early Middle Ages*, 103; Goldberg, *Struggle for Empire*, 176 & Ehlers, *Die Integration Sachsens in das fränkische Reich*, 304
135   Ibid. 224–227 & 231–232 & Rembold, *Conquest and Christianization*, 175
136   Riche, *The Carolingians*, 186; Thompson, *Feudal Germany*, 19; Gallee, *Old Saxon Texts*, XVII; Head, *Medieval Hagiography*, 237–238 & 243; Ehlers, *Die Integration Sachsens in das fränkische Reich*, 158; Goetz, *Life in the Middle Ages*, 73 & Greer, *Commemorating Power in Early Medieval Saxony*, 23
137   Ibid.; Carroll, "The Bishoprics of Saxony," 226; Leidinger, "Zur Christianisierung des Ostmünsterlandes," 41–42 & Greer, *Commemorating Power in Early Medieval Saxony*, 32
138   Carroll, "The Bishoprics of Saxony," 226. It is speculated that Freckenhorst may have been built over a former pe-Christian sanctuary/idol/shrine; see Leidinger, "Zur Christianisierung des Ostmünsterlandes," 9–10 & 25–27
139   Ibid. 233; Reuter, *The Annals of Fulda*, 33 & 65 & 130 & Goldberg, *Struggle for Empire*, 163
140   Ibid. 234–235
141   Ibid.
142   Carroll, "The Bishoprics of Saxony," 222–223
143   Ibid.
144   Nyberg, *Monasticism in North-Western Europe*, 24; Fletcher, *The Conversion of Europe*, 226–227 & Dutton, *Carolingian Civilization*, 425–427
145   Ibid. 29–30
146   Dutton, *Carolingian Civilization*, 437–438; Nelson, *The Annals of St. Bertin*, 80; Reuter, *The Annals of Fulda*, 36 & Rimbert, *Anskar*, 100–102
147   Derry, *A History of Scandinavia*, 34; Wood, *The Missionary Life*, 132; Dutton, *Carolingian Civilization*, 437–438; Sullivan, "Carolingian Missionary Theories," 275–276; Tschan, *History of the Archbishops of Hamburg-Bremen*, 50–51 & 80–81 & Rimbert, *Anskar*, 102–103
148   Thompson, *Feudal Germany*, 396–399 & 452 & 473 & 476–477 & 483 & Cantor, *The Civilization of the Middle Ages*, 214
149   Reuter, *Germany in the Early Middle Ages*, 162–163; Tschan, *History of the Archbishops of Hamburg-Bremen*, 83–85 & 157–158; Barford, *The Early Slavs*, 210–218 & 220–223 & 258–261; Barraclough, *The Origins of Modern Germany*, 38–43; Fletcher, *The Conversion of Europe*, 421 & 435–440; Melleno, "Between Borders," 371–372; Thompson, *Feudal Germany*, 387–450 & 490–528 & Warner, *Ottonian Germany*, 364–365
150   Ibid. 106; Rembold, *Conquest and Christianization*, 186; Carroll, "The Bishoprics of Saxony," 239–240 & Wende, *A History of Germany*, 13
151   Whitton, "The Society of Northern Europe," 127 & Hooper, *The Cambridge Illustrated Atlas of Warfare*, 30
152   We have only the perspectives of elite members of society, making any comprehensive understanding of the general populaces' religious outlook incredibly difficult to surmise.
153   Denmark converted in 965 at the behest of King Harald Bluetooth, while Norway was violently coerced into conversion by Olaf Tryggvason and St. Olaf between 995 and 1030. Iceland, Orkney, and Greenland all converted under political pressure. See Woolf, *Ancient Civilizations*, 454; Kritsch, *Theophoric Place Names*, 78; Cusack, *Conversion among the Germanic Peoples*, 22; Somerville & McDonald, *The Viking Age*, 379–402; Anderson, "Constraint and Freedom in Icelandic Conversions," 124–125 & Heather, *Christendom*, 402
154   Thompson, *Feudal Germany*, 449–450

Conclusion

The goal of the present work has been to contextualize and chronicle the Christianization of Saxony as it relates to the Frankish conquest, as well as demonstrate the myriad conversion strategies employed during that process, be they incentivizing or coercive. However, as indicated in the Introduction, rather than relegating these strategies to Early Medieval Saxony as a historical anomaly, we can establish direct connections to conversion methodologies subsequently employed around the globe. This final chapter will demonstrate those connections as they relate to the ten overlapping "push and pull" conversion factors outlined in the Introduction, including violence, gifts, legal enforcement, slavery, economic exploitation, eradicating paganism, geographic restructuring, promoting a cult of the saints, marriage and political alliance, and theological persuasion. Upon establishing the significance of these categories for global Christianization, we return to the question: what did conversion mean, and at what point was it complete?

Methods of Conversion and the Saxon Wars in Wider Perspective

1 **Violence:** Using violence to enforce conversion to Christianity was not novel to Carolingian Europe, nor was the concept of "righteous conquest." However, the Carolingian conquest of Saxony demonstrates (over a relatively short period) the multiple ways violence could be employed. At its most basic level, violence was a tool of empire, whereby soldiers marched against pagan enemies to conquer and convert. Charles Martel, Pippin III, and Charlemagne each used armed retinues to compel conversion in the aftermath of military victories. In these contexts, baptism and submission were synonymous, and peace treaties tended to include stipulations allowing the free operation of missionaries in Saxon territories. Boniface explicitly acknowledged that missionaries relied upon soldiers "opening up" the field for evangelism and had to maintain symbiotic relationships with imperial authorities. That reliance continued into the Colonial era. For example, Spanish and English missionaries depended upon their governments establishing "military superiority" over pagan enemies to undertake their missions.[1] Likewise, missionaries in South and East Africa could only operate effectively once Colonial governments firmly established their rule.[2]

DOI: 10.4324/9781003379157-17

While missionaries preferred peaceful conversions, if persuasion was ineffective, support for using force was not uncommon.[3] Despite avowed idealistic notions of shunning violence, monastic centers directly participated in violent conquest via arms manufacturing, supplying vital resources to armies on the march, producing literature promoting the destruction of "heathens," and accompanying soldiers into battle. Monasteries were "outposts" or "fortresses" in the war between the forces of good and evil.[4] As the Papacy gradually gained power, it was also increasingly involved in sanctioning war for conversion or "righteous conquest." For example, in 1493, inspired by the *Reconquista* that drove Moors and Jews from Spain, Pope Alexander VI condoned the Spanish conquest of the New World so long as the Natives were converted to Catholicism.[5] We are reminded here of the papal sanction of Charlemagne's conquest of the Arian Lombards and the declarations of joy in Rome following Widukind's surrender and the military defeat of the Saxons.

Pagan societies were also victims of Christian paternalist notions of Divine Providence, whereby God granted a ruler or people a sacred mission to expand Christendom. Charlemagne's dream of a "Holy Roman Empire" (or *Pax Christiana*) was rooted in a fusion of Christianity and the Roman imperial ethos. However, over the centuries following Charlemagne's demise, the idea was continually reborn under various manifestations, perhaps most blatantly in the Colonial American notion of "Manifest Destiny."[6] Early American writers wrote in providential terms about the New World, which God conveniently cleared for settlers by eradicating Native populations with disease.[7] This notion resulted in a kind of "civil religion" in the United States, which, as Richardson notes, lent itself well to justifying war and making proclamations of "American exceptionalism" while simultaneously embodying the role of "redeemer nation."[8] The resulting merger of religion with nationalism continues to play a prominent role in twenty-first-century American life, where, for many, the U.S. flag is essentially a sacred symbol.[9]

Christianization coupled with imperialism almost universally provokes violent backlashes where ecclesiastical institutions and their adherents are targeted.[10] Throughout this work, examples were demonstrated during the foundations of the early German Church, and throughout the Carolingian era in Frisia, among western Slavs, in Viking raids, and, repeatedly, with the Saxons. However, while most pagans fought back, they seldom had the means to resist the forces amassed against them effectively. In addition, massacres (such as what occurred in Verden), the threat of being enslaved, rapine, scorched earth campaigns, and legal statutes threatening capital punishment were all effective measures of terrifying populations into compliance. For example, when natives rejected Christianity in the New World, Christopher Columbus burned them at the stake.[11] Similarly, when Acoma Indians revolted against abuses hoisted on them by Spanish soldiers and Franciscan missionaries, they were attacked, mutilated (every male over 25 had a foot cut off), and children under age 12 were given over to missionaries as servants.[12]

In Saxony, following their submission, violence was also a useful means of "redirection." Saxons who were, at best, nominally Christian, became increasingly conscripted against peripheral enemies that remained predominantly pagan, which not only served the imperial ambitions of the Frankish Empire but also reframed Saxon identity and the targets of Saxon animosity. We see similar examples in Colonial contexts, where a "divide and rule" strategy directly correlates to utilizing newly Christian populations against their pagan kin or nearby enemies.

How was Christianization via violence justified? Historically, this concept is less paradoxical than we might assume. The God of the Bible was a God of war.[13] Numerous Bible verses attest to this, but one will suffice here:

> The Lord goes forth like a soldier, like a warrior he stirs up his fury;
> he cries out, he shouts aloud, he shows himself mighty against his foes.[14]

Outside the Biblical context, political rulers from Antiquity onward frequently attributed violence to Yahweh or used God to justify violence.[15] Constantine and Clovis allegedly solidified their conversions following victories in battle, which had been made possible only by the participation of the Christian God.[16] Carolingian chronicles also attributed military victories to God.[17] This was aided by the continuing notion of "divine kingship" (a pagan holdover), whereby the ruler was an appointed representative of the gods.[18] Therefore, the ruler's decisions, including war, acquired a sacred dimension. In the context of Christianity, this is evident beginning with Constantine, who, following his conversion, became the de facto leader of the Church.[19] However, the custom lingered on in European Colonial societies well into the modern era.[20]

As psychologist Philip Zimbardo famously demonstrated in his prison experiments, people are more likely to inflict violence if they believe a higher authority sanctions their actions. In the case of religious violence, actions were justified because they were sanctioned by God, the highest authority of all.[21] Violence was also justified by the demonization of paganism and the consequent dehumanization of pagan practitioners.[22] Biblical passages, Christian scholars from Antiquity, Early Medieval pastoral literature, legal mandates, Church councils, and literary depictions from the Central Middle Ages up through to the modern era all equated paganism with the Satanic. Pagan gods were devils in disguise, while pagan customs were forms of devil worship. As a result, pagans and their deities were worthy of scorn and rightfully targeted for annihilation; they were on the wrong side in the great cosmic war between good and evil.[23] That sentiment operated alongside an apocalyptic mindset, in which believers were to prepare themselves for the imminent End of Days and the appearance of the Antichrist.[24] The soul was, therefore, in essence, a battleground wherein individuals decided which cosmic power (God or Satan) they gave their loyalty to.[25] In the New World, Franciscan missionaries were especially cognizant of this notion and felt great urgency in converting the "simple souls" of natives before the Second Coming of Christ.[26]

In the twelfth-century *Deeds of the Franks*, our most robust primary source on the First Crusade, the predominantly Norman-French crusaders marched east to fight the Turks, the "enemies of God."[27] Famously, they were rallied to arms by Bishop Adhemar of Le Puy's cry, "God wills it!"[28] What followed was a series of horrific massacres and battles, won in the name of Christ and justified by the demonization of their victims. By the thirteenth century, bishops were even overseeing "sword blessings" for new German knights, which invoked God to bless the knight's blade so that it might defend Christians against "the rage of heathens" and confound "the enemies of the Cross of Christ."[29]

The demonization of non-Christians continued to be a consistent feature of European life, imperialism, and conversion during the 800-year period following the "success" of the First Crusade. It was used to justify violence against remaining European pagans as well as for slaughtering heretics, witches, Muslims, Jews, and the myriad indigenous peoples Europeans encountered during Colonialism.[30] In the United States, Cotton Mather defined Native Americans as "the devil's most devoted children," while Spanish colonizers labeled indigenous territory a "land of uncivilized dogs."[31] The derogatory racialization of pagans increasingly exacerbated such dehumanizing descriptions. For example, St. Augustine (and Isidore of Seville) laid the foundations of the notion that Africans were cursed descendants of Ham (a son of the Biblical Noah).[32] Subsequent Christian writers continued to find Biblical justifications for the origins of those deemed "Other." Huns, Mongols, Muslims, and Magyars were all variously equated with the lost tribes of Gog and Magog, Satanic enemies of the Church who, in the book of Revelation, usher in the apocalypse.[33]

There has been endless debate over the extent to which religion contributes to or exacerbates violence and war. Often these debates get bogged down in a frustrating inability to define "religion."[34] However, the American anthropologist Weston La Barre's description of religion as humanity's "way of dealing with the unknown" may be helpful, even if (admittedly) it is somewhat vague.[35] People seek to make order out of chaos and establish meaning in their lives, which helps answer the "Big Questions." That process coincides with identity formation, whereby an individual's sense of "self" is tied to how they embody meaning. Once meaning has been established, it "grounds" individuals and orients the direction of their lives. As a result, when those building blocks of meaning are challenged, people become defensive and lash out.

It is perhaps telling that the English word "war" is derived from the Anglo-Saxon *werra*, meaning "chaos" or "confusion," and is likely related to the Old Saxon *werran*—"to bring into confusion."[36] Consequently, as Mark Juergensmeyer has noted, one possible way of thinking about war "is as a way of imagining and struggling with chaos."[37] This juxtaposes the oft-cited notion proposed by Carl von Clausewitz that war is "merely the continuation of policy by another means" and, therefore, strictly a *political* act.[38] As John Keegan has observed, the problem with Clausewitz's theory is that it is "too neat" and "idealistic" in that it presupposes the existence of nation-states and rational calculation, whereas, in reality, war "antecedes the state" and "dissolves rational purpose."[39] On this latter point, Karen Armstrong has characterized war as a "surrender to reptilian ruthlessness," originating from "interlocking" motivations that may be biological, social, material, or ideological.[40] How, then, should we approach the connection between religion and war?

Until the mid-twentieth century, most people in virtually every society would have described themselves as "religious"—in the sense of adhering to a spiritual belief system.[41] Religion permeated every aspect of life, including war. Therefore, it is impossible to draw lines between religion and violence because violence was perpetuated by religious peoples who would have interpreted their participation in war through the lens of religious belief.[42] Further, following the scientific revolution and the gradual rise of secularism, adherence to particular religious traditions may have lapsed; however, the impulse to interpret conflict in terms of "meaning" remained. As a result, nation, race, political party, and many other identity factors tied to meaning have periodically been "dressed" in religious garb, creating new "sacred" symbols and myths.[43] The problem is that, while violence coupled with grand narratives of meaning does not necessarily makes it more likely, it does facilitate an absolutist "all or nothing" mindset encouraging the dehumanization and demonization of enemies.[44] This is especially the case in notions of "cosmic war," wherein the enemy is not simply a competitor for resources or power but the embodiment of evil.[45]

2 **Gifts:** Economic incentives and political patronage are explicitly connected with conversion following Constantine. When Charlemagne parlayed with Saxon nobles, an effective strategy for securing their conversion and loyalty was incentivizing them with gift-giving. Currency, precious items, access to vital resources, ownership of land and estates, and political titles were all offered to ease their submission. Charlemagne used this strategy to secure Widukind's capitulation and conversion, just as Louis the Pious did to gain Harald Klak as a newly Christianized vassal.

The conversion of Harald Klak provoked a backlash in Denmark, a reaction that we find in similar colonial contexts. For example, Hindu nationalists have demonstrated their frustration with Indians converting to Christianity, claiming that converts are "seduced" by material wealth and promises of security.[46] In addition, akin to the Danish context, Hindu nationalists have been suspicious of conversion because of its role in breaking down indigenous cultural values; conversion was seen as a tool of British imperialism used to destroy the essence of being "Indian."[47] In both contexts, conversion (or resistance) was a symbolic declaration of political allegiance or submission.

Gift-giving within Colonial mission contexts has also been a useful means of demonstrating the prosperity and technological superiority of the Colonial society. For example, as Charles Farhadian has discussed, among the Dani of Irian Jaya in the Central Highlands of Western New Guinea, missionaries offered the gospel message alongside practical items such as salt, steel axes, and shovels.[48] At the same time, Western medicine was used to successfully treat natives, demonstrating the power of the Christian God.[49]

3 **Legal Enforcement:** Paganism throughout the Roman world was declared illegal following Constantine's conversion and the policies of his successor Theodosius. Throughout the Early Middle Ages, political rulers continued to criminalize paganism via assembly declarations, edicts, and law reforms. In the Saxon context, this process is most visible in the implementation of capitularies, wherein pagan customs were outlawed (often on pain of death), and participation in Christian rituals became mandatory. Simultaneously, the Church was integrated within the legal process at an administrative level via their oversight of judicial assemblies, which was coupled with dispensing penance obligations for individuals who continued to engage in pagan or "inappropriate" customs. As a result, in addition to problematic ritual behavior, indigenous cultural markers such as attire, burial methods, art, and so forth were targeted for eradication. The criminalization of pagan customs continued into the Colonial era and was a staple of virtually every mission encounter. For example, traditional dancing and tattooing practices in the Pacific Islands were forbidden because they were deemed "heathen vestiges."[50] Likewise, Tainos in the Caribbean were prohibited from painting themselves or displaying nudity.[51] Throughout the New World, the Spanish also targeted indigenous religious customs associated with psychoactive plants such as peyote or psilocybin mushrooms, deeming the visionary experiences they brought about "satanic trickery."[52]

4 **Slavery:** Throughout global history, the most common justification for slavery has been acquiring a free labor source. Slavery existed across every known society regardless of tribe or religion. However, in Christian societies, slavery could also be justified as a method of exposing pagan captives to Christianity and securing their conversion.[53] In Saxony, captives might be taken to Francia to work on estates; however, simultaneously, Saxon children or political hostages were given over to ecclesiastical "handlers" assigned the task of "reeducating" their pagan hostages. Once their reeducation was complete, Saxons were sent back home to encourage the conversion of their kin.

By employing a strategy of "separation" and "reeducation," gradually, Saxon hostages could be used to control Saxony from within and further facilitate Saxon integration within Franco-Christian civilization. It was an effective strategy, one that was replicated in Colonial missionary encounters around the globe. Missionaries used it with Igbo children in Nigerian schools, Franciscans used it among nobles in sixteenth-century Mexico and the Mayan Yucatan, the Portuguese did the same to orphans in Goa, French "White Fathers" and "Sisters" did likewise to orphans in Algeria, while North American missionaries attempted similar objectives with Native American children in boarding schools or "praying towns" (often with horrific results).[54] In each case, the goal was essentially the same: destroy indigenous cultural patterns deemed incompatible with "civilized" Western Christian culture and replace them with more desirable beliefs and customs.[55] In the United States, this concept of "ethnocide" was blatantly expressed in the notion "kill the Indian, save the man," articulated under various guises over four centuries.[56] Likewise, in the Peruvian Andes and throughout Amazonia, as part of the *reduccion* system, natives were removed from pagan sites and settlements (which were destroyed) and resettled into Jesuit church towns to sever links to their cultural past.[57] The same strategy was employed in Australia, where Aborigines were forcefully removed from their homes and settled in reserves.[58]

John and Jean Comaroff have addressed this phenomenon in their research on the Tswana people of South Africa, where they proposed a "colonization of consciousness" model in which government authorities and missionaries attempt to bring about a change in self-perception among natives to realign them with the values of the Colonial society.[59] By controlling education, access to knowledge, and the dissemination of information, the Church incentivized assimilation while simultaneously policing thought. For example, missionaries used education in South Africa as a means of "cultural rewiring" that would encourage students to accept Colonial rule, which operated alongside the simultaneous control of pathways to employment.[60] Of course, Colonial societies themselves had long been victims of the same process. Representatives of the dominant religious ideology, be they Catholic or Protestant, policed European thought by accusing non-conformists of heresy, witchcraft, or being in league with the devil (which could result in unpleasant visits from an inquisitor).[61] These operated alongside the threat of ex-communication, whereby people became social or political pariahs and destined for eternal damnation.[62]

Setting aside various forms of "reeducation" and social coercion, many aspects of the Biblical message also appealed to enslaved people. For example, African-Americans slaves in the United States gravitated toward inspiring liberationist passages in the Bible, such as the escape of the Israelites from Egypt or the Second Coming of Christ.[63] However, while Southern plantation owners actively suppressed indigenous African customs, they were sometimes hesitant to promote the Christianization of their slaves because of the general taboo surrounding the enslavement of Christians and their fear of Africans generating resistance based on Biblical notions of spiritual egalitarianism.[64]

5 **Economic Exploitation:** Due to their conquest, Saxons were legally required to support the Church. Tithing was mandatory, and Saxons had to provide for local priests and bishops via slaves, resources, and labor for construction projects. Per Alcuin's letters, tithing, in particular, was a significant contributor to Saxon anger and rebellion. While voluntary tithing continues today in Christian church services worldwide, the original imposition of tithing on Saxons or other coerced converts can be labeled "exploitive" because tithes were *not* given voluntarily. We see similar policies in various outposts of the Spanish New World, such as among the Tarahumaras of northern Mexico, where missionaries were encouraged to organize new converts into tax-paying labor forces so their parishes might become economic assets of the empire.[65] The Tarahumaras were, in turn, expected to provide food and housing for local priests and contribute to the mission's expansion and success.[66] Colonial

authorities, corporations, and missionaries (though not always aligned) operated similarly with natives along the Amazon, many of whom were systematically enslaved and forced to work in rubber plantations.[67]

Sporadically, missionaries advocated on behalf of the natives against Colonial abuses. Perhaps the most famous example comes from Bartolome de las Casas, who, in the sixteenth century, persistently condemned Spain's slave-based *encomienda* system and the myriad abuses therein.[68] Yet, despite such protests, by encouraging the suppression of indigenous customs and forms of subsistence, missionaries (intentionally or not) aided in creating a state of economic dependency that reinforced natives' subservience to Western and ecclesiastical institutions.[69]

We can add to tithing and labor requirements simultaneous predatory schemes such as selling indulgences or encouraging people to pay for forged relics. Turn on the TV today, and similar activity remains visible in the so-called prosperity gospel, that is, if you convert and give money to God's church, God will bless you with material, physical, and spiritual abundance, which wealthy televangelists espouse to audiences in their mega-churches.[70]

6 **Eradicating Paganism:** Throughout the ancient world, tribes demonstrated the power of their gods by capturing or destroying idols associated with their enemies. However, before the development of monotheistic proselytizing *exclusivist* religions, there was seldom a desire to eradicate alternative religious systems in their entirety. Polytheism is, by its very nature, inclusive, local, and adhesive. By contrast, the Judeo-Christian traditions explicitly advocate religious imperialism. There is one truth, and believers are given a moral imperative to seek converts.[71] Ideological antagonism is, therefore, by default, "baked in."[72] To some extent, Judaism and early Islam mitigated this impulse by maintaining a closed emphasis on tribal religion. However, the growing Jewish diaspora and Muslim conquests increasingly made that impulse less practical.

Early Christians also struggled to navigate their self-definition as either a continuation of Judaism or a new religion transcending tribal affiliation. Following the ministry of Paul (Saul of Tarsus), the latter of these identities became more common as Christianity took root among "Jews and Gentiles" alike. It was solidified by the Romanization of Christianity, which merged (Nicene) Christian thought with the Roman administrative and political infrastructure, resulting in the establishment of Christianity as the official religion of the Empire.[73]

The conversion of Roman emperors ushered in a series of xenophobic laws and programs targeting pagan cults. Pagan customs, idols, and places of worship were criminalized, appropriated, or destroyed.[74] For example, in Alexandria, in 391, a Christian mob destroyed the Serapeum, a famous shrine dedicated to the god Serapis, after which the deity's statue was dragged through the streets.[75] We saw several examples of this in Early Medieval Germany. In Saxony, Frisia, and Thuringia, pagan cult sites increasingly came under attack during the Bonifatian era, which saw the armies of Charles Martel destroying Frisian shrines and Boniface tearing down the sacred oak at Geismar. A generation later, Charlemagne destroyed the Irminsul. Many pagan sites encountered in Medieval chronicles, hagiography, and pastoral literature were also transformed into Christian places of worship or pilgrimage. This pattern continued into the Colonial era, with Western governments and missionaries actively suppressing, demolishing, or appropriating indigenous pagan temples and idols.[76] For example, the Spanish built churches over Aztec temples and destroyed indigenous mountain shrines in the Andes.[77]

7 **Geographic Restructuring:** Pilgrimage sites, be they new or former pagan ones, were used to establish sacred space and economically support the development of local churches. Those local churches were usually connected to larger monastic (sometimes fortified) complexes, each subject to administrative bishoprics. In Saxony, the development of ecclesiastical institutions increased urbanization, facilitated the spread of Christian ideas, and assisted in creating a new geography of political and spiritual power. This was coupled with the "twin processes" of deportation and colonization and an extraordinary acquisition of land by the Church.[78] The increasing ecclesiastical control of land, vital resources, and currency production further enhanced the power of Church magnates and encouraged a system of dependency for the general population. As indicated earlier, a similar process to what happened in Saxony occurred in various colonial settings. For example, American missionaries in the United States advocated for the deportation and removal of Natives to reservations, which broke down tribal ways of life and fostered a state of dependency requiring Natives to rely on Church and government institutions.[79] Similarly, in Mexico, the Church restructured the land into parish districts, controlled vital resources, and accumulated vast wealth (enhancing the power of local bishops).[80]

8 **Promoting a Cult of the Saints:** The cult of the saints had several functions. First, saints' lives were meant to be inspiring examples of Christian living as well as demonstrations of the power of God. Saints' holiness and their miracles could then be used to establish places of spiritual power that might replace or transform pagan places of worship. Saints appear to have sometimes taken on the attributes of pagan deities, while the relics associated with their names replaced pagan idols. One prominent example of this can be seen in the Mexican Virgin of Guadalupe cult, which seems to have transferred to Mary elements of Tonantzin, an Aztec mother goddess.[81] Saints' relics were also valuable assets; missionaries, bishops, rulers, and noble families all utilized them as a form of economic investment. As a result, in addition to facilitating conversion, the cult of the saints ultimately continued to bolster the gentrification of the Church.

9 **Marriage and Political Alliance:** The gentrification of the Church was, in part, also a byproduct of conversion being used to cement political alliances. In Antiquity and throughout Medieval Europe, noble families or tribal groups might convert to garner favor, gain settlement rights, secure political autonomy, or deflect enemies from finding a pretext for invasion.[82] Others found it

useful to convert as part of marriage contracts whereby elite families of different kingdoms fused into a broader ruling class.[83] Conversion as a stipulation of political alliance also features prominently in colonial mission encounters. For example, the Iroquois embraced Christianity to secure their relationship with the French.[84] (Their conversion was more a symbolic matter of behavior and performance than belief.) In addition, while conversion via marriage could be used to secure alliances, it was often a less grandiose affair. For example, in the sixteenth century, Malaysian women were often pressured to convert as part of their marriage to Portuguese settlers.[85]

10 **Theological Persuasion:** Missionaries in the field faced several daunting challenges, not the least of which included securing protection and financial support for their missions. As a result, missionaries often employed a top-down conversion strategy by first targeting rulers and nobles for conversion. This strategy originated in Antiquity, with missionaries seeking out Roman senators and wealthy estate owners for conversion.[86] However, social elites were efficient and practical converts across virtually all mission contexts, not only because they offered missionaries patronage but because they also compelled their subjects to convert. In Early Medieval Saxony, we saw this pattern demonstrated by several prominent missionaries, including Boniface, the two Hewalds, and Lebuinus.

However, when attempts to garner conversion among elites failed, missionaries often turned toward marginalized community members, such as slaves, the poor, criminals, women, and the sick or disabled, with whom they could provide charity and healing.[87] For example, in Frisia, the missionary Wulfram rescued two boys from being sacrificed, while in Nordalbingia, Ansgar advocated for escaped slaves. The appeal to alienated or marginalized individuals has always been a marker of success throughout the history of Christian missions, for example, among women and Untouchables in India, with Chinese peasants in the aftermath of famines, among African-American slaves in the United States, or with shunned Igbo witches in Nigeria.[88] In these contexts, conversion could be an especially appealing way of establishing meaning amid suffering.

What message did missionaries present to the pagans they encountered? Initially, missionaries had two communication goals: (1) present the fundamental teachings of Christian theology and (2) undermine local pagan cosmology. The first goal included presenting the story of humanity's fall into sin and the need for redemption, attained through acknowledging Christ's sacrifice on the cross.[89] That acknowledgment was then demonstrated via baptism. In contrast to the pagan oral cultures they encountered, missionaries could also ground their theology in texts, a technology that must have inspired awe among potential converts.[90] Typically, animist and illiterate societies are more susceptible to conversion and Colonial powers, primarily due to their religions' localized and dynamic nature and a lack of resources for mobilizing effective resistance. Missionaries fare far worse with people who have established religious books or the military strength to resist imperial power and limit their mobility.

As a result, comparatively few Christian converts were gained in China, Japan, India, or the Islamic world.[91]

The second goal, undermining pagan cosmology, required breaking down indigenous modes of thought through persuasion. Demonizing pagan deities, desacralizing nature, or undermining faith in pagan deities' ability to protect their shrines and people was accomplished by destroying pagan idols and displaying the economic, technological, and military superiority of Christian kingdoms over pagan ones. To some extent, redefining pagan deities as "trickster devils" allowed pagans to see themselves as victims of malicious forces who deceived them. This, at least, is often a common interpretation by converts who look back on their former religion or by subsequent writers seeking to explain the beliefs of their ancestors, such as we saw with the Saxon Poet. Roger Lohman has discussed this phenomenon as it relates to New Guinea, where, following conversion, locals still believed pagan deities or spirits were real; they simply reinterpreted them as demons.[92] Charles Keyes has noted similar patterns among Pwo Karen converts in Thailand.[93] In psychological terms, this "denigration" process may alleviate pain caused by cultural rupture and identity crisis, which often accompany religious conversion.[94]

To achieve their goals, missionaries had to be able to communicate with the people they were interacting with. This is true on a technical level, in that missionaries often had to use translators or learn local languages; French Jesuit missionaries were especially good at this when ministering to Iroquois along the St. Lawrence in Canada, New York, and Vermont.[95] However, it is also true on a conceptual level in that certain Christian theological ideas (such as sin or salvation) had to be conveyed but were often confusing for people who had no precedent for them.

Before the Frankish conquest, Saxons likely had notions of communal luck, divine reciprocity, maintaining reputation, and making amends for grievances. Actions had consequences for individuals and the community. However, the idea that people are born "fallen" and tainted with sin, for which the only resolution is salvation, was a novel concept.[96] In several Colonial mission contexts, we see indigenous peoples grappling with the awkwardness of incorporating the idea of sin, which often led to various forms of reframing. For example, among the Aguaruna people in northern Peru, sin essentially became equated with the fear of retaliation; only, rather than fearing vengeance from a wronged enemy (the traditional mode of thinking), an individual feared the judgment of God.[97]

Akin to what we saw in the *Heliand*, Christian concepts had to be disseminated in a way that locals would comprehend, a process that lent itself to various forms of syncretism, adoption, and adhesion.[98] In addition, outside of rare urban areas, most converts would not have had routine access to missionaries or churches. Therefore, they would have been left to their own devices in integrating and developing Christian themes, which is how we end up with Medieval healing charms invoking pagan entities alongside Christ or the saints. As the anthropologist Stephen Glazier has noted concerning modern Rastafarians, despite the theologically exclusive nature of Christian doctrine, "conversion is not an all-or-nothing proposition," and established ritual behavior is exceedingly difficult to suppress quickly and so often continues to exist alongside the newly adopted faith.[99]

Christianity, from the beginning, was a predominantly urban phenomenon, and it remained so in most mission contexts, which required urban ecclesiastical centers to be effective.[100] Urban centers also had the benefit of drawing potential converts into new commerce systems, which facilitated the exchange of goods and ideas or fostered a state of dependency in which the Church established economic dominance.[101] Only after a Christianized urban center was established could missionaries concentrate more fully on the countryside, a process that often took generations to bear fruit.[102]

For missionaries working in rural areas, those willing to adopt or learn local customs tended to fare better in establishing rapport with natives. While Spanish missionaries and English Puritans in the colonial period tended to devalue this method (to put it mildly), French Jesuits, Moravians, and Quakers typically took a more conscientious approach toward conversion and integration. In the case of the Moravians and Quakers, this was partly due to their ideological pacifism and mystical notions of recognizing every individual's divine "inner light."[103] Meanwhile, Jesuits had modest success adapting indigenous culture for their own purposes, for example, with Chinese converts, by insisting on similarities between Christian morality and Confucian ethics.[104]

Conclusion

What did conversion mean, and at what point was it considered "complete"? The purpose of the present work has not been to critique Christianity, religion, or the conversion experience. There is much wisdom in global religious traditions, and people can undoubtedly undergo profound transformative spiritual experiences. However, when considering conversion, the archetypal examples of individual experiences we encounter with Paul, St. Augustine, or later saints and mystics are, in broad terms, exceedingly rare. Instead, most historical scenarios involving religious conversion pertain to social groups facing various forces of coercion and incentivization. It is also clear that, initially, most people say "no" to conversion.[105] In cases where they say "yes," spiritual experience and belief are not prerequisites.[106] Instead, conversion more often signified to whom or what an individual or group owed their loyalty; it demonstrated allegiance. Commitment to conversion was, therefore, often shaky, dynamic, and prone to misunderstanding.[107] Converts were especially likely to revert to prior religious affiliations or customs during periods of crisis.[108] However, crises could also incentivize conversion if current spiritual practices failed to yield results. As a result, conversion was also often *experimental*, with converts testing out the efficacy of a deity's power (either with or without rejecting alternative powers).

The frequent condemnation of syncretic elements, pagan holdovers, apostasy, and relapses into paganism all attest to the superficial and nominal nature of Early

Medieval conversions across Europe. As a result, it took generations of exposure and gradual absorption for the general populace to understand the fundamentals of what they had converted to. Beyond the Medieval context, this same pattern was replicated across the Colonial world, where various forms of syncretism were present during the initial conversion period or continue to exist today.[109] As Marshall Eakin has noted, syncretism, such as what we observe in phenomena like Mesoamerican "folk Catholicism," is a "striking" example of "the failure of spiritual conquest."[110] Local deities operated alongside (or fused with) the Christian God or various saints.[111] For instance, missionaries and natives in the United States equated the Great Spirit with the Christian God, while Jesuits in Canada sometimes presented Christ as an "enhanced" version of the local "trickster" deity.[112] Peter Gose has demonstrated that, in the Peruvian Andes, missionaries used the indigenous term *Viracocha* to refer to God.[113] However, this caused confusion because *Viracocha* was actually a term referring to native ancestor spirits that emerged from Lake Titicaca.[114] We are forced to wonder how Andean natives would have conceptualized the Christian God? As we saw concerning the Old Saxon *Heliand*, with its references to *middilgard*, demonic wights, the workings of Fate, and Christ as a mighty *drohtin*, these translation ambiguities are not trivial. Today, pre-Christian spirits remain revered by Catholics in Latin America, in the rituals of West African/Haitian Vodun, by Japanese Christians at Shinto shrines, or among Chinese Christians who are simultaneous "folk Buddhists."[115] Likewise, in northern Ghana, Christian converts pour libations to call upon ancestors or former deities, and Caribbean people practice "obeah"—magical rituals fusing West African, Hindu, and Christian traditions.[116]

Beyond syncretism, following the initial conversion period, subsequent Christians did not choose to become Christians for most of history. Instead, Christianity became "hereditary."[117] An individual was Christian not because of belief, spiritual experience, or choice but because that is what their families told them, and there was little room for deviation. As a result, assessing the point at which conversion can be considered "complete" regarding societal groups is incredibly problematic, especially if conversion is reductively interpreted as an *event*. Barring the less attested individual conversion experiences, it is more helpful to see societal conversion as a gradual dynamic process, one that goes through stages of encounter, resistance, full or partial rejection of the past, declarations of new allegiance, ritual enactment, cultivation of belief, and reform. By the time that process is finished (if it ever truly is), the religion arrived at is not representative of a monolithic static entity but rather a singular demonstration of an idea prone to limitless reinterpretation.

Notes

1 Cueller & Woodley, "North American Mission and Motive," 65 & Williamson, *The Penguin History of Latin America*, 101
2 Maxon, *East Africa*, 126 & Thompson, *A History of South Africa*, 156
3 Rambo, *Understanding Religious Conversion*, 91 & Heather, *Christendom*, 325
4 This is how Bernard of Clairvaux described Clairvaux in his twelfth-century writing. See Raiswell & Winter, *The Medieval Devil*, 124–127

5 Gose, "Converting the Ancestors," 141; Williamson, *The Penguin History of Latin America*, 98 & Guitar, "Negotiations of Conquest," 116

6 Green, "A Response to the Postcolonial Roundtable," 20 & Butler et al., *Religion in American Life*, 338

7 Cueller & Woodley, "North American Mission and Motive," 72 & Taylor, *American Colonies*, 43. Note that similar language was used in the 1980s and 1990s concerning HIV, the "Gay Plague" that God had unleashed on a sinful population.

8 Richardson, "American Exceptionalism as Prophetic Nationalism," 121–127

9 For a few additional colonial examples, see Butler et al., *Religion in American Life*, 173–176 & Merrill, "Conversion and Colonialism in Northern Mexico," 139

10 Ibid. 34–35. Anthony Reid has discussed one example in nineteenth-century Vietnam during the reign of Ming Manh, who, in a reactionary move, criminalized Christianity, ordered the destruction of churches, and demanded all Christian converts renounce their religion on pain of death. See Reid, *A History of Southeast Asia*, 225–226

11 Ibid. 27

12 Ibid. 33–34

13 Armstrong, *Fields of Blood*, 115

14 Coogan et al., *The New Oxford Annotated Bible*, 1024

15 Heather, *Christendom*, 264 & 357

16 According to his biographer Eusebius, Constantine saw the "Chi-Rho" symbol in the sky alongside the message "by this sign, conquer." See Heather, *Christendom*, 4

17 Ibid. 203

18 Heather, *Christendom*, 8; Green, *The Carolingian Lord*, 225 & 231 & Cathey, *Old Saxon*, 9

19 Ibid. 125 & 135

20 Meyer et al., *The Course of Mexican History*, 160

21 Eller, *Introducing the Anthropology of Religion*, 257–258

22 Lincoln, *Gods and Demons, Priests and Scholars*, 86

23 Cosmic dualism was a prominent feature in Mesopotamian, Zoroastrian, and Gnostic religions, each of which likely influenced Judeo-Christian thought. See Raiswell and Winter, *The Medieval Devil*, 46–47 & 69; Lincoln, *Gods and Demons, Priests and Scholars*, 32 & Armstrong, *Fields of Blood*, 40–45

24 Ibid. 92–95 & 112 & Armstrong, *Fields of Blood*, 144–145

25 Rambo, *Understanding Religious Conversion*, 130 & 134

26 Williamson, *The Penguin History of Latin America*, 99

27 Dass, *The Deeds of the Franks*, 1–17

28 Ibid. 43–108 & Heather, *Christendom*, 475

29 Shinners, Medieval Popular Religion, 295–296

30 Cueller & Woodley, "North American Mission and Motive," 66; Armstrong, *Fields of Blood*, 212–240; Butler et al., *Religion in American Life*, 25; Guitar, "Negotiations of Conquest," 121. An estimated 100,000 "witches" were killed in Germany alone. See Cawthorne, *Witch Hunt*, 107

31 Ibid. 63 & Hawk & Twiss, "An American Hermeneutic of Colonization," 51

32 Ezigbo and Williams, "Converting a Colonialist Christ," 90–93

33 Raiswell & Winter, *The Medieval Devil*, 237. Likewise, Colonial missionaries believed Native Americans were descendants of the lost ten tribes of Israel. See Mendoza, "Converted Christians, Shamans, and the House of God," 200

34 Cavanaugh, *The Myth of Religious Violence*, 57

35 La Barre, *The Ghost Dance*, 9–12 & 24

36 Juergensmeyer, *God at War*, 22

37 Ibid.

38 Von Clausewitz, *On War*, 86–87

39 Keegan, *A History of Warfare*, 3–6

40 Armstrong, *Fields of Blood*, 10 & 58
41 Cavanaugh, *The Myth of Religious Violence*, 4–5
42 Juergensmeyer, *God at War*, 71–72
43 Cavanaugh, *The Myth of Religious Violence*, 24–25 & 55 & Armstrong, *Fields of Blood*, 17 & 279–280
44 Juergensmeyer, *God at War*, 69
45 Ibid. 79–80 & Eller, *Introducing the Anthropology of Religion*, 259–260
46 Menon, "Converted Indians and their Trickster Heroes," 43
47 Ibid. 51 & Viswanathan, "Literacy in the Eye of India's Conversion Storm," 273–278
48 Farhadian, "Comparing Conversions among the Dani of Irian Jaya," 55–56
49 Ibid. 57
50 Fischer, *A History of the Pacific Islands*, 109
51 Guitar, "Negotiations of Conquest," 126
52 Schultes et al., *Plants of the Gods*, 144 & 156
53 An argument sometimes used by American plantation owners. See Butler et al., *Religion in American Life*, 254–255
54 Lindenfeld, *World Christianity and Indigenous Experience*, 32, 43, 53, 63, 78, & 181; Rambo, *Understanding Religious Conversion*, 89; Butler et al., *Religion in American Life*, 231–232 & Naylor, *North Africa*, 156–157
55 Williamson, *The Penguin History of Latin America*, 100
56 Hawk & Twiss, "An American Hermeneutic of Colonization," 50–54 & Cueller & Woodley, "North American Mission and Motive," 68
57 Gose, "Converting the Ancestors," 147–149 & Pollock, "Conversion and 'Community' in Amazonia," 167
58 Macintyre, *A Concise History of Australia*, 146–147
59 Hawk & Twiss, "An American Hermeneutic of Colonization," 55 & Comaroff & Comaroff, *Of Revelation and Revolution*, 4–6 & 199 & 310–313
60 Thompson, *A History of South Africa*, 126 & 172
61 Jacoby, *Strange Gods*, 60; Raiswell & Winter, *The Medieval Devil*, xiv & 135 & Eller, *Introducing the Anthropology of Religion*, 269
62 Heather, *Christendom*, 560–566
63 Butler et al., *Religion in American Life*, 112
64 Ibid. 109–112
65 Merrill, "Conversion and Colonialism in Northern Mexico," 129–135
66 Ibid. 136
67 Pollock, "Conversion and 'Community' in Amazonia," 168–169 & 182
68 Barton, *A History of Spain*, 122–123; Williamson, *The Penguin History of Latin America*, 15 & Guitar, "Negotiations of Conquest," 121
69 Pollock, "Conversion and 'Community' in Amazonia," 184; Taylor, *American Colonies*, 59; Smith, *A Concise History of New Zealand*, 43 & Thompson, *A History of South Africa*, 129
70 Butler et al., *Religion in American Life*, 432–433
71 Rambo, *Understanding Religious Conversion*, 68 & Eller, *Introducing the Anthropology of Religion*, 273
72 MacMullen, *Christianizing the Roman Empire*, 19
73 Heather, *Christendom*, xxiii & 150–151 & Naylor, *North Africa*, 52
74 Ibid. 85 & 107 & 114–118; Armstrong, *Fields of Blood*, 168–174 & Eller, *Introducing the Anthropology of Religion*, 269
75 Jacoby, *Strange Gods*, 47–48 & Naylor, *North Africa*, 51
76 Butler et al., *Religion in American Life*, 13–14; Eller, *Introducing the Anthropology of Religion*, 270 & Williamson, *The Penguin History of Latin America*, 99
77 Ibid. 27–28 & Gose, "Converting the Ancestors," 160
78 Heather, *Christendom*, 390

79 Cueller & Woodley, "North American Mission and Motive," 67

80 Eakin, *The History of Latin America*, 210

81 Williamson, *The Penguin History of Latin America*, 102

82 Merrill, "Conversion and Colonialism in Northern Mexico," 138

83 Heather, *Christendom*, 399

84 Greer, "Conversion and Identity," 184

85 Reid, *A History of Southeast Asia*, 111–112

86 MacMullen, *Christianizing the Roman Empire*, 65

87 The Greek philosopher Celsus disparagingly criticized Christian missionaries for avoiding the educated and wise and instead specifically targeting the ignorant, stupid, and children. However, Celsus' criticism is unfounded, as missionaries' many appeals to educated social elites make clear. See MacMullen, *Christianizing the Roman Empire*, 37

88 Lindenfeld, *World Christianity and Indigenous Experience*, 108–109 & 199; Kling, *A History of Christian Conversion*, 469–473 & 572–573 & Rambo, *Understanding Religious Conversion*, 88–89 & 133

89 Clayton, "Preaching and Teaching," 163–164

90 Heather, *Christendom*, 254

91 Rambo, *Understanding Religious Conversion*, 35–36 & 47

92 Lohman, "Turning the Belly," 112–113

93 Keyes, "Why the Thai are not Christians," 272

94 Rambo, *Understanding Religious Conversion*, 54

95 Butler et al., *Religion in American Life*, 44; Greer, "Conversion and Identity," 181–182 & Taylor, *American Colonies*, 107–111

96 Rambo has discussed the role of sin in conversion narratives regarding members of the Church of Christ, who undergo an experience of "coming to brokenness," a self-loathing state of being in which individuals take personal responsibility for their corrupt nature and acknowledge their sin as a contributor to the death of Jesus. See Rambo, *Understanding Religious Conversion*, 71–72

97 Priest, "I Discovered My Sin," 97 & 103

98 Ibid. 98 & Heather, *Christendom*, 67

99 Glazier, "'Limin wid Jah,'" 154–158

100 MacMullen, *Christianizing the Roman Empire*, 83 & Heather, *Christendom*, 21

101 Butler et al., *Religion in American Life*, 34

102 Merrill, "Conversion and Colonialism in Northern Mexico," 147

103 Butler et al., *Religion in American Life*, 101–106 & Thompson, *A History of South Africa*, 58–59

104 Hsia, "Translating Christianity," 96 & Holcombe, *A History of East Asia*, 172

105 Rambo, *Understanding Religious Conversion*, 35

106 Greer, "Conversion and Identity," 182 & Merrill, "Conversion and Colonialism in Northern Mexico," 152–154

107 Rambo, *Understanding Religious Conversion*, 76–77 & Heather, *Christendom*, 404–405

108 Fisher, *A History of the Pacific Islands*, 109 & Larkin & Meyer, "Pentecostalism, Islam and Culture," 291

109 Greer, "Conversion and Identity," 184–187; Gose, "Converting the Ancestors," 140–141; Pollock, "Conversion and 'Community' in Amazonia," 170–174; Jordan, "The Glyphomancy Factor," 297: Williamson, *The Penguin History of Latin America*, 101 & Sued-Badillo, "From Tainos to Africans in the Caribbean," 113

110 Eakin, *The History of Latin America*, 130

111 Meyer et al., *The Course of Mexican History*, 164 & Lindenfeld, *World Christianity and Indigenous Experience*, 44

112 Hawk & Twiss, "An American Hermeneutic of Colonization," 49 & Butler et al., *Religion in American Life*, 44
113 Gose, "Converting the Ancestors," 142
114 Ibid.
115 Butler et al., *Religion in American Life*, 242
116 Obeng, "Religious Interactions in Pre-Twentieth-Century West Africa," 155 & Khan, "Africa, Europe, and Asia in the Making of the Caribbean," 409–410
117 Robert Anderson has discussed this phenomenon as it relates to modern Icelanders. See Anderson, "Constraint and Freedom in Icelandic Conversions," 127

Bibliography

Abram, Christopher. *Myths of the Pagan North: The Gods of the Norsemen*. London, Continuum International Publishing Group, 2011.

Adam of Bremen and Timothy Reuter. *History of the Archbishops of Hamburg-Bremen*. Translated by Francis J. Tschan, New York, Colombia University Press, 2002.

Algeo, John, and Thomas Pyles. *The Origins and Development of the English Language*. 5th ed., Thomson Wadsworth, 2005.

Almgren, Bertil, Charlotte Blindheim, Yves D. Bouard, Torsten Capelle, and Arne E. Christensen Jr. *The Viking*. London, Senate Publishing LTD, 1999.

Altet, Xavier B. *The Early Middle Ages: From Late Antiquity to A.D. 1000*. Cologne, Taschen, 2002.

Anderson, Robert T. "Constraint and Freedom in Icelandic Conversions." *The Anthropology of Religious Conversion*, edited by Andrew Buckser and Glazier Rowman, Lanham, MD, Littlefield Publishers, 2003, pp. 124–30.

Andren, Anders. "Old Norse and Germanic Religion." *The Oxford Handbook of the Archaeology of Ritual and Religion*, edited by Timothy Insoll, Oxford, Oxford University Press, 2011, pp. 845–49.

Angerer, Michael L. "Beyond 'Germanic' and 'Christian' Monoliths: Revisiting Old English and Old Saxon Biblical Epics." *Journal of English and Germanic Philology*, vol. 120, no. 1, Jan. 2021, pp. 73–92.

Appleby, David F. "Spiritual Progress in Carolingian Saxony: A Case from Ninth Century Corvey." *The Catholic Historical Review*, vol. 82, no. 4, Oct. 1996, pp. 599–613.

Arblaster, Paul. *A History of the Low Countries*. 2nd ed., New York, Palgrave Macmillan, 2012.

Archer, Christon I., John R. Ferris, Holger H. Herwig, and Timothy H. Travers. *World History of Warfare*. Lincoln, University of Nebraska Press, 2002.

Armstrong, Karen. *Fields of Blood: Religion and the History of Violence*. Anchor Books, 2014.

Arnold, Benjamin. *Medieval Germany, 500–1300: A Political Interpretation*. New York, Macmillan Press, 1997.

Arrhenius, Birgit. "Kinship and Social Relations in the Early Medieval Period in Svealand Elucidated by DNA." *The Scandinavians from the Vendel Period to the Tenth Century: An Ethnographic Perspective*, edited by Judith Jesch, Woodbridge, The Boydell Press, 2002, pp. 55–56.

Aslan, Reza. "Cosmic War in Religious Traditions." *The Oxford Handbook of Religion and Violence*, edited by Michael Jerryson, Mark Juergensmeyer, and Margo Kitts, Oxford, Oxford University Press, 2013, pp. 262–66.

Asser, John, Simon Keynes, and Michael Lapidge. *Alfred the Great: Asser's Life of King Alfred and Other Contemporary Sources*, London, Penguin Group, 2004.

Augustyn, Prisca. *The Semiotics of Fate, Death, and the Soul in Germanic Culture: The Christianization of Old Saxon*. New York, Peter Lang Publishing, 2002. Berkeley Insights in Linguistics and Semiotics 50.

Augustyn, Prisca. "Thor's Hammer and the Power of God: Poetic Strategies in the Old Saxon Heliand Gospel." *Daphnis*, vol. 33, no. 1/2, 2004, pp. 33–51.

Ausenda, Giorgio. "Jural Relations among the Saxons before and after Christianization." *The Continental Saxons from the Migration Period to the Tenth Century: An Ethnographic Perspective*, edited by Dennis Green and Frank Siegmund, Woodbridge, The Boydell Press, 2003, pp. 113–19.

Austin-Broos, Diane. "The Anthropology of Conversion: An Introduction." *The Anthropology of Religious Conversion*, edited by Andrew Buckser and Glazier Rowman, Lanham, MD, Littlefield Publishers, 2003, pp. 2–3.

Axboe, Morten. "Danish Kings and Dendrochronology: Archaeological Insights into the Early History of the Danish State." *After Empire: Towards an Ethnology of Europe's Barbarians*, edited by Giorgio Ausenda, Woodbridge, The Boydell Press, 1995, pp. 221–31.

Bachrach, Bernard S. *Charlemagne's Early Campaigns (768–777): A Diplomatic and Military Analysis*. Boston, Brill, 2013, History of Warfare 82.

Bachrach, Bernard S., editor. *Liber Historiae Francorum*. Lawrence, KS, Coronado Press, 1973.

Bachrach, Bernard S. *Merovingian Military Organization, 481–751*. Minneapolis, University of Minnesota Press, 1972.

Bachrach, Bernard S., and David S. Bachrach. "Saxon Military Revolution, 912–973?: Myth and Reality." *Early Medieval Europe*, vol. 15, no. 2, 2007, pp. 186–222.

Bachrach, Bernard S., and David S. Bachrach. *Warfare in Medieval Europe, c. 400–c. 1453*. New York, Routledge, 2017.

Bachrach, David S. "The Military Organization of Ottonian Germany, c. 900–1018: The Views of Bishop Thietmar of Merseburg." *The Journal of Military History*, vol. 72, no. 4, Oct. 2008, pp. 1061–88.

Backman, Clifford R. *The Worlds of Medieval Europe*. 2nd ed., Oxford, Oxford University Press, 2009.

Baer, Marc D. "History and Religious Conversion." *The Oxford Handbook of Religious Conversion*, edited by Lewis R. Rambo and Charles E. Farhadian, Oxford, Oxford University Press, 2014, pp. 25–35.

Bailey, Michael. "Witchcraft and Demonology in the Middle Ages." *The Routledge History of Witchcraft*, edited by Johannes Dillinger, New York, Routledge, 2020, pp. 48–49.

Baldoli, Claudia. *A History of Italy*. New York, Palgrave Macmillan, 2009.

Ballhatchet, Kenneth, and Helen Ballhatchet. "Asia." *The Oxford Illustrated History of Christianity*, edited by John McManners, Oxford, Oxford University Press, 1990, pp. 490–510.

Banaszkiewicz, Jack. "Widukind on the Saxon Origins." *Acta Poloniae Historica*, vol. 91, 2005, pp. 25–54.

Banghard, Karl. "Noch einmal zum 'Paderborner Odin'." *Gesellschaft zur Förderung der Archäologie in Ostwestfalen*, vol. 14, 2019, pp. 70–77.

Bannister, L. *Finding the Vikings: A Tour of Historical Sites in Scandinavia* (Unpublished master's thesis). 1999. Prescott College, Ann Arbor, MI, pp. 24–25.

Barford, P. M. *The Early Slavs: Culture and Society in Early Medieval Eastern Europe*. Ithaca, NY, Cornell University Press, 2001.

Barlow, Rolph. *The Letters of Alcuin.* New York, The Forest Press, 1909.

Barney, Stephen A. *Word-Hoard: An Introduction to Old English Vocabulary.* 2nd ed., New Haven, CT, Yale University Press, 1985.

Barney, Stephen A., et al., editors. *The Etymologies of Isidore of Seville*, Cambridge, Cambridge University Press, 2006.

Bartlett, Robert, editor. *The Medieval World Complete.* London, Thames & Hudson, 2001.

Barton, Simon. *A History of Spain.* 2nd ed., New York, Palgrave Macmillan, 2009.

Barraclough, Geoffrey. *The Origins of Modern Germany.* New York, W.W. Norton & Company, 1984.

Bauer, Karl. "Die Quellen für das sog. Blutbad von Verden." *Westfälische Zeitschrift,* vol. 92, 1936, pp. 40–73.

Bauer, Katja. *Buße und Strafe im Frühmittelalter: Das Verhältnis von Bußenstrafrecht und peinlichem Strafrecht in den fränkischen Gesetzen für die Friesen, Sachsen und Thüringer (802/803).* Universitätsverlag Halle-Wittenberg, 2017.

Becher, Matthias. *Charlemagne.* New Haven, CT, Yale University Press, 2003.

Becher, Matthias. "Non enim habent regem idem Antiqui Saxones... Verfassung und Ethnogenese in Sachsen während des 8. Jahrhunderts." *Studien zur Sachsenforschung,* vol. 12, 1999, pp. 1–31.

Bede. *The Reckoning of Time.* Translated by Faith Wallis, Liverpool, Liverpool University Press, 2004.

Bede, and D. H. Farmer. *Ecclesiastical History of the English People with Bede's Letter to Egbert and Cuthbert's Letter on the Death of Bede.* Translated by Leo Shirley-Price, London, Penguin Group, 1990.

Behr, Hans-Joachim. "Die Sachsenkriege Karls des Großen und der Besuch Papst Leos III. in Paderborn 799 im Gedächtnis der Nachwelt." *Westfälische Zeitschrift,* vol. 150, 2000, pp. 211–33.

Bennett, Judith M. *Medieval Europe: A Short History.* 11th ed., New York, McGraw-Hill, 2011.

Billington, Sandra. "The Midsummer Solstice as It Was, or Was Not, Observed in Pagan Germany, Scandinavia and Anglo-Saxon England." *Folklore,* vol. 119, no. 1, Apr. 2008, pp. 41–57.

Bitel, Lisa. "Gender and the Initial Christianization of Northern Europe (to 1000 CE)." *The Oxford Handbook of Women and Gender in Medieval Europe,* edited by Judith M. Bennett and Ruth M. Karras, Oxford, Oxford University Press, 2013, pp. 417–26.

Blair, John. "Overview: Anglo-Saxon Identity." *The Oxford Handbook of Anglo-Saxon Archaeology,* edited by Helena Hamerow, David A. Hinton, and Sally Crawford, Oxford, Oxford University Press, 2011, pp. 728–29.

Blair, John. "The Anglo-Saxon Period (c.440–1066)." *The Oxford Illustrated History of Britain,* edited by Kenneth O. Morgan, Oxford, Oxford University Press, 1993, pp. 66–72.

Boniface. *The Letters of Saint Boniface.* Translated by Ephraim Emerton, New York, Columbia University Press, 1940, Records of Civilization, Sources and Studies 31.

Boretius, Alfred. *Translations and Reprints from the Original Sources of European History.* Translated by D C. Munro, 5th ed., vol. VI, Philadelphia, University of Pennsylvania Press, 1900.

Bosman, Frank G. "'Teach us the Secret Runes'. The Lords Prayer in Heliand." *Perichoresis,* vol. 14, no. 2, 2016, pp. 39–51.

Both, Frank. "Eine sächsische Hofwüstung des späten 8. und des 9. Jhs. bei Hoogstede, Ldkr. Grafschaft Bentheim." *Nachrichten aus Niedersachsens Urgeschichte,* vol. 60, 1991, pp. 101–12.

Bradbury, Jim. *The Routledge Companion to Medieval Warfare*. New York, Routledge, 2004.

Brehaut, Ernest. *An Encyclopedist of the Dark Ages: Isidore of Seville*. New York, Columbia University Press, 1912.

Bremmer, Rolf H. *Introduction to Old Frisian: History, Grammar, Reader, Glossary*. Amsterdam, John Benjamin's Publishing Company, 2009.

Bremmer, Jr., Rolf H. "Changing Perspectives on a Saint's Life: Juliana." *Companion to Old English Poetry*, edited by Henk Aertsen and Rolf H. Bremmer, Jr., Amsterdam, VU University Press, 1994, pp. 201–10.

Bremmer, Jr., Rolf H. "Old English Heroic Literature." *Companion to Old English Poetry*, edited by David F. Johnson and Elaine Trehame, Oxford, Oxford University Press, 2005, pp. 78–87.

Brennecke, Hanns C. "Deconstruction of the So-Called Germanic Arianism." *Arianism: Roman Heresy and Barbarian Creed*, edited by Guido M. Berndt and Roland Steinacher, New York, Routledge, 2016, pp. 121–23.

Brink, Stefan. "Law and Legal Customs in Viking Age Scandinavia." *The Scandinavians from the Vendel Period to the Tenth Century: An Ethnographic Perspective*, edited by Judith Jesch, Woodbridge, The Boydell Press, 2002, pp. 90–102.

Brooks, Nicholas. "The Social and Political Background." *The Cambridge Companion to Old English Literature*, edited by Malcolm Godden and Michael Lapidge, Cambridge, Cambridge University Press, 2013, pp. 3–5.

Brown, Warren C. *Violence in Medieval Europe*. New York, Routledge, 2014.

Brown, Thomas. "The Transformation of the Roman Mediterranean, 400–900." *The Oxford Illustrated History of Medieval Europe*, edited by George Holmes, Oxford, Oxford University Press, 1988, pp. 2–10.

Brunner, Heinrich. *Deutsche Rechtsgeschichte*. 2nd ed., vol. I, Leipzig, Duncker & Humblot, 1906.

Buchholz, Peter. "Perspectives for Historical Research in Germanic Religion." *History of Religions*, vol. 8, no. 2, Nov. 1968, pp. 111–38.

Buchholz, Peter. "Religious Foundations of Group Identity in Prehistoric Europe: The Germanic Peoples." *Scripta Instituti Donneriani Aboensis*, vol. 15, 1993, pp. 321–34.

Buckser, Andrew. "Social Conversion and Group Definition in Jewish Copenhagen." *The Anthropology of Religious Conversion*, edited by Andrew Buckser and Glazier Rowman, Lanham, MD, Littlefield Publishers, 2003, pp. 80–81.

Buse, Dieter K. *The Regions of Germany: A Reference Guide to History and Culture*. Westport, CT, Greenwood Press, 2005.

Butler, Jon, et al. *Religion in American Life: A Short History*. Oxford, Oxford University Press, 2003.

Butt, John J. *Daily Life in the Age of Charlemagne*. Westport, CT, Greenwood Press, 2002.

Caesar, Julius, and Aulus Hirtius. *The Gallic War*. Translated by Carolyn Hammond, New York, Oxford University Press, 1996.

Campbell, James, editor. *The Anglo-Saxons*. London, Penguin Group, 1991.

Campbell, Joseph. *The Masks of God: Primitive Mythology*. New York, Penguin Books Ltd., 1969.

Cantor, Norman F. *The Civilization of the Middle Ages*. New York, Harper Perennial, 1994.

Capelle, Torsten. "Anglische, sächsische und angelsächsische Holzschnitzkunst." *Nachrichten aus Niedersachsens Urgeschichte*, vol. 553, 1984, pp. 117–32.

Carroll, Christopher. "The Bishoprics of Saxony in the First Century after Christianization." *Early Medieval Europe*, vol. 8, no. 2, 1999, pp. 219–45.

Cathey, James E., editor. *Heliand: Text and Commentary*. 1st ed., Morgantown, West Virginia University Press, 2002.

Cathey, James E. *Old Saxon*. Muenchen, LINCOM EUROPA, 2000. Languages of the World/Materials 252.

Cathey, James E. "The Historical Setting of the *Heliand*, the Poem, and the Manuscripts." *Perspectives on the Old Saxon Heliand: Introductory and Critical Essays, with an Edition of the Leipzig Fragment*, edited by Valentine A. Pakis, Morgantown, West Virginia University Press, 2010, pp. 3–25.

Cavanaugh, William T. *The Myth of Religious Violence: Secular Ideology and the Roots of Modern Conflict*. Oxford, Oxford University Press, 2009.

Cawthorne, Nigel. *Witch Hunt: History of a Persecution*. London, Arcturus Publishing Limited, 2003.

Cichy, Eva. "Die Eresburg, Marsberg-Obermarsberg, Hochsauerlandkreis." *Frühe Burgen in Westfalen*, vol. 36, 2014, pp. 1–40.

Chadwick, Henry. "The Early Christian Community." *The Oxford Illustrated History of Christianity*, edited by John McManners, Oxford, Oxford University Press, 1990, pp. 40–60.

Clayton, Mary. "Preaching and Teaching." *The Cambridge Companion to Old English Literature*, edited by Malcolm Godden and Michael Lapidge, Cambridge, Cambridge University Press, 2013, pp. 163–64.

Clements, Jonathan. *A Brief History of the Vikings: The Last Pagans or the First Modern Europeans?* London, Constable & Robinson Ltd., 2005.

Coleman, Simon. "Continuous Conversion? The Rhetoric, Practice, and Rhetorical Practice of Charismatic Protestant Conversion." *The Anthropology of Religious Conversion*, edited by Andrew Buckser and Glazier Rowman, Lanham, MD, Littlefield Publishers, 2003, pp. 16–18.

Collins, Roger. *Charlemagne*. London, Macmillan Press Ltd., 1998.

Collins, Roger. *Early Medieval Europe 300–1000*. 2nd ed., London, Macmillan Education, 1999.

Colum, Padraic. *Nordic Gods and Heroes*. New York, Dover Publications, 1996.

Comaroff, Jean, and John Comaroff. *Of Revelation and Revolution: Christianity, Colonialism, and Consciousness in South Africa*. Vol. 1, Chicago, IL, The University of Chicago Press, 1991.

Coogan, Michael, et al., editors. *The New Oxford Annotated Bible with Apocrypha*. 4th ed., Oxford, Oxford University Press. 2018.

Cotterell, Arthur. *The Encyclopedia of Mythology*. New York, Annes Publishing Limited, 1996.

Cosack, Erhard. "Neue Spuren sächsischer Krieger in der Barenburg, bei Eldagsen, Region Hannover, und die Schlacht am Süntel 782 n. Chr." *Nachrichten aus Niedersachsens Urgeschichte*, vol. 86, 2017, pp. 233–50.

Cosman, Madeleine P. *Medieval Wordbook: More than 4,000 Terms and Expressions from Medieval Culture*. New York, Fall River Press, 2007.

Costambeys, Marios, et al. *The Carolingian World*. Cambridge, Cambridge University Press, 2012.

Coupland, Simon. "Carolingian Arms and Armor in the Ninth Century." *Viator*, 21, 1990, 29. *ProQuest*. Web. 15 Mar. 2020.

Crossley-Holland, Kevin. *The Anglo-Saxon World: An Anthology*. New York, Oxford University Press, 1999.

Cuellar, Gregory L., and Randy S. Woodley. "North American Mission and Motive." *Evangelical Postcolonial Conversations: Global Awakenings in Theology and Praxis*, edited by Higuera Smith, Jayachitra Lalitha, and L. D. Hawk, Downers Grove, IL, InterVarsity Press, 2014, pp. 63–72.

Cunliffe, Barry. *Europe between the Oceans, Themes and Variations: 9000 BC-AD 1000*. New Haven, CT, Yale University Press, 2011.

Cusack, Carole M. "Between Sea and Land: Geographical and Literary Marginality in the Conversion of Medieval Frisia." *Religions*, vol. 12, no. 580, 28 July 2021, pp. 2–10.

Cusack, Carole M. *Conversion among the Germanic Peoples*. London, Cassell, 1998.

Cusack, Carole M. "Pagan Resistance to Charlemagne's Mission: 'Indigenous' Religion and 'World' Religion in the Early Middle Ages." *The Pomegranate*, vol. 13, no. 1, 2011, pp. 33–51.

Dass, Nirmal. *The Deeds of the Franks and Other Jerusalem-Bound Pilgrims*. Lanham, MD, Rowman & Littlefield Publishers, 2011.

Davidson, Hilda E. *Gods and Myths of Northern Europe*. Baltimore, MD, Penguin Books, 1964.

Davidson, Hilda E. *Myths and Symbols in Pagan Europe: Early Scandinavian and Celtic Religions*. Syracuse, NY, Syracuse University Press, 1988.

Davidson, Hilda E. *Saxo Grammaticus The History of the Danes, Books I–IX*. Translated by Peter Fisher, Cambridge, D.S. Brewer, 1980.

Davidson, Hilda E. *The Lost Beliefs of Northern Europe*. New York, Routledge, 1993.

Davies, Norman. *Europe: A History*. New York, Oxford University Press, 1996.

Davis, Jennifer R. *Charlemagne's Practice of Empire*. Cambridge, Cambridge University Press, 2015.

Davis, Raymond. *The Lives of the Eighth-Century Popes (Liber Pontificalis): The Ancient Biographies of Nine Popes from AD 715 to AD 817/Translated with an Introduction and Commentary by Raymond Davis*. 2nd ed., vol. 13, Liverpool, Liverpool University Press, 2007, Translated Texts for Historians.

Dean, Sidney E. "Felling the Irminsul." *Medieval Warfare*, vol. 5, no. 2, 2015, pp. 15–20.

De Jong, Mayke. "Carolingian Monasticism: The Power of Prayer." *The New Cambridge Medieval History, c.700–c.900*, edited by Rosamond McKitterick, Cambridge, Cambridge University Press, 2015, pp. 624–25.

De Jong, Mayke. *The Penitential State: Authority and Atonement in the Age of Louis the Pious, 814–840*. Cambridge, Cambridge University Press, 2009.

Delvaux, Matthew C. "Colors of the Viking Age: A Cluster Analysis of Glass Beads from Hedeby." *Journal of Glass Studies*, vol. 60, 2018, pp. 41–68.

Derks, Ton, and Nico Roymans, editors. *Ethnic Constructs in Antiquity: The Role of Power and Tradition*. Amsterdam, Amsterdam University Press, 2009, pp. 321–37.

Derry, T. K. *A History of Scandinavia*. Minneapolis, University of Minnesota, 1979.

Dessens, Alexander. *Res Voluntaria, Non Necessaria: The Conquest and Forced Conversion of the Saxons under Charlemagne*. 2013. Louisiana State University. https://digitalcommons.lsu.edu/gradschool_theses/1275/.

Dettmer, Jos. *Der Sachsenführer Widukind nach Geschichte und Sage*. Wurzburg, Leo Woerl, 1879.

DeVun, Leah. *The Shape of Sex: Nonbinary Gender from Genesis to the Renaissance*. New York, Columbia University Press, 2021.

Dewey, Tonya K. *An Annotated English Translation of the Old Saxon Heliand: A Ninth-Century Biblical Paraphrase in the Germanic Epic Style*. Lewiston, NY, The Edwin Mellen Press, 2011.

Diaconus, Paulus. *History of the Langobards by Paul the Deacon*. Translated by William D. Foulke, Philadelphia, University of Pennsylvania, 1906.

Dickinson, Robert E. "The Development and Distribution of the Medieval German Town: I. The West German Lands." *Geography*, vol. 27, no. 1, Mar. 1942, pp. 9–21.

Dickinson, Robert E. "Rural Settlements in the German Lands." *Annals of the Association of American Geographers*, vol. 39, no. 4, Dec. 1949, pp. 239–63.

Dillon, Myles, and Nora Chadwick. Edison, NJ *The Celtic Realms*. Castle Books, 2003.

Dobat, Andres S. "Danevirke Revisited: An Investigation into Military and Socio-Political Organisation in South Scandinavia (c. AD 700 TO 1100)." *Medieval Archaeology*, vol. 52, 2008, pp. 27–67.

Dörfler, Walter. "Rural Economy of the Continental Saxons from the Migration Period to the Tenth Century." *The Continental Saxons from the Migration Period to the Tenth Century: An Ethnographic Perspective*, edited by Dennis Green and Frank Siegmund, Woodbridge, The Boydell Press, 2003, pp. 137–41.

Drew, Katherine F. *The Laws of the Salian Franks*. Philadelphia, University of Pennsylvania Press, 1991.

Dryakhlov, Vladimir. "The Amulets of German Merovingian Aristocracy." *Archaeologia Lituana*, vol. 19, 2018, pp. 207–17.

DuBois, Thomas A. *Nordic Religions in the Viking Age*. Philadelphia, University of Pennsylvania Press, 1999.

Durant, Will. *Caesar and Christ: A History of Roman Civilization and of Christianity from their beginning to A.D. 325*. New York, Simon and Schuster, 1944, The Story of Civilization III.

Durant, Will. *The Age of Faith: A History of Medieval Civilization — Christian, Islamic, and Judaic — from Constantine to Dante: AD. 325–1300*. New York, Simon and Schuster, 1950, The Story of Civilization IV.

Dutton, Paul E., editor. *Carolingian Civilization: A Reader*. 2nd ed., Toronto, ON, University of Toronto Press, 2009.

Dutton, Paul E. *Charlemagne's Mustache: And Other Cultural Clusters of a Dark Age*. New York, Palgrave Macmillan, 2004.

Eckhardt, Karl A. *Die Gesetze des Karolingerreiches, 714–911*. Vol. III, Weimar, Böhlaus, 1934, Germanenrechte: Texte und Übersetzungen 2.

Ehlers, Caspar. "Between Marklo and Merseburg." *Journal of the North Atlantic*, vol. 8, 2015, pp. 134–40.

Ehlers, Caspar. *Die Integration Sachsens in das fränkische Reich (751–1024)*. Vol. 231, Vandenhoeck & Ruprecht, 2007, Veröffentlichungen des Max-Planck-Instituts für Geschichte.

Ehlers, Caspar. "Könige, Klöster und der Raum: Die Entwicklung der kirchlichen Topographie Westfalens und Ostsachsens in karolingischer und ottonischer Zeit'." *Westfälische Zeitschrift*, vol. 153, 2003, pp. 189–216.

Effros, Bonnie. "De partitions Saxoniae and the Regulation of Mortuary Custom: A Carolingian Campaign of Christianization or the Suppression of Saxon Identity?" *Revue belge de philologie et d'historie*, vol. 75, no. 2, 1995, pp. 267–86.

Effros, Bonnie. *Merovingian Mortuary Archaeology and the Making of the Early Middle Ages*. Berkeley, University of California Press, 2003.

Einhard, with a foreword by Sydney Painter. *The Life of Charlemagne*. Ann Arbor, The University of Michigan Press, 1960.

Eller, Jack D. *Introducing the Anthropology of Religion: Culture to the Ultimate*. 3rd ed., New York, Routledge, 2022.

Elsakkers, Marianne. "Raptus Ultra Rhenum: Early Ninth-Century Saxon Laws on Abduction and Rape." *Amsterdamer Beitrage zur alteren Germanistik*, vol. 52, 1999, pp. 27–54.

Emmerson, Richard K., editor. *Key Figures in Medieval Europe: An Encyclopedia.* New York, Routledge, 2016.

Ezigbo, Victor I., and Reggie L. Williams. "Converting a Colonialist Christ." *Evangelical Postcolonial Conversations: Global Awakenings in Theology and Praxis*, edited by Higuera Smith, Jayachitra Lalitha, and L. D. Hawk, Downers Grove, IL, InterVarsity Press, 2014, pp. 90–93.

Falk, Avner. *Franks and Saracens: Reality and Fantasy in the Crusades.* New York, Routledge, 2018.

Farhadian, Charles E. "Comparing Conversions among the Dani of Irian Jaya." *The Anthropology of Religious Conversion*, edited by Andrew Buckser and Glazier Rowman, Lanham, MD, Littlefield Publishers, 2003, pp. 55–57.

Farmer, David. *The Oxford Dictionary of Saints.* 5th ed., Oxford, Oxford University Press, 2003.

Faulkner, Thomas. "Carolingian Kings and the Leges Barbarorum." *Historical Research*, vol. 86, no. 233, Aug. 2013, pp. 445–50.

Faulkner, Thomas. *Law and Authority in the Early Middle Ages: The Frankish Leges in the Carolingian Period.* Cambridge, Cambridge University Press, 2016.

Fehring, Günter P. *The Archaeology of Medieval Germany.* Translated by Ross Samson, New York, Routledge, 1991.

Ferguson, Robert. *The Vikings: A History.* New York, Penguin Group, 2009.

Filotas, Bernadette. *Pagan Survivals, Superstition and Popular Cultures, in Early Medieval Pastoral Literature (500–1000).* 2000. Universite de Montreal. PhD dissertation.

Fischer, Steven R. *A History of the Pacific Islands.* 2nd ed., New York, Palgrave Macmillan, 2013.

Fleming, Robin. *Britain after Rome: The Fall and Rise 400 to 1070.* London, Penguin Group, 2010.

Fletcher, Richard. *The Conversion of Europe: From Paganism to Christianity 371–1386 AD.* London, Fontana Press, 1998.

Flierman, Robert. *Saxon Identities, AD 150–900.* London, Bloomsbury Publishing Plc, 2017.

Fortson, Benjamin W. *Indo-European Language and Culture: An Introduction.* Malden, MA, Blackwell Publishing, 2004.

Fortunatus, Venantius. *Venantius Fortunatus: Personal and Political Poems.* Translated by Judith George, Liverpool, Liverpool University Press, 1995.

Fouracre, Paul. "Frankish Gaul to 814." *The New Cambridge Medieval History, c.700–c.900*, edited by Rosamond McKitterick, Cambridge, Cambridge University Press, 2015, pp. 95–102.

Fraesdorff, David. "The Power of Imagination: The Christianitas and the Pagan North during Conversion to Christianity (800–1200)." *The Medieval History Journal*, vol. 5, no. 2, 2002, pp. 309–32.

France, John, and Kelly DeVries, editors. *Warfare in the Dark Ages.* New York, Routledge, 2016.

Frank, Roberta. "Germanic Legend in Old English Literature." *The Cambridge Companion to Old English Literature*, edited by Malcolm Godden and Michael Lapidge, Cambridge, Cambridge University Press, 2013, pp. 84–85.

Freeborn, Dennis. *From Old English to Standard English.* New York, Macmillan Press, 1998.

Frederick, Jill. "Warring with words: Cynewulf's Juliana." *Companion to Old English Poetry*, edited by David F. Johnson and Elaine Trehame, Oxford, Oxford University Press, 2005, pp. 70–71.

Freise, Eckhard. "Widukind in Attigny." *1200 Jahre Widukinds Taufe*. Paderborn, Bonifatius-Druckerei, 1985, pp. 12–45.

Frenschkowski, Marco. "Witchcraft, Magic and Demonology in the Bible, Ancient Judaism and Earliest Christianity." *The Routledge History of Witchcraft*, edited by Johannes Dillinger, New York, Routledge, 2020, pp. 23–24.

Fried, Johannes. "The Frankish Kingdoms, 817–911: The East and Middle Kingdoms." *The New Cambridge Medieval History, c. 700–c. 900*, edited by Rosamond McKitterick, Cambridge, Cambridge University Press, 2015, pp. 144–64.

Friedrich, Martin. "Jesus Christ between Jews and Heathens: The Germanic Mission and the Portrayal of Christ in the Old Saxon *Heliand.*" *Perspectives on the Old Saxon Heliand: Introductory and Critical Essays, with an Edition of the Leipzig Fragment*, edited by Valentine A. Pakis, Morgantown, West Virginia University Press, 2010, pp. 271–72.

Fulbrook, Mary. *A Concise History of Germany*. 2nd ed., Cambridge, Cambridge University Press, 1991.

Fuller, Susan D. "Pagan Charms in Tenth-Century Saxony? The Function of the Meresburg Charms." *Monatshefte*, vol. 72, no. 2, 1980, pp. 162–70.

Funck-Brentano, Fr. *A History of Gaul: Celtic, Roman and Frankish Rule*. New York, Barnes and Noble, Inc., 1993.

Gallée, J. H., editor. *Old-Saxon Texts*. Leiden, E.J. Brill, 1894.

Gaskoin, C. J. B. *Alcuin: His Life and His Work*. Cambridge, Cambridge University Press, 1904.

Geary, Patrick J. *Before France & Germany: The Creation & Transformation of the Merovingian World*. Oxford, Oxford University Press, 1988.

Gebhardt, Walter. *Karl und Widukind*. Lincoln, NE, Preuss, 2009.

Gibbon, Edward. *The History of the Decline and Fall of the Roman Empire: Abridged Edition*. London, Penguin Group, 2005.

Gibbs, Marion E., and Sidney M. Johnson, editors. *Medieval German Literature*. New York, Routledge, 1997.

Gillis, Matthew B. *Heresy and Dissent in the Carolingian Empire: The Case of Gottschalk of Orbais*. Oxford, Oxford University Press, 2017.

Glazier, Stephen D. "'Limin' wid Jah': Spiritual Baptists Who Become Rastafarians and Then Become Spiritual Baptists Again." *The Anthropology of Religious Conversion*, edited by Andrew Buckser and Glazier Rowman, Lanham, MD, Littlefield Publishers, 2003, pp. 149–58.

Glover, Terrot R. *Life and Letters in the Fourth Century*. Cambridge, Cambridge University Press, 1901.

Gneuss, Helmut. "The Old English language." *The Cambridge Companion to Old English Literature*, edited by Malcolm Godden and Michael Lapidge, Cambridge, Cambridge University Press, 2013, pp. 20–21.

Godden, Malcolm. "Biblical Literature: The Old Testament." *The Cambridge Companion to Old English Literature*, edited by Malcolm Godden and Michael Lapidge, Cambridge, Cambridge University Press, 2013, pp. 219–22.

Godman, Peter, editor. *Poetry of the Carolingian Renaissance*. Norman, University of Oklahoma Press, 1985.

Goetz, Hans-Werner. *Life in the Middle Ages: From the Seventh to the Thirteenth Century*. Notre Dame, IN, University of Notre Dame Press, 1993.

Goldberg, Eric J. "Popular Revolt, Dynastic Politics, and Aristocratic Factionalism in the Early Middle Ages: The Saxon Stellinga Reconsidered." *Speculum*, vol. 70, no. 3, July 1995, pp. 467–501.

Goldberg, Eric J. *Struggle for Empire: Kingship and Conflict under Louis the German, 817–876*. Ithaca, NY, Cornell University Press, 2006.

Gonzalez, Justo L. *The Story of Christianity: The Early Church to the Dawn of the Reformation*. 2nd ed., vol. I, New York, HarperCollins, 2010, II vols.

Gooren, Henri. "Anthropology of Religious Conversion." *The Oxford Handbook of Religious Conversion*, edited by Lewis R. Rambo and Charles E. Farhadian, Oxford, Oxford University Press, 2014, pp. 85–92.

Gose, Peter. "Converting the Ancestors: Indirect Rule, Settlement Consolidation, and the Struggle over Burial in Colonial Peru, 1532–1614." *Conversion: Old Worlds and New*, edited by Kenneth Mills and Anthony Grafton, Rochester, NY, University of Rochester Press, 2003, pp. 140–65.

Grahn-Hoek, Heike. "The Thuringi, the Peculiarities of Their Law, and Their Legal Relations to the Gentes of Their Time, Chiefly According to the Lex (Angliorum et Werinorum hoc est) Thuringorum and the Other Leges barbarorum of the Early Middle Ages." *The Baiuvarii and Thuringi: An Ethnographic Perspective*, edited by Janine Fries-Knoblach, Heiko Steuer, and John Hines, Woodbridge, The Boydell Press, 2014, pp. 293–94.

Green, Dennis H. *Language and History in the Early Germanic World*. Cambridge, Cambridge University Press, 2000.

Green, Dennis H. *The Carolingian Lord*. Cambridge, Cambridge University Press, 1965.

Green, Dennis H. "Three Aspects of the Old Saxon Biblical Epic, the Heliand." *The Continental Saxons from the Migration Period to the Tenth Century: An Ethnographic Perspective*, edited by Dennis Green and Frank Siegmund, Woodbridge, The Boydell Press, 2003, pp. 254–55.

Green, Dennis H., and Frank Siegmund, editors. *The Continental Saxons from the Migration Period to the Tenth Century: An Ethnographic Perspective*. Woodbridge, The Boydell Press, 2003.

Green, Gene. "A Response to the Postcolonial Roundtable: Promises, Problems and Prospects." *Evangelical Postcolonial Conversations: Global Awakenings in Theology and Praxis*, edited by Kay Smith, Jayachitra Lalitha, and L. D. Hawk, Downers Grove, IL, InterVarsity Press, 2014, pp. 19–20.

Greer, Allan. "Conversion and Identity: Iroquois Christianity in Seventeenth-Century New France." *Conversion: Old Worlds and New*, edited by Kenneth Mills and Anthony Grafton, Rochester, NY, University of Rochester Press, 2003, pp. 177–87.

Greer, Sarah. *Commemorating Power in Early Medieval Saxony: Writing and Rewriting the Past at Gandersheim and Quedlinburg*. Oxford, Oxford University Press, 2021.

Gregory of Tours. *The History of the Franks*. Translated by Lewis Thorpe, London, Penguin Group, 1974.

Grimm, Jacob. *Teutonic Mythology*. Vol. I, New York, Dover Publications, 1966, IV vols.

Grimm, Jacob. *Teutonic Mythology*. Vol. II, New York, Dover Publications, 1966, IV vols.

Grünewald, Christoph. "Westfalen zwischen Franken und Sachsen." *Archäologie in Deutschland*, vol. 1, Jan. 1999, pp. 20–23.

Guitar, Lynne A. "Negotiations of Conquest." *The Caribbean: A History of the Region and Its Peoples*, edited by Stephen Palmie and Francisco A. Scarano, Chicago, IL, The University of Chicago Press, 2011, pp. 116–26.

Haferland, Harald. "The Hatred of Enemies: Germanic Heroic Poetry and the Narrative Design of the *Heliand*." *Perspectives on the Old Saxon Heliand: Introductory and*

Critical Essays, with an Edition of the Leipzig Fragment, edited by Valentine A. Pakis, Morgantown, West Virginia University Press, 2010, pp. 213–19.

Halle, Uta. "Archaeology in the Third Reich. Academic Scholarship and the Rise of the 'Lunatic Fringe.'" *Archaeological Dialogues*, vol. 12, no. 1, 2005, pp. 91–102.

Halsall, Guy. *Barbarian Migrations and the Roman West, 376–568*. Cambridge, Cambridge University Press, 2007.

Halsall, Guy. "The Sources and Their Interpretation." *The New Cambridge Medieval History, c.500–c.700*, edited by Paul Fouracre, Cambridge, Cambridge University Press, 2015, pp. 67–68.

Hamerow, Helena. *Early Medieval Settlements: The Archaeology of Rural Communities in Northwest Europe 400–900*. Oxford, Oxford University Press, 2002.

Harrison, Perry N. "Historical Infanticide and the 'Massacre of the Innocents' in the Old Saxon Heliand." *Neophilogous*, vol. 102, 2018, pp. 203–15, https://doi.org/10.1007/s11061-017-9551-7.

Hawk, Daniel, and Richard L. Twiss. "An American Hermeneutic of Colonization." *Evangelical Postcolonial Conversations: Global Awakenings in Theology and Praxis*, edited by Kay H. Smith, Jayachitra Lalitha, and L D. Hawk, Downers Grove, IL, InterVarsity Press, 2014, pp. 47–55.

Haywood, John. *The Penguin Historical Atlas of the Vikings*. London, Penguin Books, 1995.

Head, Thomas, editor. *Medieval Hagiography: An Anthology*. New York, Routledge, 2001.

Heather, Peter. *Christendom: The Triumph of a Religion*. London, Allen Lane, 2022.

Heather, Peter. *Empires and Barbarians: The Fall of Rome and the Birth of Europe*. Oxford, Oxford University Press, 2009.

Hedeager, Lotte. "Scandinavia." *The New Cambridge Medieval History, c.500–c.700*, edited by Paul Fouracre, Cambridge, Cambridge University Press, 2015, pp. 501–19.

Hefner, Robert W. "Introduction: World Building and the Rationality of Conversion." *Conversion to Christianity: Historical and Anthropological Perspectives on a Great Transformation*, edited by Robert W. Hefner, Berkeley, University of California Press, 1993, pp. 7–8.

Helfenstein, James. *Comparative Grammar of the Teutonic Languages*. London, Macmillan and Co., 1870.

Helmold. *The Chronicle of the Slavs*. Translated by Francis J. Tschan, New York, Octagon Books, Inc., 1966. Records of Civilization: Sources and Studies XXI.

Henderson, Ernest F. *A History of Germany in the Middle Ages*. London, George Bell & Sons, 1894.

Hennessy, Kathryn, and Gareth Jones, editors. *Fashion: The Definitive Visual Guide*. 2nd ed., New York, DK Publishing, 2019.

Henning, Joachim. "Slavery or Freedom? The Causes of Early Medieval Europe's Economic Advancement." *Early Medieval Europe*, vol. 12, no. 3, 2003, pp. 269–77.

Heine, Hans-Wilhelm. "Archäologische Burgenforschung in Südniedersachsen." *Nachrichten aus Niedersachsen Urgeschichte*, vol. 66, no. 1, 1997, pp. 259–76.

Hillgarth, J N., editor. *Christianity and Paganism, 350–750: The Conversion of Western Europe*. Philadelphia, University of Pennsylvania Press, 1986.

Hines, John, editor. *The Anglo-Saxons from the Migration Period to the Eighth Century: An Ethnographic Perspective*. Woodbridge, The Boydell Press, 1997, Studies in Historical Archaeoethnology 2.

Hines, John. "The Conversion of the Old Saxons." *The Continental Saxons from the Migration Period to the Tenth Century: An Ethnographic Perspective*, edited by Dennis Green and Frank Siegmund, Woodbridge, The Boydell Press, 2003, pp. 304–05.

Hodges, Richard. "Frisians and Franks: Argonauts of the Dark Ages." *Archaeology*, vol. 37, no. 1, Jan. 1984, pp. 26–31.

Holcombe, Charles. *A History of East Asia: From the Origins of Civilization to the Twenty-First Century*. Cambridge, Cambridge University Press, 2011.

Holland, A. W. *Germany*. London, Adam & Charles Black, 1914, The Making of the Nations.

Honselmann, Klemens. "Die Annahme des Christentums durch die Sachsen im Lichte sächsischer Quellen des 9. Jahrhunderts." *Westfälische Zeitschrift*, vol. 108, 1958, pp. 201–19.

Honselmann, Klemens. "Paderborn 777, Urbs Karoli: Karlsburg." *Westfälische Zeitschrift*, vol. 130, 1980, pp. 398–402.

Hooper, Nicholas, and Matthew Bennett. *The Cambridge Illustrated Atlas of Warfare: The Middle Ages, 768–1487*. Cambridge, Cambridge University Press, 1996.

Höpken, Constanze. "Religion, Cult, and Burial Customs." *The Oxford Handbook of the Archaeology of Roman Germany*, edited by Simon James and Stefan Krmnicek, Oxford, Oxford University Press, 2020, pp. 258–60.

Howorth, Henry H. "The Early Intercourse of the Danes and the Franks." *Transactions of the Royal Historical Society*, vol. 6, 1877, pp. 147–82.

Howorth, Henry H. "The Early Intercourse of the Danes and the Franks: Part II." *Transactions of the Royal Historical Society*, vol. 7, 1878, pp. 1–29.

Howorth, Henry H. "The Ethnology of Germany. Part I. The Saxons of Nether Saxony." *The Journal of the Anthropological Institute of Great Britain and Ireland*, vol. 6, 1877, pp. 364–78.

Howorth, Henry H. "The Ethnology of Germany. Part IV. The Saxons of Nether Saxony. Section II." *The Journal of the Anthropological Institute of Great Britain and Ireland*, vol. 9, 1880, pp. 406–36.

Hsia, R P. "Translating Christianity: Counter-Reformation Europe and the Catholic Mission in China, 1580–1780." *Conversion: Old Worlds and New*, edited by Kenneth Mills and Anthony Grafton, Rochester, NY, University of Rochester Press, 2003, pp. 96–97.

Hummer, Hans J. "Franks and Alamanni: A Discontinuous Ethnogenesis." *Franks and Alamanni in the Merovingian Period: An Ethnographic Perspective*, edited by Ian Wood, Woodbridge, The Boydell Press, 1998, pp. 9–10.

Hunt, Lynn, Thomas R. Martin, Barbara H. Rosenwein, R. P. Hsia, and Bonnie G. Smith. *The Making of the West: Peoples and Cultures*. 2nd ed., vol. A, New York, Bedford/ST. Martin's, 2005.

Hutton, Ronald. "How Pagan Were Medieval English Peasants?" *Folklore*, vol. 122, no. 3, Dec. 2011, pp. 235–49.

Innes, Matthew. *State and Society in the Early Middle Ages: The Middle Rhine Valley, 400–1000*. Cambridge, Cambridge University Press, 2004.

IJssennagger, Nelleke L. "Between Frankish and Viking: Frisia and Frisians in the Viking Age." *Viking and Medieval Scandinavia*, vol. 9, 2013, pp. 69–98.

Isenberg, Gabriele. "Nach den Sachsenkriegen Karls des Großen: Neue Bedrohung aus dem Norden." *Westfälische Zeitschrift*, vol. 164, 2014, pp. 9–25.

Jacoby, Susan. *Strange Gods: A Secular History of Conversion*. New York, Vintage Books, 2016.

James, Edward. *The Franks*. Oxford, Basil Blackwell Ltd., 1988.

James, Edward. "The Northern World in the Dark Ages, 400–900." *The Oxford Illustrated History of Medieval Europe*, edited by George Holmes, Oxford, Oxford University Press, 1988, pp. 64–95.

James, William. *The Varieties of Religious Experience*. New York, Penguin Group, 1985.

Jeep, John M., editor. *Medieval Germany: An Encyclopedia*. New York, Routledge, 2016.

Jellema, Dirk. "Frisian Trade in the Dark Ages." *Speculum*, vol. 30, no. 1, Jan. 1955, pp. 15–36.

Johnson, David F. "Old English Religious Poetry: Christ and Satan and The Dream of the Rood." *Companion to Old English Poetry*, edited by Henk Aertsen and Rolf H. Bremmer, Jr., Amsterdam, VU University Press, 1994, pp. 163–76.

Jolly, Karen L. *Popular Religion in Late Saxon England: Elf Charms in Context.* Chapel Hill, The University of North Carolina Press, 1996.

Jones, Colin. *The Cambridge Illustrated History of France.* Cambridge, Cambridge University Press, 1994.

Jordan, David K. "The Glyphomancy Factor: Observations on Chinese Conversion." *Conversion to Christianity: Historical and Anthropological Perspectives on a Great Transformation*, edited by Robert W. Hefner, Berkeley, University of California Press, 1993, pp. 296–97.

Jordanes. *The Origin and Deeds of the Goths.* Translated by Charles C. Mierow, Princeton, NJ, Princeton University Press, 1908.

Jørgensen, Lise. "Rural Economy: Ecology, Hunting, Pastoralism, Agricultural and Nutritional Aspects." *The Scandinavians from the Vendel Period to the Tenth Century: An Ethnographic Perspective*, edited by Judith Jesch, Woodbridge, The Boydell Press, 2002, pp. 136–37.

Juergensmeyer, Mark. *God at War: A Meditation on Religion and Warfare.* Oxford, Oxford University Press, 2020.

Kahler, Erich. *The Germans.* New York, Routledge, 2019.

Kapović, Mate, editor. *The Indo-European Languages.* 2nd ed., New York, Routledge, 2017.

Karras, Ruth M. "Pagan Survivals and Syncretism in the Conversion of Saxony." *The Catholic Historical Review*, vol. 72, no. 4, Oct. 1986, pp. 553–72.

Kaufmann, J. E., and H. W. Kaufmann. *The Medieval Fortress: Castles, Forts, and Walled Cities of the Middle Ages.* Cambridge, MA, Da Capo Press, 2004.

Kee, Howard C. "From the Jesus Movement toward Institutional Church." *Conversion to Christianity: Historical and Anthropological Perspectives on a Great Transformation*, edited by Robert W. Hefner, Berkeley, University of California Press, 1993, pp. 54–55.

Keefer, Sarah L. "Old English Religious Poetry." *Companion to Old English Poetry*, edited by David F. Johnson and Elaine Treharne, Oxford, Oxford University Press, 2005, pp. 24–25.

Keegan, John. *A History of Warfare.* New York, Alfred A. Knopf, Inc., 1993.

Kelly, Henry A. *The Devil at Baptism: Ritual, Theology, and Drama.* Eugene, OR, Wipf and Stock Publishers, 1985.

Kendrick, T D. *A History of the Vikings.* New York, Dover Publications, Inc., 2004.

Kennedy, Charles W. *The Caedmon Poems.* London, George Routledge & Sons Ltd., 1916.

Khamnueva-Wendt, Svetlana, et al. "Classification of Buried Soils, Cultural, and Colluvial Deposits in the Viking Town of Hedeby." *Geoarchaeology*, vol. 35, no. 3, 26 Dec. 2019, pp. 1–25.

Khan, Aisha. "Africa, Europe, and Asia in the Making of the Caribbean." *The Caribbean: A History of the Region and Its Peoples*, edited by Stephen Palmie and Francisco A. Scarano, Chicago, IL, The University of Chicago Press, 2011, pp. 409–10.

Kibler, William W., et al., editors. *Medieval France: An Encyclopedia.* New York, Routledge, 2016.

King, P. D. *Charlemagne: Translated Sources.* Lancaster, P.D. King, 1987.

Klaeber, Fr., editor. *The Later Genesis and Other Old English and Old Saxon Texts Relating to the Fall of Man.* Heidelberg, Carl Winter's Universitätsbuchhandlung, 1913.

Kling, David W. *A History of Christian Conversion.* Oxford, Oxford University Press, 2020.

Klocke, Fr. v. "Um das Blutbad von Verden und die Schlacht am Süntel 782." *Westfälische Zeitschrift*, vol. 93, 1937, pp. 151–92.

Knibbs, Eric. *Ansgar, Rimbert and the Forged Foundations of Hamburg-Bremen.* New York, Routledge, 2016.

Kobylinski, Zbigniew. "The Slavs." *The New Cambridge Medieval History, c.500–c.700*, edited by Paul Fouracre, Cambridge, Cambridge University Press, 2015, pp. 536–38.

Koch, Alexander. "Friesisch-sächsische Beziehungen zur Merowingerzeit Zum Fund einer Bügelfibel vom Typ Domburg auf dem sächsischen Gräberfeld von Liebenau, Ldkr. Nienburg (Weser)." *Nachrichten aus Niedersachsens Urgeschichte*, vol. 68, 1999, pp. 67–87.

Kolner, Floris. *The Indiculus superstitionum et paganiarum: a controversy reviewed.* 2018. Universiteit Utrecht. MA thesis. https://dspace.library.uu.nl/handle/1874/365039.

König, Ekkehard, and Johan van der Auwera, editors. *The Germanic Languages.* New York, Routledge, 1994.

König, Daniel G. "Charlemagne's 'Jihad' Revisited: Debating the Islamic Contribution to an Epochal Change in the History of Christianization." *Medieval Worlds*, vol. 3, 2016, pp. 3–40.

Kosto, Adam J. "Hostages in the Carolingian World (714–840)." *Early Medieval Europe*, vol. 11, no. 2, 2002, pp. 123–47.

Krappe, Alexander H. "The Valkyries." *The Modern Language Review*, vol. 21, no. 1, Jan. 1, pp. 55–73.

Kristoffersen, Elisabeth. *Pacifying the Saxons—An Interpretative Reading of the Heliand.* 2013. Universitetet I Oslo, MA thesis. https://www.duo.uio.no/handle/10852/38506

Kritsch, Tara-Kim. *Theophoric Place Names: A Comparative Study of Sacral Place Names in the German-Speaking World.* 2019. Háskóli Íslands, MA thesis. ttp://hdl.handle.net/1946/34390.

Krull, Regine. "Das Widukind Museum Enger: Geschichtsb." *Deutschen Museumsbund*, 2011, Berlin. Keynote speech.

Kurlander, Eric. *Hitler's Monsters: A Supernatural History of the Third Reich.* New Haven, CT, Yale University Press, 2018.

La Barre, Weston. *The Ghost Dance.* Maidstone, Crescent Moon Publishing, 2020.

Lalitha, Jayachitra. "Postcolonial Feminism, the Bible and the Native Indian Women." *Evangelical Postcolonial Conversations: Global Awakenings in Theology and Praxis*, edited by Kay H. Smith, Jayachitra Lalitha, and L D. Hawk, Downers Grove, IL, Inter-Varsity Press, 2014, pp. 79–80.

Lambek, Michael, editor. *A Reader in the Anthropology of Religion.* Oxford, Blackwell Publishing, 2002.

Lambert, Peter. "Heroisation and Demonisation in the Third Reich: The Consensus-Building Value of a Nazi Pantheon of Heroes." *Totalitarian Movements and Political Religions*, vol. 8, no. 3–4, 2007, pp. 523–46.

Lambert, Peter, and Björn Weiler, editors. *How the Past Was Used: Historical Cultures, c. 750–2000.* Oxford, Oxford University Press, 2017.

Lammers, Walther. "Die Stammesbildung bei den Sachsen." *Westfälische Forschungen: Mitteilungen des Provinzialinstitutes für Westfäkusche Landes und Volkskunde.* Vol. 10, Verlag Aschendorff in verbindung mit Böhlau Verlag, 1957, pp. 25–57.

Landon, Christopher Thomas. "Conquest and Colonization in the Early Middle Ages: The Carolingians and Saxony, c. 751–842." Order No. 10634383 University of Toronto (Canada), 2017. Ann Arbor: *ProQuest.* Web. 8 Mar. 2020.

Landon, Christopher Thomas. "Economic Incentives for the Conquest of Saxony." *Early Medieval Europe*, vol. 28, no. 1, 2020, pp. 26–56.

Langen, Ruth. "Die Bedeutung von Befestigungen in den Sachsenkriegen Karls des Großen." *Westfälische Zeitschrift*, vol. 139, 1989, pp. 181–211.

Lapidge, Michael. "The Saintly Life in Anglo-Saxon England." *The Cambridge Companion to Old English Literature*, edited by Malcolm Godden and Michael Lapidge, Cambridge, Cambridge University Press, 2013, pp. 260–61.

Larkin, Brian, and Birgit Meyer. "Pentecostalism, Islam and Culture." *Themes in West Africa's History*, edited by Emmanuel K. Akyeampong, Athens, Ohio University Press, 2006, pp. 291–93.

Larrington, Carolyne. *The Poetic Edda*. Oxford, Oxford University Press, 1996.

Last, Martin. "Die Bewaffnung der Karolingerzeit." *Nachrichten aus Niedersachsens Urgeschichte*, vol. 41, 1972, pp. 77–93.

Lauder, Toofie. *Legends and Tales of the Harz Mountains*. London, Hodder and Stoughton, 1871.

Laux, Friedrich. "Kleine karolingische und ottonische Scheibenfibeln aus Bardowick, Ldkr. Lüneburg." *Nachrichten aus Niedersachsens Urgeschichte*, vol. 67, 1998, pp. 9–28.

Lebecq, Stephane. "The Northern Seas (Fifth to Eighth Centuries)." *The New Cambridge Medieval History, c.500–c.700*, edited by Paul Fouracre, Cambridge, Cambridge University Press, 2015, pp. 643–55.

Leeming, David. *The Oxford Companion to World Mythology*. Oxford, Oxford University Press, 2009.

Leidinger, Paul. "Zur Christianisierung des Ostmünsterlandes im 8. Jahrhundert und zur Entwicklung des mittelalterlichen Pfarrsystems." *Westfälische Zeitschrift*, vol. 154, 2004, pp. 9–52.

Leyser, K. "Henry I and the Beginnings of the Saxon Empire." *The English Historical Review*, vol. 83, no. 326, Jan. 1968, pp. 1–32.

Leyser, K. "The German Aristocracy from the Ninth to the Early Twelfth Century. A Historical and Cultural Sketch." *Past & Present*, no. 41, Dec. 1968, pp. 25–53.

Lincoln, Bruce. *Gods and Demons, Priests and Scholars: Critical Explorations in the History of Religions*. Chicago, IL, The University of Chicago Press, 2012.

Lindenfeld, David. *World Christianity and Indigenous Experience: A Global History, 1500–2000*. Cambridge, Cambridge University Press, 2021.

Lintzel, Martin. "Untersuchungen zur Geschichte der alten Sachsen." *Sachsen und Anhalt: Jahruch der Historischen Kommission für die Provinz Sachsen und für Anhalt*. Vol. 10, Magdeburg, Selbstverlag der Historischen Kommission Auslieferung durch Ernst Holtermann, 1934.

Lipscomb, Suzannah, et al. *A History of Magic, Witchcraft & the Occult*. London, DK Publishing, 2020.

Lohmann, Ivar. "Turning the Belly: Insights on Religious Conversion from New Guinea Gut Feelings." *The Anthropology of Religious Conversion*, edited by Andrew Buckser and Glazier Rowman, Lanham, MD, Littlefield Publishers, 2003, pp. 112–13.

Longerich, Peter. *Heinrich Himmler: A Life*. Oxford, Oxford University Press, 2012.

Loyn, H R., and John Percival, editors. *The Reign of Charlemagne: Documents on Carolingian Government and Administration*. New York, St. Martin's Press, 1976, Documents of Medieval History 2.

Lübeck, Konrad. "Das Kloster Fulda und die Sachsenmission." *Fuldaer Studien*. Vol. 3, Parzeller & Co., 1951, pp. 47–74.

Lund, Niels. "Scandinavia, c. 700–1066." *The New Cambridge Medieval History, c.700–c.900*, edited by Rosamond McKitterick, Cambridge, Cambridge University Press, 2015, pp. 206–10.

Lundburg, Matthew D. *Christian Martyrdom and Christian Violence: On Suffering and Wielding the Sword*. Oxford, Oxford University Press, 2021.

Macdowall, Simon. *Germanic Warrior, 236–568 AD*. Oxford, Osprey Publishing, 1996.

Macintyre, Stuart. *A Concise History of Australia*. 3rd ed., Cambridge, Cambridge University Press, 2009.

Mackay, Angus, and David Ditchburn, editors. *Atlas of Medieval Europe*. New York, Routledge, 2002.

MacMullen, Ramsay. *Christianizing the Roman Empire, A.D. 100–400*. New Haven, CT, Yale University Press, 1984.

Marcellinus, Ammianus. *Ammianus Marcellinus with an English Translation by John C. Rolfe*. Translated by John C. Rolfe, Cambridge, MA, Harvard University Press, 1935–1939, 3 vols.

Marcellinus, Ammianus. *The Roman History of Ammianus Marcellinus: During the Reigns of the Emperors Constantius, Julian, Jovianus, Valentinian, and Valens*. Translated by C D. Yonge, London, George Bell & Sons, 1902.

Markus, Robert A. "From Rome to the Barbarian Kingdoms (330–700)." *The Oxford Illustrated History of Christianity*, edited by John McManners, Oxford, Oxford University Press, 1990, pp. 87–88.

Marsden, Richard. "Biblical Literature: The New Testament." *The Cambridge Companion to Old English Literature*, edited by Malcolm Godden and Michael Lapidge, Cambridge, Cambridge University Press, 2013, pp. 243–45.

Maxon, Robert. *East Africa: An Introductory History*. 3rd ed., Morgantown, West Virginia University Press, 2009.

Mayr-Harting, Henry. "Charlemagne, the Saxons, and the Imperial Coronation of 800." *The English Historical Review*, vol. 111, no. 444, Nov. 1996, pp. 1113–33.

Mayr-Harting, Henry. "The West: The Age of Conversion (700–1050)." *The Oxford Illustrated History of Christianity*, edited by John McManners, Oxford, Oxford University Press, 1990, pp. 92–119.

McKinney, Mary E. *The Saxon Poet's Life of Charles the Great*. New York, Pageant Press, 1956.

McKitterick, Rosamond. *Charlemagne: The Formation of a European Identity*. Cambridge, Cambridge University Press, 2008.

McKitterick, Rosamond. *History and Memory in the Carolingian World*. Cambridge, Cambridge University Press, 2004.

McKitterick, Rosamond. *The Frankish Kingdoms under the Carolingians, 751–987*. New York, Routledge, 2014.

McManners, John. "Introduction." *The Oxford Illustrated History of Christianity*, edited by John McManners, Oxford, Oxford University Press, 1990, pp. 11–13.

McManners, John. "The Expansion of Christianity (1500–1800)." *The Oxford Illustrated History of Christianity*, edited by John McManners, Oxford, Oxford University Press, 1990, pp. 304–18.

McNeill, John T., and Helena M. Gamer, editors. *Medieval Handbooks of Penance: A Translation of the Principal Libri Poenitentiales and Selections from Related Documents*. New York, Colombia University Press, 1990.

Meier, Dirk. "Man and Environment in the Marsh Area of Schleswig-Holstein from Roman Until Late Medieval Times." *Quarternary International*, vol. 112, 2004, pp. 55–69.

Meier, Dirk. "The North Sea Coastal Area: Settlement History from Roman to Early Medieval Times." *The Continental Saxons from the Migration Period to the Tenth Century: An Ethnographic Perspective*, edited by Dennis Green and Frank Siegmund, Woodbridge, The Boydell Press, 2003, pp. 38–39.

Melleno, Daniel. "Between Borders: Franks, Danes, and Abodrites in the trans-Elben World up to 827." *Early Medieval Europe*, vol. 25, no. 3, 2017, pp. 359–85.

Mendoza, Marcela. "Converted Christians, Shamans, and the House of God: The Reasons for Conversion Given by the Western Toba of the Argentine Chaco." *The Anthropology of Religious Conversion*, edited by Andrew Buckser and Glazier Rowman, Lanham, MD, Littlefield Publishers, 2003, pp. 200–05.

Menon, Kalyani D. "Converted Innocents and Their Trickster Heroes: The Politics of Proselytizing in India." *The Anthropology of Religious Conversion*, edited by Andrew Buckser and Glazier Rowman, Lanham, MD, Littlefield Publishers, 2003, pp. 43–51.

Meredith, Martin. *The Fortunes of Africa: A 5000-Year History of Wealth, Greed, and Endeavor*. New York, PublicAffairs, 2014.

Merrill, William L. "Conversion and Colonialism in Northern Mexico: The Tarahumara Response to the Jesuit Mission Program, 1601–1767." *Conversion to Christianity: Historical and Anthropological Perspectives on a Great Transformation*, edited by Robert W. Hefner, Berkeley, University of California Press, 1993, pp. 129–54.

Metzenthin, E. C. "The 'Heliand': A New Approach." *Studies in Philology*, vol. 21, no. 3, July 1924, pp. 502–39.

Meyer, Michael C., et al. *The Course of Mexican History*. 8th ed., Oxford, Oxford University Press, 2007.

Milis, Ludo J., editor. *The Pagan Middle Ages*. Woodbridge, The Boydell Press, 1998.

Moorehead, John. "Ostrogothic Italy and the Lombard Invasions." *The New Cambridge Medieval History, c.500–c.700*, edited by Paul Fouracre, Cambridge, Cambridge University Press, 2015, pp. 151–52.

Morris, Francis M. "Cross-North Sea Contacts in the Roman Period." *Oxford Journal of Archaeology*, vol. 34, no. 4, 2015, pp. 415–38.

Morrissey, Robert. *Charlemagne and France: A Thousand Years of Mythology*. Translated by Catherine Tihanyi, Notre Dame, IN, University of Notre Dame Press, 1997.

Motz, Lotte. "The Goddess Nerthus: A New Approach." *Amsterdamer Beiträge zur älteren Germanistik*, vol. 36, 1992, pp. 1–20.

Müller-Wille, Michael, et al. "The Transformation of Rural Society, Economy and Landscape during the First Millennium AD: Archaeological and Palaeobotanical Contributions from Northern Germany and Southern Scandinavia." *Geografiska Annaler. Series B, Human Geography*, vol. 70, no. 1, 1988, pp. 53–68.

Murphy, G. R. *The Heliand: The Saxon Gospel*. Oxford, Oxford University Press, 1992.

Murphy, G. R. *The Saxon Savior*. Oxford, Oxford University Press, 1989.

Murphy, Ronald. "The Old Saxon Heliand." *Perspectives on the Old Saxon Heliand: Introductory and Critical Essays, with an Edition of the Leipzig Fragment*, edited by Valentine A. Pakis, Morgantown, West Virginia University Press, 2010, pp. 34–52.

Musset, Licien. *The Germanic Invasions: The Making of Europe 400–600 A.D.* New York, Barnes & Noble, Inc., 1975.

Naylor, Phillip C. *North Africa: A History from Antiquity to the Present*. Austin, University of Texas Press, 2015.

Nees, Lawrence. *Early Medieval Art*. Oxford, Oxford University Press, 2002.

Neill, Stephen. *A History of Christian Missions*. Vol. 6, Penguin Group, 1990, The Penguin History of the Church.

Nelson, Janet L. *Charles the Bald*. New York, Routledge, 2013.

Nelson, Janet L. *King and Emperor: A New Life of Charlemagne*. Berkeley, University of California Press, 2019.

Nelson, Janet L. "Religion and Politics in the Reign of Charlemagne." *Religion and Politics in the Middle Ages: Germany and England by Comparison*, edited by Ludger Körntgen and Dominick Waßenhoven, Berlin, De Gruyter, 2013, pp. 21–26.

Nelson, Janet L. *The Annals of St. Bertin: Ninth-Century Histories, Vol. I*, Manchester, Manchester University Press, 1991.

Nelson, Janet, and Alice Rio. "Women and Laws in Early Medieval Europe." *The Oxford Handbook of Women and Gender in Medieval Europe*, edited by Judith M. Bennett and Ruth M. Karras, Oxford, Oxford University Press, 2013, pp. 106–07.

Newman, Paul B. *Daily Life in the Middle Ages*. Jefferson, NC, McFarland & Company, Inc., 2001.

Nicolle, David. *Carolingian Cavalryman AD 768–987*. Oxford, Osprey Publishing, 2005.

Nicolle, David. *The Age of Charlemagne*. London, Osprey Publishing, 1984.

Nicolle, David. *The Conquest of Saxony AD 782–785*. Oxford, Osprey Publishing, 2014.

Nielsen, Hans F. *The Germanic Languages: Origins and Early Dialectical Interrelations*. Tuscaloosa, The University of Alabama Press, 1998.

Nielsen, Karen. "Saxon Art between Interpretation and Imitation: The Influence of Roman, Scandinavian, Frankish, and Christian Art on the Material Culture of the Continental Saxons AD 400–1000." *The Continental Saxons from the Migration Period to the Tenth Century: An Ethnographic Perspective*, edited by Dennis Green and Frank Siegmund, Woodbridge, The Boydell Press, 2003, pp. 197–229.

Nielsen, Svend. "Urban Economy in Southern Scandinavia in the Second Half of the First Millennium AD." *The Scandinavians from the Vendel Period to the Tenth Century: An Ethnographic Perspective*, edited by Judith Jesch, Woodbridge, The Boydell Press, 2002, pp. 204–05.

Niles, John D. "Pagan Survivals and Popular Belief." *The Cambridge Companion to Old English Literature*, edited by Malcolm Godden and Michael Lapidge, Cambridge, Cambridge University Press, 2013, pp. 123–34.

Niles, John D. "Pre-Christian Anglo-Saxon Religion." *The Handbook of Religions in Ancient Europe*, edited by Lisbeth B. Christensen, Olav Hammer, and David Warburton, New York, Routledge, 2013, pp. 304–05.

Noble, Thomas F. "Carolingian Religion." *Church History*, vol. 84, no. 2, June 2015, pp. 287–307.

Noble, Thomas F. *Charlemagne and Louis the Pious: Lives by Einhard, Notker, Ermoldus, Thegan, and the Astronomer*. University Park, Pennsylvania State University Press, 2009.

Noble, Thomas F. *Soldiers of Christ: Saints and Saints' Lives from Late Antiquity and the Early Middle Ages*. 2nd ed., University Park, Pennsylvania State University Press, 2000.

Northcott, Kenneth. "An Interpretation of the Second Merseburg Charm." *The Modern Language Review*, vol. 54, no. 1, 1 Jan. 1959, pp. 45–46.

Nyberg, Tore, editor. *Monasticism in North-Western Europe, 800–1200*. New York, Routledge, 2018.

O'Brian, Katherine. "Values and Ethics in Heroic Literature." *The Cambridge Companion to Old English Literature*, edited by Malcolm Godden and Michael Lapidge, Cambridge, Cambridge University Press, 2013, pp. 101–07.

Oman, Charles. *The Dark Ages, 476–918*. Coppell, TX, Rivingtons, 2017.

Obeng, Pashington. "Religious Interactions in Pre-Twentieth-Century West Africa." *Themes in West Africa's History*, edited by Emmanuel K. Akyeampong, Athens, Ohio University Press, 2006, pp. 154–55.

Orosius, *Seven Books of History against the Pagans*. Translated by A T. Fear, Liverpool, Liverpool University Press, 2010.

Owen, Francis. *The Germanic People: Their Origin, Expansion, & Culture*. New York, Barnes and Noble, Inc., 1993.

Ozment, Steven. *A Mighty Fortress: A New History of the German People*. New York, Harper-Collins, 2004.

Palmer, James. "The 'Vigorous Rule' of Bishop Lull: Between Bonifatian Mission and Carolingian Church Control." *Early Medieval Europe*, vol. 13, no. 3, pp. 249–76.

Palmer, James. "Defining Paganism in the Carolingian World." *Early Medieval Europe*, vol. 15, no. 4, 2007, pp. 402–25.

Parsons, David. "Some Churches of the Anglo-Saxon Missionaries in Southern Germany: A review of the Evidence." *Early Medieval Europe*, vol. 8, no. 1, 1999, pp. 31–67.

Paxton, Frederick S. *Anchoress & Abbess in Ninth-Century Saxony: The Lives of Liutbirga of Wendhausen and Hathumoda of Gandersheim*. Washington, DC, The Catholic University of America Press, 2009.

Payne, John F. *English Medicine in the Anglo-Saxon Times*. Oxford, Clarendon Press, 1904.

Pearson, A F. "Barbarian Piracy and the Saxon Shore: A Reappraisal." *Oxford Journal of Archaeology*, vol. 24, no. 1, 2005, pp. 84–85.

Pierce, Marc. "An Overview of Old Saxon Linguistics, 1992–2008." *Perspectives on the Old Saxon Heliand: Introductory and Critical Essays, with an Edition of the Leipzig Fragment*, edited by Valentine A. Pakis, Morgantown, West Virginia University Press, 2010, pp. 66–67.

Pinson, Koppel S. *Modern Germany: It's History and Civilization*. 2nd ed., New York, The Macmillan Company, 1966.

Pohl, Walter. *The Avars: A Steppe Empire in Central Europe, 567–822*. Ithaca, NY, Cornell University Press, 2018.

Pollock, Donald K. "Conversion and 'Community' in Amazonia." *Conversion to Christianity: Historical and Anthropological Perspectives on a Great Transformation*, edited by Robert W. Hefner, Berkeley, University of California Press, 1993, pp. 167–91.

Pounds, Norman J. *An Historical Geography of Europe, 450 BC–AD 1330*. Cambridge, Cambridge University Press, 1973.

Priest, Robert J. "'I Discovered my Sin': Aguaruna Evangelical Conversion Narratives." *The Anthropology of Religious Conversion*, edited by Andrew Buckser and Glazier Rowman, Lanham, MD, Littlefield Publishers, 2003, pp. 97–103.

Pulsiano, Phillip, and Kirsten Wolf, editors. *Medieval Scandinavia: An Encyclopedia*. New York, Routledge, 2016.

Raaijmakers, Janneke. *The Making of the Monastic Community of Fulda, c. 744–c. 900*. Cambridge, Cambridge University Press, 2014.

Raffield, Ben. "The Slave Markets of the Viking World: Comparative Perspectives on an 'Invisible Archaeology'." *Slavery & Abolition*, vol. 40, no. 4, 2019, pp. 682–705.

Raiswell, Richard, and David R. Winter, editors. *The Medieval Devil: A Reader*. Toronto, University of Toronto Press, 2022. Readings in Medieval Civilizations and Cultures XXIV.

Rambo, Lewis R. "Anthropology and the Study of Conversion." *The Anthropology of Religious Conversion*, edited by Andrew Buckser and Glazier Rowman, Lanham, MD, Littlefield Publishers, 2003, pp. 212–13.

Rambo, Lewis R. *Understanding Religious Conversion*. New Haven, CT, Yale University Press, 1993.

Rampton, Martha, editor. *European Magic and Witchcraft: A Reader*. Toronto, University of Toronto Press, 2018, Readings in Medieval Civilizations and Cultures XX.

Rauch, Irmengard. *The Old Saxon Language: Grammar, Epic Narrative, Linguistic Interference*. New York, Peter Lang, 1992.

Reid, Anthony. *A History of Southeast Asia: Critical Crossroads*. Chichester, Wiley Blackwell, 2015.

Reinhardt, Kurt F. *Germany: 2000 Years, The Rise and Fall of the "Holy Empire."* 2nd ed., vol. 1, New York, Frederick Ungar Publishing Co., 1985, 3 vols.

Rembold, Ingrid. *Conquest and Christianization: Saxony and the Carolingian World, 772–888*. Cambridge, Cambridge University Press, 2018.

Rembold, Ingrid. "The Poeta Saxo at Paderborn: Episcopal Authority and Carolingian Rule in Late Ninth-Century Saxony." *Early Medieval Europe*, vol. 21, no. 2, 2013, pp. 169–96.

Rembold, Ingrid. "Quasi una gens: Saxony and the Frankish World, c. 772–888." *History Compass*, 2017, pp. 1–14, https://doi.org/10.1111/hic3.12385.

Reuter, Timothy. *Germany in the Early Middle Ages, c. 800–1056*. New York, Longman Group UK Limited, 1991.

Reuter, Timothy. *The Annals of Fulda: Ninth-Century Histories, Vol. II*, Manchester, Manchester University Press, 1992.

Richards, Julian D. "An Archaeology of Anglo-Saxon England." *After Empire: Towards an Ethnology of Europe's Barbarians*, edited by Giorgio Ausenda, Woodbridge, The Boydell Press, 1995, pp. 57–58.

Richardson, Kurt A. "American Exceptionalism as Prophetic Nationalism." *Evangelical Postcolonial Conversations: Global Awakenings in Theology and Praxis*, edited by Higuera Smith, Jayachitra Lalitha, and L. D. Hawk, Downers Grove, IL, InterVarsity Press, 2014, pp. 121–27.

Riche, Pierre. *Daily Life in the World of Charlemagne*. Philadelphia, University of Pennsylvania Press, 1988.

Riche, Pierre. *The Carolingians: A Family who Forged Europe*. Translated by Michael I. Allen, 2nd ed., Philadelphia, University of Pennsylvania Press, 1994.

Rimbert. *Anskar: The Apostle of the North. 801–865*. Translated by Charles C. Robinson, London, The Society for the Propagation of the Gospel in Foreign Parts, 1921.

Ring, Trudy, et al., editors. *Northern Europe: International Dictionary of Historic Places*. Vol. 2, New York, Routledge, 1995, 5 vols.

Rives, J. "Human Sacrifice among Pagans and Christians." *The Journal of Roman Studies*, vol. 85, 1995, pp. 65–85.

Robben, Fabian. "Veränderungen und Kontinuitäten während des Christianisierungsprozesses in Nordwestdeutschland im archäologischen Befund am Beispiel von Säuglingsbestattungen an frühen Kirchen in Nordwestdeutschland." *Archäologische Informationen*, vol. 34 no. 1, 2011, pp. 87–95.

Roberts, Michael. *The Humblest Sparrow: The Poetry of Venantius Fortunatus*. Ann Arbor, The University of Michigan Press, 2009.

Robinson, F. N. "A Note on the Sources of the Old Saxon 'Genesis'." *Modern Philology*, vol. 4, no. 2, Oct. 1906, pp. 389–96.

Robinson, Orrin W. *Old English and Its Closest Relatives: A Survey of the Earliest Germanic Languages*. Stanford, CA, Stanford University Press, 1992.

Ruehl, Martin A. "German Horror Stories: Teutomania and the Ghosts of Tacitus." *Arion: A Journal of Humanities and the Classics*, vol. 22, no. 2, 2014, pp. 129–90.

Rundnagel, Erwin. "Der Mythos vom Herzog Widukind." *Historische Zeitschrift*, vol. 155, no. 3, 1937, pp. 475–505.

Russell, James C. *The Germanization of Early Medieval Christianity: A Sociohistorical Approach to Religious Transformation*. Oxford, Oxford University Press, 1994.

Salway, Peter. "Roman Britain (c.55 BC-C. AD 440)." *The Oxford Illustrated History of Britain*, edited by Kenneth O. Morgan, Oxford, Oxford University Press, 1993, pp. 45–49.

Schäferdiek, Knut. "Der Schwarze und der Weiße Hewald." *Westfälische Zeitschrift*, vol. 146, 1996, pp. 9–24.

Schäferdiek, Knut. "Germanic and Celtic Christianities." *The Cambridge History of Christianity: Constantine to c.600*, edited by Augustine Cassiday and Frederick W. Norris, Cambridge, Cambridge University Press, 2007, pp. 53–64.

Schieffer, Rudolf. "Die Anfänge der westfälischen Domstifte." *Westfälische Zeitschrift*, vol. 138, 1988, pp. 175–90.

Schlesinger, Walter. "Early Medieval Fortifications in Hesse: A General Historical Report." *World Archaeology*, vol. 7, no. 3, Feb. 1976, pp. 243–60.

Schmid, Karl. "Der Sachsenherzog Widukind als Monich auf der Reichnau Ein Beitrag zur Kritik des Widukind-Mythos." *Jahrbuch des Instituts für Frühmittelalterforschung*, vol. 17, 24 Sept. 1983, pp. 255–77.

Schmid, Karl. "Die Nachfahren Widukinds." *Deutsches Archiv für Erforschung des Mittelalters*, Vol. 20, Böhlau Verlag, 1964, pp. 1–48.

Schmidt, Ferdinand. *Charlemagne*. Translated by George P. Upton, Chicago, A.C. McClurg & Co., 1910, Life Stories for Young People.

Scholz, Bernard W., and Barbara Rogers. *Carolingian Chronicles: Royal Frankish Annals and Nithard's Histories*. Ann Arbor, The University of Michigan Press, 1972.

Schreg, Rainer. "Farmsteads in Early Medieval Germany — Architecture and Organization." *Arqueologia de la Arquitectura*, vol. 9, 2012, pp. 247–65.

Schrijver, Peter. *Language Contact and the Origins of the Germanic Languages*. New York, Routledge, 2014.

Schultes, Richard E., et al. *Plants of the Gods*. 2nd ed., Rochester, NY, Healing Arts Press, 2001.

Schwikart, Ernst. *Journey through Lower Saxony*. Würzburg, Verlaghaus Würzburg GmbH & Co. KG, 2009.

Scott, Mariana. *The Heliand: Translated from the Old Saxon/ by Mariana Scott*. Chapel Hill, The University of North Carolina Press, 1966.

Screen, Elina. "The Importance of the Emperor: Lothar I and the Frankish Civil War, 840–843." *Early Medieval Europe*, vol. 12, no. 1, 2003, pp. 25–51.

Seebohm, Frederic. *Tribal Custom in Anglo-Saxon Law*. London, Longmans, Green, and Co., 1911.

Sermon, Richard. "From Easter to Ostara: the Reinvention of a Pagan Goddess?" *Time and Mind: The Journal of Archaeology, Consciousness and Culture*, vol. 1, no. 3, Nov. 2008, pp. 331–44.

Shaw, Philip A. *Pagan Goddesses in the Early Germanic World: Eostre, Hreda and the Cult of Matrons*. London, Bristol Classical Press, 2011.

Shinners, John, editor. *Medieval Popular Religion, 1000–1500: A Reader*. 2nd ed., Toronto, Higher Education University of Toronto Press, 2008. Readings in Medieval Civilizations and Cultures II.

Shuler, Eric. "The Saxons within Carolingian Christendom: Post-conquest Identity in the Translations of Vitus, Pusinna, and Liborius." *Journal of Medieval History*, vol. 36, 2010, pp. 39–54.

Siegmund, Frank. "Social Relations among the Old Saxons." *The Continental Saxons from the Migration Period to the Tenth Century: An Ethnographic Perspective*, edited by Dennis Green and Frank Siegmund, Woodbridge, The Boydell Press, 2003, pp. 83–88.

Sievers, Eduard, editor. *Heliand.* Halle, Verlag Der Buchhandlung Des Waisenhauses, 1878.

Simek, Rudolf. *Dictionary of Northern Mythology.* Translated by Angela Hall, Cambridge, D.S. Brewer, 1993.

Simek, Rudolf. "Continental Germanic Religion." *The Handbook of Religions in Ancient Europe*, edited by Lisbeth B. Christensen, Olav Hammer, and David Warburton, New York, Routledge, 2013, pp. 292–301.

Sindbæk, Søren M. "The Lands of 'Denemearce': Cultural Differences and Social Networks of the Viking Age in South Scandinavia." *Viking and Medieval Scandinavia*, vol. 4, 2008, pp. 169–208.

Słupecki, Leszek. "Slavic Religion." *The Handbook of Religions in Ancient Europe*, edited by Lisbeth B. Christensen, Olav Hammer, and David Warburton, New York, Routledge, 2013, pp. 338–39.

Smith, Edward W. *The Echo of Odin: Norse Mythology and Human Consciousness.* Jefferson, NC, McFarland & Company, Inc., 2018.

Smith, Julia M. "Religion and Lay Society." *The New Cambridge Medieval History, c.700-c.900*, edited by Rosamond McKitterick, Cambridge, Cambridge University Press, 2015, pp. 670–71.

Smith, Kay H., et al., editors. *Evangelical Postcolonial Conversations: Global Awakenings in Theology and Praxis.* Westmont, IL, InterVarsity Press, 2014.

Smith, Philippa M. *A Concise History of New Zealand.* 2nd ed., Cambridge, Cambridge University Press, 2012.

Snyder, Christopher A. *The Britons.* Oxford, Blackwell Publishing, 2003.

Somerville, Angus A., and R. A. McDonald, editors. *The Viking Age: A Reade.* 3rd ed., Toronto, University of Toronto Press, 2020. Readings in Medieval Civilizations and Cultures XIV.

Speidel, Michael P. *Ancient Germanic Warriors: Warrior Styles from Trajan's Column to Icelandic Sagas.* New York, Routledge, 2004.

Springer, Matthias. *Die Sachsen.* Stuttgart, W. Kohlhammer, 2004.

Springer, Matthias. "Location in Space and Time." *The Continental Saxons from the Migration Period to the Tenth Century: An Ethnographic Perspective*, edited by Dennis Green and Frank Siegmund, Woodbridge, The Boydell Press, 2003, pp. 11–32.

Springer, Matthias. "Was Lebuins Lebensbeschreibung über die Verfassung Sachsens wirklich sagt, oder warum man sich mit einzelnen Wörtern beschäftigen muß." *Westfälische Zeitschrift*, vol. 148, 1998, pp. 241–59.

Squatriti, Paolo. "Digging Ditches in Early Medieval Europe." *Past and Present*, vol. 176, Aug. 2002, pp. 11–65.

Stadler, Peter. "Avar Chronology Revisited, and the Question of Ethnicity in the Avar Qaganate." *The Other Europe in the Middle Ages: Avars, Bulgars, Khazars, and Cumans*, edited by Florin Curta and Roman Kovalev, Leiden, Brill, 2008, pp. 47–82.

Steffen, Lloyd. "Religion and Violence in Christian Traditions." *The Oxford Handbook of Religion and Violence*, edited by Michael Jerryson, Mark Juergensmeyer, and Margo Kitts, Oxford, Oxford University Press, 2013, pp. 103–15.

Stenton, Frank. *Anglo-Saxon England.* 3rd ed., Oxford, Oxford University Press, 1971.

Steuer, Heiko. "The Beginnings of Urban Economies among the Saxons." *The Continental Saxons from the Migration Period to the Tenth Century: An Ethnographic Perspective*, edited by Dennis Green and Frank Siegmund, Woodbridge, The Boydell Press, 2003, pp. 166–73.

Steuer, Heiko. "Thuringians and Bavarians Location in Space and Time and Social Relations." *The Baiuvarii and Thuringi: An Ethnographic Perspective*, edited by Janine Fries-Knoblach, Heiko Steuer, and John Hines, Woodbridge, The Boydell Press, 2014, pp. 120–21.

Stevenson, Edward L. *The Geography/Claudius Ptolemy*. Translated and edited by Edward Luther Stevenson: with an introduction by Joseph Fischer. New York, Dover Publications, 1991.

Stofferahn, Steven. "Staying the Royal Sword: Alcuin and the Conversion Dilemma in Early Medieval Europe." *The Historian*, vol. 71, 2009, pp. 461–77.

Stofferahn, Steven A. "Resonance and Discord: An Early Medieval Reconsideration of Political Culture." *Historical Reflections*, vol. 36, no. 1, 2001, pp. 1–13.

Stone, Rachel. "Carolingian Domesticities." *The Oxford Handbook of Women and Gender in Medieval Europe*, edited by Judith M. Bennett and Ruth M. Karras, Oxford, Oxford University Press, 2013, pp. 228–29.

Sued-Badillo, Jalil. "From Tainos to Africans in the Caribbean." *The Caribbean: A History of the Region and Its Peoples*, edited by Stephen Palmie and Francisco A. Scarano, Chicago, IL, The University of Chicago Press, 2011, pp. 112–13.

Sullivan, Richard E. "Carolingian Missionary Theories." *The Catholic Historical Review*, vol. 42, no. 3, Oct. 1956, pp. 273–95.

Sullivan, Richard E. "Early Missionary Activity: A Comparative Study of Eastern and Western Methods." *Church History*, vol. 23, no. 1, Mar. 1954, pp. 17–35.

Sullivan, Richard E. "The Carolingian Missionary and the Pagan." *Speculum*, vol. 28, no. 4, Oct. 1953, pp. 705–40.

Swanton, Michael, editor. *The Anglo-Saxon Chronicle*. New York, Routledge, 1998.

Sykes, Brian. *Saxons, Vikings, and Celts: The Genetic Roots of Britain and Ireland*. New York, W.W. Norton & Company, 2006.

Sypeck, Jeff. *Becoming Charlemagne: Europe, Baghdad, and the Empires of A.D. 800*. New York, HarperCollins, 2006.

Tacitus, Publius. *The Agricola and The Germania*. Stilwell, Digireads.com Publishing, 2008.

Tacitus, Publius. *The Histories and The Annals*. Translated by Clifford H. Moore and John Jackson, vol. II, New York, William Heinemann LTD, 1931, III vols.

Talbot, C. H., editor. *The Anglo-Saxon Missionaries in Germany*. London, Sheed and Ward, 1954.

Thiebaux, Marcelle. *The Writings of Medieval Women: An Anthology*. 2nd ed., New York, Routledge, 2012.

Thietmar. *Ottonian Germany: The Chronicon of Thietmar of Merseburg*. Translated by David A. Warner, Manchester, Manchester University Press, 2001.

Thompson, James W. *Feudal Germany*. Chicago, IL, University of Chicago Press, 1928.

Thompson, Leonard. *A History of South Africa*. 4th ed., New Haven, CT, Yale University Press, 2014.

Thorpe, Benjamin. *North German and Netherlandish Popular Traditions and Superstitions*. Vol. 3, London, Edward Lumley, 1852, 3 vols. Northern Mythology, Comprising the Principal Popular Traditions and Superstitions of Scandinavia, North Germany, and the Netherlands.

Tiefenbach, Heinrich. *Altsächsisches Handwörterbuch/A Concise Old Saxon Dictionary*. Berlin, De Gruyter, 2010.

Todd, Malcolm. *The Early Germans*. 2nd ed., Malden, Blackwell Publishing, 2004.

Tornaghi, Paola. "Anglo-Saxon Charms and the Language of Magic." *Aevum*, vol. 84, no. 2, May 2010, pp. 439–64.

Van Dam, Raymond. "Merovingian Gaul and the Frankish Conquests." *The New Cambridge Medieval History, c.500–c.700*, edited by Paul Fouracre, Cambridge, Cambridge University Press, 2015, pp. 212–13.

Verhulst, Adriaan. "Economic Organisation." *The New Cambridge Medieval History, c.700–c.900*, edited by Rosamond McKitterick, Cambridge, Cambridge University Press, 2015, pp. 507–08.

Verhulst, Adriaan. *The Carolingian Economy*. Cambridge, Cambridge University Press, 2002.

Versloot, A. P. "The Geography and Dialects of Old Saxon: River-basin Communication Networks and the Distributional Patterns of North Sea Germanic Features in Old Saxon." *Frisians and their North Sea Neighbours: From the Fifth Century to the Viking Age*, edited by John Hines and Nelleke IJssennagger, Woodbridge, The Boydell Press, 2017, pp. 126–27.

Viswanathan, Gauri. "Literacy in the Eye of India's Conversion Storm." *Conversion: Old Worlds and New*, edited by Kenneth Mills and Anthony Grafton, Rochester, NY, University of Rochester Press, 2003, pp. 273–78.

Vitensis, Victor. *Victor of Vita: History of the Vandal Persecution*. Translated by John Moorhead, Liverpool, Liverpool University Press, 1992.

Von Clausewitz, Carl. *On War*. Translated by Peter Paret, Princeton, NJ, Princeton University Press, 1976.

Von Heung-Sik Park, Seol. "Die Stände der Lex Saxonum." *Concilium medii aevi*, vol. 2, 1999, pp. 197–210.

Von Schnurbein, Stefanie. *Norse Revival: Transformations of Germanic Paganism*. Leiden, Brill, 2016, Studies in Critical Research on Religion 5.

Von Schwerin, Claudius F. *Leges Saxonum und Lex Thuringorum*. Hannover, Claudius Freiherrn von Schwerin, 1918. Monumenta Germaniae historica. Fontes iuris Germanici antiqui in usum scholarum separatim editi 4, www.dmgh.de/mgh_fontes_iuris_4/index.htm#page/(3)/mode/1up.

Wallace-Hadrill, J M. *The Fourth Book of the Chronicle of Fredegar, with its continuations/ Translated from the Latin with Introduction by J.M. Wallace-Hadrill*. Westport, CT, Greenwood Press, 1981.

Wallace-Hadrill, J M. *The Frankish Church*. Oxford, Clarendon Press, 1983.

Wamers, Egon. "Carolingian Pfalzen and Law." *Danish Journal of Archaeology*, vol. 6, no. 2, 2017, pp. 149–63.

Wangerin, Laura. "The Governance of Ottonian Germany in Historiographical Perspective." *History Compass*, 2015, pp. 1–10, https://doi.org/10.1111/hic3.12367.

Wattenbach, Wilhelm, editor. *Die Übertragung des hl. Alexander von Rudolf und Meginhart*. Leipzig, Alfred Lorentz, 1940.

Welch, Martin. "Pre-Christian Practices in." *The Oxford Handbook of the Archaeology of Ritual and Religion*, edited by Timothy Insoll, Oxford, Oxford University Press, 2011, pp. 863–70.

Wells, Peter S. *Barbarians to Angels: The Dark Ages Reconsidered*. New York, W.W. Norton & Company, Inc., 2008.

Wemple, Suzanne F. *Women in Frankish Society: Marriage and the Cloister 500 to 900*. Philadelphia, University of Pennsylvania Press, 1981.

Wende, Peter. *A History of Germany*. New York, Palgrave Macmillan, 2005.

White, Ethan D. "The Goddess Frig: Reassessing an Anglo-Saxon Deity." *Preternature: Critical and Historical Studies on the Preternatural*, vol. 3, no. 2, 2014, pp. 284–310.

Whitton, David. "The Society of Northern Europe in the High Middle Ages, 900–1200." *The Oxford Illustrated History of Medieval Europe*, edited by George Holmes, Oxford, Oxford University Press, 1988, pp. 118–128.

Wickham, Chris. *The Inheritance of Rome: Illuminating the Dark Ages, 400–1000*. London, Penguin Group, 2009.

Widukind, Bachrach BS, Bachrach DS. *Deeds of the Saxons/Widukind of Corvey; Translated with an Introduction and Notes by Bernard S. Bachrach and David S. Bachrach*. Washington, DC, The Catholic University of America Press; 2014.

Williams, Gareth. "Atrocity or Apology?" *Medieval Warfare*, vol. 5, no. 2, 2015, pp. 21–24.

Williamson, Edwin. *The Penguin History of Latin America*. London, Penguin Group, 2009.

Willibald. *The Life of Saint Boniface*. Translated by George W. Robinson, Cambridge, MA, Harvard University Press, 1916.

Wolfram, Herwig. *History of the Goths*. Translated by Thomas J. Dunlap, 2nd ed., Berkeley, University of California Press, 1988.

Wolfram, Herwig. *The Roman Empire and Its Germanic Peoples*. Translated by Thomas Dunlap, Berkeley, University of California Press, 1997, pp. 1–314. Press, 1979.

Wood, Ian N. "Christianization and the Dissemination of Christian Teaching." *The New Cambridge Medieval History, c.500–c.700*, edited by Paul Fouracre, Cambridge, Cambridge University Press, 2015, pp. 712–25.

Wood, Ian N. "Pagan Religions and Superstitions East of the Rhine from the Fifth to the Ninth Century." *After Empire: Towards an Ethnology of Europe's Barbarians*, edited by Giorgio Ausenda, Woodbridge, The Boydell Press, 1995, pp. 257–64.

Wood, Ian N. "Religion in Pre-Carolingian Thuringia and Bavaria." *The Baiuvarii and Thuringi: An Ethnographic Perspective*, edited by Janine Fries-Knoblach, Heiko Steuer, and John Hines, Woodbridge, The Boydell Press, 2014, pp. 319–24.

Wood, Ian N. *The Merovingian Kingdoms, 450–751*. 2nd ed., New York, Longman Group Ltd., 1994.

Wood, Ian N. *The Missionary Life: Saints and the Evangelisation of Europe 400–1050*. New York, Routledge, 2014.

Wood, Ian N. "The Northern Frontier: Christianity Face to Face with Paganism." *The Cambridge History of Christianity: Early Medieval Christianities, c.600–c.1100*, edited by Thomas F. Noble and Julia Smith, Cambridge, Cambridge University Press, 2008, pp. 230–31.

Woolf, Greg, editor. *Ancient Civilizations: The Illustrated Guide to Belief, Mythology, and Art*. San Diego, CA, Thunder Bay Press, 2005.

Wormald, Patrick. "Kings and Kingship." *The New Cambridge Medieval History, c.500–c.700*, edited by Paul Fouracre, Cambridge, Cambridge University Press, 2015, pp. 574–75.

Wright, Joseph. *An Old High-German Primer with Grammar, Notes, and Glossary*. Oxford, Clarendon Press, 1888.

Yenne, Bill. *Hitler's Master of the Dark Arts: Himmler's Black Knights and the Occult Origins of the SS*. Minneapolis, MN, Zenith Press, 2010.

Youngs, Samuel J. "A Transcript of Submission: Jesus as Fated Victim of Divine Vengeance in the Old Saxon Heliand." *Religions*, vol. 12, no. 306, 21 Apr. 2021, pp. 1–16.

Zimmerman, Christiane, and Hauke Jöns. "Cultural Contacts between the Western Baltic, the North Sea Region and Scandinavia: Attributing Runic Finds to Runic Traditions and Corpora of the Early Viking Age." *Frisians and Their North Sea Neighbours: From the Fifth Century to the Viking Age*, edited by John Hines and Nelleke IJssennagger, Woodbridge, The Boydell Press, 2017, pp. 251–52.

Index